LAST RIGHTS

THE DEATH OF AMERICAN LIBERTY

JAMES BOVARD

The
LIBERTARIAN
INSTITUTE

LAST RIGHTS

THE **DEATH** OF
AMERICAN LIBERTY

JAMES BOVARD

Last Rights:
The Death of American Liberty

© 2023 by James Bovard
All rights reserved.

Published in the United States of America by

The Libertarian Institute
612 W. 34th St.
Austin, TX 78705

LibertarianInstitute.org

ISBN-13: 979-8-9884031-8-0

Table of Contents

1. Tyranny Comes to Main Street

Americans today have the "freedom" to be fleeced, groped, wiretapped, injected, censored, injected, ticketed, disarmed, beaten, vilified, detained, and maybe shot by government agents. Politicians are hell-bent on protecting citizens against everything except Uncle Sam. Is America becoming a Cage Keeper Democracy where voters merely ratify the latest demolition of their rights and liberties?

"We live in a world in which everything has been criminalized," warned Supreme Court Justice Neil Gorsuch.[1] There are now more than 5,200 separate federal criminal offenses, a 36% increase since the 1990s, along with tens of thousands of state and local crimes. More laws mean more violators who can be harshly punished on command, resulting in the arrests of more than 10 million Americans each year. Thanks to the Supreme Court, police can lock up anyone accused of "even a very minor criminal offense" such as an unbuckled seatbelt.

The Founding Fathers saw property rights as "the guardian of every other right." But today's politicians never lack a pretext for plundering private citizens. Despite being charged with no crime, half a million Americans have been robbed by government agents on the nation's sidewalks, highways, and airports in recent decades. Federal law enforcement agencies arbitrarily confiscate more property from Americans each year than all the burglars steal nationwide.[2] The IRS pilfered more cash from private bank accounts because of alleged paperwork errors than the total looted by bank robbers nationwide. Federal bureaucrats blocked landowners from farming or building on a hundred million acres of their own property because of puddles, ditches, or other suspected wet spots.

Police have killed more than 25,000 citizens since the turn of the century, but the federal government does not even bother compiling a body count. SWAT teams use battering rams and flash-bang grenades to attack 50,000 homes a year, routinely terrorizing people suspected of dastardly crimes like spraying graffiti or running poker games. Cops in many cities have been caught planting guns on hapless targets, while corrupt police labs fabricated tens of thousands of bogus drug convictions. Police unions have more sway over government policy than anyone on the wrong end of a baton or Taser. Despite perpetual promises of reform, most police who brutalize private citizens still automatically receive legal immunity. Federal Judge Don Willett derided the "Constitution-free zone" courts created where "individuals whose constitutional rights are violated at the hands of federal officers are essentially remedy-less."[3]

Gun owners are America's fastest-growing criminal class. One state after another is enacting "Show us the gun and we'll find the crime" laws. Judges and politicians are justifying mass disarmament in the name of "freedom from fear" — as if no one will be safe until government controls every trigger. Federal agencies consider all 20+ million marijuana users who own firearms to be felons (unless their last name is Biden). Presidents Donald Trump and Joe Biden both retroactively outlawed widely-owned firearm accessories, creating new legions of potential jailbirds. At the same time many federal agencies are stockpiling automatic weapons, Biden calls for banning semiautomatic pistols and rifles owned by 50 million Americans.

Politicians and bureaucrats exploited the COVID-19 pandemic to forbid any activities they chose, from going to church to buying garden seeds. Governors in most states effectively banned hundreds of millions of citizens from leaving their homes. Shutting down entire states was the equivalent of sacrificing virgins to appease angry viral gods. In Los Angeles, citizens were prohibited from going outside for a walk or bike ride. Tens of thousands of small businesses were bankrupted by shutdown orders, while federal "relief" spurred a $600 billion worldwide fraud stampede. Most Americans suffered COVID infections despite government decrees that Supreme Court Justice Samuel Alito labeled "previously unimaginable restrictions on individual liberty."[4] Government officials endlessly invoked "science and data" to sanctify their power. But many pandemic policies were simply Political Science 101, using deceit and demagoguery to domineer humanity.

Government decrees are blighting more lives than ever before. Vague laws convert bureaucrats into czars who dictate as they please. More than a thousand occupations have been closed to anyone who fails to kowtow to absurd state licensing requirements, from fortune tellers in Massachusetts to anyone rubbing feet in Arizona. Tens of thousands of drivers have been injured and hundreds killed thanks to red light traffic ticket cameras notorious for multiplying collisions. The Equal Employment Opportunity Commission made it a federal crime to refuse to hire ex-convicts.[5] The Americans with Disabilities Act has spurred half a million "discrimination" lawsuits, including by narcoleptics who fell asleep on the job and by a deaf guy outraged about missing captions on porn videos.

Schoolchildren are being sacrificed on an altar of social justice. From No Child Left Behind to Common Core, federal dictates have subverted academic standards and squandered billions of hours of kids' lives. Teacher unions have worked to destroy local control of education, prevent teacher accountability, deny parents any voice in their children's education, and pointlessly shut down schools during the pandemic. In lieu of literacy, government schools are redefining gender and indoctrinating kids with values that many parents detest. When mothers and fathers raised hell at school board meetings, the Biden administration and the FBI labeled them as terrorist suspects.

Politicians are increasingly dividing Americans into two classes — those who work for a living and those who vote for a living. Subsidy programs have multiplied even faster than congressional ethics scandals. Federal aid propelled college tuition increases that turned ex-students into a new debtor class endlessly clamoring for relief. Farm subsidies wreak chaos in markets while providing a gravy train for affluent landowners. Federal mortgage policies have been "wrecking ball benevolence," whipsawing the housing market and spawning the 2007–08 collapse that reduced the net worth of black and Hispanic households by 50%. The number of handout recipients has more than doubled since 1983, and the feds are now feeding more than 100 million Americans. Government grants are eventually followed by government restrictions, and dependence often turns into submission. The ultimate victim of handouts could be democracy itself: politicians cannot undermine self-reliance without subverting self-government.

While politicians boast of bestowing freebies, taxes have become a financial Grim Reaper. The Internal Revenue Service is Washington's ultimate sacred cow because it delivers trillions of dollars to allow politicians to work miracles (or at least get re-elected). Americans are forced to pay more in taxes than their total spending on food, clothing, and housing. Tax codes have become inscrutable at the same time the IRS pummels people with ten times more penalties than in earlier decades. The Biden administration is racing to hire 87,000 new IRS agents and employees to squeeze far more money out of both rich and poor taxpayers. Inflation has become the cruelest tax as the dollar's purchasing power fell 17% since Biden took office, fleecing any citizen with a savings account.

The federal government is generating so many absurdities nowadays that even cynics cannot keep up. The Transportation Security Administration epitomizes Washington's boneheaded command-and-control approach to modern perils. TSA's Whole Body Scanners doused tens of millions of travelers with radiation while taking nude pictures of them. TSA's groin-grabbing "enhanced pat-downs" spark thousands of sexual assault complaints from women every year. TSA terrorist profiles have warned of travelers who are either staring intently or avoiding eye contact, or who fidget, yawn, or sweat heavily; anyone who is whistling and/or staring at their feet; Boston blacks wearing backward baseball caps; and anyone who "expresses contempt" for TSA Security Theater antics.

Federal surveillance leaves no refuge for dissent. Government agencies are secretly accumulating mountains of data that could be used for "blackmail, stalking, harassment and public shaming" of American citizens, according to a 2023 federal report.[6] The National Security Agency has stalked Americans via their cellphones, covertly installed spyware onto personal computers, and treated anyone "searching the Web for suspicious stuff" like a terrorist suspect. The Patriot Act spurred the illegal seizure of personal and financial information from tens of millions of Americans. Customs agents can seize and copy the cellphones, laptop drives, and private papers of any American crossing the U.S. border. The Drug Enforcement Administration is building a secret nationwide network of license plate scanners to track every driver. Federally funded "fusion centers" are stockpiling Suspicious Activity Reports on tourists who photograph landmarks, "people who avoid eye contact," and anyone "reverent of individual liberty." The FBI's "terrorist warning signs" include hotel guests using "Do Not Disturb" signs and the Gadsden "Don't Tread on Me" flag.

At the same time spying on citizens skyrocketed, Washington dropped an Iron Curtain around itself. The government is committing more crimes than citizens will ever know. Whistleblowers and journalists are hounded as if exposing official lies is a heresy against democracy. Every year, the federal government slaps a "secret" label on trillions of pages of information — enough to fill 20 million filing cabinets. Any document which is classified is treated like a holy relic that cannot be exposed without damning the nation. Self-government has been defined down to paying, obeying, and wearing a federal blindfold. There are plenty of laws to protect government secrets but no law to protect democracy from federal secrecy.

The First Amendment is becoming a historic relic. Federal Judge Terry Doughty recently condemned the Biden administration for potentially "the most massive attack against free speech in United States history."[7] That verdict was ratified in September 2023 by a federal appeals court ruling slamming the White House and federal agencies for actions that resulted in "suppressing millions of protected free speech postings by American citizens." Federal agencies pirouetted as a "Ministry of Truth," according to the court rulings. Censorship converts citizens into captives. Federal censorship tainted the 2020 and 2022 elections, suppressing tens of millions of tweets, YouTube videos, and Facebook posts from conservatives and Republicans. White House officials even ordered Facebook to delete humorous memes, including a parody of a future television ad: "Did you or a loved one take the COVID vaccine? You may be entitled…"

Rather than the Rule of Law, we have a government of threats, intimidation, and browbeating. "Government of the people" defaulted into "government for the people," which degenerated into perennially punishing people for their own good. Twenty-five years ago, Supreme Justice Ruth Bader Ginsburg warned against permitting federal agencies "the extraordinary authority… to manufacture crimes."[8] Entrapment schemes proliferate as G-men fabricate crimes to justify budget increases. The FBI, pretending that rosary beads could be extremist symbols, is targeting traditional Catholics across the nation because of their conservative moral values. The FBI entitles its legions of confidential informants to commit more than 5,000 crimes a year, dragging many unlucky bystanders to their legal doom. The number of inmates in federal prison increased 500% since 1980, and America has the highest incarceration rate in the world. Politicians are more anxious to control citizens than to protect them. More people are busted each year for marijuana possession than for all violent crimes combined, while the futile War on Drugs causes more fatalities than ever before.

Every recent administration has expanded and exploited the dictatorial potential of the presidency. Former President Richard Nixon shocked Americans in 1977 when he asserted during a television interview: "When the president does it, that means that it is not illegal."[9] But Nixon's slogan is the Oval Office maxim for the new millennium. Presidents now only need to find a single federal lawyer who says, "Yes, Master!" President George W. Bush's lawyers secretly decided that neither federal law nor the Constitution could limit the power of the president, who could declare martial law or authorize torture at his whim. President Barack Obama claimed a prerogative to assassinate Americans he labeled terrorist suspects.[10] President Donald Trump boasted of "an absolute right to do what I want to with the Justice Department."[11] In 2022, President Biden proclaimed that "liberty is under assault."[12] But he was referring solely to a few court rulings he disapproved, not to the federal supremacy he championed for almost 50 years in the Senate and the White House.

The authoritarian trendline in American political life is more important than the name or party of any officeholder. "One precedent in favor of power is stronger than a hundred against it," as Thomas Jefferson warned during the American Revolution. Unfortunately, there are a hundred precedents in favor of government now for each precedent in favor of liberty. There is a "No harm, no foul" attitude towards violating the Constitution, and Washington almost always hides the harm. The sheer power of federal agencies such as the FBI is becoming one of the gravest perils to American democracy.

Elections are becoming demolition derbies that threaten to wreck the nation. Historian Henry Adams observed a century ago that politics "has always been the systematic organization of hatreds." Nowadays, politics seems hell-bent on multiplying hatred. Enraged activists are increasingly tarring all their opponents as traitors. Many of the protestors who spent years vehemently denouncing Trump were not opposed to dictators per se; they simply wanted different dictates. More than half of Americans expect a civil war "in the next few years," according to a recent survey.[13]

Americans are indoctrinated in public schools to presume that our national DNA guarantees that we will always be free. But few follies are more perilous than presuming that individual rights are safe in perpetuity. None of the arguments on why liberty is inevitable can explain why it is becoming an endangered species. Yet many people believe that liberty will inevitably triumph because of some "law of history" never enacted by God, a convocation of cardinals, or even the Arkansas state legislature. Presuming that freedom is our destiny lulls people against political predators.

Federal Judge Learned Hand warned in 1944: "Liberty lies in the hearts of men and women; when it dies there, no constitution, no law, no court can save it." But Americans are more likely to encounter liberty in history books instead of their own lives. Many young people are unaware of bygone eras when Americans could travel without being groped, buy a beer or smoke a cigar without committing a federal offense, or protest without being quarantined in an Orwellian "free-speech zone."[14] Is the spirit of liberty dead? Almost a third of young American adults support installing mandatory government surveillance cameras in private homes to "reduce domestic violence, abuse, and other illegal activity."[15]

We have an Impunity Democracy in which government officials pay no price for their crimes. Americans today are more likely to believe in witches, ghosts, and astrology than to trust the federal government. Washington's legitimacy is in tatters thanks to a long train of bipartisan perfidy. If government is lawless, elections merely designate the most dangerous criminals in the land.

At a time when foreign democracies are collapsing like dominos, can America avoid becoming the "elective despotism" the Founding Fathers dreaded? The first step to reviving liberty is to recognize how far politicians have stretched their power. But nothing can safeguard freedom except the bravery of citizens who refuse to be shackled.

2. Seizure Fever

"The right of property is the guardian of every other right, and to deprive the people of this, is to deprive them of their liberty."

— Arthur Lee of Virginia (1775)[1]

Seizure fever is toxifying law enforcement across the nation. For more than 30 years, federal, state, and local government agencies have plundered citizens on practically any harebrained accusation or pretext. The perpetual failure to curb official rapacity is a milestone in the dissolution of American liberty and constitutional rights.

In 1970, Congress authorized seizing assets from mobsters, racketeers, and drug kingpins. But the target list kept expanding, and federal agents can now confiscate private property based on 400 different federal laws.[2] A Justice Department lawyer told the Supreme Court that the feds can rightfully take possession of any property involved in legal violations except for "a minor infraction such as a parking offense."[3] Indiana Solicitor General Thomas Fisher declared in 2019 that the government is entitled to confiscate any car or truck that exceeds the speed limit.

Federal agencies have used legal flimflams to snare more than $50 billion in private property since 2000.[4] Government officials can "seize now, prove later" (or maybe never) thanks to a "legal fiction."[5] Government agencies pretend that they are suing the actual property, not the owner. While criminal charges against persons require proof beyond a reasonable doubt, accusations against property require little or no evidence. Most federal seizures are done administratively, and a simple memo entitles government to commandeer as it pleases. As DEA agent Sean Waite explained: "We don't have to prove that the person is guilty… It's that the money is presumed to be guilty."[6] How can you prove that a $20 bill in your wallet was never nefariously used a decade ago?

The Piracy Pedigree of Contemporary Plundering

In 1992, a Justice Department newsletter conceded: "Like children in a candy shop, the law enforcement community chose all manner and method of seizing and forfeiting property, gorging ourselves in an effort which soon came to resemble one designed to raise revenues." The same year, a federal appeals court warned that it was "enormously troubled by the government's increasing and virtually unchecked use of the civil forfeiture statutes and the disregard for due process that is buried in those statutes."[7] In 1993, another federal appeals court questioned whether forfeiture policies were driven by "an insatiable appetite for a source for increased agency revenue."[8]

But the Supreme Court repeatedly upheld forfeitures that made a mockery of due process. In 1996, the Court ruled on a case involving John Bennis, a steelworker who picked up a prostitute and parked on a Detroit street while driving home from work.[9] Police swooped in upon the two of them as she was "performing a sex act on him," as one newspaper delicately reported in that genteel era. Because they were caught in flagrante, police seized his car. (Detroit police confiscated nearly 3,000 cars in 1995 in anti-prostitution crackdowns.)

The co-owner of the 1977 Pontiac was John's wife, Tina Bennis, who was outraged to lose her property because of her spouse's dalliance. But the Justice Department blamed Tina because she did not "prove that she took all reasonable steps to prevent illegal use of the car." Are wives obliged to hire detectives to stalk their husbands any time they reach for the car keys?

To justify the seizure, Chief Justice William Rehnquist reeled in a Spanish pirate ship that attacked U.S. ships in 1822. Since the Pontiac, like the pirate ship, was involved in a criminal offense, there was no violation of due process in its seizure. Rehnquist did not deign to explain the legal equivalence of piracy in the 1820s and oral sex in the 1990s. Rehnquist decreed: "The government may not be required to compensate an owner for property which it has already lawfully acquired under the exercise of governmental authority."[10]

Justice John Paul Stevens dissented, warning that the logic of the decision "would permit the States to exercise virtually unbridled power to confiscate vast amounts of property where professional criminals have engaged in illegal acts," including hotels where prostitutes ply their trade. Stevens also pointed out that the decision encouraged reckless driving, since Bennis could have kept the Pontiac if he had not parked while the hooker earned her fee.

In the 1820s, pirates inflicted a few million dollars in damage on American ships. But the Bennis decision helped unleash thousands of pirates in police cars who confiscated tens of billions of dollars from individuals and businesses in the following decades.

Asset forfeiture became the most controversial law enforcement abuse of the 1990s. Legislation curtailing forfeiture was championed by both liberal and conservative members of Congress, as well as by the American Civil Liberties Union (ACLU) and the National Rifle Association (NRA). But the Clinton administration derailed reform efforts by promising to make administrative fixes that never occurred. Deputy Attorney General Eric Holder complained that requiring "clear and convincing evidence" before confiscating private property would cripple the feds' ability to protect Americans. Holder portrayed the Justice Department as a helpless giant at the mercy of any forfeiture victim who disputed federal charges.

Congress eventually enacted the brazenly mistitled Civil Asset Forfeiture Reform Act of 2000, which doubled the number of laws federal prosecutors could use to seize private property.[11] That law authorized three years in prison for individuals who allegedly make "frivolous" legal claims to retrieve their seized property. But government agents faced no penalty for lying to confiscate people's cash, cars, and other property. The law spurred a tenfold increase in confiscations, reaching $4.3 billion by fiscal year 2012.

President Donald Trump gushed in 2017 that forfeiture was raw power at its best: "How simple could anything be. I love it." When Trump met with sheriffs from across the nation, he joked about destroying the career of a Texas legislator who sought to curb forfeiture abuses.[12] Trump's first Attorney General, Jeff Sessions, had been the biggest forfeiture zealot in the U.S. Senate. Prior to joining the Trump administration, Sessions absurdly declared that 95% of people hit by forfeiture have "done nothing in their lives but sell dope."[13]

During the 2020 campaign, Joe Biden promised to repeal the pro-forfeiture changes that Sessions made in 2017. But as Chairman of the Senate Judiciary Committee, Biden had written or championed many of the laws that spawned pervasive abuses. Thus far, the Biden administration has done nothing to curb federal forfeitures excesses.

The Canine Constitutional Veto

The Fifth Amendment states that "No person shall be… deprived of life, liberty, or property, without due process of law."

Except by dogs.

The Supreme Court declared in 1967: "Wherever a man may be, he is entitled to know that he will remain free from unreasonable searches and seizures."

Except by dogs. A wag of a tail or a tilt of a dog's head is sufficient to establish "probable cause" to waive a citizen's right to be free from warrantless searches.

Late in the last century, laboratory tests proved that the vast majority of U.S. currency had sufficient microscopic traces of illicit drugs to trigger a canine alert. Regardless, such alerts have been endlessly cited to "prove" that cash is tainted by cocaine or other narcotics and thus can be forfeited. In 1998, Federal Judge James Moran groused that relying on dog sniffs to justify seizures meant "the property of virtually any person traveling with a substantial amount of cash would be subject to forfeiture." Chicago attorney Stephen Komie lamented in 2019 that ordinary citizens' rights have no chance "because the dog will never come and testify and you can't cross-examine a dog."[14]

Supreme Court Justices have splattered judicial holy water on "search warrants on a leash." Even dogs who alert 100% of the time, with a huge number of false positives, are considered sufficiently trustworthy to serve as "probable cause on four legs."[15] *Washington Post* columnist Radley Balko quipped, "It's no wonder one police department scrapped any pretense of fairness and just named its drug dog 'Guilty.'"[16]

In 2021, drug dogs aided and abetted an $86 million FBI robbery of safe deposit boxes. The FBI raided U.S. Private Vaults, a Beverly Hills, California, company that provided customers with secure storage compartments. The search warrant specifically prohibited the feds from seizing the contents of 369 private safe deposit boxes, but the FBI broke into them regardless and sought to "confiscate thousands of gold and silver bars, Rolex watches, and gem-studded earrings, bracelets and necklaces," as well as over a million dollars in poker chips. The FBI's search warrant effectively labeled all of the customers as criminals: "Only those who wish to hide their wealth from the DEA, IRS, or creditors would instead choose to pay to store actual cash at a single storefront operation owned by the likes of [U.S. Private Vaults' co-owners]."[17]

Alerts by drug dogs sufficed to seize the cash. The FBI also claimed that the fact that some of the money was wrapped in old rubber bands indicated that the owners were drug dealers. Confiscation was also justified because one of the box holders had a vehicle with Illinois license plates. One FBI agent submitted a post-raid affidavit: "Based on my training and experience in money laundering investigations, Chicago, Illinois, is a hub of both drug trafficking and money laundering."[18] Robert Johnson, a lawyer representing seven of the box holders, observed: "The government's theory is that having cash makes you a presumptive criminal, and I think every American should be worried about that."[19] The *Los Angeles Times* reported: "Many box holders have agreed to give up a portion of their cash and property after deciding it was not worth spending tens of thousands of dollars in legal fees — or more — to recover the rest."[20] A federal judge eventually forced the FBI to return the seized property to some of the box holders.

Highway Robbery

Between 2001 and 2014, lawmen seized more than $2.5 billion in cash from 60,000 travelers on the nation's highways — with no criminal charges in the vast majority of cases.[21] Federal, state, and local law enforcement have institutionalized shakedowns on the nation's highways to the point that "forfeiture corridors are the new speed traps," as *Mother Jones* observed.[22]

Police can almost always find a pretext to pull someone over. Gerard Arenberg, executive director of the National Association of Chiefs of Police, told me in a 1996 interview: "We have so damn many laws, you can't drive the streets without breaking the law."[23] The *Washington Post* reported that police set up "rolling checkpoints on busy highways and pulled over motorists for minor violations, such as following too closely or improper signaling," and "looked for supposed 'indicators' of criminal activity, which can include such things as trash on the floor of a vehicle, or abundant energy drinks."[24]

In Tenaha, Texas, authorities confiscated $3 million from motorists passing through East Texas.[25] The names of the court filings capture Tenaha's rapacity, such as *State of Texas v. One Gold Crucifix*. "The police had confiscated a simple gold cross that a woman wore around her neck after pulling her over for a minor traffic violation. No contraband was reported, no criminal charges were filed, and no traffic ticket was issued," the *New Yorker* noted.[26] If drivers "refused to part with their money, officers threatened to arrest them on false money laundering charges and other serious felonies," an ACLU lawsuit charged.[27] Tenaha police stopped a 27-year-old black man who worked as a chicken slicer in an Arkansas Tyson plant and fleeced him of $3,900 after accusing him of "driving too close to the white line."[28] After police warned Jennifer Boatright that they would take custody of her children if she refused to surrender thousands of dollars she

13

carried to buy a used car, she burst into tears and thought: "Where are we? Is this some kind of foreign country, where they're selling people's kids off?"[29] The ACLU lawsuit and the Texas legislature compelled the town to cease the abusive seizures in 2012. However, most victims never got their property back.[30]

Perverse incentives propel plunder. Police in many states use confiscated property to pay their own salaries, bonuses, and vacations. A Missouri police chief said that forfeiture money was "like pennies from heaven... that get you a toy."[31] Federal agencies partner with local and state law enforcement to enable them to evade state laws limiting seizures of private property. Under a program euphemistically called "equitable sharing" (which sounds better than "shared plunder"), local and state law enforcement agencies retain most of the property they seize when they team up with the feds.

In South Carolina, police keep 95% of assets they commandeer. Drivers' cash is routinely seized after they are stopped for picayune offenses. As the *Greenville News* reported:

> Ramando Moore was cited for having an open container [of alcohol] in Richland County in 2015; he lost $604. Plexton Denard Hunter was pulled over for a seatbelt violation in 2015 in Richland County and had $541 seized. Tesla Carter, another seatbelt violation, this time in Anderson in 2015. She lost $1,361.[32]

Most police seizures of cash involved less than a thousand dollars — a trivial amount for serious drug traffickers. "Black men... represent 13% of the state's population. Yet 65% of all citizens targeted for civil forfeiture in the state are black males," according to a 2019 investigation by South Carolinian newspapers.

In Phelps County, Missouri, police have seized millions of dollars in cash and property from people traveling on Interstate 44. Two-thirds of Phelps County forfeiture victims have Hispanic names.[33] Phelps County deputies justify seizures simply by asserting that the owners are shady characters — with evidence such as "driving a rental vehicle... bloodshot eyes, nervousness or even air fresheners hanging from the rearview mirror."[34] Drivers were commonly stopped for failing to signal before changing lanes, another tell-tale sign of drug trafficking. Phelps County police "almost never file state criminal charges against those whose cash they seize, nor does it make big drug seizures during these stops targeting cash," reported a 2020 investigation by St. Louis Public Radio.

In 2021, the feds partnered with local police to commence robbing armored cars.[35] Though 36 states have legalized marijuana for recreational and/or medical use, federal law continues to prohibit engaging in cannabis transactions. Local police in California and Kansas began stopping and searching armored cars owned by Empyreal Logistics, which transported cash from licensed marijuana dispensaries. More than a million dollars was taken and split between local and federal lawmen. The FBI justified the seizures because the proceeds were derived from narcotics crimes or money laundering — even though state law in California explicitly permits the transport of money from legal cannabis operations.[36] In May 2022, the feds and California police departments agreed to return the seized money after Empyreal signed a settlement declaring that "San Bernardino deputies are not highway robbers as previously reported in the media."[37] Alas, the official statement did not deter a local paper, the *Riverside Press-Enterprise*, from summarizing the resolution: "The San Bernardino County Sheriff's Department has agreed to stop operating like highway robbers."[38]

Fleecing Flyers

The Drug Enforcement Administration pays tens of millions of dollars to informants in the travel business who provide confidential passenger information.[39] Anyone who pays cash for a ticket can be reported as a drug dealer or accomplice. Airline employee tipoffs have spurred thousands of cash seizures, but narcotics are discovered in less than 1% of cases. Informants routinely collect 25% of the value of any property the government seizes based on their accusations.

"You make it, we'll take it" is the unofficial motto of DEA's Asset Forfeiture program, which confiscated more than $4 billion in cash since 2007. DEA agents, many of them operating in airports, routinely "rely on their immediate, on-the-spot judgment" to justify seizing other people's money, the Inspector General reported. DEA agents justify seizures based on clues such as "traveling to or from a known source city for drug trafficking, purchasing a ticket within 24 hours of travel, purchasing a ticket for a long flight with an immediate return, purchasing a one-way ticket, and traveling without checked luggage." But "source city" includes almost any major city in the United States. California destinations are especially suspect, since Los Angeles is considered "a well-known source city for marijuana and other types of narcotics" and Fresno is "known for large quantities of outdoor grown marijuana."[40]

Most cash seizures occurred "without preexisting intelligence of a specific drug crime," the Inspector General reported. DEA agents "approach travelers and ask if they would be willing to answer a few questions, a process that often ends with them either asking for permission to search the person's bags or having a dog sniff them for drugs," *USA Today* noted.[41] In one case, a DEA agent plucked $70,000 from a checked suitcase "without doing any more investigation or attempting to question the owner at the airport — instead simply putting a receipt in the bag and sending it on to its final destination."[42] A retired DEA task force supervisor told *USA Today*: "We want the cash. Good agents chase cash. It was just easier to get the asset, and that's where you make a dent in the criminal organization."[43] The fact that prior seizures made no dent in the overall level of drug trafficking is irrelevant to DEA windfalls.

DEA is paying numerous TSA agents across the nation to alert them when they detect ample cash during screening. Josh Gingerich was traveling from Chicago home to the Sacramento area in 2018 when a TSA agent notified DEA agents about $29,000 in cash in his backpack. According to Gingerich, who purchases and resells trucks, DEA agents "claimed to smell marijuana on a plastic bag filled with dirty laundry in his backpack… Officers dumped the clothes, filled the bag with cash, then brought it to the drug dog." The agents found no drugs, but an alleged scent sufficed to seize the money.[44]

TSA and DEA agents automatically confiscate the cash of any domestic traveler they detect with more than $5,000 — their magic threshold for money being "suspicious." In August 2019, 57-year-old Rebecca Brown was flying out of Pittsburgh International Airport while carrying a Tupperware container with her father's life savings — $82,373. Her 79-year-old father was showing signs of mental decline and was worried about keeping so much cash in his house. Brown was transporting the stash to her home in Boston where she planned to set up a joint bank account. A TSA agent noticed the money while scanning Brown's carry-on luggage and alerted a DEA agent who asked Brown some questions and then announced he was seizing the cash. The DEA agent put Brown's money "into a plastic bag and told her someone would be in touch with her," the *Washington Post* reported.[45] The cash grab prevented her father from fixing up his old pickup truck and getting badly needed dental surgery. After a lawsuit challenging the seizure was publicized, DEA sent Brown a letter rotely declaring: "After further review, a decision has been made to return the property." The Institute for Justice's Dan Alban, a savvy attorney who has thwarted many outrageous federal cash seizures, observed: "This is something that we know is happening all across the United States. We've been contacted by people who have been traveling to buy used cars or buy equipment for their business and had their cash seized."

Sidewalk Snitches

Forfeiture turns police into sidewalk dictators. In 1992, *USA Today* reported that Washington, D.C., police routinely stop black citizens and "confiscate small amounts of cash and jewelry on the streets and in parks — even when no drugs are found or charges filed." Local resident Ben Davis groused: "I've got money in both pockets, but I don't know how much. The assumption is, if I can't tell you exactly how much I have, it must be from criminal enterprise."[46] D.C. police refrained from using those heavy-handed tactics on well-coiffed lobbyists lunching in the K Street Corridor.

Twenty-two years later, the *Washington Post* reported that D.C. police officers had made more than 10,000 seizures since 2009 — including more than a thousand cash seizures of less than $20 — a total of more than $5 million. Most of the victims were not charged with criminal or civil offenses; instead, they were simply given a receipt itemizing their losses. The District charges up to $2,500 "simply for the right to challenge a police seizure in court, which can take months or even years to resolve," the *New Yorker* noted.[47] While D.C. police entitle themselves to rifle through the pockets of anyone they label suspicious, they fail to make arrests in 90% of the city's robberies.

Traipsing the sidewalks of New York is riskier than most residents realize. The *New York Daily News* reported in 2015: "An arcane 134-year-old process... means the NYPD can take the possessions — cars, cash, computers — of anyone who gets stopped, even if it's for jaywalking and even if that person never gets convicted or even charged."[48] In 2016, the *Village Voice* reported: "For decades, the NYPD has been taking the money and possessions of anyone it arrests, or even stops on the street, under the legal pretense of civil forfeiture."[49] Victims are rarely charged with criminal offenses. Police make it extremely difficult for innocent victims to reclaim wallets, cars, jewelry, or other goods. Bronx Councilman Ritchie Torres declared: "The reality of civil forfeiture is that it penalizes poverty," since "constitutional rights are reserved only for those who can afford it." The NYPD complained that it was unfair to expect them to track the forfeitures because it would require "a manual count of over half a million invoices each year."[50]

Baltimore police made almost 5,000 cash seizures in 2017, pocketing more than $2 million.[51] The *Baltimore Sun* noted: "Under Maryland law, police are allowed to seize money that is found during investigations." As long as police say they are "investigating" drugs, gambling, dirt bikes, whatever — owners are out of luck. Even though most of the victims were not arrested or convicted, the police refused to return 94% of their takings. Since most Baltimore residents do not possess law school degrees, they could not distinguish between official forfeiture actions and the notorious street robberies by the Baltimore Police Gun Trace Task Force.

Grand Theft Auto

Politicians and police are increasingly stealing anything with four wheels. Many states and localities already have laws authorizing police to confiscate autos from people accused of drunk driving — regardless of whether a person is convicted of any offense. Minnesota police confiscated a $40,000 sports utility vehicle because the owner got liquored up while sitting in his driveway testing the new vehicle's audio system.[52] Chicago suburbs enacted ordinances to seize a car if teenage drivers are out past 11:00 PM. District of Columbia police seized so many cars from purported customers of prostitutes that they lost count; many confiscated cars were destroyed by vandals who plundered police impoundment lots.[53]

In Memphis, police seize vehicles of any drivers who speak to a decoy fake prostitute on the street (no proposition or consummation necessary). Memphis Police Chief Cerelyn Davis champions confiscating cars of alleged reckless drivers "even if the case gets dropped in court."[54] Memphis Mayor Jim Strickland recommended conducting mass public demolitions of the cars of reckless drivers. Memphis residents "were compelled to pay large fees to recover their vehicles even when they had not been convicted of any crime," the *New York Times* reported.

Albuquerque police seized the equivalent of one vehicle for every 25 households in the city. The New Mexico legislature banned pre-conviction seizures of private property, but Albuquerque politicians decided that state law did not apply to its programs. The city continued aggressively commandeering cars from anyone suspected of various crimes. The city seized so many vehicles — more than 8,000 vehicles since 2010 — that it considered building a new facility to store its pirated fleet. Most of the seized cars were not owned by the drivers who were accosted by police.[55] In 2018, Federal Judge James Browning ruled that the city "has an unconstitutional institutional incentive to prosecute forfeiture cases, because, in practice, the forfeiture program sets its own budget and can spend, without meaningful oversight, all of the excess funds it raises from previous years."

Wayne County, Michigan, "seized thousands of cars in 2017 under the auspices of marijuana enforcement," *Reason* magazine reported.[56] Michigan voters legalized the recreational use of marijuana in a referendum, but police continued targeting vehicles suspected of drug violations even when no marijuana was found. Jarrett Skorup of the Mackinac Center for Public Policy observed: "The vehicles are worth very little, typically around $1,000 or $2,000. These are very likely low-income people, people that can't afford to sit around without a vehicle for three weeks or afford an attorney to go challenge it."[57] Police routinely offer to return cars for $900 — cheaper than hiring a lawyer to fight the abuse and waiting perhaps years for the county to formally initiate forfeiture action. The Michigan legislature in 2011 permitted forfeiture revenue to go straight into police budgets, spurring "seizing things like money out of birthday cards and lawnmowers," according to one retired State Police officer.

Chicago police have impounded more than a quarter million vehicles since 2010 for offenses ranging from "possession of paint intended for graffiti or defacement," "playing music too loudly," littering, "interfering with a funeral procession," and other offenses.[58] Chicago relies on "towing without telling," violating a state law requiring giving fair notice to vehicle owners. ACLU staff attorney Ben Ruddell said Chicago was "charging exorbitant fees in a way that it knows is likely to make it so folks never get their cars out of impoundment."[59] Roughly a quarter of the cars impounded are later sold for scrap prices because the owners cannot afford to ransom them after a deluge of exorbitant towing and storage fees. A 2019 lawsuit charged that, thanks to such policies, "thousands of cars are in effect stolen from citizens of Chicago and sold without proper notice and due process."[60]

Drivers can lose their vehicles for failing to kowtow to federal commands.[61] In 2015, angry Customs Service agents seized a new Ford F-250 truck to punish a Kentucky farmer who took their photos. Gerardo Serrano was traveling to visit kinfolk in Mexico when he snapped a few cellphone pictures at the border checkpoint in Eagle Pass, Texas. Customs agents protested that he was not allowed to take pictures. (Customs policy on this issue is unclear.) "One of the agents unlocked Serrano's door, unbuckled his seatbelt, and yanked him out of the car," according to his subsequent lawsuit. Serrano angrily declared: "Listen, you can't yank me out like that. I'm an American, you can't do that to me." After Serrano was handcuffed, an agent growled, "I'm sick of hearing about your rights. You have no rights here." An agent grabbed his phone and demanded Serrano give him the passcode. Serrano replied, "Go get a warrant." Even though he was on the verge of exiting the U.S., the agents vigorously searched his truck. One agent yelled "We got him!" after finding a magazine with five rounds for the pistol Serrano was licensed to carry. Serrano had left his SIG Sauer home, since he knew private firearms were not permitted in Mexico, but had forgotten about that magazine. (Serrano is a piker compared to the U.S. Marshals Service, which lost track of two million bullets.)[62] Customs confiscated his truck because it was "being used to transport 'arms or munitions of war,'" the *Washington Post* reported.[63] The feds made no effort to nail him as an arms trafficker; instead, they just wanted his Ford F-250. The feds notified Serrano that he would have to post a $3,800 bond — equal to 10% of the truck's value — if he wanted to dispute the seizure in court. Serrano paid the money but could not sue the agency until it filed a formal notice of forfeiture. After two years and no formal notice, Serrano finally filed suit, spurring a *Washington Post* profile of the case. Less than 24 hours later, Customs notified him that he could pick up his truck any time he wanted.

Home Heists

"A man's home is his castle" is null and void in the age of forfeiture.

Philadelphia police have confiscated more than a thousand homes since 2005. In 2012, an elderly black couple in West Philadelphia saw their small home assailed by several vans of heavily armed cops who warned: "We'll give you ten minutes to get your things and vacate the property." The Philadelphia city government had authorized police "to enter, seize, and seal the premises, without any prior notice." The couple had lived in the house for almost 50 years, but after their son was enticed to sell $60 worth of marijuana to a confidential informant, the government claimed the property. In 2014, police evicted a Greek immigrant couple after their son sold $40 worth of drugs in the front yard.[64] The *New Yorker* noted that "homes in Philadelphia are routinely seized for unproved minor drug crimes, often involving children or grandchildren who don't own the home." Louis Rulli of the University of Pennsylvania Law School observed: "For real-estate forfeitures, it's overwhelmingly African-Americans and Hispanics. It has a very disparate race and class impact."[65]

Philly's victims faced a Kafkaesque gauntlet to retrieve their property. "The typical forfeiture case required the defendant to appear in court four times. Adding up lawyer's fees and work hours lost, you're looking at thousands of dollars of expense to contest a forfeiture," a *Washington Post* analysis concluded.[66] Hearings would be repeatedly rescheduled at prosecutors' whim — and "if a defendant missed a hearing, their property could be summarily taken," the *Philadelphia Inquirer* noted.[67] The city government "treated its citizens like ATMs, ensnaring thousands of people in a system designed to strip people of their property and their rights," according to attorney Darpana Sheth.

Conway, South Carolina, police spent years trying to seize the small house of an elderly black widow. Ella Bromell had lived in the hardscrabble neighborhood for most of her life. The *Greenville News* reported that the problem "started in 2007 when people in her neighborhood were selling drugs outside of her home while she was at work or asleep." Bromwell "put up 'No Trespassing' signs and a fence. She trimmed bushes so passing police could see her porch easier." She was traumatized by the repeated government attempts to evict her from her home: "For nearly a decade, Bromell has been hiding inside, curtains and blinds drawn." In 2017, Judge William Seals, Jr., slammed the seizure attempt: "Law enforcement failed to produce any evidence that… the defendant had any actual knowledge of the criminal drug activity taking place at the residence."[68]

In December 2020, the police chief and mayor of Highland Park, Michigan, conducted a warrantless surprise inspection of a 13,000 square foot former church owned by Polish immigrants. Justyna and Matt Kozbial had multiple state licenses to grow marijuana, but the local officials confiscated the building regardless. Police refused to formally charge the

Kozbials, leaving them in Kafkaesque legal purgatory. The building was pillaged by vandals after the government seized it. After the Kozbials filed a lawsuit, the city admitted there was nothing to justify the seizure and offered to give the building back if the Kozbials would buy two new cars for the police department from a local Ford dealership. Marc Deldin, the Kozbials' attorney, complained, "It was a shakedown with a badge and a lawyer."[69]

At the federal level, Immigration and Customs Enforcement (ICE) agents "have become house-flippers, using… 'civil asset forfeiture' to steal houses from people they say were involved in crime, then selling the houses to fund… more seizures of more houses," author Cory Doctorow declared.[70] In a confidential seizure handbook, ICE agents are instructed to secure a warrant to search a property and to "bring along a private real estate expert to help appraise the property's value."[71] ICE warned its bounty hunters: "If total liabilities and costs incurred in seizing a real property or business exceed the value of the property, the property should not be seized." As a report in the *Intercept* noted:

> The manual instructs agents seeking to seize a property to work with confidential informants, scour tax records, and even obtain an interception warrant to determine whether "a telephone located on the property was used to plan or discuss criminal activity" in order to justify seizing the property.[72]

A single alleged phone call suffices to nullify the owner's title to his house, vivifying how the forfeiture deck is stacked.

Conniving Behind Closed Doors

Historian Lord Acton warned in 1861: "Everything secret degenerates, even the administration of justice." Across the nation, secrecy shrouds forfeiture's worst abuses.[73]

The New York State Police's multibillion-dollar forfeiture program was such a shambles that it failed to even track the cash and vehicles they seized, according to a 2015 audit.[74]

In Kentucky, almost 90% of the state's 323 law enforcement agencies ignored their legal obligation to file a report on their forfeiture harvests with the state government. The lawmen faced no penalty for their breaches.[75]

In 2017, Texas law enforcement agencies confiscated more than $50 million but kept no records on how many victims were never charged with a crime. The *Texas Tribune* noted that "state lawmakers, at the urging of prosecutors and law enforcement, have resisted attempts to report more detailed information about asset forfeiture to the public."[76]

Most states do not even report how much property they seize via forfeiture, and 14 states "do not appear to require any form of property tracking, leaving in doubt even such basic questions as what was seized and how much it was worth, who seized it… and why it was seized," the Institute for Justice reported. A top forfeiture official for Albuquerque explained in 2014 why his city didn't track how much property it confiscated: "I think they would rather not talk about those numbers because then it starts becoming more of a bullet-point for people that are trying to fight the program."[77]

Barely 1% of property seized by the feds is ever returned in part because the recovery process is hellishly complex.[78] The feds have gone to bizarre lengths to assure that forfeiture remains inscrutable. In 2004, the Justice Department ordered hundreds of federal depository libraries around the nation to remove and destroy its publications titled "Civil and Criminal Forfeiture Procedure," "Select Criminal Forfeiture Forms," and "Asset Forfeiture and Money Laundering Resource Directory." The outlawed documents "include information on how citizens can retrieve items that may have been confiscated by the government during an investigation," protested American Library Association president Michael Gorman.[79] The Justice Department canceled the bonfires after the mutiny of the librarians.

Federal agencies are also buttressing forfeiture with a propaganda campaign perhaps inspired by *National Lampoon*. In 1973, the *Lampoon* published an iconic cover showing a revolver pressed against a nervous dog's head: "If you don't buy this magazine, we'll kill this dog." In June 2019, the FBI posted a video on Twitter of adorable puppies who would supposedly all die unless the feds can continue confiscating private property without a criminal conviction. The FBI proclaimed: "Civil forfeiture laws are helping the FBI and its partners get dogs rescued from dogfighting rings positioned to be treated, rehabilitated, and moved into better situations." One critic summarized the video's subtle message: "Surrender the Fifth Amendment or the dog dies."[80] In reality, dogs are involved in less than 0.01% of all forfeiture cases, and almost all such cases result in criminal convictions. The video did not mention that the FBI's dogfighting crackdowns routinely killed the "rescued" dogs to save the expense of maintaining them.

The Forfeiture Dynamo

Deputy Attorney General Eric Holder boasted to Congress in 1999 that forfeiture laws allow the feds to "separate the criminal from his profits... thus removing the incentive that others may have to commit similar crimes tomorrow."[81] But the fundamental incentive driving forfeiture abuses since 1984 has been the ability of federal, state, and local agencies to keep seizures for themselves. More than 500 police departments and law enforcement task forces rely on forfeitures for 20% or more of their budgets. The District of Columbia police budget includes provisions for spending forfeiture proceeds for the next four years.[82]

Routine forfeiture procedures are often difficult to distinguish from garden variety extortion. Police and prosecutors routinely treat forfeiture funds like lottery winnings to spend as they please. Manhattan District Attorney Cy Vance spent almost a quarter million dollars from a forfeiture fund on "fine dining, first-class airfare, and luxurious hotels."[83] In Texas, forfeitures financed margarita machines and trips to Hawaii.[84] Houston cops gave $600,000 in forfeiture proceeds to a nonprofit political ally of the police department.[85] Georgia revenue agents spent millions of dollars of confiscated assets to "buy trinkets, travel, engraved firearms, tactical gear, a fleet of cars... commemorative Super Bowl badges, golf carts, $130 sunglasses — even stress balls shaped like beer mugs and wine bottles."[86] The money was raised in part by confiscating convenience stores that were accused of technical violations of regulations for video gambling machines (which are legal in Georgia).

The Chicago Police Department used millions of forfeiture dollars to create a junior National Security Agency to spy on city residents. Without notifying the Chicago City Council, the police department bought software to enable it to crack cellphone encryption and track users, conduct warrantless intercepts of phone calls, and track and record license plates around the city.[87] Chicago police also covertly used forfeiture proceeds to purchase a secretive drone network to surveil drivers, pedestrians, and other "terrorist related issues." That revelation occurred solely because a hacker released internal emails from the Chicago city government.[88]

The U.S. Commission on Civil Rights warned in 2017 that allowing law enforcement agencies to keep what they seize "creates an inherent conflict of interest" which undermines "public trust in the police." John Yoder, the Justice Department's forfeiture chief in the 1980s, lamented in 2014 that forfeiture "has turned into an evil itself, with the corruption it engendered among government and law enforcement coming to clearly outweigh any benefits."[89]

Forfeiture is a rigged game in which low-income Americans suffer worst. Justice Clarence Thomas wrote in 2017: "These forfeiture operations frequently target the poor and other groups least able to defend their interests in forfeiture proceedings."[90] Similarly, Texas Supreme Court Justice Don Willett declared in a 2014 dissent: "Civil forfeiture... now disproportionately ensnares those least capable of protecting themselves, poor Texans who usually capitulate without a fight because mounting a defense is too costly."[91] "Due process" in forfeiture cases often depends solely on the media coverage an abuse receives. Sporadic government defeats are no consolation to forfeiture victims who cannot afford a lawyer to fight for their rights.

Conclusion: Forfeiture as a Failure of Democracy

In February 2019, the Supreme Court issued a rare rebuke to the forfeiture regime. Indiana police confiscated a $41,000 Land Rover after its drug addict driver sold $225 worth of drugs. The driver sued, claiming that the forfeiture violated the Constitution's prohibition on excessive fines. Justice Ruth Bader Ginsburg, writing for the Court, declared: "The protection against excessive fines has been a constant shield throughout Anglo-American history: Exorbitant tolls undermine other constitutional liberties."[92] In a concurring opinion, Justice Clarence Thomas stressed that the Fourteenth Amendment, which recognized that state and local governments had no prerogative to violate citizens' rights, was spurred in part by outrageous Southern legislation in the wake of the Civil War. Thomas quoted a congressman who asserted in 1866 that the excessive fines inflicted by Alabama's laws were "almost reenacting slavery."

But the Supreme Court has dismally failed to uphold a "constant shield" against excessive fines in recent history. Forfeiture victims who are wrongfully stripped of their life savings may feel like police are "reenacting slavery" — since the fruits of years of labor vanish in a moment. As North Carolina convenience store owner Lyndon McLellan groused when federal agents unjustifiably seized his bank account without warning: "It took me 13 years to save that much money, and 13 seconds for the government to take it away."[93]

For decades, the Supreme Court has blindfolded itself to law enforcement abuses and upheld forfeitures that should have "shocked the conscience." Rather than standing up for decency and due process, the Supreme Court became a silent partner in the fleecing of legions of Americans. Perpetual law enforcement looting could not occur without perennial political and judicial complicity.

Similar shamelessness prevailed at many state and local courts. When the South Carolina Supreme Court upheld a state forfeiture law in 2022, Chief Justice Donald Beatty dissented, scoffing at an "illusion of due process" that bowed to "precedent regarding an ancient legal fiction… because this is the way things have always been, and then it insulates the fiction from further scrutiny behind an unassailable presumption of constitutionality."[94]

Forfeiture abuses reveal how "legal fictions" ravage individual rights. Forfeiture proceedings are often akin to medieval tribunals where judges listened to priests reciting ritual phrases prior to announcing whether another heretic must be burned. Perhaps the biggest "legal fiction" is that laws still constrain government agents. The notion that government must have unlimited power to punish anyone suspected of a crime is the same dogma that has propelled tyranny for thousands of years.

3. The War on Gun Owners

"A man's rights rest in three boxes: the ballot box, the jury box, and the cartridge box."

— Escaped slave and abolitionist Frederick Douglass, 1867

Federal, state, and local governments have turned tens of millions of peaceful gun owners into felons whose lives can be destroyed at the whim of a prosecutor or a president. As crime soars in cities across the nation, self-defense is now supposedly the worst offense.

Politicians have long trumpeted their contempt for gun owners. In a 1994 Supreme Court case, the Clinton administration portrayed gun owners as the legal equivalent of drug dealers, asserting that "one would hardly be surprised to learn that owning a gun is not an innocent act."[1] Before Eric Holder became Attorney General in 2009, he urged public schools to preach an antigun message every single day and proclaimed that "we need to… really brainwash people into thinking about guns in a vastly different way."[2] President Biden has called for banning the most popular rifles and pistols owned by Americans.

Gun owners are pariahs for media outlets that portray any privately owned firearm as a school-massacre-in-waiting. *New Republic*, one of the most influential liberal magazines, called for banning all private firearms and scoffed at "a reluctance to impose 'elite' culture on parts of the country where guns are popular."[3] After the Supreme Court struck down arbitrary restrictions on carrying firearms in six states in 2022, Georgetown University law professor Rosa Brooks howled, "We are essentially slaves to a document that was written more than 230 years ago by a tiny group of white slave-owning men."[4] Any limit on politicians' power to forcibly disarm private citizens is the new slavery.

You Might Be a Federal Firearms Felon If…

Because Congress and presidents refuse to recognize state laws, the feds have a pretext to forcibly disarm and imprison almost 10% of the American public. Federal supremacy is the largest single cause of illicit gun ownership in America. But the vast majority of unindicted firearm felons have never been arrested for violence.

Potheads are America's biggest gun offenders. Thirty-six states have voted or passed legislation to authorize medicinal use of marijuana, and many states also permit recreational use of marijuana. But federal agencies consider those laws null and void. The Bureau of Alcohol, Tobacco, Firearms and Explosives (ATF) prohibits gun and ammunition sales to anyone who uses of marijuana or other narcotics, claiming that they pose a risk of "irrational or unpredictable behavior."

ATF Form 4473, the Firearms Transaction Record, which is mandatory for any purchase from a licensed gun dealer, specifically inquires whether the "applicant is an unlawful user of marijuana."[5] Nonviolent marijuana users face "up to 15 years in prison for illegal firearm possession, up to 15 years for 'trafficking in firearms' by obtaining a gun, and up to 10 years for failing to report cannabis consumption" on Form 4473.[6] In 2018, two Maine marijuana users were indicted and later convicted for federal firearms violations after they failed to disclose that they were "unlawful" users of marijuana on that form (regardless that marijuana is legal in Maine).[7]

Three months after Hawaii's first marijuana medical dispensary opened in 2017, the Honolulu Police Department ordered "legal cannabis patients to 'voluntarily surrender' any guns they own because pot is still considered an illegal drug under federal law," the *Honolulu Star-Advertiser* reported.[8] Honolulu Police Chief Susan Ballard warned medical marijuana card holders that they had 30 days to "voluntarily surrender [their] firearms, permit and ammunition to the Honolulu Police Department or otherwise transfer ownership." Honolulu police relented after a backlash, but the legal peril remains.

Federal prosecutors are using "the nation's drug laws as a key tool to keep guns out of the wrong hands" — including those of "anti-government extremists," the *Dallas Morning News* reported in 2021. To spur a federal firearms investigation, "social media photos of someone using marijuana or other drugs will suffice."[9] Law professor Dru Stevenson asserted that federal drug laws have become, "functionally speaking, our society's primary mechanism of gun control." Defense lawyer Brian Poe observed that prosecutors use the charge as "a catch-all if they haven't been able to find anything else to charge them with." Rachel Malone, Texas director for Gun Owners of America, says: "To tell Texans you can't purchase a firearm if you have a compassionate [marijuana] use card is unconscionable. We should not force people to choose between gun ownership and taking care of themselves."[10]

Most states that permit medicinal marijuana have registries of authorized users. The ATF could potentially access most of those marijuana user registries and then conduct mass arrests in states that mandate firearms registration. That type of roundup is not politically feasible at the moment. But a few highly publicized shootings by marijuana users could provide engraved invitations for prosecutors to become superstars.

The marijuana gun ban is being challenged in multiple lawsuits. In 2022, the Justice Department justified the ban by invoking previous government prohibitions on gun ownership by Catholics, American Indians, and panhandlers. Federal Judge Allen Wyrick slammed the feds for relying on "ignominious historical restrictions"[11] and rejected the government's claim that a person's "mere status as a user of marijuana justifies stripping him of his fundamental right to possess a firearm."[12] Challenging that ruling, the Justice Department modified its argument and justified disarming potheads because the government previously locked up "lunatics." As *Reason*'s Jacob Sullum noted: "According to the Biden administration, it was perfectly reasonable to put cannabis consumers in the same category as… children, 'armed revolutionaries,' and 'mental defectives.'"[13]

More than 52 million Americans used marijuana during 2021, according to the National Survey of Drug Use and Health, and another 10 million people used other illicit substances.[14] Actual usage is higher because some people are paranoid about confessing crimes to federally funded survey takers. Roughly 40% of American households possess firearms. Thus, roughly 25 million gun owners are probably felons because of their possession or use of marijuana or other illicit indulgences. Though most gun owners who violate marijuana laws pose no threat, federal agencies could round them up as if they were hostile Indians being confined to a reservation.

When laws create so many criminals, selective prosecution is guaranteed — or selective non-prosecution for the politically connected. Hunter Biden, the son of President Joe Biden, purchased a .38 Revolver in 2018 and signed the federal form attesting that he was not a user of illegal narcotics. However, in his 2021 memoir, Hunter Biden trumpeted stories of smoking crack cocaine in the same period he bought the gun. Biden's girlfriend at the time, the widowed wife of his brother, threw the gun into a trash can after he left it in his truck; the gun was found by an old man rummaging for recyclables.

After he turned the revolver in to the police, Secret Service agents descended on the gun shop that sold the firearm and sought to seize the paperwork tied to the sale and Hunter. As *Politico* reported:

> Any involvement by the Secret Service on behalf of the Biden family or on its own initiative would be inappropriate interference in an incident that was already being investigated by Delaware State Police with the involvement of the FBI, according to law enforcement officials.[15]

ATF rejected a Freedom of Information Act request for records on the Hunter Biden case because any response would violate Biden's "privacy."[16]

In June 2023, the Justice Department announced that it had offered a plea deal to Hunter that would involve no jail time for his firearms offense. Instead, he was entitled to enter a pretrial diversion program to deal with his drug abuses. Other private citizens received no such sweetheart deals for "lying and buying." In 2019, a federal prosecutor said that rapper Kodak Black needed "tough love," and he was sent to prison for three years for false claims on his firearms form.[17] Two months before the feds announced the plea offer for Hunter, "a woman in Iowa was sentenced to a year in prison for lying about her address and drug use on Form 4473," reported Gun Owners of America.[18] The coverup and plea deal for his son did not deter Joe Biden from perennially demanding far more prosecutions of nonviolent firearms law violators.

On September 14, federal prosecutors indicted Hunter Biden for three counts tied to lying about his gun purchase. Hunter's legal team denounced the charges as "unique and unjustified." They plan to argue in court that the indictment is invalid because the president's son is abiding by the pretrial diversion agreement he previously was offered.[19]

Confiscating Politically Incorrect Rifles

Since late in the last century, politicians have floated mass disarmament schemes. In January 1994, the Clinton administration's federal budget proposal announced: "The administration also supports a ban on semiautomatic firearms."[20] At that time, Americans owned more than 35 million semiautomatic pistols and rifles. The administration backed away from a total semiautomatic ban but pursued piecemeal prohibition.

President Bill Clinton launched a crusade to ban "assault weapons." That term has little or no coherent meaning — at least as used by politicians.

According to the Defense Department, an assault weapon is a rifle that is capable of both automatic (machine gun) fire and semiautomatic (one shot per trigger pull) fire. But most of the media implicitly defined "assault weapon" as any politically incorrect rifle. Clinton's ban prohibited the sale of rifles with bayonet lugs or grenade launchers — even though grenade launchers attached to rifles had never been used in a violent crime in the U.S. It was "picture book prohibition" — diminishing the Second Amendment on aesthetic grounds.

Fearmongering propelled the ban. Though the ban dealt with semiautomatic rifles and pistols, Clinton repeatedly claimed that all assault weapons were "automatic weapons." Ownership of machine guns has been severely restricted by the federal government since 1934, and the violent crime rate among properly registered machine gun owners is among the lowest of any group.

Congress passed the Assault Weapons Ban in 1994, which lasted for a decade. The ban was never intended to solve the crime problem, a *Washington Post* editorial admitted: "Assault weapons play a part in only a small percentage of crime. The provision is mainly symbolic; its virtue will be if it turns out to be, as hoped, a stepping stone to broader gun control."[21] *Post* columnist Charles Krauthammer, in an article headlined, "Disarm the Citizenry. But Not Yet," explained the "real logic of the ban… Its only real justification is not to reduce crime but to desensitize the public to the regulation of weapons in preparation for their ultimate confiscation."[22] Once an assault weapons law is on the books, there would be little to prevent politicians from vastly increasing the number of prohibited weapons banned under its vague provisions.

When Sen. Dianne Feinstein (D-CA) pushed to revive the ban in 2012, she estimated that the previously banned weapons were used in 50 killings nationwide per year[23] — fewer than the number of people strangled to death each year.[24] A 2013 National Institute of Justice report concluded: "Since assault weapons are not a major contributor to U.S. gun homicide and the existing stock of guns is large, an assault weapon ban is unlikely to have an impact on gun violence."

In 2019, compelling Americans to surrender "assault weapons" became "the newest purity test" for Democratic presidential candidates, according to the *Washington Post*.[25] "Hell yes, we're going to take your AR-15," proclaimed Beto O'Rourke at a Democratic Party presidential candidate debate. The AR-

15 is the most popular rifle type sold in America. (His campaign promptly turned his threat into a T-shirt sold for fundraising.) In August 2019, a CNN host asked Biden about gun owners who fear that "a Biden administration means they're gonna come for my guns." Biden replied, "Bingo, you're right, if you have an assault weapon."[26]

Biden used "assault weapon" as a catch-all term for anything he disapproves. In 2022, he condemned any firearms using 9mm ammunition (which he ludicrously labeled "high-caliber weapons").[27] Biden also condemned any gun magazines which hold more than 10 rounds.[28] Biden's standard would outlaw most of the pistols sold in the U.S. in the last decade. In November 2022, Biden called for banning all semiautomatic firearms: "The idea we still allow semiautomatic weapons to be purchased is sick. It's just sick. It has no, no social redeeming value. Zero. None."[29] Similarly, the 220-member House of Representatives Democratic Caucus solemnly announced on Twitter in 2022: "Semiautomatic rifles are weapons of war."[30] Biden would turn the clock back a hundred years on self-defense at the same time that his own bodyguards have the latest machine guns.

Antigun activists don't care about the specific meaning of "assault weapon" as long as the phrase evokes dread. Steve Dettelbach, Biden's ATF chief, repeatedly failed to define "assault weapon" in congressional testimony. As a candidate for Ohio Attorney General in 2018, Dettelbach called for banning assault weapons. At his 2022 Senate confirmation hearing, Dettelbach admitted that he "did not define the term. And I haven't gone through the process of defining that term." At a 2023 House hearing, when asked for a definition, Dettelbach replied: "If Congress wishes to take that up, I think Congress would have to do the work… but we have people at ATF who can talk… so that whatever determination you chose to make would be an informed one."[31]

President Biden hustles a fractured fairy tale to boost the ban. Biden frequently told audiences: "You couldn't buy a cannon when this [Second] Amendment was passed, so there's no reason you should be able to buy certain assault weapons."[32] But Americans were permitted to purchase cannons and anything else they chose after the nation was founded. *Washington Post* fact-checker Glenn Kessler awarded Biden "Four Pinocchios" — the harshest rating for political lies: "We have no idea where [Biden] conjured up this notion about a ban on cannon ownership in the early days of the Republic, but he needs to stop making this claim."[33]

Because "assault weapon" is a political concoction rather than a specific type of firearm, legal definitions are arbitrary and confusing — which can have fatal consequences such as in the case of Duncan Lemp (as discussed in Chapter 4, "Licensed to Kill"). Montgomery County, Maryland, police killed 21-year-old Lemp on March 12, 2020, after they saw an Instagram photo he posted of himself with a rifle, which they presumed was an Israeli rifle banned under Maryland's assault weapon law. Nine months after Lemp perished in a no-knock predawn attack, the county attorney issued a report which perfunctorily

> noted that upon further review and investigation into the IWI Tavor X95 rifle, it was determined that it was not an assault rifle… It appears that Lemp's rifle was a legal "copycat" made to look exactly like the illegal version of the IWI Tavor X95. Very minute changes such as the overall length of the weapon can mean the difference between an illegal assault rifle and a legal one.[34]

But the non-banned weapon was "close enough for government work" to exonerate police for killing Lemp in his bedroom. The county government treated its fatal mistake like a paperwork error. (In July 2022, the Supreme Court effectively invalidated the Maryland assault weapons law.)

"Very minute changes" is the key to the assault weapons controversy. Tweaks to official regulations can convert millions of American gun owners into felons overnight. Assault weapons are a "flag of convenience" for politicians' targeting the rights of gun owners. For decades, the controversy has resembled a circus shell game. Politicians talk about assault weapons as solely a moral issue — a question of pure evil — and then move the shell to forbid vast numbers of widely owned firearms. Banning assault weapons gives government a pretext to arrest or imprison legions of citizens while doing nothing to make America safer.

Since Gun Owners Are Crazy…

Since politicians have not been able to impose total prohibitions on firearms ownership, they are creating pretexts to disarm Americans on a case-by-case basis. And since a person would have to be nuts to own guns, there are plenty of opportunities for legal mischief.

Since 1968, federal law prohibited gun purchases by individuals who have been involuntarily committed to psychiatric hospitals and certified by a court as mentally unstable. But many politicians seek far more sweeping prohibitions.

In 2013, Gov. Andrew Cuomo railroaded the Secure Ammunition and Firearms Enforcement Act (SAFE) through the New York legislature. Cuomo proclaimed: "People who have mental health issues should not have guns. They could hurt themselves; they could hurt other people."[35] But tens of millions of Americans visit therapists each year, and "mental health issues" opens a prohibitionist Pandora's Box.

More than 85,000 New Yorkers lost their Second Amendment rights as a result of a "mental health" exclusion clause in the 2013 law.[36] New York University law professor James Jacobs observed: "Based on as little as a single short emergency room interview," an individual "need not even be notified that his or her name has been added to a database of persons whose firearms license must be revoked and whose firearms must be surrendered."[37] Medical professionals and others were already legally obliged to notify police if a patient "made a credible threat" of violence, but the SAFE Act was far more expansive.[38]

One of the law's first victims was a librarian who was forced to surrender his firearms in part because he (like more than ten million other Americans) had received a prescription for Xanax. A New York City public radio station reported the case of "a retired police officer who went to a Long Island hospital complaining of insomnia. A week later, sheriff's deputies confiscated his guns." County health officials were supposed to personally vet the disarmament recommendations from nurses, social workers, and others. Instead, county health officials effectively became "clerical workers, rubber-stamping the decisions," the *New York Times* reported.[39] The unjustified mass disarmament of private citizens was a harmless error — at least in the eyes of New York politicians.

A similar nationwide "mental health" gun grab occurred in the final weeks of the Obama administration. Spurred by the White House, the Social Security Administration ruled that up to 75,000 disability recipients a year who were labeled "mental defectives" ("the same unscientific and unspecific standard that the Supreme Court approved in 1927 when legalizing the sterilization of the mentally ill and other eugenic treatments"[40]) would be forced to surrender their firearms. Sen. Charles Grassley (R-IA) complained:

> The disorders list [for banning gun ownership] included eating
> disorders and other disorders that merely impact sleep or caused

restlessness or even "feelings of inadequacy," illustrating that the regulation was not limited to people with serious mental disorders that caused them to be dangerous.[41]

The Social Security Administration was not required to prove anyone was mentally ill before nullifying their rights. Instead, as NRA-ILA observed, "[t]he rule forces affected beneficiaries to file a petition for 'restoration' of rights and to somehow prove their possession of firearms would not harm public safety or the public interest."[42] The ACLU opposed the mandate because it "reinforces the harmful stereotype that people with mental disabilities, a vast and diverse group of citizens, are violent." Congress and the Trump administration speedily overturned the new rule in 2017.

The push for mental health gun seizures was turbocharged after 19-year-old Nikolas Cruz attacked Marjory Stoneman Douglas High School in Parkland, Florida, on February 14, 2018. Eight sheriff's deputies cowered outside while Cruz's rampage left 17 dead. Cruz should have been previously arrested numerous times because of violence and threats at school. Cruz had posted on YouTube: "I'm going to be a professional school shooter." Even though he used his own name for that comment, the FBI claimed that they "could not determine his true identity." But school authorities refrained from charging him because of an Obama administration school grant program that sought to curb the "school-to-prison" pipeline for minority students (Cruz was Hispanic). In 2022, the Justice Department paid $127 million to survivors and family members of the Parkland massacre, admitting the FBI's culpability for failing to follow up on explicit tips regarding Cruz's pending shooting spree.[43]

The botched government response to a brazen threat did not deter legislators from speedily enacting "red flag" laws to authorize instantly disarming people suspected of violent tendencies. President Trump propelled that campaign when he declared that law enforcement should "take the guns first, go through due process second."[44]

Maryland was one of the first states to enact an "extreme risk protective order" law. At 5:17 AM on November 5, 2018, two cops banged on the door of 61-year-old Gary Willis in Ferndale, Maryland. Willis was asleep and came to the door holding a gun. The police told him to put the gun down, and he complied. However, after police handed him the gun seizure court order, police claimed that he "became irate." He allegedly picked up his gun, a scuffle followed, and a policeman shot and killed Willis. Anne Arundel

County Police Chief Timothy Altomare commented later that day: "If you look at this morning's outcome, it's tough for us to say, 'Well, what did we prevent?'… What would've happened if we didn't go there at 5 AM?"[45] Willis would not have been dead, for starters. The police department refused to disclose any solid information on why Willis was raided. His niece told the *Baltimore Sun*: "I'm just dumbfounded. My uncle wouldn't hurt anybody… They didn't need to do what they did."[46] The Maryland law entitled "law enforcement officers, physicians, mental health specialists, and… housemates, spouses, dating partners… and anyone 'related to the respondent by blood, marriage, or adoption'" to file a request to forcibly disarm a target.[47] Almost no evidence is necessary to spur a gun confiscation raid.

By early 2021, 19 states and the District of Columbia had enacted "red flag" laws. Shortly after taking office, President Biden announced: "I want to see a national Red Flag Law and legislation to incentivize states to enact their own Red Flag Laws." Biden's Justice Department intervened in a 2021 Supreme Court case that many antigun activists viewed as a model for government officials forcibly protecting people against themselves.

In 2015, after an elderly couple living in Cranston, Rhode Island, had a heated argument, Edward Caniglia placed an unloaded revolver on the table and taunted his wife: "Why don't you just shoot me and get me out of my misery?" His wife was spooked and left to stay overnight in a hotel. When he didn't answer a phone call the next morning, she called the police and asked them to check on him.

Police arrived and browbeat Edward Caniglia into getting a psychiatric examination at a hospital. He agreed to do so only after police promised not to seize his handguns. The shrinks certified him as sane (at least by prevailing Rhode Island standards), but police confiscated his guns while he was gone. Both he and his wife requested that the guns be returned. Police refused to do so until Caniglia, who had no history of violence or abusing firearms, filed a lawsuit claiming that his constitutional rights had been violated. A federal appeals court upheld the gun seizure to give "elbow room" to police who "must act as a master of all emergencies [and are] 'expected to… provide an infinite variety of services to preserve and protect community safety.'"[48]

That ruling scorned prior Supreme Court rulings, including a 1980 declaration: "It is a basic principle of Fourth Amendment law that searches and seizures inside a home without a warrant are presumptively unreasonable."[49] But prosecutors persuaded federal judges that a private home deserved no sanctity from police intrusions. According to a Biden administration brief, constitutional rights were moot because the Cranston cops were simply dealing with "an impending safety threat through a warrantless seizure of a potentially mentally unstable person and an entry into his residence for the limited purpose of removing firearms."[50] For Biden's legal team, "confiscating" became "removing" as smoothly as one of Falstaff's minions turned "stealing" into "conveying." The Biden administration presumed that search warrants were unnecessary any time government officials assert that it is "reasonable" to enter someone's house "to ensure public health and safety." And who defines "reasonableness"? The same government officials who barge into people's homes.

The Supreme Court unanimously rejected Biden's position in the Rhode Island Red Flag gun case. Justice Clarence Thomas wrote that the case involved the "very core" of the Fourth Amendment, "the right of a man to retreat into his own home and there be free from unreasonable governmental intrusion."[51] The court refused to give police "an open-ended license" to enter homes and seize firearms without a warrant.

A few weeks after that Supreme Court defeat, the Biden administration released its model gun confiscation order legislation. Individuals targeted by such orders could be automatically disarmed and would have the legal burden to prove they are no risk. The model bill included a long list of categories of people and professions that could nominate targets for red flag raids. The NRA noted: "The Biden administration endorses granting any school employee a veto on a student's right to keep and bear arms up to two years after they were enrolled."

Anyone who vigorously criticizes and opposes politicians and bureaucrats could be labeled a sick person who cannot be trusted with a gun. How easy should it be to forcibly disarm peaceful citizens? Pennsylvania Governor Tom Wolf posted a graphic online showing how Red Flag laws provide "no fuss, no muss" disarmament. After a woman sees a Facebook friend post "photos of guns and cryptic messages," she calls the police who petition a judge to "temporarily" seize his guns. The Facebook post provides "proof" the guy is a threat who must be forcibly disarmed.[52] The vapid standard that Wolf championed would suffice to confiscate weapons from any gun owner who publicly criticized the government. Red Flag laws are also an engraved invitation to "swatting" — filing false reports to provoke police raids on hapless citizens.

In June 2022, Congress passed the Bipartisan Safer Communities Act to pay state governments to enact red flag laws. That law mandated more due process protections than currently exist in some states. But the Biden administration ignored the "due process" technicality and speedily shoveled federal funds to encourage gun bans by any state. In July 2023, Republican senators protested to Attorney General Merrick Garland that the Justice Department "has funded every state that applied with a 'red flag' gun confiscation law on the books without enforcing Congress's 'due process' requirements… to bribe pro-gun states into passing gun confiscation laws."[53] A senior advisor for the Bureau of Justice Assistance declared that federal grants could be used in states without red flag laws to pay for "media campaigns or public service announcements that would encourage the state to incorporate that type of law… to potentially create that law within their state."[54] But federal agencies are not supposed to use tax dollars for propaganda.

There is scant evidence that red flag laws curb bloodshed. An analysis in the journal *Psychiatric Services* concluded that "Connecticut's [red flag] law was associated with a net increase in suicides." A 2020 RAND Corporation analysis of the results of red flag orders "found no qualifying studies showing that extreme risk protection orders decreased any of the eight outcomes we investigated," including "violent crime" and "suicide."[55] In 2021, RAND analysts warned that "policies targeting individuals based on risk factors would result in an extremely high rate of false positives," in the "order of one in a million" for people who will commit mass shootings.

The Presidential Magic Felony Wand

With a single edict, a president can turn hundreds of thousands of peaceful gun owners into felons.

On October 1, 2017, Stephen Paddock fired hundreds of rounds from his window in the Mandalay Bay hotel in Las Vegas into a crowd attending a country music concert below. Sixty people were killed, and more than 400 wounded. Paddock was using a bump stock, an attachment to rifles that enables more rapid scattershot fire. The FBI took charge of the investigation and disclosed almost nothing about either the killings or the killer.

After the shooting caused a national uproar, President Trump vowed that "bump stocks are going to be gone." Trump declared: "I'm writing that [ban order] out myself. I don't care if Congress does it or not."[56] Trump discovered a new constitutional loophole for topics that spur frenetic presidential tweets.

Federal agencies had previously repeatedly ruled that bump stocks were unregulated firearm parts that did not convert semiautomatic weapons into machine guns.[57] Bump stocks had not been used in any other mass shooting. The *Washington Post* noted that law enforcement agencies did not use bump stocks because they made guns fire inaccurately.[58] Regardless, Trump tweeted that "we will BAN all devices that turn legal weapons into illegal machine guns."[59]

In 2018, the ATF reclassified guns with bump stocks as illegal machine guns because "such devices allow a shooter of a semiautomatic firearm to initiate a continuous firing cycle with a single pull of the trigger." But that was not how bump stocks actually operate. Even Sen. Dianne Feinstein, a perennial gun control champion, admitted that the Trump administration's position "hinges on a dubious analysis claiming that bumping the trigger is not the same as pulling it."[60] *Arizona Republic* columnist Joanna Allhands observed that the Justice Department "performs verbal gymnastics," claiming that "the shooter's finger and arm are part of the mechanism that makes this miraculous change."[61]

Gun owners purchased half a million bump stocks after the feds had repeatedly declared that they were legal to possess. When the Justice Department sought public comments on the proposed ban, the vast majority of 180,000 respondents strongly opposed criminalizing bump stock possession. Didn't matter.

Anyone who fails to destroy or surrender their bump stock faces a penalty of $250,000 and up to ten years in prison. After the federal ban took effect, the ATF reported that "less than 1% of gun owners turned in their bump stocks."[62] However, many bump stocks were reportedly lost in boating accidents.

A lawsuit by 23 state attorneys general asserted that the ATF rule "categorically expands the text of the criminal statute in a way that Congress couldn't possibly have intended." In March 2021, a federal appeals court in Cincinnati struck down the ban, declaring:

> Granting the executive the right both to determine a criminal statute's meaning and to enforce that same criminal statute poses a severe risk to individual liberty... It is not the role of the executive — particularly the unelected administrative state — to dictate to the public what is right and what is wrong.[63]

In December 2021, another federal appeals court panel deadlocked on a bump stock ban case, splitting 8 to 8, thereby leaving in place a lower court decision upholding the ban. The appeals court justified the ban: "No doubt many people believe that rifles equipped with bump stocks share the same dangerous traits that led Congress to ban machine guns."[64] The appeals court thus created a new legal standard — "no doubt many people believe" — for sanctifying arbitrary decrees. Elsewhere, a U.S. Navy/Marine Corps Court of Appeals overturned a bump stock conviction based on "the instinctive distaste against men languishing in prison unless the lawmaker has clearly said they should."[65] Litigation on this issue continues.

Biden did not let the Trump "presidential magic felony wand" go idle. Shortly after Biden took office, the ATF proposed to outlaw up to 40 million stabilizing braces used for pistol shooting.[66] Mike Maharrey of the Tenth Amendment Center observed that a pistol brace "serves as a stabilizer that enables a shooter to fire with one hand. Pistol braces are popular with disabled people who can't use both arms." The ATF had previously ruled in 2012 and 2017 that such braces were an accessory not subject to federal restrictions.

On April 8, 2021, Biden announced, "A stabilizing brace... essentially, it makes that pistol a hell of a lot more accurate and a mini-rifle."[67] He decreed that millions of pistol braces would henceforth be treated as the legal equivalent of sawed-off shotguns under federal law. Because pistol braces can be concealed, the Biden administration sought to treat anyone who possessed such devices as a bank-robber-in-waiting. In a June 2023 speech, Biden bizarrely claimed that putting a brace on a pistol "makes them where you can have a higher-caliber weapon — a higher-caliber bullet — coming out of that gun."[68] Even CNN fact-checkers groaned over that howler.

Anyone who fails to file an application with ATF, get fingerprinted, submit to a background check, and pay a $200 tax could face five years in prison for each pistol brace they possess. Forty-eight Republican senators signed a letter to Attorney General Garland complaining that the proposed rule "would turn millions of law-abiding Americans into criminals overnight, and would constitute the largest executive branch-imposed gun registration and confiscation scheme in American history." The Biden administration failed to offer a clear or coherent definition of what it was banning. Instead, the ATF created a byzantine "check list" which gun owners could use to "count up their points" on their pistols and braces to see whether they were felonious. After the Biden administration issued the final regulation in early 2023, 25 state attorneys general and the NRA sued. An NRA official declared that the ATF "is declaring that they will effectively decide on a case-by-case basis" whether a firearm is subject to the new prohibition.[69]

While Trump and Biden yanked the rug out from under existing gun owners, governors and state lawmakers heroically banned guns that don't exist. After the New York legislature enacted his SAFE Act, Gov. Cuomo boasted, "You can overpower the extremists with intelligence and with reason and with commonsense." But a federal judge later ruled that parts of the SAFE Act were "entirely indecipherable." Because Cuomo wanted the title of "the nation's toughest antigun governor," the SAFE Act idiotically decreed that gun owners were permitted to load only seven rounds into ten-round magazines.[70] Most New York gun owners ignored the law's registration requirement.

The Golden State is the home to America's most visionary prohibitionists. California's Unsafe Handgun Act outlawed the sale of any semiautomatic handgun manufactured after 2013 that does not possess a trigger that would "stamp microscopically the handgun's make, model, and serial number onto each fired shell casing." California legislators congratulated themselves on discovering the "silver bullet" for stopping violence — even though that microstamping technology did not exist. The result is a de facto ban on all new semiautomatic handguns produced after 2013.

A federal appeals court upheld the law in 2018 because there was no proof that "microstamping is technologically infeasible" — even though not a single gun manufacturer could produce firearms meeting the legislative standard.[71] The California Supreme Court also upheld the law in 2018, declaring: "Impossibility can occasionally excuse noncompliance with a statute. But impossibility does not authorize a court to go beyond interpreting a statute and simply invalidate it."[72] Banning new pistols via the microstamping mandate is as much of a constitutional infringement as prohibiting newspapers from publishing unless their printing presses have zero carbon footprint. The California legislature neglected to require criminals to leave their shell casings at the scene of a shooting, thereby making the law even more inane.

Self-Reliance or Sacrificial Animals?

When President Obama announced an array of new restrictions on firearms in early 2016, he declared: "These actions won't prevent every act of violence, or save every life — but if even one life is spared, they will be well worth the effort."[73] Obama implied that privately owned guns never save a single life — a common refrain by gun ban advocates. Instead, guns are presumably a sheer menace that politicians must eradicate. In some states, courts uphold police denials of firearms permits "under the dogmas that handguns can never be effectively used by private citizens for self-defense," as lawyer and scholar Stephen Halbrook testified to Congress.[74]

Firearms are far more effective for self-defense than many politicians and pundits admit. Florida State University criminologist Gary Kleck observed that "in the vast majority of cases in which a victim has a handgun, the criminal surrenders or flees."[75] Federal Judge Stephen McGlynn noted in an April 2023 court decision that "there are up to 2.5 million instances each year in which civilians used firearms for home defense."[76] A 2013 Centers for Disease Control (CDC) report recognized that "self-defense can be an important crime deterrent" and noted that "almost all national survey estimates indicate that defensive gun uses by victims are at least as common as offensive uses by criminals" and occur up to three million times per year.[77]

During the urban riots beginning in May 2020, far more Americans recognized that "no one is coming" when their lives are in deadly peril. Shortly before those riots, several governors banned gun stores from opening to serve their customers as part of COVID lockdowns. Elsewhere, gun sales skyrocketed as citizens feared a collapse of public order.

A federal appeals court condemned the gun store closure order issued by Ventura County, California, at the start of the pandemic. While politicians shuttered gun stores, bike shops were kept open because politicians considered them "essential." Judge Lawrence VanDyke declared that the Second Amendment "means nothing if the government can prohibit all persons from acquiring any firearm or ammunition. But that's what happened in this case." The 48-day closure of gun shops and firing ranges "wholly prevented law-abiding citizens in the County from realizing their right to keep and bear arms."[78]

On Memorial Day 2020, Minneapolis police officer Derek Chauvin brutally killed George Floyd, and riots erupted in many cities across the nation. The *Washington Post* portrayed the violence as "an anti-racism uprising."[79] The media spin was epitomized by a CNN chyron — "Fiery But Mostly Peaceful Protests" — beneath a burning building.[80] The media continued focusing on the purported ideals of demonstrators long after mass looting, arson, and killings erupted. Law professor David Bernstein observed: "Big-city mayors made a partisan or ideologically motivated decision to refuse to deploy the police to quash rioting… to show solidarity with left-wing protestors."[81]

After Minneapolis Mayor Jacob Frey ordered police to stand down and abandon a precinct headquarters, the building was burned down, and looting and burning engulfed much of the city, leaving several people dead, dozens stabbed or shot, and scores of police officers injured. Fifteen hundred properties suffered up to $500 million in damage.[82] Mayor Frey shrugged off the damage as "just brick and mortar."[83] The city's homicide rate doubled after the riots.

New York City Mayor Bill de Blasio responded to violent protests by announcing that he wanted police to use "a light touch because people are undeniably angry for a reason."[84] The chief of a New York Police Department union complained: "We are being told to stand down. We have a city that's being destroyed."[85] For hours, police failed to respond to desperate calls after looting broke out, and they stood aside when the flagship Macy's store on 34th Street was plundered. Almost 500 stores were looted or burned.[86]

Seattle Mayor Jenny Durkan forced police to abandon a precinct headquarters. Demonstrators quickly swarmed that area and proclaimed an autonomous zone. Durkan justified their action by referring to it as a "block party" heralding a "summer of love."[87] The following month, Durkan admitted that the autonomous zone helped spur a 525% increase in crime in Seattle.[88] The city's murder rate doubled in 2020. By 2021, police were so overwhelmed by a crime surge that they ceased investigating sexual assaults involving adults, according to the *Seattle Times*.[89]

After violence erupted in Chicago, Mayor Lori Lightfoot hectored defenseless residents: "Do not pick up arms and try to be the police. If there's a problem, call 911. We will respond. But… do not take matters into your own hands." But the 911 system completely collapsed during widespread looting and shooting.[90] Chicago's poorest neighborhoods were ravaged by mobs that pillaged local store owners, who were mostly minorities. In the first weekend of June 2020, 85 people were shot and 24 murdered in the city — likely the most violent weekend in Chicago history.[91] Chicago police failed to respond to more than 400,000 high-priority emergency service calls in 2021, including 14,955 assaults in progress, 1,352 reports of a person shot, and almost a thousand cases of a person stabbed.[92]

The wisdom on relying passively on police for protection was settled on May 24, 2022, at Robb Elementary School in Uvalde, Texas. Salvador Ramos, a deranged 18-year-old with almost no firearms experience, entered the school and began shooting children with a semiautomatic rifle. Police with rifles were inside the school within three minutes. At least 19 police officers, some with body armor, loitered outside the classroom while the killing continued. A police commander justified the delay because the door was locked and officers didn't have a key. But it was unlocked, and no policeman had attempted to enter the room. Almost 400 local, state, and federal law officers converged on the scene. Students were calling 911 and pleading for help. Desperate parents rushed to the scene. One mother was handcuffed, and others were knocked to the ground. Federal marshals arrested one parent for "intervening in an active investigation."[93] The rampaging teenager was not confronted until 77 minutes after his shooting spree started. Nineteen students and two teachers were killed.

A Texas Department of Public Safety lieutenant explained to CNN that the police did not confront the shooter because "they could've been shot." Fox News's Janice Dean groused: "It's like a fireman not going into a building because they might get burned."[94] Texas Department of Public Safety Director Steve McCraw condemned the slow response:

> The officers had weapons; the children had none. The officers had body armor; the children had none. The officers had training; the subject had none. One hour, 14 minutes, and 8 seconds. That's how long children waited, and the teachers waited, in Room 111 to be rescued.[95]

Millions of violent assaults occur each year that police fail to prevent. Politicians have no legal liability for seizing or banning the guns that individuals could have used to save their lives or protect their families. As a federal appeals court ruled in 1982: "There is no constitutional right to be protected by the state against being murdered by criminals or madmen."[96]

Instead, politicians pretend they are entitled to forcibly disarm citizens in order to harvest votes from people who fear or hate guns.

Police failures and pervasive violence spurred far more citizens to purchase firearms. Columnist Don Feder noted: "In 2020, the number of women buying guns more than doubled."[97] Derrick Morgan, national chief of the Black Gun Owners Association, commented: "A lot of people are reaching out to us, mainly new gun owners and people who wouldn't have considered owning a gun or firearm for their protection."[98]

In June 2022, the Supreme Court struck down laws that arbitrarily denied concealed carry permits to the vast majority of citizens in six states. Justice Thomas wrote: "Because the State of New York issues public-carry licenses only when an applicant demonstrates a special need for self-defense, we conclude that the State's licensing regime violates the Constitution." Thomas summarized the absurdity of the status quo: "We know of no other constitutional right that an individual may exercise only after demonstrating to government officers some special need." The ruling put an end to an absurd situation in New York City, where the NYPD estimated that up to two million illegal guns were circulating — in part due to restrictive laws that criminalized self-defense.[99] Among the most eloquent critics of New York's prohibitions were the Black Attorneys of Legal Aid and the Bronx Defenders lawyers group. Their brief to the Court declared: "Each year, we represent hundreds of indigent people whom New York criminally charges for exercising their right to keep and bear arms. For our clients, New York's licensing requirement renders the Second Amendment a legal fiction." The brief pointed out that their clients have been "deprived... of their jobs, children, livelihoods, and ability to live in this country... because [they] exercised a constitutional right."[100]

Many Democratic governors rushed to issue new regulations that made a mockery of the Supreme Court ruling. Gov. Kathy Hochul encouraged citizens to rat out neighbors who possessed both guns and bad ideas: "Now you can talk to their neighbors online and find out whether or not this person has been spouting, uh, you know, philosophies that indicate they have been radicalized, and that's how we protect our citizens as well."[101] The Deputy Commissioner of the New York Police Department responded to the Supreme Court notice by notifying police that "anyone carrying a firearm is presumed to be carrying unlawfully until proven otherwise."[102]

The rising number of people who carry concealed weapons is a sign of a new American self-reliance. For the average citizen walking down a dark street late at night, a promise from a politician is worth less than a .38 Special. In the past decade, "more than twenty states have adopted new laws deregulating the carrying of firearms," which Ryan McMaken of the Mises Institute points out is a "sign of failing trust in government."[103]

Give Us Your Guns, Or We Will Kill You.

In a June 2022 speech calling for Congress to restrict firearm ownership, Biden asserted that he respected "the concerns of lawful gun owners."[104] But after Biden changes the law, millions of those same individuals could be criminals whom Biden is entitled to disarm and imprison.

Federal and state laws have already turned tens of millions of citizens into "felons-in-waiting" who can be legally destroyed at prosecutors' convenience. What will happen if the government decides to vigorously enforce firearms prohibitions?

In 2018, Rep. Eric Swalwell, a California congressman and a flash-in-the-pan Democratic presidential candidate, called for government confiscation of all assault weapons. When a conservative activist suggested that gun grabbers wanted a war, Swalwell replied: "And it would be a short war, my friend. The government has nukes. Too many of them. But they're legit."[105] Swalwell did not specify how many bombs he would be willing to drop to end gun violence.

In a 2021 speech championing gun control, Biden scoffed: "If you wanted or if you think you need to have weapons to take on the government, you need F-15s and maybe some nuclear weapons."[106] (Tell that to the Taliban.) But Americans resisting mass gun confiscation will not need to defeat the feds. They would merely need to wait until government agents commit horrific blunders which turn millions more Americans against Washington. That pattern has repeated itself in prior gun crackdowns gone awry.

Many rural gun owners are as unlikely to surrender their guns as they are to give up their Bibles. Escalating government force will create martyrs that multiply resistance. The British government's heavy-handed repression of all Bostonians for a "tea party" by a smattering of activists helped turn the Thirteen Colonies against King George. Seeking to forcibly commandeer millions of weapons will result in clashes which the government will sometimes lose — especially given the record of police cowering during mass shooting events.

Any attempt to enforce widespread gun confiscation will require suspending Americans' constitutional right to trial by jury. An Idaho jury found Ruby Ridge defendants not guilty in 1993 after "government witnesses cause case to collapse," as the *Washington Post* noted.[107] In 1994, a Texas jury rejected charges that Branch Davidians were guilty of murdering federal agents in a verdict the *New York Times* described as a "stunning defeat" for the feds.[108] Juries might resist convicting firearms violators the way that Massachusetts juries in the 1850s refused to enforce the Fugitive Slave Act. Juries would not defer to the assertion of federal agents who behaved like foreign invaders.

The First Amendment could be another crackdown casualty. During the final day at Waco, FBI loudspeakers continually broadcast, "This is not an assault," while FBI tanks flattened 20% of the Davidians' home prior to a mass conflagration — which was preceded by the FBI firing incendiary pyrotechnic grenades at the residence.[109] The videos of the FBI tank assault undercut the FBI's post-debacle spin and swayed many Americans to conclude that the federal power posed a grave peril to domestic tranquility. Nowadays, most people have a cellphone which includes a video camera. Film clips of federal agents smashing into homes and assailing defiant citizens could become more incendiary than any presidential tweet. If the government responds to incriminating videos by totally blocking Internet access to suppress the videos, it will lose the support of vast numbers of Americans who are not firearm zealots.

Presidents, Congress, and their bureaucratic allies cannot count on local officials carrying out Washington's commands. Sheriffs in New York State, New Mexico, and Colorado have already publicly refused to enforce what they consider unjust gun laws. Martial law would be necessary to carry out sweeping firearms seizures in many parts of America. But that would be perilous because many National Guard members might balk at carrying out such orders, especially after enforcement efforts killed innocent neighbors. Losing the loyalty of the troops would be the final straw.

Gun grabbers forget how this nation came to exist. The American Revolution was sparked by a gun grab gone awry at Lexington and Concord, Massachusetts. In a 1999 decision, Federal Judge Sam Cummings explained:

> The individual right to bear arms… was a crucial factor in the
> Colonists' victory over the British Army in the Revolutionary War…
> A foundation of American political thought during the Revolutionary
> period was the well-justified concern about political corruption and
> governmental tyranny.[110]

The Founders appreciated the wisdom of William Blackstone, the most respected British legal expert of the 18th century, who stressed that individuals' owning arms was vital "to restrain the violence of oppression."[111] As Professor Joyce Lee Malcolm documented in her 1994 book *To Keep and Bear Arms: The Origins of an Anglo-American Right*, the Second Amendment was based on the "anti-government… legacy from seventeenth- and eighteenth-century England."[112] Malcolm called the Second Amendment "the safety valve of the Constitution… If parchment barriers proved inadequate, the people could protect their liberties or alter their government."[113]

Discussions on federal gun control measures often focus on whether specific guns serve "sporting purposes." But if the Founding Fathers had specified that citizens could possess guns only for hunting ducks and deer, the Constitution never would have been ratified. The Founders were inspired by British political philosopher John Locke, who had warned almost a century earlier: "I have no reason to believe that he, who, after taking away my rights (or my ability to defend them), will treat me better than a slave." That sentiment has echoed throughout our history. As Black Panthers leader Huey Newton declared in 1967: "Any unarmed people are slaves, or are subject to slavery at any given moment."[114] As black gun rights advocate Maj Toure asserted: "You don't need 30 rounds to hunt, but you need far more than that when you're being hunted."[115]

"Claiming you need a gun to protect yourself against the government is ludicrous," Rep. Swalwell announced in 2018.[116] But politicians ban guns so that no one can resist their decrees. In late 2019, New Zealand Prime Minister Jacinda Ardern banned possession of most semiautomatic firearms and many shotguns.[117] When the COVID pandemic began, she dictated endless lockdowns, placing the entire capital city under "snap lockdowns" any time a single COVID case was detected. In October 2020, the government announced that it was creating "quarantine centers" for anyone who tested positive and refused to obey government orders. One Twitter wag scoffed, "New Zealand went from gun bans to concentration camps in less than a year."[118] Ardern's iron-fist policies made her a worldwide progressive hero but failed to prevent almost two million New Zealanders (including herself) from getting infected by COVID. She resigned in 2023 after announcing that she had had a mental breakdown.

Conclusion

Gun owners are supposed to trust politicians who say that they merely want guns registered, or specific firearms and ammo magazines banned, or specific types of people forcibly disarmed. When an assault weapons ban fails to end shootings, politicians may demand that all rifles be prohibited and confiscated. After that ban fails to end violence, politicians will claim they must seize all handguns. Each failed intervention justifies further bans until either self-defense is abolished or political legitimacy collapses.

Gun owners would be criminally naïve to expect Washington politicians to respect their rights better in the future than they did in the past. Any firearms crackdown will be applauded by politicians and activists who hate gun owners even more than they hate guns. How far will firearms prohibition go? On March 24, 2023, Biden announced that he wanted to "keep guns out of the hands of domestic political advisors."[119] The White House did not disclose whether Biden's advisors personally owned firearms. At a White House anti-gun event on September 22, 2023, Biden bizarrely proclaimed: "I've been to every mass shooting."[120] Scorekeepers viewed Biden's blather as a harmless error as long as he remained on the side of the angels.

It is folly to expect fair play on gun owners' rights when politicians openly seek pretexts to disarm as many Americans as possible. Gun owners cannot expect government agents to reasonably enforce unreasonable laws. What right do legislators have to decree that anyone who puts more than 7 rounds into a 10-round magazine is an outlaw? Or that anyone who sells a gun that lacks a nonexistent stamping trigger is a menace to humanity? Prohibiting gun ownership leaves private citizens in servile dependency on government employees for the preservation of their own lives.

Private firearm ownership is the last best check on tyranny. Banning firearms is a declaration of war on all limits on political power. Politicians who proudly seek to destroy the Second Amendment cannot be trusted to respect any other constitutional right. The civil disobedience of peaceful gun owners is one of the best hopes for the survival of American liberty.

4. Licensed to Kill

Politicians and judges have turned police into a privileged class with a license to oppress other Americans. Court decisions assure that police officers are rarely liable when they shoot innocent people, smash into the wrong houses, or rape women they handcuff. Wrongful killings by police spark brief uproars and promises of reform. But no fundamental rollback of law enforcement's lethal power and prerogatives has occurred.

The vast majority of Americans justifiably support the police when they confront or apprehend violent predators. However, judges, politicians, and police unions have effectively exempted hundreds of thousands of individuals from the Rule of Law. Law professor Joanna Schwartz observed in 2023 that Supreme Court decisions have been "so deferential to police that officers can stop, arrest, search, beat, shoot, or kill people who have done nothing wrong without violating their rights."[1]

Why Police Killings Don't Count

In 1994, Congress enacted the Violent Crime Control and Law Enforcement Act, spawning far more federal subsidies for state and local law enforcement, including funding for a hundred thousand new police officers. The bill also created 50 new criminal offenses that would result in skyrocketing prison populations in the following 15 years.

As Congress readied the 356-page bill, critics warned that police departments were out of control and deserved no new federal funding. The ACLU and the NRA jointly called for President Bill Clinton to appoint a national commission to investigate "lawlessness in law enforcement." The Mollen Commission was shocked by "the incompetence and the inadequacies of the [New York Police Department] to police itself." The commission's chief counsel noted that police corruption was "characterized by brutality, theft, abuse of authority and active police criminality." Similar scandals rocked Los Angeles, Chicago, and many other cities.

To mollify critics, the 1994 Crime Bill required the Attorney General to "acquire data about the use of excessive force by law enforcement officers" across the nation and to "publish an annual summary of the data acquired." Congress effectively ordered the Justice Department to tally how often police kill private citizens. To placate police unions, the law specified that the data would not "reveal the identity of the victim or any law enforcement officer."

Two years later, a Justice Department report lamented that "systematically collecting information on use of force" by law enforcement was "difficult given... the sensitivity of the issue." Instead, the Justice Department launched "a police-public contact survey to ask questions about the use of both appropriate and inappropriate force during police-public encounters." Professor James Fyfe observed: "Since dead people can't participate in such a survey, this work tells us nothing about how often police kill." The federal government was deluging state and local law enforcement agencies with billions of dollars in aid, but it was too much to ask recipients for honest body counts.

Seven years after the 1994 Crime Bill was enacted, the Justice Department finally issued a report that tacitly presumed that anyone who was gunned down by police deserved to die. "Policing and Homicide, 1976–1998," labeled everyone who died after a police shooting as "felons justifiably killed by police." There were thousands of people shot unjustifiably by police in those decades, but their innocence vanished in bureaucratic jargon. The Justice Department was so embarrassed by the report's "lack of distinction between justifiable police shootings and murders, that it did not send out its usual promotional material announcing the report," according to the *New York Times*.[2]

According to the Justice Department, police killings were statistically negligible and damn near irrelevant: "Felons justifiably killed by police represent a tiny fraction of the total population. Of the 183 million whites in 1998, police killed 225; of the 27 million blacks, police killed 127." The report left no doubt about the Justice Department's allegiance: "The use of deadly force against a police officer is almost never justified, while the use of deadly force by police often is."

In the following years, controversies about police killings periodically percolated to the surface. A 2011 investigation by the *Las Vegas Review Journal* noted: "No one anywhere comprehensively tracks the most significant act police can do in the line of duty: take a life." When asked why the agency failed to track police killings, FBI spokesman William Carr replied: "We don't have a mandate to do that. It would take a request from Congress for us to collect that data." The stark mandate in the 1994 law was not permitted to disturb the FBI's repose.

Police killings became a hot topic nationwide after a policeman in Ferguson, Missouri, killed 18-year-old Michael Brown in August 2014. Angry protestors raged in the streets after false reports that Brown had raised his hands and said, "Don't shoot." The Obama Justice Department investigated and concluded that Brown was fatally shot after he scuffled with a policeman and sought to seize his gun. A separate Justice Department report found that the Ferguson Police Department systemically violated the rights of black residents and almost everyone else who fell under their sway.

Attorney General Eric Holder responded to the uproar over the Ferguson shooting by declaring that "we must seek to rebuild trust between law enforcement and the local community."[3] But the feds continued ignoring most police killings. The *Wall Street Journal* noted in late 2014 that some police departments "didn't view justifiable homicides by law-enforcement officers as events that should be reported. The Fairfax County Police Department in Virginia said it didn't consider such cases to be an 'actual offense,' and thus doesn't report them to the FBI."[4] FBI data omitted all killings by federal agents.

After failing to obey the 1994 law during his six years as Attorney General, Holder endorsed collecting national police shooting data shortly before he left office in 2015. But his replacement, Attorney General Loretta Lynch, side railed the effort: "One of the things we are focusing on at the Department of Justice is not trying to reach down from Washington and dictate to every local department how they should handle the minutiae of record keeping."[5] But it wasn't "minutiae" for the families of police victims. Lynch asserted: "The real issues are: 'What steps are we all taking to connect communities… with police and back with government?'"[6] Many police departments behaved recklessly in part because the Justice Department always covered for them at the Supreme Court. Obama's "Justice Department has supported police officers every time an excessive-force case has made its way" to a Supreme Court hearing, the *New York Times* noted.[7]

Spurred by the lack of reliable federal data, the *Washington Post* and *The Guardian* began tracking individual shootings by police across the nation. *The Guardian* relied on crowdsourcing on the Internet to compile its report, revealing that police killed 1,134 people across the nation in 2015. This was two-and-a-half times higher than the death toll the FBI reported the previous year. Jim Bueermann, a former police chief and president of the Police Foundation, asserted: "These shootings are grossly underreported. We are never going to reduce the number of police shootings if we don't begin to accurately track this information."[8]

Many of the killings by police were justified, taking down armed robbers or other attackers. However, more than 20% of the police killings occurred after a non-violent crime or an attempted traffic or street stop.[9] Patrick Ball, a statistician and United Nations consultant, estimated in 2016 that "one-third of all Americans killed by strangers are killed by police" and that "eight to ten percent of all American homicide victims are killed by the police."[10]

The FBI was not the only federal agency that scorned tracking police killings. The Centers for Disease Control's National Vital Statistics System tracks the causes of all deaths in the United States. That database, based on state death certificates, is known for being 99% accurate except for the "law-enforcement related mortality" category. A 2017 Harvard University study found that most police killings in 2015 were "wrongly classified as not having been the result of interactions with officers." Many police killings were instead categorized as "accidental injuries" or "undetermined."[11] More than 30 people were killed by police in Oklahoma in 2015, but "none of them were counted on death certificates," Harvard's Justin Feldman observed.[12] A 2021 study published in the *Lancet*, a British medical journal, found that most killings by police in the U.S. had been misreported over the prior 40 years, thereby greatly understating the amount of carnage officialdom inflicted on Americans.[13]

Congress had supposedly solved that problem. In late 2014, Congress passed the Death in Custody Reporting Act to compel states and federal agencies to fully report fatalities of people they had sought to arrest or detain. But the FBI and other agencies ignored the law. The Government Accountability Office reported in 2021 that "FBI officials told us that they had not been informed of this responsibility to collect data on police use of excessive force."[14] Instead, the FBI announced that it might shut down the police use of force database because local agencies continued refusing to provide the data.[15] Federal statistics continued to be so flawed that the FBI official records included "only about one-third of the 7,000 fatal police shootings" counted by the *Post* between 2015 and 2021.[16]

What happens when the official scorekeepers ignore police rampages and killings?

Flash-Bang First, Ask Questions Later

What happens when the Supreme Court preemptively grants legal immunity to 18,000 law enforcement agencies?

Half a million violent SWAT raids on American homes.

The SWAT acronym originally stood for "Special Weapons Attack Team" but was euphemized to "Special Weapons and Tactics." An Indiana appeals court characterized SWAT raids as a "military-style assault," while a federal appeals court labeled the flash-bang grenades that police routinely detonate as "bombs." An ACLU report characterized SWAT raids as violent events where swarms of police officers, "armed with assault rifles and grenades, approach a home, break down doors and windows (often causing property damage), and scream for the people inside to get on the floor (often pointing their guns at them)."[17] Failure to instantly submit to SWAT raiders can be a capital offense. A *New York Times* investigation found that "at least 81 civilians and 13 law enforcement officers died in raids from 2010 through 2016. Scores of others were maimed or wounded."[18]

There are now more than 30,000 SWAT teams in the nation's law enforcement agencies. Forty years ago, only a few thousand SWAT raids occurred each year. Now, there are 50,000 or more SWAT raids per year, according to the nation's foremost authority, Professor Peter Kraska of Eastern Kentucky University.

SWAT raids have targeted "people suspected of running illegal poker games, brewing moonshine and neglecting pets."[19] In Michigan, a SWAT team raided a private home to seize "any and all evidence pertaining to graffiti including but not limited to, spray paint containers, markers, notebooks, and photographs."[20] The Greenwich, Connecticut, SWAT team was deployed any time the lottery jackpots exceeded one million dollars. In Massachusetts, SWAT teams were deployed to preempt possible rioting after a Red Sox game, "providing security for a Dalai Lama lecture," and roaming "Halloween celebrations looking out for unspecified 'gang-related activity.'"[21]

SWAT raids would not have proliferated unless the police were effectively immune from both damages and decency. As early as 1603, English courts recognized that law officers were obliged to knock and announce their purpose before entering a private citizen's home. But in a 1995 brief to the Supreme Court, the Clinton administration flushed the Fourth Amendment. The Justice Department stressed that "various indoor plumbing facilities… did not exist" in the 1600s when the "knock-and-announce" rule was adopted. Making a grand concession to civil liberties, the Clinton administration admitted that if police "officers knew that… the premises contain no plumbing facilities… then invocation of the destruction-of-evidence justification for an unannounced entry would be unreasonable." A 1997 Supreme Court decision effectively sanctified no-knock raids whenever police claimed a "reasonable suspicion" that evidence might be destroyed.[22]

No-knock raids quickly became standard operating procedures across the nation. San Antonio Police Chief William McManus explained in 2010, "If it's a small quantity [of drugs], you're probably not going to find too many police investigators that are going to knock."[23] The *New York Times* noted in 2017 that no-knock warrants were routinely granted permitting "the most extreme force in pursuit of the smallest amounts of drugs, since a few grams are more quickly flushed than a few bales."[24] That absurdity was comically foreshadowed during Supreme Court oral arguments in 1995. Criminal defense lawyer John Wesley Hall scoffed that "the more drugs you've got, the more right you have to an announcement" by the police at the front door instead of a surprise assault. (I was ejected from the Supreme Court press box for laughing boisterously at that line, which almost no one else in the courtroom found amusing.)[25]

SWAT attacks on American homes have been fueled by a federal arms buildup. Beginning in the 1990s, the Pentagon deluged local police with thousands of machine guns, hundreds of armored personnel carriers, scores of grenade launchers, and more than a million other pieces of military hardware. *Business Insider* described the program: "It's like eBay for cops with leftover war equipment, except everything is free and you only pay for shipping and handling."[26] President Obama lamented in 2015: "We've seen how militarized gear can sometimes give people the feeling like there's an occupying force…[it] can alienate and intimidate residents and make them feel scared."[27] Obama sounded like an innocent bystander to the multibillion-dollar windfall of Pentagon armaments provided to police departments during his presidency. Even worse, prior to 2017, the Pentagon "required that any transferred equipment be 'placed into use within one year of receipt,'"[28] creating a perverse incentive for military-style assaults on American homes.

The Pentagon has provided more than $7 billion worth of surplus military equipment to cops,[29] helping bring out the worst in many law enforcement agencies. Georgia police departments that took surplus military gear "fatally shot about four times as many people as those that didn't… The more equipment a [police] department receives, the more people are shot and killed, even after accounting for violent crime, race, income, drug use and population," the *Atlanta Journal-Constitution* reported in 2020.[30] Police departments receiving large amounts of surplus military equipment "increases civilian deaths by roughly 129%," according to a 2017 academic analysis in *Research & Politics*.[31]

Flash-bang grenades epitomize the current relation between police and private citizens. A 2019 federal appeals court decision noted that the grenades are "four times louder than a 12-gauge shotgun blast" with "a powerful enough concussive effect to break windows and put holes in walls."[32] Flash-bangs burn hotter than lava and have started more than 50 fires across the nation.[33] As criminal defense lawyer Clay Conrad observed in 2010, flash-bangs are "just an assault. These things are designed to blind and deafen… You're intentionally injuring people."[34]

SWAT teams routinely presume that they are entitled to blast anyone they search.[35] El Monte, California, Assistant Police Chief Bill Ankeny admitted:

> We throw flash-bang grenades… We do bang on the door and make an announcement — "It's the police" — but it kind of runs together. If you're sitting on the couch, it would be difficult to get to the door before they knock it down.[36]

The Little Rock, Arkansas, SWAT team ignited flash-bangs in almost all of their narcotics search raids between 2011 and 2013. The SWAT team in Kansas City, Missouri, uses flash-bangs for up to 90% of the warrants they serve.[37] A federal appeals court in 2019 condemned that SWAT team for its "flash-bang first, ask questions later" approach, igniting bombs to carry out a search warrant of a peaceful household even after a resident had offered to open the front door.[38]

Flash-bangs have killed, maimed, or injured more than 50 people since 2000, according to a ProPublica investigation. In Billings, Montana, a 12-year-old girl was severely burned after a SWAT team's flash-bang exploded next to her as she slept in her bedroom.[39] In a 2014 Georgia raid, a police officer tossed a flash-bang into the crib of a nineteen-month-old baby, severely injuring him. In 2017, the Indiana Supreme Court overturned a drug conviction because a SWAT team conducted an "unreasonable" "military-style assault" that exploded a flash-bang bomb near a nine-month-old baby. An ACLU analysis found that Massachusetts SWAT teams faced a "25–50-percent chance of finding children" when violently carrying out search warrants.[40] Flash-bangs are far more destructive than the vast majority of narcotics which spur SWAT raids.

A toxic combination of new technology and traditional sloth are making police raids more perilous. Law enforcement in nine states are using software called CloudGavel to email judges who often reply within minutes approving no-knock raid applications. Few judges ask any questions of police. Instead, e-warrant applications are accepted as the Word of God. As Professor Kraska noted: "The whole system has devolved into a perfunctory bureaucracy that doesn't take any care or due diligence for how it's done."[41]

No-knock SWAT raids at wrong addresses have become a national scandal. Some police departments responded by defining the problem almost out of existence. In 2003, the NYPD admitted that 10% of the 450 no-knock raids it admitted conducting each month were "wrong-door raids." That estimate became public after "a wrong-door raid resulted in the homeowner's death: when police broke into the home of 57-year-old Alberta Spruill and threw in a flash-bang grenade, the shock gave her a fatal heart attack," *Vox* noted.[42]

The right to batter down front doors tacitly includes the right to kill any citizen who defends his home. Police routinely claim that no-knock raids are justified because their targets have legally registered firearms, thereby justifying preemptive government violence. The *New York Times* noted: "After being awakened by the shattering of doors and the detonation of stun grenades, bleary suspects reach for nearby weapons — at times realizing it is the police, at others mistaking them for intruders — and the shooting begins."[43] Techdirt.com noted in 2019: "As anyone other than cops seems to comprehend, startling people in their own homes with explosives and kicked-in doors tends to make everything more dangerous for everyone."[44]

The word of a single imaginary informant can sanctify a front attack on the homes of peaceful Americans. On January 29, 2019, 20 Houston police officers attacked a home where heroin was allegedly being sold. Disabled Navy veteran Dennis Tuttle, 59, and his wife, Rhogena Nicholas, 58, and their family dog were killed in the opening seconds of a drug raid that left four officers wounded. On February 15, Houston police officials admitted that Gerald Goines, the officer who got the search warrant, had lied. No informant had claimed that Tuttle was selling heroin. Goines had not even bothered to learn the names of the people residing in the house before the raid. The local CBS station, KHOU, examined 109 cases in which Goines had been involved: "In every one of those cases in which he claimed confidential informants observed guns inside, no weapons were ever recovered."[45] A grand jury indicted 11 Houston Police Department officers "in connection to the raid, charging them with engaging in organized criminal activity and other first-degree felonies that could result in life sentences," the *Houston Chronicle* reported. Goines was charged with murder.[46]

SWAT raids have proliferated in part because their targets often live "on the wrong side of town." Blacks were three times more likely than whites to be the targets of SWAT raids, according to an ACLU analysis.[47] The *New York Times* estimated that half the civilians killed in SWAT raids were black or Hispanic.[48]

SWAT teams are routinely called out to deal with people threatening to take their own lives. As the *San Antonio Express-News* reported, "A 48-year-old armed man was killed in a hail of gunfire early Saturday by a special operations police squad during what police said was an attempt to stop him from committing suicide." Almost a hundred killings by police occurred in 2015 after "police had been alerted over a suicidal person or someone who was harming him- or herself," *The Guardian* reported.[49] Former Boston cop and criminology professor Tom Nolan observed: "It's certainly counter-productive to have a fully armed militarized SWAT team respond to potentially suicidal suspects who are looking for ways out like suicide-by-cop situations."[50]

SWAT attacks have multiplied practically on automatic pilot. An ACLU report lamented: "The militarization of policing in the United States has occurred with almost no public oversight... Agencies that monitor and provide oversight over the militarization of policing are virtually nonexistent."[51] Nobody has solid information on the total number of SWAT raids, and "efforts by news and watchdog groups to compile national figures have been frustrated by police stonewalling," as the *New York Times* noted[52] After Maryland police wrongfully raided a mayor's house and killed his dogs, the state required police to report on every SWAT raid. Between 2010 and 2014, police in Maryland conducted over 8,000 SWAT raids, killing nine people and injuring almost a hundred. The grim statistics spurred the

Maryland legislature to end SWAT recordkeeping. But Maryland cops retained prerogatives that spurred a brutal killing (as discussed in Chapter 3, "The War on Gun Owners") that the national media ignored.

At 4:42 AM on March 12, 2020, a Montgomery County, Maryland, SWAT team arrived outside of the bedroom where 21-year-old Duncan Lemp slept next to his pregnant girlfriend in his parents' house in affluent Potomac, Maryland. One team of SWAT cops used a battering ram to smash in the front door of the Lemp home while setting off flash-bang grenades. Simultaneously, another cop stepped up to a bedroom window, smashed it with a fireman's pike tool, and pulled back the curtains. Two flash-bang grenades were thrown into the bedroom. Another police officer stepped up to the broken window with a rifle and quickly shot Lemp five times. The official report noted that "other members of the SWAT team were tasked with deploying 'flashbangs' outside the residence to disorient the senses of the occupants of the house as to what was happening."

Lemp had been outspoken on social media about his distrust of government and his support for gun rights. His last tweet declared: "The Constitution is dead." Three months later, so was Lemp. Before he was killed, he had texted his mother that he might be targeted by police "because I exercise my constitutional rights."[53]

Police repeatedly changed their story on the raid that killed Lemp. Lemp had no history of violence and had not threatened anyone. But Montgomery County prosecutors claimed the violent no-knock raid was justified "due to Lemp being 'anti-government,' 'anti-police,' currently in possession of body armor, and an active member of the Three Percenters" (a militia group that Lemp's parents said Duncan never joined). The official report that whitewashed the killing stressed that a "confidential source" tipped off police that Lemp possessed firearms and "had made 'anti-police' statements in the past."[54] The police also justified the raid by falsely claiming that Lemp possessed an illegal Israeli assault weapon.

Police claimed that Lemp was going for his rifle when he was killed. But citizens were obliged to take the police's word since they chose not to make any video recordings of their attack. According to lawyer Rene Sandler, Montgomery County allowed the SWAT team to "opt out of the truth and transparency by not being required to wear body camera or videotaping a no-knock raid."[55] After Lemp was gunned down, a policeman walked through the house videotaping the wreckage, including Lemp's mother sitting on her bed weeping inconsolably.

Lemp's political views and gun ownership made him a pariah in the most liberal county in Maryland. The county government refused to reveal whether police ever considered any alternative to peacefully detain or arrest Lemp prior to attacking his bedroom.

Lemp's mother, Mercedes Lemp, told me: "I will always wonder whether the police intended to kill Duncan from the start — there was never a search... the way they conducted themselves seems as if they intended to kill him even before the raid began."[56] The cop who gunned down Lemp in his bedroom faced no charges because police are automatically absolved for killing people with ideas politicians disapprove. Lemp's fate confirmed the old saying: Just because you're paranoid doesn't mean they aren't out to get you.

Shoot First, Think Later

Why have police departments become so reckless in their attacks on the citizenry?

In the wake of the Civil War, freed Southern blacks were terrorized by lynch mobs and other attackers. Congress responded by enacting the Civil Rights Act of 1871, commonly referred to as the Ku Klux Klan Act. Because Southern local and state governments failed to restrain violence, Section 1983 of that law authorized lawsuits against any person acting "under color of" law who caused a "deprivation of any rights... secured by the Constitution and laws." The law enabled individual victims to directly sue government officials in federal court for abuses, providing an escape hatch from local and state judges who scorned certain classes of victims.

Almost a century later, in 1967, the Supreme Court poked a hole in the 1871 law by declaring that government officials who acted in "good faith" when violating citizens' rights could not be sued. And how can judges tell if people have "good faith"? They work for the government. This was a radical departure from almost two centuries of American jurisprudence which previously held officials strictly liable for violating constitutional rights. Instead, the Supreme Court invented the doctrine of "qualified immunity."

Fifteen years later, the Supreme Court vastly expanded this de facto exemption from the Rule of Law in the case of *Harlow v. Fitzgerald*. Two White House aides in the Nixon administration conspired to fire an Air

Force official who had exposed a multibillion-dollar Pentagon scandal during congressional testimony. The Supreme Court sided with the Nixon staffers and granted government officials immunity from lawsuits unless their conduct violated "clearly established statutory or constitutional rights of which a reasonable person would have known."[57] But the Court's "reasonable" standard became more irrational with each passing decade. Prior to this decision, a government official's malice or bad faith was often the decisive factor in lawsuits charging them with abuse of power.[58]

According to the Supreme Court, ignorance of the law is no excuse except for government officials who trample the law. Regardless of centuries of court rulings that clearly demarcate citizens' constitutional rights, the Supreme Court decided that government officials deserved immunity unless a prior court case had condemned almost exactly the same abusive behavior. The Supreme Court grants qualified immunity almost every time because "the plaintiff could not produce a precedent with facts close enough" to their case.[59] Federal Judge Don Willett declared in 2018 that "qualified immunity smacks of unqualified impunity, letting public officials duck consequences for bad behavior — no matter how palpably unreasonable — as long as they were the first to behave badly."

In a 2015 case absolving a reckless shooting that killed a motorist, Justice Sonia Sotomayor angrily dissented that the Court's decision "tells [police] officers that they can shoot first and think later, and it tells the public that palpably unreasonable conduct will go unpunished."[60] Three years later, Justice Sotomayor complained that the Supreme Court's "one-sided approach to qualified immunity transforms the doctrine into an absolute shield for law enforcement, gutting the deterrent effect" on constitutional rights.[61]

The Court's rulings have been driven by faith in arbitrary power and superiority of government officials. The Court has granted or expanded qualified immunity to officialdom more than 10 times as often as it has denied immunity, spurring University of Chicago law professor William Baude to denounce its "pro-immunity crusade."[62] In 2012, the Supreme Court declared: "The public good can best be secured by allowing officers charged with the duty of deciding upon the rights of others, to act upon their own free, unbiased convictions, uninfluenced by any apprehensions."[63] But the American Revolution occurred thanks to the ravages of British officials who were "uninfluenced by any apprehensions" of punishment.

How does the Supreme Court's pro-government idealism play out in the real world? As *Reason* reported, courts have

> approved qualified immunity for cops who allegedly shot people without cause, sicced a dog on a man who was surrendering, tased a driver who was stopped for failing to buckle his seatbelt, and ordered a 17-year-old boy to disrobe and masturbate so they could take pictures of his erect penis.[64]

Federal courts granted qualified immunity in 2022 to police who wrongfully arrested an Ohio man who had mocked them on Facebook.[65]

The Supreme Court's rulings on qualified immunity have preemptively nullified thousands of jury verdicts. Until recent decades, juries routinely had the final word on whether Americans' rights had been violated by government officials. But juries never hear cases after judges grant immunity. Federal Judge James Browning stated that "jury trials are the most democratic expression of what police action is reasonable and what action is excessive. If the citizens of New Mexico decide that state actors used excessive force or were deliberately indifferent, the verdict should stand."[66]

The Right to Destroy Innocent People

To serve and protect, police must be allowed to slander and destroy. Cops in many states and localities have acquired the right to lie about the shootings, searches, and practically anything else. Police have routinely planted drugs, guns, and other evidence to incriminate innocent people, while police labs have engaged in wholesale fraud blighting tens of thousands of lives.

Supreme Court rulings turned a trickle of police perjury into a torrent. In 1967, the Supreme Court, in the case of *McCray v. Illinois*, gave policemen the right to keep secret the name of their "reliable informant" they used to get search warrants or target people for arrest. Law professor Irving Younger observed at the time: "The *McCray* case almost guarantees wholesale police perjury. When his conduct is challenged as constituting an unreasonable search and seizure… every policeman will have a genie-like informer to legalize his master's arrests."[67] The Supreme Court created a judicial playing field on which police were the only witnesses who can safely lie.

In 1983, the Supreme Court ruled that government officials are immune from lawsuits even when their brazen lies in court testimony resulted in the conviction of innocent people. The court fretted that "the alternative of limiting the official's immunity would disserve the broader public interest."[68] Honest government was not one of the "broader public interests" the Court recognized that day.

In 1994, the Mollen Commission reported that "the practice of [NYPD] police falsification in connection with such arrests is so common in certain precincts that it has spawned its own word: 'testilying.'" Federal appeals court chief judge Alex Kozinski observed in 1995: "It is an open secret long shared by prosecutors, defense lawyers and judges that perjury is widespread among law enforcement officers."[69] Former San Jose, California, Police Chief Joseph McNamara observed that "hundreds of thousands of law-enforcement officers commit felony perjury every year testifying about drug arrests."[70]

In Tulia, Texas, Tom Coleman, an undercover cop on the federally funded Panhandle Drug Task Force, carried out drug stings in 1999 that resulted in the arrests of 46 people — equal to 10% of the black population of the town. There were no independent witnesses to back up Coleman's accusations of pervasive drug dealing in the low-rent farming community. As the United Press International noted, Coleman "made no video or audio recordings during his 18-month investigation. No drugs were found during the drug sweep and later he said his only notes were scribbled on his leg." But his leg and his word sufficed for mass arrests, including 12 people sentenced to prison who had no prior criminal record. "Dozens of children became virtual orphans as their parents were hauled to jail. In the coming months, 19 people would be shipped to state prison, some with sentences of 20, 60, or even 99 years," the *Village Voice* reported.[71] The NAACP of Texas denounced the crackdown as "the ethnic cleansing of young male blacks of Tulia."[72] For his exploits, Coleman received the Texas Lawman of the Year[73] award, presented by Texas Attorney General (and future U.S. Senator) John Cornyn. Defense lawyers and civil rights activists eventually exposed Coleman's vast frauds. Gov. Rick Perry pardoned 35 convicts who had been wrongfully tarred by his accusations, but not until after some of them had spent four years in prison. Coleman was later convicted of perjury but was sentenced only to probation.[74]

Almost a thousand people have seen their convictions overturned in recent decades in cases that involved perjury or false reports by police or prosecutors. A 2018 *New York Times* investigation of police lying revealed "an entrenched perjury problem several decades in the making that shows little sign of fading."[75] More than 100 NYPD "employees accused of 'lying on official reports, under oath, or during an internal affairs investigation' were punished with as little as a few days of lost vacation," the New York Civil Liberties Union reported in 2018.[76]

It's a small step from fabricating guilt on the witness stand to creating guilt by planting evidence. Many police shootings have been exonerated by "throwdown" guns carried for emergency frame-ups. In 2001, a federal investigation resulted in the arrest of 13 Miami police connected to fabricating evidence or planting guns at the scene of three people whom the police unjustifiably killed.[77] In 2018, eight members of the Baltimore Gun Trace Task Force were convicted for planting guns on police shooting victims and other abuses. Police carried toy guns in their glove compartments or kept BB guns in their trunks to place at the scene of police shootings that might otherwise look like murder. More than 800 court cases were dismissed or overturned because of the Gun Trace Task Force's crime spree.[78]

That scandal percolated for years because Maryland treats planting evidence as the equivalent of jaywalking. A Baltimore policeman was convicted in 2018 of "fabricating evidence in a case in which his own body camera footage showed him placing drugs in a vacant lot and then acting as if he had just discovered them." A man was jailed for six months for those drugs before the charge was dropped. The policeman kept his job because, as the *Baltimore Sun* explained: "Under Maryland law, officers are only removed automatically if convicted of a felony. Fabricating evidence and misconduct in office are both misdemeanors."[79] An ACLU lawyer groused that he "cannot imagine a more screwed-up, idiotic way of trying to manage a police department or any other public office" than continuing to employ a cop convicted for fabricating evidence.

Bogus drugs produce more scandals than police throwdown guns. In 2019, Jackson County, Florida, sheriff's deputy Zach Wester was charged with 50 counts of racketeering, false imprisonment, fabricating evidence, and drug possession for framing more than a hundred motorists he stopped. Wester would pull cars over for crossing the center line and then plant baggies of narcotics in their vehicles. As *Reason* reported:

> Wester kept unmarked bags of marijuana and methamphetamines in the trunk of his patrol car, manipulated his body cam footage, planted drugs in people's cars, and falsified arrest reports to railroad innocent people under the color of law. His victims, many of whom had prior

records or were working to stay sober, had their lives upended. One
man lost custody of his daughter.[80]

Wester's perfidy exceeded his mastery of his body cam, and his videos
undid him. He was sentenced to 12 years in prison for planting drugs.[81]

While planting drugs usually involves a smattering of victims,
Massachusetts shattered all records. In 2012, Massachusetts State Police drug
lab chemist Annie Dookhan was arrested for falsifying tens of thousands of
drug tests, "always in favor of the prosecution," as *Rolling Stone* reported.[82]
Dookhan would add narcotics to tests which came back negative or would
boost the weight so that a person could be convicted of drug dealing instead
of mere possession. Her zealotry knew no bounds, such as the day "she
testified under oath that a chunk of cashew was crack cocaine."[83] Dookhan's
brazen lab frauds went unnoticed even though she routinely certified samples
as illicit narcotics without ever testing them. Supervisors marveled at her
productivity, and colleagues called her "Superwoman."

Five months after the Dookhan scandal broke, another Massachusetts
state lab chemist, Sonja Farak, was arrested at home and charged with
tampering with evidence as well as heroin and cocaine possession. The state
Attorney General's office quickly announced that it "did not believe Farak's
alleged tampering would undermine any cases."[84] Massachusetts Governor
Deval Patrick assured the media: "The most important take-home, I think,
is that no individual's due process rights were compromised" by Farak's
misconduct.[85]

No such luck. Farak had personally abused narcotics from her first day
on the job in 2004 — sometimes even cooking crack cocaine on a burner in
the lab and snorting meth and cocaine in courthouse bathrooms when she
was called to testify. She detailed her abuses in hundreds of pages of diaries.
But the state attorney general's office insisted that she had only started
consuming narcotics on the job a few months before her arrest, and they
blocked all efforts to expose the full extent of Farak's abuses. Massachusetts
government officials could not be bothered to rectify the unjust convictions.
Slate reported in 2015 that "district attorneys take the position that…
prosecutors have no special duty to notify defendants that their convictions
might have been obtained with evidence that was falsified by government
employees."[86] Most of the victims could not afford lawyers to challenge their
convictions.

More than 50,000 convictions were overturned, and the ACLU hailed "the largest dismissal of criminal cases as a result of one case in the history of the United States of America."[87] Hundreds of convicts were released from prison. But, as Anthony Benedetti of the Committee for Public Counsel Services, observed, "the damage has been done. Jobs have been lost, people have been unable to get jobs, housing has been lost, some people have been deported."[88] More than 20 states have had crime lab scandals since the turn of the century.[89]

Police Unions' Right to Rampage

While judges routinely exempt police from the Constitution, police unions assure that law enforcement officers are also often exempt from democracy.

Police unions arose out of the chaos of the riots that afflicted many cities in the 1960s. According to the *New York Times*, "Newly formed police unions leveraged fears of lawlessness and an era of high crime to win" special contract privileges. Critics complained that "officers empowered to protect the public instead were protected from the public."[90] Police union contracts overrode the city charter in Detroit and the state law in Illinois.[91]

Political clout can confer a license for tyranny. The Mollen Commission concluded in 1994 that the Patrolmen's Benevolent Association, representing 29,000 New York City cops, "often acts as a shelter for and protector of the corrupt cop." Three years later, the New York State Senate passed a bill to "eliminate the New York City Police Commissioner's ability to fire corrupt or brutal officers," as the *New York Times* reported. The *Times* sneered: "History demonstrates that rank-and-file Assembly members will vote in favor of any bill sought by the city police unions, no matter how idiotic." Former Portland, Oregon, Mayor Sam Adams lamented the impossibility of firing cops who had wrongfully shot civilians: "This was as bad a part of government as I'd ever seen. The government gets to kill someone and get away with it."[92]

Las Vegas had one of America's highest rates of killings by police, but investigations were stymied because "police unions balked at inquest reforms, first by advising members not to testify at the hearings and then helping officers file a lawsuit challenging the new system's constitutionality," according to the *Las Vegas Review Journal*.[93] The system was so deferential to police that, in cases "where an officer shoots but only wounds or misses entirely… the district attorney looks at the case only if the shooting subject is being prosecuted," the *Review Journal* noted.

Unions have finagled legislation that assures cops of special treatment after they shoot civilians. Maryland police were protected by a "Law Enforcement Officers Bill of Rights" that prohibited questioning a police officer for 10 days after any incident in which he used deadly force. In Prince George's County, Maryland, "a lawyer or a police union official is always summoned to the scene of a shooting to make sure no one speaks to the officer who pulled the trigger," the *Washington Post* reported. Union lawyers were kept busy because that police department had the highest rate of shooting civilians in the nation. A 2001 *Washington Post* investigation revealed: "Between 1990 and 2001 Prince George's police shot 122 people… Almost half of those shot were unarmed, and many had committed no crime."[94] All the shootings, including those that killed 47 people, were ruled "justified." The Maryland legislature purportedly repealed the Law Enforcement Officers Bill of Rights law in 2021, but the replacement law was quickly exploited to cover up police abuses. Yanet Amanuel of the ACLU of Maryland groused: "Every time there is an opportunity to give the community control of the police, Maryland Democrats at every level who say they support police accountability squander it by backing amendments pushed by the Fraternal Order of Police (FOP)."[95]

Thirteen other states have similar "law enforcement bills of rights" that give sweeping privileges to police accused of crimes, including automatic delays before they have to answer any questions about their shootings. The Florida Law Enforcement Officer Bill of Rights entitles police to receive "all witness statements… and all other existing evidence… before the beginning of any investigative interview of that officer."[96] In a 2019 *George Washington Law Review* article on delays in interviewing police who shoot citizens, one police chief commented that "showing evidence in advance allows [police] to tailor their lies to fit the evidence." Another police chief observed that that process simply gives police suspects "time to fabricate a better lie."[97] In July 2023, the NYPD Civilian Complaint Review Board agreed to permit police to "watch surveillance footage, bystander videos and other video recordings [including body cam] that investigators plan to ask them about before giving their versions of what happened," Gothamist reported.[98] Police had made almost 150 false or misleading official statements to the review board since 2020.

Collective bargaining is tied to higher police brutality. In 2003, the Florida Supreme Court ruled that sheriff deputies were entitled to unionize. A 2019 University of Chicago study found that "collective bargaining rights led to about a 40% increase in violent incidents of misconduct among sheriffs' offices."[99] The study also noted that collective bargaining agreements "can lower the probability of detecting misconduct" by law enforcement. Economist Rob Gillezeau analyzed data from the history of police unionization and found that "after officers gained access to collective bargaining rights, there was a substantial increase in killings of civilians," National Public Radio reported in 2020.[100]

Police union contracts routinely mandate censorship and secrecy. In 2016, a hacker posted online hundreds of police union contracts poached from the Fraternal Order of Police website. *The Guardian* analyzed the disclosures and found that "more than a third featured clauses allowing — and often mandating — the destruction of records of civilian complaints, departmental investigations, or disciplinary actions after a negotiated period of time."[101] Small towns and big cities' contracts contained "'expungement' clauses [which] allowed for records of formal investigations and written reprimands to be 'purged' after a few years or, in some cases, months." Unions guaranteed that private citizens would have no access to the records of prior criminal misconduct by police. The police union contract in Ralston, Nebraska, specified that the city government was "bound to 'make every reasonable effort' to prevent a photograph of the officer [involved in any disciplinary action] from being released to the public or news media."

Unions assure that police who kill civilians routinely enjoy both impunity and anonymity. Nationwide, police departments refused to disclose the names of 20% of the police who killed people in 2015. The *Washington Post* reported:

> In Chicago, police in 2015 shot and killed nine people... The [collective bargaining] contract prohibits the department from identifying an officer to the media unless the shooting results in criminal or administrative charges. An officer who killed two people in one shooting disclosed his own name when he sued the estate of one of those he killed, citing emotional trauma.[102]

A 2016 report by the Chicago Police Accountability Task Force concluded: "The collective bargaining agreements between the police unions and the City have essentially turned the code of silence into official policy."[103]

Philadelphia police shot 400 people between 2007 and 2015. In 2015, Police Chief Charles Ramsey began releasing the names of cops who shot people. The Fraternal Order of Police speedily responded by filing "an unfair-labor-practice charge, saying that Ramsey had made the change without negotiating with the union."[104] Unfortunately, people killed by police were not available to file "unfair labor practices" against the union. Two years later, the Pennsylvania House of Representatives passed a bill prohibiting "any public official from identifying a police officer who has discharged his firearm or used force to kill or seriously injure someone." The ACLU's Elizabeth Randol growled, "A functioning democracy doesn't hide public employees who seriously injure or kill someone."[105] David Simon, the writer who masterminded the television series *Homicide* and *The Wire*, observed: "Without a name, there's no way for anyone to evaluate an officer's performance independently, to gauge his or her effectiveness and competence, to know whether he or she has shot one person or 10."[106]

After Baltimore police killed 13 people in 2008, the city government ceased disclosing the names of the cops who fired fatal shots. The mayor also refrained from revealing to the Baltimore City Council the details or costs of lawsuit settlements regarding police brutality and other abuses. In the following five years, the city paid out more than $20 million for more than a hundred settlements for police abuses. Baltimore included a clause in lawsuit settlements prohibiting police victims from "discussing any facts or allegations… with the news media."[107]

In 2019, a federal appeals court struck down Baltimore's gag order for police brutality victims in a case that began when Ashley Overbey, a 25-year-old black woman, was beaten, tased, handcuffed, and arrested after she called the police to her home after a burglary.[108] When asked why she was being arrested, a policeman told Overbey: "Because you talk too much, bitch."[109] Overbey sued, and the city settled for $63,000. The city revoked half the settlement two years later when Overbey spoke to the *Baltimore Sun*. City lawyers claimed that Baltimore had a right to avoid "harmful publicity" and that the victim had "sold her [speech] rights."[110] One federal judge derided Baltimore's settlement policy as "hush money" for police victims. The appeals court noted that "'mistrust of governmental power'… is one of the 'premises' of the First Amendment, and we think it well-warranted here."[111]

California "had the nation's strictest laws on disclosing police personnel records, due in large part to the lobbying efforts of powerful law enforcement unions that wanted to keep the files confidential," the *Los Angeles Times* reported.[112] But that was supposed to change thanks to a 2021 law to compel disclosure. Many localities responded to the new law by destroying police misconduct records.

The biggest disclosure occurred inadvertently when a small state agency replied to an information request from student journalists. They were sent a secret list exposing 12,000 California police officers convicted of murder, child molesting, shoplifting, and other crimes, as well as "cops who trafficked drugs, cops who stole money from their departments and even one who robbed a bank wearing a fake beard," the San Jose *Mercury News* reported.[113] The list also revealed many police who drove while drunk or drugged, sometimes killing other drivers, as well as cops who "sexually assaulted subjects, took bribes, filed false reports and committed perjury." Attorney General Xavier Becerra threatened to file criminal charges against the student journalists if they did not destroy those records.[114]

In June 2023, California was bracing for a police standards commission to "decertify or suspend 3,000 to 3,500 police officers each year for serious misconduct under a new state law."[115] But Gov. Gavin Newsom and the legislature reached a Solomonic compromise: delaying until at least 2027 the disclosure of the names of rogue cops — therefore enabling them to remain on police forces. "California has always been a black hole for police transparency," groused David Loy of the First Amendment Coalition.[116]

Secrecy is the default in most locales when governments settle police misconduct cases. A 2022 *Washington Post* investigation found that city governments paid over $3 billion to settle misconduct lawsuits against police between 2010 and 2020, and that "more than 1,200 officers in the departments surveyed had been the subject of at least five payments. More than 200 had 10 or more."[117] An NYPD "transparency" website omitted the names of nine out of the ten NYPD officers tagged most often in police misconduct lawsuits that cost the city $7 million. Seven of the officers had been named in 20 or more lawsuits, but the NYPD protected their reputations with an extremely narrow standard for disclosure.[118] Most local governments didn't bother tracking the names of the perpetrators who spurred the lawsuits: "Few cities or counties track claims by the names of the officers involved — meaning that officials may be unaware of officers whose alleged misconduct is repeatedly costing taxpayers." Shielding the names assures repeat police abuses.

The Right to Accost Everybody

There are almost endless pretexts for arresting people nowadays because federal, state, and local politicians and officials have criminalized daily life with hundreds of thousands of edicts. Capt. Steve Powell of the Colorado State Patrol said: "Ninety percent of the cars out there are doing something that you can pull them over for. There are a jillion reasons people can be stopped — taillights, windshields cracked, any number of things."[119]

Once again, police can thank the Supreme Court for their privileges. In 2001, the Supreme Court upheld the arrest of Gail Atwater, a Texas mother who was driving her pickup truck at 15 miles per hour near her home in Lago Vista. Because her children were not wearing seatbelts, she was denounced, handcuffed, and taken away by an abusive cop whose tirade left her children "terrified and hysterical." The provision of the Texas code that Atwater violated did not authorize arrests; instead, it merely authorized a $50 fine. But that technicality was brushed.

A majority of Supreme Court Justices recognized that "Atwater's claim to live free of pointless indignity and confinement clearly outweighs anything the City can raise against it specific to her case." But five Justices rubberstamped her arrest anyhow. The Supreme Court declared: "If an officer has probable cause to believe that an individual has committed even a very minor criminal offense in his presence, he may, without violating the Fourth Amendment, arrest the offender." The Court warned that permitting arrests only for offenses for which legislators authorized arrests could result in a "systematic disincentive to arrest." So instead, the Court created a systematic incentive for jailing peaceful citizens. The Court also fretted that curbing police's right to arrest people for petty offenses could result in "personal liability" for officers who make such arrests.

Justice O'Connor, in a stout dissent, warned that "such unbounded discretion [by police] carries with it grave potential for abuse." O'Connor mocked the Court majority for claiming there was no evidence of "an epidemic of unnecessary minor-offense arrests." Police make more than ten million arrests each year, including vast numbers of nonviolent offenses. But they are all irrelevant as long as Supreme Court Justices didn't get busted.

Because police have pretexts to pull over almost whomever they please, "driving while female" can be perilous. A 2008 study by a University of Missouri professor (and former policeman) Timothy Maher found that "pulling over a driver to get a closer look" at an attractive female was a widespread police abuse.[120] A Pennsylvania state trooper confessed: "I asked women to expose their breasts to me — expose your breasts and you're out of trouble. That was my rush." The same trooper "visited the hospital bedside of a pregnant woman who had attempted suicide, and groped her breasts and masturbated," the *Philadelphia Inquirer* reported.[121]

Police are up to four times more likely than other Americans to engage in domestic violence.[122] "In many departments, an officer will automatically be fired for a positive marijuana test, but can stay on the job after abusing or battering a spouse," the *New York Times* noted in 2013.[123] A 2019 *USA Today* investigation found more than 3,000 allegations of rape, child molestation, and other sexual misconduct leveled against police officers. A 2016 federally funded survey found 405 forcible rape charges against police officers between 2005 and 2013, 636 charges for "forcible fondling," 209 for forcible sodomy, 98 for indecent exposure, 58 for sexual assault with an object, and 186 for statutory rape. That study relied on online news searches because "surprisingly little is known about the crimes committed by law enforcement officers, in part because there are virtually no official nationwide data collected."[124] Chief Bernadette DiPino of the Sarasota Police Department in Florida observed that police sexual abuses are "happening probably in every law enforcement agency across the country. It's so underreported and people are scared that if they call and complain about a police officer, they think every other police officer is going to be then out to get them."[125]

Ninety percent of the police chiefs in a University of Missouri survey indicated that police sexual misconduct was a serious problem. A 2016 Justice Department report revealed that Baltimore police "were coercing women, especially sex workers, into sex to avoid arrest."[126] A District of Columbia policeman was fired after being convicted for sexually abusing a 19-year-old woman he enticed into his patrol car while on duty. A D.C. police trial board overturned the firing after hearing testimony that the assailant was a "nice guy" and that his assault was "totally out of character."[127]

The numbers on police rape would be far higher if most states did not tacitly permit cops to extort sexual favors from handcuffed women. Most major city police departments have "no policy explicitly prohibiting police sexual misconduct against members of the public," according to author Andrea Ritchie.[128] Thirty-five states permit policemen to "evade sexual assault charges by claiming that such an encounter — from groping to intercourse — was consensual," *BuzzFeed* reported in 2018.[129] A *New York*

Times editorial derided such laws as the "police rape loophole."[130] In 2016, a Phoenix police officer was "acquitted of sexual assault even though he admitted to having oral sex with a handcuffed woman in his patrol car, claiming she had seduced him." The first time a California police officer is convicted of having sex with someone he took into custody, it is only a misdemeanor offense; only repeat offenders need fear felony charges. *BuzzFeed* reported that in several states, "sexual assault laws require an accuser to prove that an officer used their authority in an overt effort to coerce."[131] Police "who rape have plenty of weapons at their disposal: the threat of arrest, the access to a victim's personal records, and the aura of immunity that comes from carrying a badge," *BuzzFeed* noted.

In 2017, two NYPD plainclothes cops arrested Anna Chambers, a petite 18-year-old Brooklyn resident who they detected smoking marijuana in a parked car. While Chambers was handcuffed in an unmarked police van, the two officers took turns raping her. She was forced to perform oral sex on both of them, and a hospital test revealed one of the officer's semen in her vagina. But the police officers, who dumped Chambers on the sidewalk after finishing with her, claimed the sex was consensual; they did not arrest her, issue a citation, or even file any paperwork on the encounter. They were initially charged with kidnapping and raping Chambers but were permitted to plead guilty to 11 lesser charges, including misconduct. They were also permitted to resign instead of being fired, and they received no jail time — only five years of probation. The judge blamed Chambers for bribing the policemen.[132]

The uproar from the Chambers case spurred the New York legislature to prohibit police from having sex with arrestees. But laws permitting police to sexually exploit people in their custody have not been changed in most states because it was "politically unpopular to push laws that target cops and anger their powerful unions," *BuzzFeed* reported.

Conclusion

The automatic absolution of law enforcement is one of Washington's most predictable charades. Politicians are perpetually prone to perceive insufficient submission as the real problem in America. Attorney General William Barr told the Fraternal Order of Police in 2019: "We must have zero tolerance for resisting police."[133] Unless one assumes that police are both infallible and perfectly benevolent, compelling every American to submit to any police command is the death of a free society. Barr had previously championed granting legal immunity to the FBI sniper who gunned down an Idaho mother holding her baby in a cabin door.[134]

Rather than "equality before the law," police get "free shots" at private citizens. Americans never consented to being tyrannized and subjugated by police for endless petty offenses. Police have too much power because politicians have too much power. Politicians criminalize daily life and then tell police, "Be nice," or mandate sensitivity training. Instead of making police accountable, some progressive prosecutors are sufficing with turning shoplifting into an entitlement program.

As long as cops have pretexts to harass and assail millions of peaceful Americans every day, outrages will continue. The proliferation of police abuses could not have occurred unless the Supreme Court perennially placed G-men on a pedestal. How did preserving "law and order" degenerate into exempting police from the Constitution? America is becoming a two-tiered society: those whom the law fails to bind and those whom the law fails to protect. But, as Senator John Taylor warned in 1822: "There are no rights where there are no remedies."[135]

5. COVID Crackdown Catastrophes

"You're not going to get COVID if you have these vaccinations."
— President Joe Biden, July 21, 2021[1]

The COVID-19 pandemic opened a Pandora's Box of perils to freedom, prosperity, and health. Though judges torpedoed a few despotic decrees, politicians fanned pandemic fears to seize nearly absolute power. Despite pervasive abuses, not a single government official spent a day in jail for the most politically exploited pandemic in American history.

Politicians effectively promised to banish all COVID risk by obliterating individual liberty. But according to the Centers for Disease Control, most Americans still contracted COVID despite "the greatest intrusions on civil liberties in the peacetime history of this country," as Justice Neil Gorsuch declared in 2023. Those lockdowns destroyed millions of jobs, spurred hundreds of thousands of bankruptcies,[2] and sparked far more suicides, alcoholism, and drug abuse.

Chinese Chicanery, American Coverup

The Chinese government first admitted that a pandemic had broken out in the city of Wuhan in early 2020. Though the Chinese military-affiliated Wuhan Institute of Virology had been experimenting with bats for years, the Chinese government insisted the new virus came from a nearby marketplace. But the lead scientists involved with bat research had all been struck down by COVID-19 symptoms shortly before the Chinese government denied any responsibility.

The outbreak of COVID-19 spurred one of the most brazen coverups in modern U.S. history. The National Institute for Health had been financing gain-of-function research at the Wuhan Institute of Virology. That type of research seeks to genetically alter organisms to enable the spread of viruses into new species. Such research is extremely dangerous; as MIT professor Kevin Esvelt asked in 2021, "Why is anyone trying to teach the world how to make viruses that could kill millions of people?"[3] The risks were compounded because the Wuhan Institute had a very poor safety rating. Two years earlier, the State Department confidentially "warned other federal agencies about safety issues at Wuhan labs studying bat COVID," but the public disclosure of that alert was delayed until 2022.

In late January 2020, top federal scientists recognized that the pandemic could obliterate their reputations. Dr. Francis Collins, the director of the National Institutes for Health, wrote in an email that "a swift convening of experts in a confidence-inspiring framework is needed or the voices of conspiracy will quickly dominate, doing great potential harm to science and international harmony." The "conspiracy" was the facts of the matter. Anthony Fauci, the chief of the National Institute for Allergy and Infectious Diseases (NIAID), speedily enlisted a handful of trusted scientists to gin up a paper supposedly "proving" that the virus could not have originated in the lab. A top NIAID scientist accepted the task of debunking the lab leak story because, as he emailed a colleague, "Tony doesn't want his fingerprints on origin stories."[4] The *Lancet*, one of the most respected medical journals in the world, enlisted in the coverup with an op-ed by 27 scientists who proclaimed: "We stand together to strongly condemn conspiracy theories suggesting that COVID-19 does not have a natural origin."[5] Official bribery bolstered the same conclusion. In September 2023, a senior CIA analyst told a congressional committee that six key CIA analysts had been bribed by the agency to abandon their conclusion that COVID originated in a lab leak.[6]

Further "proof" was provided by a torrent of accusations of racism against anyone who publicly suggested that the virus originated in a Chinese lab. The State Department's Global Engagement Center added a federal fist to the debate, pressuring Twitter to suppress hundreds of thousands of accounts (including thousands of average Americans) in early 2020 for the crime of suggesting that COVID originated in a lab. In congressional testimony, Fauci repeatedly lied, denying that the U.S. government had financed gain-of-function research at the Wuhan Institute.

If COVID-19 had been initially recognized as the result of one of the biggest government boondoggles in history, it would have been far more difficult for American politicians and government scientists to pirouette as saviors as they seized sway over daily life.

Regardless of the source of the pandemic, Western governments were awed by how the brutal Chinese lockdowns supposedly thwarted the spread of the virus. President Donald Trump asserted on February 29: "China seems to be making tremendous progress. Their numbers are way down... They've been talking to our people, we've been talking to their people, having to do with the virus."[7]

The Trump administration initially downplayed the peril from COVID but soon embraced repressive responses. On March 16, 2020, Trump endorsed "15 Days to Slow the Spread" — a slogan that would live in infamy. Trump promised: "If everyone makes this change or these critical changes and sacrifices now, we will rally together as one nation and we will defeat the virus and we're going to have a big celebration together."[8] Freezing the economy and daily life would magically vanquish the virus. A reporter asked whether Trump was "considering instituting a nationwide lockdown, a nationwide quarantine." Trump replied, "At this point, not nationwide, but... at this moment, no, we're not." But the small print on a CDC flyer handed to reporters specifically called for shutting down schools and many businesses in most of the nation.[9] (The calamitous effects of school lockdowns will be examined in Chapter 6, "Schools Gone Wild.")

On March 22, Trump proudly proclaimed: "I'm a wartime president... This is a different kind of war than we've ever had."[10] On April 13, Trump revealed, "The federal government has absolute power. It has the power. As to whether or not I'll use that power, we'll see."[11] *Politico* reported that Trump's Justice Department was considering asking Congress to approve suspending habeas corpus for the duration of the pandemic. Norman Reimer of the National Association of Criminal Defense Lawyers warned that the proposed policy "means you could be arrested and never brought before a judge until they decide that the emergency or the civil disobedience is over." Pre-arrest power could be used to detain anyone suspected of being infected or failing to obey lockdown orders.

The World Health Organization announced that "3.4% of reported COVID-19 cases have died."[12] That calculation was profoundly flawed from the start, since there were no reliable estimates of how many people had COVID infections. Regardless, the WHO estimate quickly became canonized, and the media derided lower estimates as "misinformation."[13] The actual fatality rate was less than 1%, and far less than 1% for the non-elderly.

The WHO mortality claim spurred widespread panic. *New York Times* science reporter Donald McNeil urged American politicians to "go Medieval" on COVID-19 with tactics "from the era of the Black Death... pen terrified citizens up inside their poisoned cities... Harsh measures horrify civil libertarians, but they often save lives, especially when they are imposed in the early days."[14] Valorizing Black Death repression set the tone for reporters and editors as frightened as Army paratroopers leaping into their first firefight. (McNeil was a co-winner of the 2020 Pulitzer for Public Service.)

Federal agencies blundered massively from the start of the pandemic. The CDC sent out contaminated COVID tests that gave false readings to state and local health departments, undercutting efforts to track the virus.[15] The Food and Drug Administration blocked the speedy development and deployment of private testing that could have provided Americans with far better awareness of the perils they faced.[16] Instead of access to life-saving medical results, Americans were obliged to settle for Trump's ludicrous assertion that "anybody that needs a test gets a test." He also claimed the tests were "perfect."

In the name of saving lives, politicians entitled themselves to destroy an unlimited number of livelihoods. Most governors responded to COVID-19 by dropping the equivalent of a Reverse Neutron Bomb — something which destroys the economy while leaving human beings unharmed. But the only way to assume people were uninjured was to presume their lives were totally detached from their jobs, bank accounts, mortgage and rent payments, and friends and family.

Government bureaucrats quickly became a new priesthood sanctifying endless sacrifices in the name of public health. Within six weeks of the start of lockdowns, almost 40% of households earning less than $40,000 per year had someone who recently lost their job, according to the Federal Reserve.[17] A *JAMA Psychiatry* analysis warned that stay-at-home orders and rising unemployment were a "perfect storm" for higher suicide rates.[18] A California health organization estimated that up to 75,000 Americans could die from "despair" as a result of the pandemic, unemployment, and government restrictions.[19] From the start, politicians ignored the collateral damage from their repressive policies.

Oregon Governor Kate Brown banned residents from leaving their homes except for "essential work," buying food, and other narrow exemptions, and also banned all recreational travel. Shortly before Thanksgiving, Brown urged citizens to summon the police if they noticed neighbors having too many guests for the big dinner — a proposal that one Oregon local official declared "turned people into 'second-rate slaves' in their own homes."[20]

Maryland Governor Larry Hogan asserted that "every Marylander can be a hero, just by staying home," after he dictated a "shelter-at-home" order. Anyone who violated his edict faced a $5,000 fine and a year in prison. Maryland politicians destroyed more than 400,000 jobs, resulting in almost 20% of the workers in the state filing for unemployment compensation. The *Washington Post* reported that Maryland's COVID "restrictions have crippled the economy and paralyzed daily life since mid-March." But the shutdowns failed to prevent COVID cases from increasing fiftyfold or the death toll from rising a hundredfold.

Michigan Governor Gretchen Whitmer placed almost the entire state under house arrest, dictating a $1,000 fine for anyone who left their home to visit family or friends.[21] Business owners faced up to three years in prison for refusing to close their operations. Whitmer prohibited purchasing seeds for spring planting after she decreed that it was a "nonessential" activity. (Purchasing state lottery tickets was still an "essential" activity.) Unemployment soared to 24% statewide. After the Michigan Supreme Court decreed that Whitmer was effectively a lawless dictator who had illegally extended a "state of emergency," Whitmer's appointees simply issued "new COVID-19 emergency orders that [were] nearly identical to her invalidated emergency orders," as the Mackinac Center noted.[22]

After New Jersey Governor Phil Murphy shut down almost every business in the state and compelled residents to remain in their homes, Fox News host Tucker Carlson asked him about the constitutionality of his executive order. "That's above my pay grade, Tucker," Murphy responded with a laugh. "I wasn't thinking of the Bill of Rights when we did this." The Bill of Rights did not impede police arresting citizens for any imagined offense. In the first months of the lockdown, Newark, New Jersey, police issued thousands of tickets for "[c]ommitt[ing] any unauthorized or otherwise unlawful act during the threat or imminence of danger in any emergency" jeopardizing health or safety. The offenses, punishable by up to 6 months in prison and a $1,000 fine, included COVID scofflaws caught "hanging out," "sitting on milk crate," "sitting on bench smoking," "standing outside enjoying the weather," "being in the street in the company of another," and "standing without a mask," as journalist Michael Tracey reported.[23]

Any politician who recited the phrase "science and data" became entitled to outlaw any activity he chose. The mayor of Louisville, Kentucky, banned drive-in church services at the same time he permitted drive-through liquor stores to remain open.[24] Los Angeles Mayor Eric Garcetti banned all unnecessary "travel, including, without limitation, travel on foot, bicycle, scooter, motorcycle, automobile, or public transit."[25] The mayor offered no evidence that people strolling on sidewalks or parks spurred COVID cases. Garcetti also "ordered all residents living in the city 'to remain in their homes.'" In a hat tip to the protestors that had roiled many American cities in 2020, Garcetti's order exempted "participating in an in-person outdoor protest while wearing a face covering, maintaining social distancing, and observing the Los Angeles County Protocol for Public Demonstrations." The order also exempted people who work in "'music, film and television production' and private golf courses that follow state guidelines."[26]

New York Governor Andrew Cuomo issued a deluge of decrees after the state legislature gave him "authorization of absolute power," as the *New Yorker* declared.[27] The *New York Times* proclaimed: "Andrew Cuomo Is the Control Freak We Need Right Now."[28] Cuomo justified imposing a state-wide lockdown: "If everything we do saves just one life, I'll be happy." Potentially saving one life entitled the governor to sabotage the efforts of almost 20 million people to take care of themselves and their families. Cuomo denounced anyone who disobeyed his edicts and condemned sheriffs as "dictators" for refusing to enforce his mask mandate inside people's homes.[29] The *New Yorker* explained that Cuomo and his aides saw the battle over COVID policy as "between people who believe government can be a force for good and those who think otherwise." Ordering citizens to "stay at home," padlocking schools, and bankrupting businesses miraculously vindicated government as "a force for good." Cuomo won an Emmy Award for his "masterful use of television" during the pandemic.[30] New York had among the highest COVID death rates despite Cuomo's idealistic repression. Ten days after Cuomo issued his lockdown order, his aides "began drafting a 'preface' for a possible 'book' on Cuomo's 'leadership' and 'decision-making,'" the *New York Post* later reported.[31]

Politicians sought to placate angry citizens with a tidal wave of handouts that eventually exceeded $5 trillion. "COVID fraud" became redundant after federal programs were looted by shysters around the globe.[32] Unemployment benefits were offered to anyone who filed a form and concocted a false name. "Overseas organized crime groups flooded state unemployment systems with bogus online claims, overwhelming antiquated computer software benefits in blunt-force attacks that siphoned out millions of dollars," NBC News reported. Prison inmates, drug gangs, and Nigerian racketeers pilfered the program. One swindler collected unemployment benefits from 29 different states. In the first year of the pandemic, Maryland detected more than 1.3 million fraudulent unemployment claims — equal to 20% of the state's population. Up to $400 billion in unemployment benefits were wrongly paid out.

Beginning in June 2020, the feds distributed $813 billion in Paycheck Protection Program (PPP) loans to businesses. Trump's Treasury Secretary Steven Mnuchin boasted that PPP is "supporting an estimated 50 million jobs." But many of those jobs existed solely in the imagination of political appointees. The Small Business Administration (SBA), which administered the program, ludicrously claimed that PPP loans saved more jobs than the total number of employees in at least 15 industries.[33] The SBA effectively told people, "Apply and sign and tell us that you're really entitled to the money," according to Justice Department Inspector General Michael Horowitz.[34]

The feds gave PPP loans to "342 people who said their name was 'N/A.'" After 15 Illinois jailbirds used PPP loans to pay their bail, cynics scoffed that the program should be named the Prisoner Paycheck Program.[35] PPP loans went to more than a thousand "ghost businesses" in Markham, Illinois — indicative of a nationwide problem of deluging nonexistent companies with federal cash. In Florida, a PPP loan was used to bankroll a murder-for-hire plot that left a TSA agent dead.[36] An NBC News investigation found that almost $600 billion may have been lost to fraud.[37]

"Science and Data" Shenanigans

Shutdown advocates appealed to science like righteous priests invoking God and the Bible to sanctify scourging enemies.[38] But the "science" was often farcically unreliable. Mandatory mask mandates became the new version of the Emancipation Proclamation. *Washington Post* columnist Leana Wen claimed that mask mandates "protect our freedom" by preventing "the need for lockdowns" (which she later championed).[39] As COVID case numbers soared, many states and locales decreed that anyone going to grocery stores or practically anyplace else must wear a face covering. One California mayor announced that anyone not wearing a mask in public was guilty of "an act of domestic terrorism."[40]

Government officials imposed heavy fines on anyone not wearing a mask — and then urged people to wear utterly unreliable cloth masks so that medical personnel could have all of the surgical and N95 masks.[41] Mandating wearing unreliable masks was on par with wearing dunce caps inscribed, "Save me, Big Brother!" High rates of compliance with mask mandates utterly failed to prevent second and third waves of COVID infections. A 2022 comprehensive evaluation of dozens of studies found no significant difference in COVID outcomes between the 39 states with mask mandates and 11 states with no mandates.[42]

COVID prohibitions spawned millions of new narcs. A *New York Times* piece headlined "Social Distancing Informants Have Their Eyes on You" noted: "In some cities and counties, vigilantism has been encouraged by municipalities that have set up special phone numbers, apps or online forms to report violations."[43] Two hundred thousand complaints were registered in Massachusetts alone, including against a maskless female stripper at Kittens Gentlemen's Club and a deluge of accusations against people whose masks had slipped beneath their nose.[44] The *New York Times* reported, "Some liberals said they thought that calling out violators was a civic duty and a matter of public health." Many East Germans felt the same way about notifying the Stasi about anti-communist mutterings overheard while queueing to buy cabbages.

The lockdowns failed to prevent almost nine million Americans from testing positive for COVID by late June 2020. The CDC warned that the actual number of cases could be ten times higher.[45] The World Health Organization's COVID-19 envoy David Nabarro warned that "lockdowns just have one consequence that you must never, ever belittle, and that is making poor people an awful lot poorer."[46] Actually, there was never a true lockdown. Instead, affluent people stayed home, while the comparatively downtrodden delivered their groceries, fancy meals, and endless knick-knacks from Amazon.

Some politicians exploited COVID to treat their domains like conquered territories. Governor Gavin Newsom decreed that severe restrictions on daily life would be perpetuated in California counties based on voter turnout, alcohol availability, and other non-health factors. Newsom never explained how people forfeited their right to freedom because their neighbors neglected to vote. California assemblyman Kevin Kiley groused: "An entire county can be kept shut down because certain areas are judged to be lacking in 'equity,' even if the whole county has relatively few cases of COVID."[47] California suffered some of the highest COVID fatality rates despite Newsom's decrees.

Nevada Governor Steve Sisloak decreed that casinos could operate at half capacity — allowing hundreds of gamblers at a time — but that churches could only allow 50 worshippers regardless of their size. The Supreme Court denied an injunction to overturn the edict. Justice Gorsuch dissented: "The First Amendment prohibits such obvious discrimination against the exercise of religion... There is no world in which the Constitution permits Nevada to favor Caesars Palace over Calvary Chapel," the church that sought the injunction.[48]

Politicians vilified individual freedom as the greatest threat to Americans' survival. Democratic presidential candidate Joe Biden vowed to impose a national shutdown to fight COVID if his science advisors recommended it. An ABC television host asked him: "Are you going to force [everyone] to wear a mask?" Biden replied: "This isn't about freedom; it's about freedom for your... neighbors... This is... the first time I've ever heard people say that doing something patriotic you can save other people's lives, impacts on their freedom. Come on. Give me a break."[49]

On September 14, Federal Judge William Stickman nullified COVID restrictions decreed by Pennsylvania Governor Tom Wolf: "Broad population-wide lockdowns are such a dramatic inversion of the concept of liberty in a free society as to be nearly presumptively unconstitutional."[50] Stickman noted that even during the Spanish Flu epidemic a century earlier, "nothing remotely approximating lockdowns were imposed." Stickman ruled that the "non-life-sustaining" label to justify shutting down businesses was "an arbitrary, ad hoc process" with government officials simply "picking winners and losers" and violating the Constitution's Due Process and Equal Protection Clauses. As the Heritage Foundation noted, Wolf's COVID enforcement team

> met in secret, kept no notes, never held recorded votes on key decisions, and none of the secret group... was a doctor or public health official... The government shuttered mom-and-pop hardware stores... while allowing large ones, like Lowe's and Home Depot, to stay open.[51]

Eloquent judicial condemnations were almost completely ignored by the media. Instead, Trump was portrayed as homicidally negligent. Trump's critics did not specify when a president became blameworthy for failing to prevent all risks in Americans' daily lives. CNN ramped up the fear with a COVID Death Counter always on the screen. But the death count was statistical garbage from the get-go. Individuals who died of gunshot wounds were counted as COVID deaths if a postmortem showed any COVID trace.

After initially supporting harsh measures, Trump vigorously criticized lockdowns imposed by governors before getting walloped by COVID himself in the final campaign stretch. According to former White House Chief of Staff Mark Meadows, Trump tested positive for COVID three days before his first debate with Biden. During that time, Trump met with many individuals but failed to disclose to them their risk of contracting COVID from him. (Trump denied Meadows's account.[52])

In the final debate between presidential candidates in October 2020, Biden blamed Trump for every COVID fatality: "220,000 Americans dead… Anyone who's responsible for that many deaths should not remain as President of the United States." Biden promised, "I will take care of this. I will end this. I'm going to shut down the virus, not the country."

Biden ran one of the most fear-based presidential campaigns in modern history. Biden talked as if every American family had lost a member or two from this pestilence. He routinely exaggerated COVID death tolls[53] a hundredfold or a thousandfold, publicly asserting that millions of Americans had been killed by COVID-19.[54] According to much of the media, it was a single-issue election: "It's the pandemic, stupid," as a *Politico* headline blared.[55] Biden was helped mightily by fearmongering media coverage. A Brookings Institution analysis noted: "Democrats are much more likely than Republicans to overestimate [COVID] harm. Forty-one percent of Democrats… answered that half or more of those infected by COVID-19 need to be hospitalized."[56] At that time, the rate of hospitalization was between 1% and 5%, but Democratic voters overestimated the risk up to twentyfold. A CNN exit poll found that the "recent rise in coronavirus cases" was the most important factor for 61% of Biden voters.[57] Biden won the presidency as a result of only 43,000 votes in three swing states.[58]

The initial congressional COVID bailout included $400 million to assist state governments in running the November election. Democrats exploited the pandemic to get a federal seal of approval for voting procedures previously shunned because of pervasive fraud — including ballot harvesting, unmanned ballot drop boxes, and deluging all potential voters with absentee ballots. Many politicians pretended that the COVID pandemic justified nullifying many protections against voter fraud crafted in the preceding centuries.

Among the constitutional casualties of the pandemic was the Elections Clause, which specified that the rules for federal elections (president and Congress) "shall be prescribed in each State by the Legislature thereof." That constitutional provision was trampled in many states. Though millions of Biden supporters had rushed to demonstrate across the nation after the killing of George Floyd, Democratic Party leaders and their media allies insisted that voting in person was too risky. Democratic Party and election officials scorned state law to rewrite the rules for the 2020 election in several swing states. Trump and his allies issued a deluge of false claims about how the 2020 election was stolen, but the changes in election procedures should have been controversial regardless.

In Wisconsin, political appointees exhorted residents to ignore state law when casting their ballots. The Wisconsin Election Commission and local election officials encouraged all "voters to unlawfully declare themselves 'indefinitely Confined' — which under Wisconsin law allows the voter to avoid security measures like signature verification and photo ID requirements," as a brief to the U.S. Supreme Court from the Attorney General of Texas declared.[59] The Wisconsin Elections Commission approved setting up to 500 unmanned ballot drop boxes in major Democratic cities in violation of Wisconsin law. In December 2020, the Wisconsin Supreme Court ruled that election officials had acted illegally, but that did not void hundreds of thousands of ballots cast illicitly. Biden carried Wisconsin by 20,000 votes.

In Pennsylvania, the state supreme court invoked a vaporous phrase in the state constitution — "Elections shall be free and equal" — to justify invalidating a state law that prohibited counting mail-in ballots that arrived after Election Day. The judges even mandated counting ballots that arrived late with no postmark.

In Michigan, Secretary of State Jocelyn Benson "unilaterally abrogated Michigan election statutes related to absentee ballot applications" by sending "unsolicited absentee-voter ballot applications by mail to all 7.7 million registered Michigan voters... without verifying voter signatures as required" by state law.[60] Wayne County, the state's most populous county (which includes Detroit), ignored "Michigan's statutory signature verification requirements for absentee ballots." More than 3 million votes were cast by absentee ballot in Michigan (57% of all votes) without verification of voter signatures. Biden won Michigan by 154,000 votes.

As the pandemic continued, religious freedom became increasingly vilified. On Thanksgiving Eve, the Supreme Court struck down New York State restrictions that limited religious gatherings to fewer than eleven people. The Court ruled that Cuomo's rules were "far more restrictive than any COVID-related regulations that have previously come before the Court… and far more severe than has been shown to be required to prevent the spread of the virus."[61] Justice Gorsuch wrote, "According to the Governor, it may be unsafe to go to church, but it is always fine to pick up another bottle of wine or shop for a new bike." The ruling horrified the liberal establishment. An ACLU official fretted to the *New York Times* that "the freedom to worship… does not include a license to harm others or endanger public health."[62]

Though many states effectively outlawed weddings to minimize the risk of COVID transmission, some freedoms were more equal than others. Politicians and bureaucrats carved a "copulation exemption" into their public health mandates. Shortly after lockdowns were imposed in most states, COVID policy superstar Anthony Fauci declared that people who hook up with strangers via Tinder were entitled to make their "choice regarding a risk."[63] While New York cops violently assaulted people for not wearing face masks, city officials sanctioned "glory holes" for sex with strangers. The city health department urged people to "be creative with… physical barriers, like walls, that allow sexual contact while preventing close face-to-face contact."[64] It also recommended to people who organize orgies: "Limit the size of your guest list. Keep it intimate." The Health Department did not specify whether "intimate" meant fewer people than a subway car in rush hour. Shortly before Thanksgiving 2020, Pennsylvania Governor Tom Wolf decreed that anyone visiting other people's homes must wear a mask. But the dress code was more casual after dinner. The Pennsylvania Department of Health produced a "Safer Sex and COVID-19" guide for people who "attend a large gathering where you might end up having sex." People attending orgies should "limit the number of partners" and "try to identify a consistent sex partner."[65] Consistently what? The Philadelphia Board of Health urged prostitutes to "shower thoroughly after each client and change clothes" and wash hands "with soap and water for at least 20 seconds." But small business owners were not allowed to open their stores no matter how long they washed their hands.

At the start of the pandemic, President Trump launched Operation Warp Speed to spur a vaccine for COVID. It normally takes five or more years to develop a new vaccine, but pharmaceutical companies pocketed hefty subsidies while rushing to develop a new injection. The announcement that Pfizer had created a new vaccine was postponed until November 9 — just after Biden was proclaimed the winner of the presidential election. Liberal political analyst Nate Silver later asserted that "liberal public health elites" had swayed Pfizer to delay the announcement until after the election to help Biden.[66] Thirty days later, the Food and Drug Administration (FDA) approved the vaccine for emergency use, despite zero independent data on the vaccine's safety. The Emergency Use Authorization meant vaccine makers had zero liability for any deaths or injuries resulting from the injections.[67]

After winning the election, Biden speedily proclaimed a goal of getting 100 million Americans vaccinated within 100 days. In his Inaugural Address on January 20, 2021, he promised to "defeat the virus." On his first day in office, he decreed that masks must be worn any time people were on federal property.[68] Biden's edict contained an unwritten "Poohbah Exemption." Hours after signing the mandate, Biden and family members were not wearing masks when they visited the Lincoln Memorial. At a daily press briefing, White House spokeswoman Jen Psaki scoffed at a reporter's question: "He was celebrating a historic day in our country… We have bigger things to worry about."[69] Biden set the tone for elected officials to brazenly violate the COVID restrictions they imposed on everyone else.[70]

On Groundhog Day 2021, the Biden Administration mandated wearing face masks on all National Park Service lands "when physical distancing cannot be maintained," including "narrow or busy trails, overlooks and historic homes." Probably 95% of the Park Service's 800+ million acres is uncrowded 98% of the time. But the new mandate entitled zealots to scream at anyone not wearing a mask, regardless of trails wide enough for 18-wheel trucks. The Outdoor Society hailed the new regulation: "If you see violations of the mask requirement: Find the closest ranger or volunteer in the area and let them know." The mandate was justified by the dread many Biden supporters felt whenever they saw unmasked human beings.[71]

The Supreme Court continued to defer mostly to the emergency proclamations of state and local officials and politicians. In a February 2021 ruling, the Court upheld Gov. Newsom's ban on singing in churches. Gorsuch dissented: "If Hollywood may host a studio audience or film a singing competition while not a single soul may enter California's churches, synagogues, and mosques, something has gone seriously awry." Gorsuch exposed the rascality behind COVID controls: "Government actors have been moving the goalposts on pandemic-related sacrifices for months, adopting new benchmarks that always seem to put restoration of liberty just around the corner."[72]

Biden Goes to War

On March 11, the first anniversary of COVID lockdowns, Biden donned rhetorical military epaulets and announced on television: "I'm using every power I have as the President of the United States to put us on a war footing to get the job done. Sounds like hyperbole, but I mean it, a war footing."[73] Biden promised that the feds will "have enough vaccine supply for all adults in America by the end of May... We're mobilizing thousands of vaccinators to put the vaccine in [everyone's] arm." Biden said that he might deign to designate the Fourth of July as Americans' shrink-wrapped "Freedom Day." If people dutifully got vaccinated, Biden said, "there's a good chance you, your families, and friends will be [permitted] to get together [in small groups] in your backyard or in your neighborhood and have a cookout or a barbecue and celebrate Independence Day." Biden converted the Fourth of July into a benchmark of submission to presidential decrees.

In his first speech to Congress on April 28, 2021, Biden portrayed himself as the heroic conqueror of COVID: "In our first 100 days together, we have acted to restore the people's faith in democracy to deliver. We're vaccinating the nation." A *Washington Post* headline aptly summarized Biden's speech: "Government is good."

To safeguard the reputation of government, the Biden administration doubled down on suppressing damning facts. The White House forced the State Department to cease its investigation into the origins of COVID-19. Facebook agreed to delete any posts or comments that suggested "COVID-19 is man-made or manufactured." The Biden administration canonized Anthony Fauci with the new title "Chief Medical Advisor to the President." This honorific entitled Fauci to blather about any issue he chose.

In a commencement speech at Emory University, Fauci announced, "COVID-19 has shone a bright light on our own society's failings."

On June 2, Biden declared that people should "exercise your freedom" to get vaccinated so Americans can enjoy a "summer of freedom."[74] On July 4, Biden proclaimed that "we are closer than ever to declaring our independence from a deadly virus." Biden sounded like a pontiff absolving his obedient flock: "We can live our lives."[75]

Biden missed no chance to tout vaccines as panaceas. At a CNN town hall on July 21, Biden promised, "You're not going to get COVID if you have these vaccinations."[76] How did Biden know that? Because the CDC months earlier had ceased keeping track of almost all "breakthrough" infections among vaccinated people except cases resulting in hospitalization or death.[77]

The following week, headlines revealed that almost 400 vaccinated people contracted COVID on holiday visits to Provincetown, Massachusetts. On July 30, the *Washington Post* and *New York Times* published leaked CDC documents warning that vaccines were utterly failing to stop COVID transmission. The *Times* tweeted, "The Delta variant is as contagious as chickenpox and may be spread by vaccinated people as easily as the unvaccinated."[78]

Biden White House COVID spokesman Ben Wakana hysterically denounced the *Washington Post* as "completely irresponsible" and flogged the *Times* with an all-caps Twitter outburst: "YOU'RE DOING IT WRONG."[79] But on August 5, CDC chief Rochelle Walensky admitted that vaccines failed to "prevent transmission" of COVID.[80] The Biden administration previously refused to even disclose the number of "breakthrough" infections occurring among White House staff.[81] The following week, a Mayo Clinic study revealed the Pfizer COVID vaccine had become only 42% effective — below the standard FDA normally required for vaccine approval.[82] At the same time the Biden administration was trumpeting false claims on vaccine efficacy, Surgeon General Vivek Murthy lamented, "Misinformation takes away our freedom to make informed decisions for ourselves and our loved ones."[83]

Biden policymakers doubled down on fear. NIH Director Francis Collins announced on CNN that "parents of unvaccinated kids should... wear masks" in their own homes. He conceded: "I know that's uncomfortable. I know it seems weird, but it is the best way to protect your kids."[84] A few hours later, Collins recanted on Twitter, perhaps after other political appointees persuaded him to stop sounding like a blithering idiot.

In mid-August, the *Washington Post* castigated the CDC for withholding COVID information, noting that its "overly rosy assessments of the vaccines' effectiveness against delta may have lulled Americans into a false sense of security."[85] CDC Director Walensky responded by promising "to develop a new forecasting and outbreak analytics center to analyze data in real time," the *Post* reported. If only the CDC had thought earlier of devoting some of its $8 billion budget to that task!

The pandemic's first political hero toppled in disgrace in the summer of 2021. Early in the pandemic, New York Governor Cuomo forced nursing homes to admit COVID-infected patients and permitted COVID-infected staffers to keep working at those homes. New York State initially reported barely half of the total of more than 12,000 New York nursing home patients who died of COVID — one out of eight nursing home residents in the state.[86] Cuomo's appointees suppressed data on nursing home deaths while he was negotiating a $5 million advance for his self-tribute book on pandemic leadership lessons, *American Crisis: Leadership Lessons from the COVID-19 Pandemic.*[87] After an official investigation of nursing home COVID deaths was followed by a deluge of sexual harassment accusations, Cuomo resigned.[88]

As vaccine efficacy faded and COVID cases surged, politicians quickly found the scapegoat. Maryland Governor Hogan accused the unvaccinated of "threatening the freedoms of all the rest of us."[89] CNN hosts condemned "the tyranny of the unvaccinated." Former Biden senior COVID advisor Andy Slavitt complained that, because of COVID fatalities, "We're not enjoying freedom. We're paying respect to people who perpetuate ignorance and liars."[90] He ridiculed Americans who objected to vaccine mandates: "Those making a spectacle of themselves & throwing their toys out of the stroller shouldn't confuse the fact that these steps are very routine & common sense by normal standards." Demonizing the unvaxxed while the COVID vaccines failed was the health policy version of "The Emperor Has No Clothes." The Biden administration browbeat Twitter, Facebook, and other social media companies into suppressing all criticism, true and false, of the vaccines. (The censorship campaign will be discussed further in Chapter 13, "Mindless Ministry of Truth.")

On August 13, the Associated Press reported that the Biden administration was considering "mandating vaccines for interstate travel." Enforcing such a policy would require the creation of COVID posses waiting to chase down anyone crossing state lines without proper papers. The Associated Press report noted that any such decree was being delayed until "Americans were ready for the strong-arming from the federal government."[91]

Biden's FDA Fix

Biden resolved to strong-arm Americans to get vaxxed. But he could not compel mass injections unless the COVID shots had the final FDA seal of approval. White House machinations spurred perhaps the most scandalous bureaucratic bait-and-switch in recent U.S. history.

When Pfizer filed an application for full approval in May 2021, FDA said it aimed to announce a decision the following January. Under White House pressure, FDA's top vaccine officials stated they could complete the analysis by September 15. But that wasn't fast enough. Acting Commissioner Janet Woodcock was concerned because "states cannot require mandatory vaccination" without FDA final approval, the chief of FDA's vaccine-review office, Marion Gruber, revealed in an email. Gruber warned that a thorough evaluation was needed due to "increasing evidence" linking the vaccine to the "development of myocarditis (especially in young males)." After Gruber balked, Woodcock placed a loyal subordinate in charge of the process, and the vaccine received full approval on August 23. Biden boasted that day of achieving a COVID "key milestone" and labeled FDA approval "gold standard," proving vaccines were safe and effective.[92] Team Biden's arm-twisting spurred a "mutiny" at FDA, *Politico* reported.[93] Gruber and her top deputy resigned in protest. The COVID vaccine's rushed approval was the pharmaceutical version of a riverboat gamble — except Biden was betting the lives and health of Americans.

To sanctify Biden's policies, the CDC formally changed the definition of vaccine from "a product that stimulates a person's immune system to produce immunity to a specific disease" to "a preparation that is used to stimulate the body's immune response against diseases."[94] The injections could still be labeled "vaccines" despite failing to prevent COVID infections. Rep. Thomas Massie (R-KY) scoffed at the "evolving definition" of vaccines: "They've been busy at the Ministry of Truth."[95]

Biden responded to the vax failures by repudiating his 2020 promise that "I wouldn't demand [vaccines] to be mandatory."[96] On September 9, 2021, Biden bet his presidency on COVID vaccines. In a televised evening speech, he announced, "My job as president is to protect all Americans."[97] Actually, his oath of office was to uphold and defend the Constitution, but no matter. Biden told viewers: "Recent data indicates there's only one confirmed positive [COVID] case per 5,000 fully vaccinated Americans per day."[98] That howler was based on the CDC's refusal to count breakthrough infections, but it was a linchpin of his calculus of compulsion. Biden issued the equivalent of a declaration of war on 80 million unvaccinated Americans, portraying them as Public Enemy No. 1, (except for postal workers, whom the White House exempted from the mandate due to the clout of postal unions). Biden castigated the unvaxxed: "We've been patient, but our patience is wearing thin. And your refusal has cost all of us." Biden's declaration sounded like a dictator's threat prior to invading a foreign nation. Biden finger-wagged: "This is not about freedom or personal choice. It's about protecting yourself and those around you — the people you work with, the people you care about, the people you love." But who would protect Americans from Biden's lawless mandates?

A month after his September COVID speech, Biden claimed that, thanks to his mandate, there were only "67 eligible Americans who aren't vaccinated." The White House Press Office added a correction to the transcript: "[million]."[99] In a CNN town hall, Biden derided vaccine skeptics as murderers who only wanted "the freedom to kill you" with COVID.[100]

Biden did not formally issue his vaccine mandate until November 5, when his appointees uncorked a 150,000-word *Federal Register* notice imposing a "jab or job" ultimatum on 17 million healthcare workers, 84 million private workers at large private companies, and millions of federal employees. The official notice touted the initial 95% claimed efficacy of COVID vaccines but downplayed the subsequent plummet. The announcement explained that the "most important inducement [for vaccination] will be the fear of job loss."[101] The notice omitted citing the provision of the Constitution that entitled presidents to destroy jobs. The ultimatum was justified, according to the *Federal Register* notice, because "vaccination mandates have generally been more effective than merely encouraging vaccination." In other words, compulsion produces submission.

To vanquish COVID, freedom was redefined as obedience to officialdom. A *Washington Post* editorial, headlined "Mandates Work," proclaimed: "Vaccines are a near-certain pass to avert misery, a protection against hospitalization and death. Isn't that freedom?"[102] Top ACLU officials, writing in the *New York Times*, proclaimed that "vaccine mandates actually further civil liberties" because they protect "people with disabilities... communities of color," and other vulnerable groups.[103]

New York City decreed that vaccination passes were required for citizens to enter restaurants, gyms, and entertainment venues. Mayor Bill de Blasio declared: "If you do get vaccinated, and you're around fully vaccinated people, you still have more freedom than folks who are not vaccinated. So, it's really strategic."[104] But not as "strategic" as politicians destroying freedom on the installment plan. Freedom could not survive any more such Pyrrhic victories. The passport regime effectively banned most blacks from many activities of daily life, since they had a much lower vaccination rate than other New Yorkers.

In Washington, D.C., the mayor's vaccine passport regime was approved by 86% of whites but only 63% of blacks.[105] An upscale Dupont Circle coffee shop welcomed patrons with ominous signs: "Masks on & Vaccine Cards Out!" That was as welcoming as the slogan: "Come Sip with the Gestapo!" (That coffee shop went out of business a few months later.)[106] California vaccine passports infuriated residents who watched their state falling to pieces. Radio host Grant Stinchfield groused that in Los Angeles, "You can [defecate] on the street, shoot drugs in [a] crack tent on the sidewalk and even steal anything [worth] less than 900 bucks but now you have to show papers to get in a restaurant or gym!?!?"[107] Former FDA press chief Emily Miller commented: "The purpose of a vaccine passport is for the #ScaredVaccinated to have a false sense of security."[108]

People who contract a virus and recover have natural immunity that subsequently protects them. But the Biden administration preferred presidential bragging rights — "100 million shots in 100 days."[109] A major Israeli study revealed that people who had COVID-19 had far better protection against the Delta variant than did people who received multiple COVID-19 vaccine injections.[110] At that time, the CDC estimated that 150 million Americans had been infected with COVID (only one in four COVID infections had been recognized and/or reported).[111] Though more than 149 million Americans had recovered from COVID, Biden policymakers —

unlike European health officials — pretended natural immunity didn't exist, thereby justifying universal vaccine compulsion.

Five months after his July 4th victory proclamation, Biden unveiled his "COVID Winter Plan" — a phrase that sounded like a contingency for a losing war. On December 14, Biden told an Ohio television station: "This is a pandemic of the unvaccinated. That's the problem. Everybody talks about freedom… not to have a shot or have a test. Well guess what? How about patriotism?"[112] Biden sounded unaware that his administration had conceded months ago that vaccines failed to prevent COVID transmission.

Two days later, Biden delivered ghoulish Christmas greetings to Americans: "We are looking at a winter of severe illness and death for the unvaccinated."[113] Five days later, Biden declared that "almost everyone who has died from COVID-19 in the past many months has been unvaccinated."[114] Once again, a bureaucratic coverup spawned a Biden falsehood. In October, the CDC had ceased publishing data showing soaring deaths among the fully vaxxed because the data "might be misinterpreted as the vaccines being ineffective," the *New York Times* later revealed.[115] Some state governments continued to publish COVID death data despite the CDC data lockdown. Oregon officially classified roughly a quarter of its COVID fatalities between August and December as "vaccine breakthrough deaths."[116] According to the Vermont Department of Health, "Half of the [COVID] deaths in August were breakthrough cases. Almost three-quarters of them in September were."[117]

Failing vaccines spurred a tidal wave of new COVID cases thanks to the Omicron variant. "Mandates have curbed almost everything except COVID-19 cases," Yahoo editor Javier David quipped.[118] Even though almost two-thirds of the U.S. population was fully vaccinated, COVID cases exploded nationwide.[119] More than a million new COVID cases were reported daily by early 2022, hitting 1.35 million cases on January 10.[120] Even though two-thirds of Maryland adults were fully vaccinated, Maryland had more COVID fatalities in January 2022 than in any previous month.[121]

The disruptions from the latest surge were exacerbated by a severe shortage of COVID tests. News broadcasts showed endless lines of people desperately waiting for tests they needed to get permission to take a flight, attend school, travel abroad, or visit parents in nursing homes.[122] Professor Eric Topol groused: "Our testing infrastructure has been horrendous since the first day of the pandemic."[123]

Prior to the 2020 election, Biden condemned Trump for a shortage of COVID tests, declaring that America needed "faster, cheaper screening tests that you could take right at home or in school."[124] In early 2021, Biden's White House rejected a proposal by health agency officials to purchase millions of rapid COVID-19 tests.[125] In September 2021, Biden promised he was "taking steps" so "every American, no matter their income, can access free and convenient tests."[126] In October, top health experts from Harvard and elsewhere pushed the Biden administration to purchase 700 million COVID-19 test kits to distribute to Americans ahead of a winter surge. Biden officials torpedoed the proposal.[127] "White House health aides believed that once Americans were vaccinated, few would need testing," the *Washington Post* reported.[128]

In lieu of tests, Biden COVID czar Jeff Zients offered positive thinking: "Everyone in America has access to free testing in an efficient and effective way."[129] The shortage of COVID tests epitomized the failure of the federal command-and-control approach that minimized private innovation. As ProPublica reported, "Many companies with at-home tests have been stymied by an FDA review process that has flummoxed experts and even caused one agency reviewer to quit in frustration."[130] Scott Lincicome, a Duke Law School lecturer, noted that the latest "fix" was "actually the president's sixth promise to subsidize and plan our way to testing abundance."[131] Other nations had plenty of tests. Germany permitted sales of more than 60 rapid COVID-19 tests, "including several made in the United States for export only." Germans could easily buy tests for a dollar, while many Americans couldn't find and purchase a test at any price.

Biden jolted True Believers in late December by declaring, "There is no federal solution [to COVID-19]. This gets solved at a state level."[132] Except, of course, for Biden's vaccine mandate. Biden's assertion was treated as one of his transient outbursts unconnected to his governance.

Team Biden's Magic Cure for COVID Nurses

Those mandates were battered in federal appeals courts before landing at the Supreme Court on January 7. Neither the Justices nor the lawyers arguing the cases mentioned the words *freedom* or *liberty* during almost four hours of legal wrangling that day. Instead, histrionics and wild-eyed exaggerations took center stage. Justice Sandra Sotomayor wailed: "We have over a hundred thousand children [with COVID] — which we've never had before

— in serious condition and many on ventilators." In reality, fewer than 3,500 kids nationwide were hospitalized with COVID[133] — fewer than were hospitalized each week for tonsillitis.[134] Justice Stephen Breyer implied that the vaccines could miraculously prevent all of the 750,000 cases that were occurring on a daily basis. Justice Elena Kagan asserted that the Biden policy is saying to healthcare providers, "The one thing you can't do is to kill your patients." Workers must get vaccinated, Kagan said, "so that… you can't be the carrier of disease."[135]

Unless the CDC approved of the disease carriers, as I noted in a *USA Today* op-ed on the morning of the Court's arguments.[136] After Biden dictated that all healthcare workers must be fully vaxxed, hospitals responded by firing thousands of nurses and other healthcare workers who refused to get injected. More than half a million healthcare workers had already had COVID-19 infections,[137] and more than 99% of them survived. However, the Biden mandate presumed that vaccines were the sole source of good health and protection and ignored post-infection immunity because of perceived "uncertainties… as to the strength and length of [natural] immunity."

The *Federal Register* notice on the new mandate dismissed concerns about the loss of healthcare staff because "there is insufficient evidence to quantify" the impact. Since the feds chose to ignore the damage, the problem didn't exist. The Cleveland Clinic fired 700 employees. In New York, a hospital closed its maternity ward and ceased delivering babies because of a shortage of vaccinated nurses after Cuomo dictated a vax mandate.[138] One health system curtailed elective and nonemergency surgeries and reduced radiology treatment in part because of a loss of health personnel due to the vaccine mandate.[139] Biden responded to shortages of critical personnel by sending in a thousand U.S. military personnel to assist hospitals, but that provided zero relief for most healthcare facilities.

The CDC "solved" the nursing shortage by permitting COVID-positive nurses to treat patients. Shortly before the Supreme Court heard the vaccine mandate cases, the CDC changed its previous guidance on healthcare workers isolating after testing positive for COVID-19.[140] COVID-19-positive nurses across the country were told to come to work and treat patients, even if they still had symptoms.[141] According to Biden policymakers, it was better for hospital patients to be treated by fever-ridden COVID-positive nurses[142] (whose COVID-19 vaccinations failed to safeguard them) than by unvaccinated nurses with no COVID.[143] Zenei Triunfo-Cortez, president of National Nurses United, said the new policy "will only result in further transmission, illness and death."[144] Vaccination status went from being a proxy for health to being a substitute for sane healthcare policy.

The Supreme Court's deliberations occurred in a netherworld that tacitly assumed that vaccines worked. But the effectiveness of the COVID booster shot had fallen to 31% by the time the Court heard the cases, according to the CDC.[145] Nobel Laureate scientist Luc Montagnier noted in the *Wall Street Journal* that Moderna and Pfizer vaccines after 30 days had no "statistically significant positive effect against Omicron infection, and after 90 days, their effect went negative — i.e., vaccinated people were more susceptible to Omicron infection."[146] The CDC later admitted that almost half the COVID deaths in early 2022 were among the fully vaxxed.[147] On January 11, Biden's FDA acting chief Janet Woodcock told a Senate committee that "most people are going to get COVID."[148] So what was the point of mandatory vaccines?

On January 13, the Court voted 6 to 3 to overturn Biden's mandate for all private employees of large companies to get vaccinated. However, the Court also voted to uphold the vaccine mandate for 10 million healthcare workers by a 5-to-4 vote. That ruling pronounced: "Ensuring that providers take steps to avoid transmitting a dangerous virus to their patients is consistent with the fundamental principle of the medical profession: first, do no harm."[149] But federal policymakers were exempt from the "do no harm" admonition. The Justices ignored Biden's welcome mat for COVID-positive nurses that obliterated the legal and moral case for mandates. Shortly after the decision was announced, the *Lancet* editorialized that healthcare workers who recovered from COVID should be exempt from vax mandates.

On the day the Supreme Court announced its verdicts, Biden redefined victory over COVID: "When I got here, we were doing fewer than 2 million tests a day. Now… We will hit approximately 15 million tests a day… That's a huge leap."[150] People "leaping" for COVID tests thanks to vaccine failures did not deter Biden's victory lap.

Freedom, Fear, and Mass Hatred

"In time, we hate that which we often fear," William Shakespeare wrote four centuries ago. A January 2022 Rasmussen poll found that 59% of

Democratic voters favored house arrest for the unvaccinated, and 45% favored locking the unvaxxed into government detention facilities. Almost half of Democrats favored empowering government to "fine or imprison individuals who publicly question the efficacy of the existing COVID-19 vaccines on social media, television, radio, or in online or digital publications."[151] Some media outlets were equally imperious and intolerant. A *Salt Lake City Tribune* editorial called on the governor to mandate a "mass vaccination campaign" deploying "the National Guard to ensure that people without proof of vaccination would not be allowed, well, anywhere."[152]

In early 2022, freedom officially became the biggest villain of the pandemic — at least north of the border. When Canadian truckers drove to Ottawa to protest a vaccine mandate, a *Washington Post* cartoonist portrayed the trucker convoy as "fascism" incarnate while a *Post* columnist derided the "toxic 'Freedom Convoy.'"[153] A Toronto *Globe and Mail* columnist wailed that the protestors had "weaponized freedom," asserting that "freedom" has become a "code for white-identity politics and the far-right's weapon of choice in the culture wars" and lamenting that politicians "have used the call for 'freedom' to promote bigoted, racist and anti-democratic ideas." CBC Radio posted an article that struggled to explain "[w]hy the word 'freedom' is such a useful rallying cry for protestors," touting an expert who asserted that the protestors' "calls for freedom renders the word meaningless."[154] But not as meaningless as the prattle from government-owned media such as the CBC.

In his State of the Union address on March 1, 2022, Biden boasted, "We achieved [victory over COVID] because we provided free vaccines, treatments, tests, and masks."[155] The vaxxes faded, the tests were flawed or late, and most people got their own masks which did little or nothing to prevent transmission. The following month, the CDC formally admitted that reported cases were "just the tip of the iceberg" and estimated that almost 200 million Americans (60% of adults and 75% of children) had already been infected by COVID.[156]

Compulsory injections remained the gold standard for many progressives. California mandated COVID vaccines for all schoolchildren in the fall of 2022, but court battles delayed that edict. New York Governor Kathy Hochul sought unsuccessfully to mandate vaccines for all schoolkids in the Empire State. But the New York State Department of Health reported in May 2022 that the Pfizer vaccine was only 12% effective for children during the Omicron surge.[157]

In a September 2022 Philadelphia speech with a fiery red background, Biden proclaimed: "Today, COVID no longer controls our lives."[158] But Biden refused to relinquish any control. The following month, the Biden administration officially extended the national emergency "as a result of the continued consequences of the COVID-19 pandemic." By this standard, as long as COVID has any "continuing consequences," Biden could retain command. As CNBC noted: "The emergency declaration gives federal agencies broad authority to expand certain programs without congressional approval."[159] Constitutional checks and balances could not be permitted to impede national salvation. The emergency finally lapsed — thanks to congressional intervention — in May 2023.

The failures of the original COVID vaccines resulted in endless boosters, each of which was rubberstamped by federal bureaucrats with little or no evidence. On January 9, 2023, Biden implored all good Americans to get jabbed again: "Everyone 6 months and up should get their updated COVID vaccine."[160] Biden's pronouncement was another triumph of hope over experience. A *Wall Street Journal* analysis noted that FDA "rushed in late August [2022] to authorize the bivalents [boosters] before clinical data were available. The CDC recommended the bivalents for all adults without any evidence that they were effective or needed." The CDC approved the boosters even though the efficacy rate in tests was as low as 22%.[161] FDA approved Pfizer's application for a fourth booster based on tests performed on eight mice.[162] That rubberstamp sufficed to justify compelling another round of boosters for anyone covered by vaccine mandates. FDA championed injecting young children with emergency use COVID vaccines even though the Centers for Disease Control estimated that more than 90% of children and adolescents had already had COVID infections as of late 2022[163] and thus had natural immunity to subsequent infection. As Leana Wen noted in the *Washington Post*: "A *Lancet* study found that those who were vaccinated but never had COVID were 4 times as likely to have severe illness resulting in hospitalization or death compared to the unvaccinated who recovered from it."[164]

The official storyline on COVID suffered further damage in early 2023 when both the FBI and the Department of Energy concluded that COVID-19 likely originated in a Chinese lab. After a senator had suggested prosecuting Fauci for false testimony on bankrolling "gain-of-function" research, Fauci howled that his critics are "really criticizing science because I represent science. That's dangerous." But not nearly as dangerous as vesting vast power in secretive federal agencies.

The Great Pandemic Follies have been based on the illusion that government could make life risk-free. But the advocates of lockdowns and endless prohibitions ignore the risk of totally disrupting hundreds of millions of lives:

• Deaths from drug overdoses set an all-time record of 108,000 in 2021, and alcohol-related deaths jumped 25% in the first year of the pandemic.[165]

• A National Bureau of Economic Research analysis estimated that young Americans suffered "171,000 excess non-COVID deaths during 2020 and 2021… a historic, yet largely unacknowledged, health emergency."[166] Many of those fatalities were "collateral damage" from shutdowns and other COVID policies.

• The Centers for Disease Control reported a 51% increase in emergency room visits for suspected suicide attempts by teenage girls in early 2021.[167]

• The number of Americans reporting struggling with depression or anxiety increased more than 300%.[168]

• During the first year of the pandemic, the number of children diagnosed with Type 2 diabetes jumped by 77%, according to the *Journal of Pediatrics*.[169]

• Millions of jobs were lost thanks to lockdowns, a major reason why life expectancy in the United States had its sharpest plunge since World War II.[170]

• A 2022 Johns Hopkins University analysis of 24 studies on lockdowns in the U.S. and Europe found "no evidence that lockdowns, school closures, border closures, and limiting gatherings have had a noticeable effect on COVID-19 mortality."[171] As former *New York Times* columnist John Tierney observed: "The lockdowns were the most radical experiment in the history of public health, implemented without evidence that they would work."[172]

The biggest pandemic wildcard is the potentially adverse effects of federally mandated vaccines. In November 2022, the NIH posted an article that blamed "fearmongering and scare tactics" by anti-vaccine activists for the reported adverse side effects of COVID vaccines.[173] In June 2022, the CDC website blithely announced: "Any side effects from getting the vaccine are normal signs the body is building protection."[174] But it wasn't a "normal sign" that FDA received more than a million reports to its Vaccine Adverse Event Reporting System (VAERS) — vastly more than for any prior vaccine in history. Those reports included unverified claims linking COVID vaccines to more than 29,000 deaths.[175] Vaccines have resulted in a sixfold increase in myocarditis in young males.[176] But aside from messing up their hearts, the vaccines didn't hurt them. Based on a Swiss medical study, up to three million Americans may have asymptomatic heart damage thanks to COVID booster shots.[177] The CDC is investigating a possible link between Pfizer vaccines and strokes in the elderly.[178]

Conclusion

Federal COVID policy has often been merely meaningless invocations. On July 25, 2023, Biden somberly announced: "We're still feeling the profound loss of the pandemic... We have over 100 people dead. That's 100 empty chairs around the kitchen table."[179] The official White House transcript crossed out Biden's statement and replaced it with a "1 million."

Since the start of the pandemic, government officials absolved themselves for every debacle they helped spawn. In 2023, Surgeon General Vivek Murthy announced that he had a "lightbulb moment" when he realized Americans were suffering from an "epidemic of loneliness and isolation." Murthy stated that people told him that they "felt isolated, invisible, and insignificant." Murthy pretended that government agencies were innocent bystanders — as if the lockdowns had not profoundly disrupted people's lives. But one more vast intrusion into private lives will finally make Americans happy, right?

Anthony Fauci lamented in 2022, "We're living in a progressively anti-science era, and that's a very dangerous thing."[180] But politicians browbeating scientists into submission was no triumph of science. The Governmental Accountability Office reported in 2022 that some CDC and FDA employees feared political retaliation if they objected to COVID policies proclaimed by the White House or top officials. CDC and FDA employees complained that "potential political interference... resulted in the alteration or suppression of scientific findings," including "politically motivated... delayed publication of COVID-19-related scientific findings."[181] Those delays battered Biden's credibility.

Fauci justified COVID mandates because average citizens "don't have the ability" to determine what is best for them.[182] But it wasn't "best" for Americans that the CDC and FDA sent out tainted COVID samples for initial testing, or that the CDC consistently deceived the American people about vaccines, fatalities, and many other topics. It wasn't "best" for Americans that officialdom sought to establish a divine right to deceive the public for their own good. It wasn't "best" for Americans that Fauci and cohorts lied about their role in bankrolling reckless research at a communist military lab that led to 7 million deaths. On September 20, 2023, the Biden administration belatedly banned the Wuhan Institute of Virology from receiving any U.S. government research funding for 10 years as punishment for its unauthorized gain-of-function experiments on bat coronaviruses.[183]

A virus with a 99+% survival rate spawned a 100% presumption in favor of despotism. From the start of the pandemic, many people who swore allegiance to "science and data" also believed that absolute power would keep them safe. Doubters became dissidents who deserved to be denounced if not banished. Citizens were assured that the biggest danger was that their rulers would have insufficient clout to force everyone else to stop working, stop worshipping, stay inside, and get injected. British philosopher John Stuart Mill warned in 1842: "Persons of timid character are the more predisposed to believe any statement, the more it is calculated to alarm them."[184] But as long as most people can be frightened, almost everyone can be subjugated.

Politicians vindicated lockdowns by claiming that all the sacrifices are justified if they "save just one life." But what about "just one freedom"? Zero freedom was the price for zero COVID, except that hundreds of millions of Americans still had COVID infections. As Brownstone Institute president Jeffrey Tucker quipped, "Mitigating disease through compulsory lockdowns is like cleaning your house by bombing it."[185] For bureaucrats and politicians, compelling submission was a victory, even when their policies fail to vanquish a virus. Vaccinations exemplify obedience — which, for politicians, became the best proxy for public health. But the government has no liability for the injections it mandates or the rights it destroys. Officialdom forced people to exchange freedom for a façade of safety. And politicians and bureaucrats still pretended to be infallible even after most Americans were hit with COVID infections.

Faith in absolute power is unscientific regardless of how many scientists pledge allegiance to Washington in return for federal funding. As historian John Barry, author of *The Great Influenza*, observed: "When you mix politics and science, you get politics."[186]

In the long run, people have more to fear from politicians than from viruses. No-fault Czars are no substitute for individual liberty. As Justice Gorsuch warned, "A leader or an expert who claims he can fix everything, if only we do exactly as he says, can prove an irresistible force." Permitting governments to seize unlimited power based on shaky extrapolations of infection rates will doom our republic. It is a fatal folly to defer to experts who promise that granting them boundless power will keep everyone else safe. Politicians were never entitled to turn the Constitution into COVID roadkill.

6. Schools Gone Wild

"The public school has become the established church of secular society."
— Author Ivan Illich, 1969

Government schooling is the most expensive "gift" most Americans ever receive. Public schools are increasingly coercive and abusive of both students and parents. Despite perpetual promises of reform and soaring government expenditures, educational standards and student learning have plunged.

More than 80% of children are enrolled in public schools, even though most parents would prefer other options but cannot afford them after paying taxes for government schools. Politicians and progressives have imposed one scheme after another that pointlessly disrupted learning and squandered a swath of kids' lives. Government schools in hundreds of cities, towns, and counties have been effectively taken over by unions, and children are increasingly exploited and stymied for the benefit of organized labor. The COVID school shutdowns were a culmination of decades of disdain for students and learning.

No Balderdash Left Behind

For most of American history, education was a task for parents, private schools, and state and local governments. But more than half a century ago, Washington politicians came to the rescue. When President Lyndon Johnson signed the Elementary and Secondary Education Act (ESEA) in 1965, he proclaimed that the Act

> represents a major new commitment of the federal government to quality and equality in the schooling that we offer our young people… We bridge the gap between helplessness and hope for more than five million educationally deprived children.

In 1979, President Jimmy Carter created the federal Department of Education as a payoff to teacher unions who had supported his 1976 campaign. But federal subsidies were no magic elixir. A 1983 federal report entitled *A Nation at Risk: The Imperative for Educational Reform* observed: "If an unfriendly foreign power had attempted to impose on America the mediocre educational performance that exists today, we might well have viewed it as an act of war."[1]

In 1994, when President Clinton signed the renewal of the Elementary and Secondary Education Act, he pledged "to set world-class education standards for what every child in every American school should know."[2] The 1994 law specified that by the year 2000, "All children in America will start school ready to learn… The high school graduation rate will increase to at least 90%… U.S. students will be first in the world in mathematics and science achievement." Congress also ludicrously promised that "every school in the United States will be free of drugs and violence" within six years.

None of those targets were achieved, so politicians proclaimed even more far-fetched goals. After George W. Bush won the presidency by portraying himself as a "compassionate conservative," he swayed Congress in 2002 to enact the No Child Left Behind Act (NCLB). NCLB was spurred by decades of bureaucratic chicanery. School test data had been manipulated to allow "all 50 state education agencies to report above-average scores for their elementary schools, with most claiming such scores in every subject area and every grade level," as former Education Department official Larry Uzzell explained.[3] NCLB promised to end the lying about school failures.

The Bush administration exploited the name of the law to convince voters that federal education intervention was succeeding. NCLB mandated that all students must be "proficient" in reading and math by 2014. It also required "adequate yearly progress" for all groups of students in every school. To achieve that Valhalla, federal subsidies were boosted and states were permitted to arbitrarily define *proficient* and revise standards as often as necessary. The feds threatened to penalize schools that failed to show "adequate progress."

NCLB was barely enacted before state education departments began slashing learning goals to protect their federal subsidies. Education Secretary Rod Paige groused in late 2002 that state education department plans to "ratchet down their standards" were "nothing less than shameful." Paige's outburst did not deter federal education bureaucrats from rubberstamping a "race to the bottom" by states:

• Michigan responded to NCLB by slashing the number of students in each school who must pass state high school English tests from 75% to 42%.

• In Washington state, the number of seventh graders who passed the math test rose by 500% after the passing grade was lowered. A headline in the Tacoma *News Tribune* read: "Schools to Get Higher Marks, Even If Students Don't."

• After New York reduced the scores required to pass state tests, an Elmira *Star-Gazette* headline captured the official charade: "Schools Improve as Standards Go Down."

A 2006 report by Education Sector, a nonprofit organization, derided NCLB for creating "a system of perverse incentives that rewards state education officials who misrepresent reality."[4] NCLB testing regimes exempted millions of students' scores from NCLB results; minorities were seven times more likely to be excluded than white students.[5] Nebraska received federal permission to exclude the test scores of more than 25% of all students — including most of the minorities in the state.[6] Some states permitted students to repeatedly take NCLB exams and then count only passing scores to produce a mirage of "adequate progress." Most states were permitted to use slippery, shameless "confidence intervals" or "margin-of-error" formulas, allowing schools to claim success even when students missed learning goals by a country mile. Wisconsin used "confidence intervals" in 2005 to reduce the number of failing school districts by 97%.

Bush tarred NCLB critics as racists, claiming they were guilty of "the soft bigotry of low expectations" for minority students.[7] Like previous federal legislation, NCLB sought to "close the achievement gap" between different races of students. However, the 2008 National Assessment of Education Progress found that "the reading scores of African-American boys in eighth grade were barely higher than the scores of white girls in fourth grade."[8] A 2010 federal survey found that "only 12% of black eighth-grade boys are proficient in math, compared to 44% of white boys."[9]

American schoolchildren wasted hundreds of billions of hours preparing for and taking tests that did little more than spawn an illusion of progress — as well as political and bureaucratic bragging rights. Harvard education professor Richard Elmore called the NCLB "the single largest, and the single most damaging, expansion of federal power over the nation's education system in history."

By 2009, most states had lowered their math or reading standards (or both) to satisfy NCLB "adequate yearly progress" targets. Arne Duncan, Obama's Education Secretary, caterwauled: "Far too many states dummied down standards… We're actually lying to children and families and saying they are prepared to be successful... It's one of the most insidious things that happened."[10] Few members of Congress noticed or cared that NCLB became the biggest national education fraud ever committed.

President Obama promised to continue federal subsidies for government schools so "the federal government can play a leading role in encouraging the... high standards we need." Obama kept the NCLB framework and vowed that all students would graduate from high school and be "college- and career-ready" by 2020. States were still obliged to miraculously make all schoolchildren proficient in math and reading by 2014.

Obama's political appointees exempted states from impossible NCLB deadlines if they adopted policies that Obama demanded. The Obama administration relied on regulatory blackmail — policymaking by extortion — to impose policies that Congress never would have enacted. Instead of striving for students of different races and ethnic groups to all reach proficiency, the Obama administration cajoled most states into setting lower academic goals for blacks and Hispanics.[11] To receive an NCLB waiver, the Obama administration required states to craft detailed plans and timetables to cut the achievement gap in half.[12]

The feds approved the District of Columbia's plan to boost the percentage of white students who passed reading tests from 88% to 94% while the percentage of black students who passed rose from 41% to 71%. At D.C.'s Wilson High School, the goal was for 67% of black students and 95% of white students to pass math tests by 2017.[13] (Cynical Washingtonians joke that Wilson High has a two-track system, and its graduates go either to Yale or to jail.)

The Obama administration approved Minnesota's plan to achieve 82% proficiency in 11th grade math for white students, 66% for Hispanic students, and 62% for black students.[14]

Alabama's plan aimed for 91.5% of white third graders and 79% of black third graders to pass math. Tim Robinson, the father of two black schoolchildren, complained to the *Tuscaloosa News*: "I think having a low bar means they can just pass them on. I think it's dumbing our race down and preparing our boys for prison."[15] The Virginia NAACP also denounced the racial double standards.[16]

In most states, the racial double-scoring was quietly adopted as simply another bureaucratic fix to keep federal cash flow into school coffers. Historian Walter Russell Mead warned: "In practical terms, this is setting up a system in which some teachers will think they've succeeded as long as the black kids in a class reach a certain low level of proficiency."[17]

The Obama administration's master plan for education compelled every state capital to erect Towers of Babel statistics that were as meaningless as Bush-era NCLB test scores. States submitted detailed forecasts of testing progress for each racial and ethnic group at every school. Washington State's spreadsheet for each school contained more than 47,000 separate lines. That was a level of education planning akin to the "five-year plans" of Soviet central planners who pretended to foretell the yields for every crop on every collective farm. Many schools were caught falsifying student test results to fulfill federal mandates.

Another Federal Classroom Coup

The biggest educational controversy of the Obama era involved bribing and browbeating state school systems into adopting the Common Core curriculum, which the *New York Times* described as "one of the most ambitious education reform projects in American history… hatched with high hopes and missionary zeal."[18] President Obama announced plans in 2009 to "reward states that come together and adopt a common set of standards and assessments." The 2009 stimulus bill included $362 million for a "consortia of states to develop assessments and measure student achievement against standards." Obama later boasted of having "convinced almost every state to develop smarter curricula."

From 1965 onwards, federal education law specifically prohibited any use of federal funds to "endorse, approve, or sanction any curriculum designed to be used in an elementary school or secondary school." But almost 40 state education departments, leaping for federal dollars, pledged to impose Common Core even before the standards were finalized. Secretary Duncan declared in 2010: "I'm ecstatic. This has been the third rail of education… We'll have states working together for the first time on curriculum, textbooks, assessment."[19] Many states were compelled to adopt the Common Core as the price of receiving a federal waiver from NCLB's impossible goals.

Professor Diane Ravitch observed that "the Common Core standards have been adopted in 46 states without any field test. They are being imposed on the children of this nation despite the fact that no one has any idea how they will affect students, teachers, or schools." The *New York Times* noted in

2019 that Common Core "standards were not rolled out with lesson plans, textbooks and widespread teacher-training programs."[20] In Maryland, schools were obliged to start using the new curriculum before bureaucrats had finished writing the lesson plans. Baltimore County School Superintendent Dallas Dance reassured parents: "We are building the plane as we fly it, but let's be clear our passengers are safe."[21] (Dance was later convicted of four charges of perjury and sent to prison.[22])

The new curriculum scorned traditional educational values and goals. When the Common Core standards were first developed, they were touted as a means to close the "achievement gap" by lowering standards so that more minorities passed tests.

Common Core Standards architect David Coleman, in a 2011 New York speech that disparaged creative writing, declared: "As you grow up in this world, you realize people really don't give a shit about what you feel or what you think." The Common Core downgraded literary classics so kids would have more time to imbibe emissions from government bureaucracies. Instead of Mark Twain's *Huckleberry Finn*, the Common Core recommended that children read the Environmental Protection Agency's *Report on Recommended Levels of Insulation*. Shakespeare could be replaced by the California Invasive Plant Council's *Invasive Plant Inventory*, another "informational text" on the Common Core list. In Massachusetts, the Common Core curriculum reduced "the amount of classic literature, poetry and drama taught in English classes by 60%."[23]

Common Core slashed mathematics standards in many states. Stanford professor Jim Milgram, who helped develop Common Core, derided the final standards for "lowering the bar" by dropping trigonometry, pre-Calculus, and Euclidean geometry. Milgram said that the process was tainted by the lobbying of state education departments who favored "making the standards as non-challenging as possible." Professor Sandra Stotsky, a former member of the Common Core Validation Committee, complained: "Common Core has carefully disguised its road to equally low outcomes for all demographic groups."[24]

Common Core math confounded parents and students alike. Comedian Louis C.K., whose daughters were vexed by the new curriculum, ridiculed it with an apocryphal example of a Common Core math problem: "Bill has three goldfish. He buys two more. How many dogs live in London?"[25] After Common Core was adopted, so many students in Montgomery County,

Maryland, failed their math tests that the school systems abolished high school final exams.

Obama administration officials castigated anyone who did not cheer for Common Core. Secretary Duncan told a convention of state superintendents of education that opposition to Common Core came from "white suburban moms" upset that "their child[ren are]n't as brilliant as they thought they were." Duncan also derided opposition to the Common Core as a "conspiracy theory in search of a conspiracy." But American Enterprise Institute fellow Frederick Hess warned that Common Core looked like "a back-door way for the federal government to exert tremendous influence over education" and "a standing invitation to further federal involvement in schooling."

Common Core proved another in a long series of federal pratfalls. The federally funded Center for Standards, Alignment, Instruction, and Learning reported in May 2019 that Common Core resulted in "significant negative effects on 4th graders' reading achievement during the 7 years after the adoption of the new standards."[26] Education Secretary Betsy DeVos commented: "This country is in a student achievement crisis, and over the past decade it has continued to worsen, especially for our most vulnerable students." The ACT college testing firm issued a report in late 2019 that warned: "Readiness levels in English, reading, math, and science have all decreased since 2015, with English and math seeing the largest decline."

Teacher Unions and the Great COVID Lockout

Since the 1970s, the National Education Association has been the leading advocate of "no-fault" teaching: whatever happens, don't blame the teacher.[27] Teacher unions have worked to destroy local control of education, subvert standards, prevent teacher accountability, and deny parents a significant voice in their children's education. Unions have launched strikes to prevent and restrict "parental interference" in public education. The *New York Times* noted in 1995 that teacher unions have been "for decades the most conspicuous voice in American education."[28]

Forbes aptly nicknamed the NEA the "National Extortion Association." Teacher unions increasingly look like conspiracies to protect incompetent teachers and impoverish taxpayers. Teacher unions are especially powerful in inner cities, where teacher pay is often highest and teacher performance is usually the worst. The *Chicago Tribune* concluded that the Chicago Teachers

Association has "as much control over operations of the public schools as the Chicago Board of Education" and "more control than is available to principals, parents, taxpayers, and voters."[29] Thanks to powerful unions, California has 300,000 teachers, but a court decision revealed that only two teachers (0.0008%) "are dismissed yearly for unprofessional conduct or unsatisfactory performance."[30]

The NEA and the American Federation of Teachers are major donors to political candidates and to liberal dark-money groups. Those unions played a decisive role in helping Biden win the 2020 election.

The power of teacher unions was an abstraction for most parents until the COVID-19 pandemic. Teacher unions claimed that their members, unlike most other American workers, were entitled to full pay and risk-free environments. Teacher unions barricaded school doors the same way that segregationist governors in the 1950s and 1960s refused to obey federal court orders to admit black students.

Learning losses were greatest in areas where teacher unions were strongest.[31] School shutdowns quickly and profoundly disrupted lives and blighted learning. As early as June 2020, a *Wall Street Journal* headline summarized the debacle: "The Results Are In for Remote Learning: It Didn't Work." The article noted: "In many places, lots of students simply didn't show up online… Soon many districts weren't requiring students to do any work at all, increasing the risk that millions of students would have big gaps in their learning."[32] The Center on Reinventing Public Education found that the vast majority of school districts did not require any live teaching over video. An analysis by the Centers for Disease Control (CDC) noted that only "one in three school districts expected teachers to provide instruction, track student engagement, or monitor academic progress for all students."

In his 2020 presidential campaign, Joe Biden promised that schools would re-open within a hundred days of his taking office. One month into Biden's presidency, CDC chief Rochelle Walensky announced that schools could re-open safely by taking proper precautions. But White House Press Secretary Jen Psaki announced that Walensky was merely speaking "in a personal capacity." Teacher unions flexed their muscles, and the Biden administration tacitly signed on for perpetuating school shutdowns on one pretext after another. Congress passed a Biden-pushed bill to deluge schools with $180 billion in emergency COVID funding. But schools were not required to re-open and teach in person in return for the windfall.

Teacher unions exploited the pandemic to seek to forcibly remake American society. United Teachers Los Angeles demanded "charter school moratoriums, defunding the police, and rent abatement." The *Washington Examiner* reported:

> Teachers unions in Boston, Chicago, Milwaukee, and St. Paul teamed up with the Democratic Socialists of America to say traditional public schools could not continue without changes that included a national ban on evictions, an end to voucher programs, and the abolition of standardized testing.[33]

During a 2022 strike, Minneapolis Federation of Teachers boss Greta Callahan proclaimed: "Our fight is against the patriarchy, our fight is against capitalism, our fight is for the soul of our city."[34]

Unions vilified any politician or parent who sought to re-open schools. New York City teachers marched with signs stating "//wewillnotdiefordoe [the Department of Education]." The Chicago Teachers Union proclaimed: "The push to reopen schools is based in sexism, racism, and misogyny."[35] Journalist Jonathan Chait noted: "In Washington, D.C., teachers demonstrated with 'body bags' — trash bags stuffed to resemble corpses — to protest reopening." At an October 2020 protest against opening schools, teacher union members in Prince William County, Virginia, carried child-size coffins as props.[36]

Teacher unions rallied around a simple motto: "If one teacher dies, isn't that too many?" A *Journal of the American Medical Association* analysis estimated that shutting down the schools would reduce children's life expectancy cumulatively by more than five million years, based on "lower income, reduced educational attainment, and worse health outcomes."[37] Economists Thomas Kane and Andrew McEachin estimated that the decline in student achievement could represent a "$43,800 loss in expected lifetime earnings" for each student.[38]

Politicians and unions ignored the disparate impact of shutdowns on minorities. A Brookings Institution study found that "test-score gaps between students in low-poverty and high-poverty elementary schools grew approximately 20% in math and 15% [respectively] in reading during the 2020–2021 school year."[39] Harvard professor Joseph Allen noted in late 2021: "Black and Hispanic students were twice as likely as white students to be remote and were twice as likely to have no live access to a teacher."[40] Unreliable "distance learning" produced more than a 500% increase in the number of black and Hispanic students failing classes in Montgomery County, Maryland, government schools.[41] Richmond, Virginia, schools had some of the "longest closures in the country," and student test results show "almost two years' worth of lost achievement."[42]

Some government officials sought to define the problem out of existence. Speaking to National Public Radio, a school administrator in Clayton County, Georgia, explained: "We try not to say 'learning loss,' because if they didn't learn it, they didn't lose it."[43] National Education Association president Becky Pringle scorned the phrase *learning loss* "because students are always learning."[44] After New York schools posted shocking student test results, the state government slashed standards, redefining "proficiency" downwards. Marianne Perie, the co-chair of the advisory committee for the standards, explained: "We're at this new normal. So for New York we are saying the new baseline is 2022."[45]

There was never a scientific justification for perpetually locking kids out of classrooms. CDC chief Robert Redfield declared in November 2020: "The truth is, for kids, K-12 is one of the safest places they can be."[46] *Washington Examiner* editor Tim Carney noted: "Kids learning remotely got COVID at 3 times the rate as kids learning in person" at private schools that remained open in Montgomery County, Maryland.[47] Private schools safely re-opened in many cities and states where government schools remained padlocked. By February 2021, 90% of private schools were open, but only half of public schools had opened their doors again to students.[48] Tom Carroll, superintendent of schools for the Catholic Archdiocese of Boston, observed: "The science is clear that there is no substitute for in-person learning, especially for poor and minority children most at danger of falling behind."

Propaganda in Lieu of Literacy

Teacher unions are increasingly dictating policy to the schools. In the late 1970s, the NEA denounced back-to-basics as "irrelevant and reactionary." An NEA publication asserted that such reforms were orchestrated by the "neo-conservative New Right, a mixture of taxpayer groups, fundamentalists, and a few unreconstructed racists."[49] As Professor Richard Mitchell noted in his 1981 classic *The Graves of Academe*, the NEA has played a crucial role in mentally debasing American public schools because its members "wanted to be not teachers but preachers, and prophets too, charging themselves with the cure of the soul of democracy and the raising up in the faith of true believers." In a September 2022 virtual town hall, American Federation of Teachers president Randi Weingarten proclaimed that teachers have become "social justice warriors."[50]

Other teacher activist associations also commandeered classrooms. In April 2022, the National Council of Teachers of English (NCTE) — the largest association of English teachers in the U.S. — went to the barricades against the printed word. NCTE declared it was time

> to decenter book reading and essay writing as the pinnacles of English language arts education. Speaking and listening are increasingly valued as forms of expression that are vital to personal and professional success… It behooves our profession… to confront and challenge the tacit and implicit ways in which print media is valorized.[51]

NCTE "behooves" children to return to oral traditions — the easiest way to close achievement gaps. NCTE hailed "new literacies" — sharing "selfies" in lieu of reading sonnets.

English teachers do not want simply to move the goalposts; instead, they aspire to make the entire playing field vanish. Rather than focusing narrowly on the written word, NCTE asserted that teachers should teach kids to "identify and disrupt the inequalities of contemporary life, including structural racism, sexism, consumerism, and economic injustice." Rather than requiring kids to read entire books, teachers should edify kiddies on "immigration, xenophobia, police brutality, racism, and environmental degradation." NCTE summons teachers to convert children into "empowered change agents."

Such aspirations might be more credible if English teachers were not dismally failing to impart reading skills. Student test scores in one Baltimore class show that almost half the juniors in high school were reading at second- and third-grade levels. Jeffrey Zwillenberg of Reading Partners Baltimore commented: "Reading is that one fundamental skill that unlocks all others."[52] But the failure of urban schools to teach reading practically assures that victimized students will be locked into a rut for their lives. "Millions of children are needlessly classified as 'disabled' when, in fact, their main problem is that nobody taught them to read when they were five and six years old," according to a report by the Thomas B. Fordham Foundation.[53]

Teacher activists have subverted phonics methods of teaching reading. As former Education Department lawyer Hans Bader observed: "Teachers know phonics works well to teach reading, but some woke teachers hate it despite knowing that, because it makes them feel like 'curriculum robots' — so they prefer ineffective methods, like social-justice reading, that are more fun for teachers."[54]

The social justice method was a disaster in places like Oakland, California, where only 19% of students learned to read competently. In 2021, the local NAACP petitioned the school district to include "explicit instruction for phonemic awareness, phonics, fluency, vocabulary, and comprehension" for students.[55] Oakland teacher Kareen Weaver, who led the fight to restore phonics methods, said: "We abandoned what worked because we didn't like how it felt to us as adults, when actually, the social-justice thing to do is to teach them explicitly how to read."

Math activists are leading the charge to banish the long-standing prejudice that $2 + 2 = 4$. The easiest way to close the math achievement gap is to pardon wrong answers. "White supremacy culture shows up in math classrooms when… students are required to 'show their work,'" according to a newsletter sent to math teachers by the Oregon Department of Education.[56] Professor Diane Ravitch noted that traditional math was being replaced by ethnomathematics — which some critics derided as "rain forest algebra" — which presumes that "traditional mathematics — the mathematics taught in universities around the world — is the property of Western Civilization and is inexorably linked with the values of the oppressors and conquerors."[57]

The California Department of Education proposed guidelines relying on *A Pathway to Equitable Math Instruction*, a document that calls for fixing "barriers to math equity" by offering teachers "opportunities for ongoing self-reflection as they seek to develop an anti-racist math practice." That document warns of the "white supremacy culture in the mathematics classroom," such as focusing on "getting the right answer."[58]

In July 2023, the state's department of education issued new guidelines that demanded that California math teachers be "committed to social justice work" to "equip students with a toolkit and mindset to identify and combat inequities with mathematics." A *Wall Street Journal* analysis noted: "California's education bureaucrats are seeking to reinvent math as a grievance study… The only big idea… is that unequal outcomes in math performance are proof of a racist society."[59] Former Assistant Secretary of Education Williamson Evers observed that California's new curriculum strives for "equity" — meaning equality of results — to be achieved by "re-engineering the teaching of math so that it is easier and sugar-coated; and making political organizing and political issues the subject of math class."[60] Math teacher activists effectively claimed a right to blight kids' lives by leaving them innumerate — but for good causes. Professor Erec Smith, co-founder of Free Black Thought, scoffed that the "ultimate message is clear: Black kids are bad at math, so why don't we just excuse them from really learning it?"[61]

History is another topic that activist teachers are hell-bent on fixing. AFT president Randi Weingarten proclaimed in 2021 that her union members have a right to teach "honest history" in government classrooms[62] and boasted, "We teach history, not hate." But, for decades, teachers and government schools have dismally failed to teach students history or much of anything else. American students are appallingly ignorant of the Constitution, American history, and American culture. Former Supreme Court Justice Sandra Day O'Connor groused in 2014 that fewer than 20% of high school seniors "can say what the Declaration of Independence is, and it's right there in the title."[63] In the most recent National Assessment of Educational Progress, only 13% of students were proficient in history. Kerry Sautner of the National Constitution Center commented: "Students are beginning to disengage from and become more fearful of expressing their opinions on history, government and other topics important to civic learning."[64] Trusting government officials to teach honest history is like relying on plantation owners to teach slaves how to escape.

Biology teachers are some of the most zealous crusaders to reform humanity while prancing in front of a classroom. In 2021, the National Science Teachers Association (NSTA) published "Gender-Inclusive Biology: A framework in action," seeking to identify "places where societal power and oppression impact specific marginalized gender groups, including transgender, intersex, and gender non-conforming people."[65] NSTA sought to rewrite the English language, replacing *women* and *men* by teaching kids to refer to *people with ovaries* and *people with testes*. Instead of referring to mothers, teachers are urged to use the phrase *gestational parent*.[66] Instead of *father*, kids are taught to use the term *XY individuals*. The report suggests replacing the word *parents* with *gene-givers* or *biological life transmitters*. *Anti-oppression* is the rallying cry for the report. To prevent oppression, teachers must not tolerate any student criticism of the new ideology: "Address casual offensive comments in the classroom promptly and firmly. Focus on the harm done to the individual and community, and coach students in repeating non-harmful forms of expression."

Across the nation, parents are getting riled by curricula indoctrinating their children. The *Washington Examiner* reported last year: "West Hartford Public Schools in Connecticut has begun to introduce gender ideology in kindergarten as part of what it calls 'social justice lessons,'" including texts that reportedly "teach 5- and 6-year-olds that their parents and doctor assigned them their sex and might have gotten it wrong." At Centennial Elementary School in Denver, Colorado, kindergarten and first grade teachers "sent out a note... the principles that would guide their instruction with 5-, 6-, and 7-year-olds... including 'queer-affirming' and 'trans-affirming' principles."[67] In Portland, Oregon, first and second graders are taught that "gender is like outer space because there are as many ways to be different genders as there are stars in the sky... Only you can know what your gender is."[68]

The San Francisco Unified School District encourages teachers to refer to children's parents as "'caregiver 1 and caregiver 2 instead of mother and father' — a practice that assumes that parents are interchangeable and incidental," Christopher Rufo of the Manhattan Institute notes.[69] At least the school system didn't copy *The Cat in the Hat* and merely label the parents "Thing One" and "Thing Two." In Michigan, teachers are encouraged to "abandon so-called gendered language, such as 'boys and girls,' and replace those terms with gender-neutral variations such as 'earthlings,' 'people with penises,' and 'people with vulvas.'"[70] A Vermont school district, as part of its new "gender inclusive language," refers to a male as a "person who produces sperm."[71]

The nation's second largest school system, the Los Angeles Unified School District, created "a year-round program glamorizing transgender identity and promoting an uncritical, 'trans-affirming' culture in the classroom," Rufo reported in 2022.[72] Teachers are encouraged to strive for the "breakdown of the gender binary" and to make classrooms "queer all school year," while a teacher training program championed "Queering Culture & Race." Schools celebrate kids being "pansexual," "gender fluid," and "two-spirit" (an American Indian term referring to a mysterious third gender). Los Angeles schools "can facilitate a child's transition from one gender to another without notifying parents." The Montgomery County,

Maryland, school system justified keeping young kids' gender transitions secret in order to protect children from their own parents.

How Parents Became Terrorists

School shutdowns, "woke" curricula, and mask mandates spurred angry protests at school board meetings. Michelle Leete, Vice President of the Virginia PTA and President of the local NAACP affiliate, vilified parents opposing a "woke" agenda: "Let them die. Don't let these uncomfortable people deter us from our bold march forward."[73] The Biden administration didn't go quite that far, but it did send the FBI to suppress critics.

Secretary of Education Miguel Cardona contacted the National School Board Association (NSBA) and requested they send a letter to President Biden seeking federal intervention. On September 29, 2021, NSBA pleaded to the White House and Justice Department: "As these acts of malice, violence, and threats against public school officials have increased, the classification of these heinous actions could be the equivalent to a form of domestic terrorism and hate crimes."[74] NSBA urged Team Biden to deploy the FBI and the Patriot Act against protesting parents (an initial draft of the letter called for sending in the National Guard to protect school boards).[75] President Biden phoned NSBA President Viola Garcia to thank her for the letter.

On October 4, Attorney General Merrick Garland announced that the FBI would speedily "convene meetings" in every state aimed at "addressing threats against school administrators, board members, teachers, and staff."[76] The Justice Department announced that its National Security Division would help determine "how federal enforcement tools can be used" to prosecute angry parents. The Biden administration effectively announced plans to drop legal nuclear bombs on school board critics.

In congressional testimony, Garland vehemently denied that "the FBI was using counterterrorism tools to target parents who protested at school board meetings," as Rep. Jim Jordan (R-OH) later noted. But an FBI whistleblower revealed that FBI counterterrorism tools were being used to target angry parents. FBI agents across the nation began interrogating parents whose names were reported on a "tip line" set up for people to phone in accusations. But FBI whistleblowers revealed that "the tip line was snaring ordinary parents who simply complained to their school board or school officials about mask mandates, school closures or other matters, including curriculum that incorporated critical race theory."[77] On May 10, 2022, congressional Republicans notified Attorney General Garland that they had evidence that the FBI

> has labeled at least dozens of investigations into parents with a threat tag created by the FBI's Counterterrorism Division... You have subjected these moms and dads to the opening of an FBI investigation... as a direct result of their fundamental constitutional right to speak and advocate for their children.

The FBI interrogated one person after a call to the tip line asserted that he was a gun owner who opposed school mask mandates and "fit the profile of an insurrectionist." The caller later admitted that he had "no specific information or observations of... any crime threats."[78] The FBI also investigated Republican elected officials "after a Democratic Party official filed a tip claiming that the Republicans had 'incited violence' by 'expressing displeasure with school districts' vaccine mandates.'" Twenty-five states abandoned the NSBA after the uproar following the 2021 letter and FBI crackdown.[79]

Conscripting Three-Year-Olds

For many students, government schooling is akin to being lashed into a dentist chair where the mind-numbing drilling never ends. President Biden has an easy solution: extending "public education for every person in America, starting as early as we can." Biden is pushing for $200 billion in federal subsidies for "universal" pre-kindergarten classes for all three- and four-year old children.[80] That policy strongly appeals to Democrats who want federally paid, "free" child care for all parents.

But the largest study ever done in the U.S. found that preschool harms youngsters. Tennessee created a monumental program to "provide free, 'high quality' preschool for children whose family income was below the poverty level," *Psychology Today* reported.[81] The program also included a control group with similar backgrounds and household incomes who did not attend preschool. The program was a disaster: "The pre-K graduates were a bit more than twice as likely to have been diagnosed as learning disordered compared to the controls," as *Psychology Today* reported. By sixth grade, the students who had attended pre-K showed "reduced performance on all academic achievement tests, a sharp increase in learning disorders, and much more rule violation and behavioral offenses than occurred in the control group." Forcing young children to attend academic classes before they were ripe for them may have "caused children to develop a hatred and rebellious attitude toward school," Dr. Peter Gray concluded.

Tennessee's stark results have not stopped the political campaign to detain far more younger children in government schools. No such luck. Biden effectively proclaimed the need to "round up all the three-year-olds" in several statements in late 2022[82] and again in July 2023.[83]

Jailbreak?

Most parents cannot afford to pay for private schooling after paying taxes for public schools. Surveys show that parents overwhelmingly prefer private schools or other school options. A 2017 poll found that 71% of Americans believe that private schools provide an excellent or good education, compared to only 44% for public schools.[84] In a 2021 poll, 74% favored entitling parents to "use the tax dollars designated for their child's education to send their child to the public or private school which best serves their needs."[85] If financial costs were not a constraint, only 34% of current school parents would send their kids to public schools.

Teacher unions have vehemently fought almost every proposal to permit parents to have more choice in their kids' schooling. When a coalition pushed a referendum to provide state scholarships for kids attending private schools, the California Teachers Association warned: "There are some proposals that are so evil that they should never even be presented to the voters."[86]

Government school pratfalls are spurring a stampede for the exit. "More than a dozen states created or expanded voucher programs in the wake of the pandemic, and more than half of all the states now offer publicly funded options to help parents pay for private educations," the *New York Times* recently noted.[87]

In June 2022, the Arizona legislature enacted what it heralded as "the most expansive school choice legislation in the nation." Every student in the state will "have access to $6,500 of the taxpayer funds to pay for customized learning solutions their parents choose" in Empowerment accounts.[88] Arizona public schools spend roughly $10,400 per student, so the total costs to taxpayers could decline if parents and students take the $6,500 and go to private schools. Teacher unions launched a "Save Our Schools Arizona" campaign for a referendum to close any escape hatch from government schools.

When the Republican-controlled North Carolina legislature advanced bills in May 2023 to expand the state's school choice option, Governor Roy Cooper panicked and proclaimed: "It's time to declare a State of Emergency for public education in North Carolina." His declaration didn't have any legal impact, but it snared bushels of headlines. The real "emergency" was the collapse in citizens' confidence in government schools: more than two-thirds of North Carolinians favored enabling students to escape public school monopolies.[89]

The Homeschooling Specter

When politicians shut down schools at the start of the pandemic, the biggest peril was parents teaching their own kids, according to some experts. A *Washington Post* headline howled: "Homeschooling during the coronavirus will set back a generation of children."[90] Homeschooling meant the return of the Dark Ages, according to Harvard Law Professor Elizabeth Bartholet: "The issue is, do we think that parents should have 24/7, essentially authoritarian control over their children from ages zero to 18? I think that's dangerous."[91]

Professor Bartholet was intensely hostile to private education across the board: "It would be deeply unfair to allow those who can afford private schools to isolate their children from public values in private schools reflecting the parents' values."[92] And what are the "public values" that some schools champion nowadays? Gender self-doubt, political indignation, and orchestrated rage for teachers' pet peeves. Are kids who have not been inoculated with "public school values" carrying a deadly mental virus?

Pandemic school shutdowns spurred a boom in homeschooling. The percentage of parents who homeschool their kids rose from 3% in 2012 to 11% in 2020–21, and rose to 16% among black families.[93] The homeschooling boom is continuing after schools have re-opened, with the number of parents homeschooling their kids in 2021–22 far higher than in pre-pandemic times.[94] Big city school systems had unprecedented enrollment declines thanks to homeschooling, a surge in private schools, and families moving away from repressive urban regimes. Public schools are also being slammed by a huge increase in truancy, especially among minority and low-income kids.

Homeschooled kids excel on tests that flummox many if not most public school kids. "Twenty years of data show that home-schooled students test higher than public school students on the ACT, and the college graduation rate of home-school alumni is nearly 10% higher than their peers," the *Washington Examiner* reported.[95] A comprehensive analysis by the Home School Legal Defense Association concluded: "Homeschoolers are still achieving well beyond their public school counterparts — no matter what their family background, socioeconomic level, or style of homeschooling."

But student achievements don't matter to the elite. Harvard's Bartholet declared: "Most children will do all right in public schools, even if some of them might do better if homeschooled. And parents will be free to make up at home what their children are not getting at school." But when did politicians, professors, and education officialdom acquire the right to inflict "solutions" designed to leave many kids worse off? When did government schools acquire the right to blight minds in the name of social justice?

Such questions are irrelevant to policymakers and progressive activists. For them, it is a self-evident truth that politicians and their appointees have a right to domineer young minds. At a 2023 award ceremony for Teacher of the Year, Biden asserted that there is "no such thing as someone else's child. Our nation's children are all our children."[96] In May 2023, a Florida fifth grade teacher announced on CNN that your "rights as a parent, those rights are gone when your child is in the public school system."[97] Iowa school board member Rachel Wall proclaimed: "The purpose of a public education is to not teach kids what the parents want. It is to teach them what society needs them to know. The client is not the parent, but the community."[98] It remains to be seen whether the Biden administration and FBI will be able to quash all opposition.

Conclusion: Let the Children Go

On May 19, 2023, Secretary Cardona tweeted: "Teachers know what is best for their kids because they are with them every day. We must trust teachers."[99] But teachers are not hired as pundits to blather on any and all subjects; they are paid to convey specific skills to students. Unfortunately, many teachers are too busy proselytizing to correct their students' grammar and math errors. They turn kids into righteous warriors in lieu of making them literate. Vast numbers of students will be left pliable for propaganda from teachers, politicians, and others. And the real problem, as Cardona proclaimed in September 2023, is uppity parents "acting as if they know what's right for kids."[100]

From No Child Left Behind to Common Core to pandemic shutdowns, government schools have squandered much of the childhoods of tens of millions of children. AFT president Randi Weingarten declared in May 2022: "Trust us to be the mind workers… We are the ones who try to help our kids critically think and know themselves and feel good about themselves."[101] In reality, many teachers are mind wreckers who piously strut before flocks who fall further behind every school year. Activist teachers endlessly claim to "teach kids to think for themselves." And how do they know kids actually think? Because they almost all agree with their teacher by the end of the school year.

At this point, the federal Education Department is as credible as a used car dealer repeatedly caught manipulating odometers. The motto of federal education policymakers is: "This time we are not lying." Yet, regardless of how badly they screw up, presidents, congressmen, and bureaucrats act entitled to vast sway over schooling.

America can no longer afford a "no-fault" federal education policy. Politicians must cease treating children's minds as a disposable resource. Generations of young kids have been sacrificed for whatever fad sweeps political and education activists. The best solution is to enable as many children as possible to exit government schools as soon as possible.

7. Ten Thousand Czars

"No person shall be... deprived of life, liberty, or property, without due process of law."

– Fifth Amendment, U.S. Constitution

Citizens are increasingly obliged to plead for bureaucratic permission to live their own lives. In day-to-day operation, governments at all levels are becoming pseudo-benevolent dictatorships. The Minnesota Supreme Court declared in 1960: "The liberty of the individual... is largely a freedom from arbitrary action by those possessed of the power of government."[1] But such lofty declarations nowadays have as much impact as a dog barking at the moon. "Due process" has been defined down to signify any process that officialdom inflicts on private citizens.

Federal agencies are issuing up to 5,000 new rules a year, as well as tens of thousands of regulatory "guidance" documents that often confer ample power to skewer wayward citizens. In a 1952 Supreme Court decision, Justice Robert Jackson declared that "the essence of our free government is 'leave to live by no man's leave, underneath the law' — to be governed by those impersonal forces which we call law."[2]

But "law" isn't what it used to be. In 1765, legal philosopher William Blackstone defined law as a "rule of civil conduct prescribed by the supreme power in a state, commanding what is right and prohibiting what is wrong." That ideal faded as a presumption of rectitude became automatically attached to government commands. In 1907, the Supreme Court stated: "'Law' is a statement of the circumstances in which the public force will be brought to bear upon men through the courts."[3] But contemporary laws routinely proclaim vague goals that entitle government agencies to castigate as they please.

Throwing Americans Out of Work

Americans' right to work was long recognized and respected by judges and politicians alike. The Supreme Court ruled in 1907 that the Constitution recognized "the right to hold specific private employment and to follow a chosen profession free from unreasonable governmental interference."[4] But courts and politicians abandoned that constitutional fealty long ago.

More than a thousand occupations now require a government license.[5] In the 1950s, only about 5% of the workforce was covered by occupational licensing; now, almost 30% of all jobs require a government permission slip. Licensing restrictions reduce employment by almost 3 million jobs and cost consumers hundreds of billions of dollars in higher prices.[6] A 2022 Institute for Justice analysis noted: "Workers in 71 occupations… face greater average burdens than entry-level emergency medical technicians."[7]

From florists in Louisiana to parking valets in West Virginia, licensing impedes citizens from earning an honest dollar. Illinois licenses "restaurant busing staff" — but plenty of dishes still get dropped on the way to the kitchen. Six states require individuals to possess a government license before being hired to place items in boxes — as if private companies would otherwise hire only Three Stooges knuckleheads. Somerville, Massachusetts, instituted licensing for fortune tellers in 2012 to "make sure that we were not dealing with people who have been convicted of fraud with respect to fortune telling."[8] Somerville also requires a license for necromancy, but necrophilia remains strictly illegal. South Dakota municipalities can "prohibit clairvoyants, phrenologists, mind readers, fortune tellers, and fakirs" (except politicians).[9]

Licensing laws are usually engineered by professional associations to protect the public from perfidious competitors charging lower prices. Several states require licenses and up to six years of education and training to become an interior designer. A zealous licensing advocate warned a Florida legislative committee in 2011 that interior design blunders caused almost 90,000 deaths per year nationwide. This zany estimate was concocted from the total national fatalities from hospital infections — all of which presumedly occurred because a non-interior designer made "poor hospital carpet choices" that spread infections. Federal Trade Commission chief Maureen Ohlhausen groused in 2017:

> The health and safety arguments about why these occupations need to be licensed range from dubious to ridiculous. I challenge anyone to explain why the state has a legitimate interest in protecting the public from rogue interior designers carpet-bombing living rooms with ugly throw pillows.[10]

Masseuses are licensed in almost all states, with some states requiring a full year of courses or experience before getting permission to knead. The Arizona State Board of Massage Therapy was created in 2003 to prohibit anyone from working as a masseuse without logging 700 hours of training and paying a licensing fee. But the law failed to stop individuals who paw fully clothed clients to help their "energy." Robert Wilson, the deputy director of the state board, caterwauled, "If they're rubbing you, they're doing massage therapy."[11] One licensed masseuse went even further, complaining to an Arizona newspaper that anyone "putting your hands on people" should be forced to get a license. At least no Arizonan has yet demanded licenses for frisky teenagers on prom night.

A New York licensed masseuse launched a MoveOn petition to stop "Alleged Lawbreakers" from using "loopholes" such as "foot rub" or "back rub."[12] The aggrieved masseuse and 700 co-signers warned that "greater restrictions and enforcement are needed throughout the State to hold those criminally accountable who are not authorized to perform such services." But most people do not view unlicensed shoulder rubs as the moral equivalent of armed robbery.

Licensing investigations are a leading source of subsidized jollies for cops. In Massapequa, New York, police infiltrated a massage parlor and received multiple massages from women later busted for being unlicensed masseuses.[13] After a Pennsylvania detective went undercover and received an illicit hand job from an unlicensed Chinese masseuse, a spokesman for the Lancaster County district attorney justified the happy ending: "If the person does not speak English, then we might need more in order to establish the crime and prove it."[14]

A dozen states now require a license for art therapy. The Virginia Board of Health Professions warned in 2020 that

> basic art tools, such as paint and glue, which contain toxic chemicals that could cause harm should they be inhaled or ingested; scissors which have sharp edges capable of causing cuts or punctures; and objects such as clay, if thrown, could be considered potentially dangers [sic].

The report did not explain why a master's degree was necessary to deter kiddies from flinging balls of clay at each other. Nor did the report reveal why graduate degrees were vital for dealing with "sharp edges" (carpenters survive without such degrees). The report stressed that licensure would enable art therapists to charge higher prices — a transcendent benefit for any government board. But licensees do not need to prove that art therapy cures anything aside from boredom. Because art therapy is an inherently vague notion, a "licensing board could go after art teachers for advertising the mental health benefits of their classes," observed Andrew Wimer of the Institute for Justice.

African-style hair braiding has recently soared in popularity, but some state governments refuse to permit individuals to braid their neighbors' hair for pay without completing a thousand hours or more of unnecessary cosmetology or barbering training. African-style braiding does not use chemicals and generates almost zero consumer complaints. After Iris Brantley set up her hair braiding business in Dallas, Texas, "the cops came to my salon — two undercover cops, and then when I looked around, five uniformed cops were standing before my client, and they... carted me off to jail like a common criminal" for "braiding without a cosmetology license."[15] Brantley kept fighting and, after almost 20 years, Texas deregulated hair braiding in 2015. Missouri maintained a strict regime until a lawsuit challenge revealed that the state licensing board literally knew nothing about braiding, spurring the legislature to repeal the law.

All states require a government license to work as a barber; many states require one year of barber school. Barber licensing illustrates the shotgun behind the licensing door. A 2014 federal appeals court ruling described how Orange County, Florida, SWAT teams

> descended on multiple target locations. They blocked the entrances and exits to the parking lots so no one could leave and no one could enter. With some team members dressed in ballistic vests and masks, and with guns drawn, the deputies rushed into their target destinations, handcuffed the stunned occupants — and demanded to see their barbers' licenses.

These barbershops had up to 25 customers waiting when SWAT teams assailed them. When one barber complained he had done nothing wrong, a police officer responded, "It's a pretty big [rule] book; I'm pretty sure I can find something in here to take you to jail for." The court decision noted: "At the conclusion of the inspection, it was determined that all of the barbers had valid licenses and that the barbershop was in compliance with all safety and sanitation rules," so police did not have to shoot anyone. All of the nine barbershops targeted were owned by blacks or Hispanics. *Washington Post* columnist Radley Balko observed that the raids were "basically fishing operations for drug crimes and to recruit confidential informants."[16] Police failed to snare an honest search warrant but used a "checking licenses" pretext to harass the barbers, intimidate the customers (including young children), and rummage through every nook and cranny of the premises. The appeals court slammed the sheriff's department for "conducting a run-of-the-mill administrative inspection as though it is a criminal raid."

More than 35 states require licenses for anyone working as a travel guide, with some states requiring years of experience and $1,500+ licensing fees. Charleston, South Carolina, justified licensing tour guides because guides were "professionals" and thus presumably had no right to speak to visitors without government permission. A federal court zapped the Charleston restriction in 2018.[17] Similarly, the District of Columbia threatened to jail unlicensed tour guides for 30 days. As a federal appeals court noted in 2014:

> In Washington, D.C., it is illegal to talk about points of interest or the history of the city while escorting or guiding a person who paid you to do so — that is, unless you pay the government $200 and pass a 100-question multiple-choice exam.[18]

The court concluded that D.C. government officials failed the history test on the First Amendment and struck down the law.

Licensing boards can become censors. In 2013, the Kentucky Board of Examiners of Psychology banned a nationally syndicated columnist from offering advice to Kentucky newspaper readers. John Rosemond had been writing an advice column for hundreds of papers for almost 40 years. After a retired shrink filed a formal complaint, Rosemond received a cease-and-desist letter and was charged with "unlicensed practice of psychology" because he was not licensed in the State of Kentucky (he was licensed as a psychologist in North Carolina). In 2015, Federal Judge Gregory Van Tatenhove ruled that Kentucky had "unconstitutionally applied" its regulations to the newspaper column: "To permit the state to halt this lawful expression would result in a harm far more concrete and damaging to society than the speculative harm which the state purportedly seeks to avoid."

Judges discovered a food loophole in the First Amendment. As the rate of obesity skyrocketed, many Americans offered slimming tips to fellow citizens. A federal judge upheld Florida's prohibition on unlicensed dietary advice in 2019 because "talking with a person about their diet isn't speech; it's the 'conduct' of practicing dietetics," as attorney Ari Bargil lamented.[19] In 2012, the North Carolina Board of Dietetics/Nutrition prohibited Steve Cooksey from blogging about his personal experience with a paleo diet. The Board warned that he was guilty of the "unlicensed practice of dietetics" for giving free personal advice to his website visitors. A federal court stomped the board's gag order in 2015.[20] But other states continue treating dietary advice on par with suicide advocacy.

Occupational licensing presumes that "government knows best," but inept or corrupt licensing boards send consumers "an inaccurate signal of quality and a false sense of security," the Federal Trade Commission warned. State medical boards routinely refuse to disclose which doctors or other medical professionals have been sanctioned for misconduct, incompetence, or criminal offenses. A 2016 investigation by the *Atlanta Journal-Constitution* found more "than 2,400 cases of doctors across the country who had sexually assaulted their patients" and more than a thousand of those "physicians were still licensed to practice medicine."[21] One Baltimore physician "was convicted of raping a gynecological patient in his office but allowed by the commission to continue practicing medicine."[22] The California Bureau of Vocational Nursing permitted nurses convicted of sexual battery or molesting female patients to continue practicing for years even after they were compelled to register as sex offenders.[23]

Massachusetts state boards gave licenses to scores of convicted sex offenders, including more than 20 electricians who routinely worked in private homes, as a 2019 *Boston Globe* investigation revealed.[24] Massachusetts licensing boards, which provide de facto work permits to 400,000 people, failed to compare the list of applicants with the registry of convicted sex offenders. The *Globe* noted: "A massage therapist... is now facing charges of raping a client, just months after getting a license while on probation for assault and battery on a police officer." The debacle resulted from perverse bureaucratic incentives: "Several people who work for the agency said the Division of Professional Licensure has a strong bias toward approving licenses, which brought in more than $28 million in fees in fiscal year 2016." The FBI launched an investigation in 2020 after a state board apparently gave licenses to hundreds of masseuses with bogus addresses and fake massage school transcripts.[25]

Licensing hinders Americans from relocating across state lines, since each state often creates its own entry barriers.[26] Balkanizing the nation boosts the profits of professionals while pointlessly blighting millions of potential careers. Arizona State University researcher Stephen Slivinski found that states that impose pervasive licensing restrictions on low-income occupations have 11% fewer entrepreneurs.[27]

Licensing is a "Do not enter" sign to the middle class. An Obama White House report in 2016 concluded that occupational licensing boosted prices for goods and services up to 16% and estimated that "unlicensed workers earn 10 to 15% lower wages than licensed workers with similar levels of education, training, and experience."[28] Labor Secretary Alexander Acosta observed in 2018:

> Excessive licensing raises the cost of entry — often prohibitively — for certain careers, locking many Americans out of good jobs. Uneven educational requirements, steep fees and long approval periods foreclose economic opportunity for those who need it most.[29]

In a 2015 decision, Texas Supreme Court Justice Don Willett observed:

> The Texas occupational licensure regime, predominantly impeding Texans of modest means, can seem a hodge-podge of disjointed, logic-defying irrationalities, where the burdens imposed seem almost farcical, forcing many lower-income Texans to face a choice: submit to illogical bureaucracy or operate an illegal business?[30]

Doggedly Damning Drivers

Crime is surging in American cities, but the official data omits the vast majority of highway robberies. Tens of thousands of American drivers have been injured and many people killed as a result of reckless revenue pursuit by local governments.

More than 500 municipalities, including most of the nation's largest cities, installed red light cameras on their streets starting two decades ago.[31] Violations routinely cost $100 a photo, and California wallops transgressors for up to $500. Local governments have partnered with private companies to build, deploy, and maintain cameras which have institutionalized "bounty hunting" at traffic intersections.

Red light cameras proliferated despite their perils. Cameras spark traffic collisions because drivers stop suddenly to avoid being fined. A 2004 study financed by the U.S. Department of Transportation revealed that the cameras were "associated with higher levels of many types and severity categories of crashes."[32] In 2005, six years after the District of Columbia set up a red light regime that generated more than 500,000 tickets, a *Washington Post* analysis revealed that "the number of crashes at locations with cameras more than doubled." The Florida Department of Highway Safety and Motor

Vehicles reported in 2016 that "fatalities from accidents doubled" at intersections with red light cameras.[33]

Numerous federal studies have shown that lengthening yellow lights is the most effective step to reduce collisions at traffic lights. "A one second increase in yellow time results in 40% decrease in severe red light related crashes," according to the Federal Highway Administration.[34] After Georgia mandated longer yellow lights in 2009, the revenue from red light cameras collapsed by up to 90% in many localities.[35]

But many governments have shortened yellow lights to boost their revenue. In 2015, the State of Maryland suspended its mandate that yellow lights need to be at least three-and-a-half seconds. Montgomery County, Maryland, reaped more than $300,000 in tickets after shortening one yellow light at a busy intersection to less than three seconds.[36] Some private companies that install and maintain red light cameras prohibit cities from extending yellow lights because it would hurt their profits.[37]

Most red light tickets are slapped on drivers who make right turns on red without coming to a dead stop. The National Highway Traffic Safety Administration concluded that zero fatalities occurred nationwide in 1998 "from an accident resulting from a right hand turn on red when the driver yielded to oncoming traffic."[38] The American Automobile Association (AAA) spokesman John Townsend labeled right-turn-on-red cameras as "the biggest scandal in automated traffic enforcement."[39] Some red light camera contracts effectively set ticket quotas that localities are required to fulfill.[40] According to the National Motorists Association, one of the largest manufacturers of red light cameras "has included clauses in their contracts that prohibit city engineers from applying engineering practices that improve compliance and reduce accidents."[41]

Some of the most brazen abuses occur in the District of Columbia, which complements its red light regime with almost a million speed camera tickets each year. The AAA denounced one D.C. speed camera near the Maryland border as "an old-fashioned, money-making, motorist rip-off speed trap right out of the 'Dukes of Hazzard.'"[42] A single camera in D.C. generated more than a hundred thousand tickets and $11 million in fines.[43] In May 2019, the D.C. government placed a single almost undetectable "work zone" sign on a major high-speed highway (which drivers mistakenly assumed was an interstate) and lowered the speed limit from 55 to 40 miles per hour. Even though no work occurred on that stretch, the city levied fines of up to $800 on drivers exceeding the covert speed limit. A federal judge concluded that D.C. was collecting fines from a "wrongfully designated construction zone" but refused to hold the local government liable because the ticketed victims did not have "standing" to sue because "they do not allege that any one of them will drive past the single remaining camera in the future."[44]

Foul play is fair play as long as government profits. The D.C. Inspector General found that the automated ticketing system was so out of control that "drivers get speeding tickets for violations they don't commit and for vehicles they've never owned."[45] City bureaucrats were proud of rigging the ticketing system. A senior D.C. government official declared: "You are guilty until you have proven yourself innocent... That has worked well for us." Even stop signs have become traps for motorists. The hidden camera at one D.C. stop sign has bilked drivers for more than a million dollars.[46]

The combination of speed cameras and shiftless bureaucrats tossed citizens into a Kafkaesque hell. On November 2, 2020, Doug Nelson, a 73-year-old Postal Service employee and Vietnam veteran, was carjacked as he returned after work to his edgy D.C. neighborhood. Nelson quickly surrendered his vehicle to pistol-wielding assailants. He filed a police report, and his car was eventually recovered, but the license plates were stolen by the thieves.[47]

In the following weeks, Nelson received thousands of dollars in tickets for speed camera violations racked up by the thieves. Nelson and his wife repeatedly notified the D.C. government of the unjust fines, but their complaints were ignored. Thanks to the fines, they were prohibited from getting a new license plate and were thus banned from driving their only vehicle. They had to pay the entire fine — which quickly rose to $5,000 — before they could legally challenge the penalties. District bureaucrats ignored the foul play until a local television station investigated, spurring the cancellation of the fines. Hannah Cox of the Foundation for Economic Education observed that D.C. bureaucrats "unjustly deprived the Nelsons of the use of their car for far longer than the carjackers did."[48]

Transportation Secretary Pete Buttigieg is championing federal funding for more speed cameras across the nation to boost "racial equity" in policing. D.C. Mayor Muriel Bowser jumped on the bandwagon, announcing a goal of tripling the number of traffic enforcement cameras on the city's streets.[49] But according to a 2018 report by the D.C. Policy Center:

> Neighborhoods where 80% or more of residents are black on average paid $322 per capita in automated traffic tickets compared to just $20 per capita in 80% white neighborhoods. Residents in black neighborhoods were 17 times more likely to receive a photo ticket.[50]

Black neighborhoods did not have a higher rate of auto crashes than other neighborhoods. Similar bias was reported in Upstate New York. Two activists complained in the *Buffalo News* in 2021 that the city's "predatory traffic ticketing" speed cameras were "balancing its budget on the backs of Black and brown residents" because "communities of color and the city's highest poverty areas" were hit hardest by the tickets.[51] A 2022 ProPublica investigation revealed that in Chicago,

> households in majority Black and Hispanic ZIP codes received [red light camera] tickets at around twice the rate of those in white areas... Black neighborhoods... have been hit with more than half a billion dollars in penalties over the last 15 years, contributing to thousands of vehicle impoundments [and] driver's license suspensions.[52]

Unnecessary and unjust tickets disrupt lives and destroy people's ability to feed their families. A 2019 study by the Federal Reserve concluded that almost half of Americans "could not afford an unexpected expense of $400 or more." The D.C. government responded to hardship cases by offering a "community service option" where low-income traffic violators could pay off tickets by working for the city at the minimum wage rate. At least the city has not yet created chain gangs sweating to pay their speed camera debts.

Why would politicians impose traffic regimes that pointlessly penalize or kill hapless citizens? Follow the money. Bribery scandals have enveloped red light cameras in Texas, Arizona, Ohio, Illinois, and elsewhere. The former top salesman for Redflex, one of the largest providers of red light cameras, testified that his company had "sent gifts and bribes to officials in at least 14 states."[53] (Redflex denied the allegation.) Several Illinois mayors were convicted of bribery in 2022 as part of a federal investigation of payoffs by a red light camera contractor. Illinois Comptroller Susana Mendoza condemned red light ticket regimes as "a program that's broken and morally corrupt" and recommended ending them across the state.[54]

Glancing Geese Veto Property Rights

How many drops of water are needed to justify commandeering private land? Unfortunately, bureaucrats and judges have been changing the answer for 50 years.

In 1972, Congress passed the Clean Water Act to, among other things, restrict the pollution of navigable waters. That law gave the Army Corps of Engineers the power to approve or deny building permits, and the EPA received the power to veto Army Corps permits. The law was not expected to be controversial because "navigable waters" was a tiny portion of U.S. territory. However, in 1975, a federal judge revealed that the law also applied to wetlands that were adjacent to navigable waters.

And thus "WOTUS" — the Waters of the United States — became perpetual legal quicksand. Federal agencies have left landowners in purgatory by changing the WOTUS definition 13 times since 1972.[55] Because the Clean Water Act imposes strict criminal liability, farmers plowing their own fields can be treated like midnight dumpers heaving barrels of dioxin into a river.

In 1988, presidential candidate George H.W. Bush, seeking votes from environmentalists, announced that "all existing wetlands, no matter how small, should be preserved." On January 21, 1989, the day after Bush's inauguration, the EPA and the Army Corps revealed a new, vastly broader definition of *wetlands*. Land that was dry 350 days a year could be classified as a "federal jurisdictional wetland." Fairness to Land Owners, an advocacy group, said the new definition doubled the amount of wetlands in the U.S. from roughly 100 million acres to 200 million acres, the vast majority owned by private citizens.

To justify commandeering private land, federal bureaucrats concocted the "glancing geese" test. Federal Judge Daniel Manion in 1992 rejected the EPA's claim of jurisdiction over private land "solely on the ground that migratory birds could, potentially, use the wetland as a place to feed or nest or as a stopover" when no evidence existed that "birds, or any other wildlife, actually used [the area] for any purpose." The EPA and Army Corps prohibited owners from using their land if photographers took bird pictures on their turf. A few clicks of a camera sufficed to nullify property rights. Federal courts continued wrangling over the "glancing geese test" until the Supreme Court spiked it in 2001.

In 1993, Federal Judge Roger Vinson denounced federal wetlands policies as a "regulatory hydra... worthy of *Alice in Wonderland*."[56] The same year, the

Clinton administration banned any activity with "environmental concern" on wetlands. A federal prosecutor admitted that the Army Corps "could require a permit to ride a bicycle across a wetland."[57] A White House press release suggested that "Congress should amend the Clean Water Act to make it consistent with the agencies' rulemaking." Previously, the Constitution required federal regulations to comply with laws Congress actually passed.

Thanks to the Clinton regulations, the Army Corps and the EPA imposed controls over sections of a development as small as 26 square feet — roughly half the size of a ping-pong table. One Rhode Island town was forced to wait for almost two years to get federal permission to do mosquito-control work on 0.009 acres of wetlands. Slapping a "federally designated wetland" label on private property "decreases the value of land by $600 an acre or more."[58] The Congressional Budget Office estimated that compensating owners for property value losses due to wetlands designations would cost at least $10 billion. However, property owners were denied a single dollar of compensation after being banned from using their land.

In a 2006 case, four Supreme Court Justices derided wetlands policy as institutionalized lawlessness. Justice Antonin Scalia, writing the majority opinion, declared that the Army Corps "exercises the discretion of an enlightened despot, relying on such factors as 'economics,' 'aesthetics,' 'recreation,' and 'in general, the needs and welfare of the people.'"[59] Scalia noted that "the average applicant for an individual [wetlands] permit spends 788 days and $271,596 in completing the process." Chief Justice Roberts slammed the Army Corps for its "essentially boundless view of the scope of its power." However, there was no court majority because a fifth Justice, Anthony Kennedy, played "King Solomon," sawing due process in half. He asserted that regulatory control would be justified if the wetlands had a "significant nexus" to navigable waters.

Voila! Federal agencies soon found a "significant nexus" everywhere. A coalition of 14 agricultural organizations later complained that the EPA and the Army Corps were using vague, arbitrary standards that "could reach any spot in the Nation that has ever been wet."[60] In 2008, the Bush administration revised federal wetlands guidelines in accordance with the ruling of the four Justices' decision in 2006.

In 2011, the Obama administration announced that it was disregarding the 2006 Supreme Court decision and would issue WOTUS regulations re-establishing federal control over private wetlands. However, before the new rules were finished, Obama appointees suspended the revision process.

In 2012, the Supreme Court slammed the EPA for wetlands foul play. Michael and Chantell Sackett spent $23,000 in 2005 to buy a small vacant lot in a residential subdivision near Priest Lake in Idaho. After they began preparing to build a house, the EPA shocked them by preliminarily classifying their property as a wetland and threatening a $75,000-a-day fine unless construction ceased. The Sacketts were prohibited from challenging that edict until EPA issued a final ruling — which EPA endlessly delayed. The Court unanimously ruled that there was no reason to believe that "the Clean Water Act was uniquely designed to enable the strong-arming [of property owners] into 'voluntary compliance' without the opportunity for judicial review." Justice Scalia mocked the EPA's definition of *wetlands*, noting that the Idaho landowners had never "seen a ship or other vessel cross their yard." Justice Samuel Alito wrote that "the reach of the Clean Water Act is notoriously unclear," and its harsh penalties "[leave] most property owners with little practical alternative but to dance to the EPA's tune."[61] Alito urged Congress to clarify the legal definition of *wetlands*, but legislators shirked their duty.

In 2014, the Obama administration finally issued its new, improved definition of *wetlands*, which coincidentally vastly increased federal jurisdiction over private lands. The proposed regulations were wildly popular — or at least so it seemed. Federal law prohibits federal agencies from launching publicity campaigns to whip up public support for their proposed regulations. Regardless, the EPA spent tax dollars on a massive covert publicity campaign on Twitter and other social media, linking to the Natural Resources Defense Council to generate positive comments for expanding federal control over more private property.[62] EPA chief Gina McCarthy bragged to Congress: "We have received over one million comments, and 87.1% of those comments... are supportive of this rule." But the Government Accountability Office condemned the EPA in 2015 for its "illegal propaganda" campaign to spur that support.[63] GAO concluded that the EPA's effort "constitutes covert propaganda, in violation of the publicity or propaganda prohibition," because recipients were unaware that the EPA was sending messages seeking positive comments on its proposed regulation. No EPA official was fined or jailed for violating federal law.

Shortly after taking office in 2017, President Trump proclaimed that Obama's wetlands rule could apply to "nearly every puddle or every ditch on a farmer's land, or everywhere else that they decide," which he denounced as "a massive power grab."[64] In early 2020, the Trump administration issued new regulatory guidance titled the Navigable Waters Protection Rule (NWPR), curtailing the power of federal agencies over wetlands.[65]

The new rules didn't stick. In June 2021, the Biden administration announced that the Trump-era rules were "leading to significant environmental degradation." *Politico* reported that Biden appointees sought a new policy "informed by lessons from the previous whipsaw of regulations."[66] Eighteen months later, the Biden administration promulgated new wetlands rules "to overcome nearly a decade of challenges to EPA powers."[67]

In 2022, the Supreme Court heard another challenge by the Sacketts on their Idaho turf. As their lawyers explained, the EPA continued demanding that the Sacketts get a federal Clean Water Act permit to build their house because

> Priest Lake is a navigable water; a non-navigable creek connects to Priest Lake; the non-navigable creek is connected to a non-navigable, man-made ditch; the non-navigable, man-made ditch is connected to wetlands; these wetlands, though separated from the Sacketts' lot by a 30-foot-wide paved road, are nevertheless "similarly situated" to wetlands alleged to exist on the Sacketts' lot... [thus creating a] "significant nexus" to Priest Lake.

The EPA persisted, even though the agency "recognizes that no water at all — surface or subsurface — flows from the Sacketts' lot to the wetlands or to the ditch across the street."[68]

All nine Supreme Court Justices agreed in a May 2023 decision that federal bureaucrats had no right to seize control over the Sacketts' property.[69] The couple's nightmare was over, but there is no way to know how many other landowners were wrongfully hog-tied by the EPA. Under the new standard the Court promulgated by a 5-to-4 vote, the EPA can no longer plant its flag on wetlands completely separate from traditional navigable waters. Justice Alito, writing for the majority, condemned the existing policy for "putting a staggering array of landowners at risk of criminal prosecution for such mundane activities as moving dirt."[70] In a concurring opinion, Justice Clarence Thomas said the ruling "curbs a serious expansion of federal authority" that turned the federal government "into something resembling 'a local zoning board.'"

It remains to be seen whether federal agencies will accede to the latest attempt to curb their arbitrary power over landowners.

Disabilities Act Debacles from Pornhub to Pizza

The Americans with Disabilities Act has become one of the premier "good intention debacles" of our times. After President George H.W. Bush signed the ADA in 1990, he hailed the law as "the world's first declaration of equality for people with disabilities."[71] President Bill Clinton announced in 1994 that the ADA "is a national monument to freedom."[72] But the ADA is designed to sacrifice some people's freedom to give special benefits to other people and to permit lawyers to plunder businesses as they please. The ADA's breadth and vagueness have spurred a deluge of absurd federal decrees and more than a half million lawsuits.

The 1990 ADA defined *disability* as "a physical or mental impairment that substantially limits one or more of the major life activities" — a far broader definition than previous federal laws to help the blind, deaf, and others with specific handicaps. The Supreme Court repeatedly struck down ADA regulations for creating excessively expansive definitions of *disability*.[73] Congress responded in 2008 by vastly expanding *disability* to include diabetes, depression, heart disease, and cancer[74] — as well as people who claim to have difficulty standing, lifting, bending, reading, concentrating, or thinking. The original ADA covered 43 million Americans, and the 2008 amendments added tens of millions of additional claimants.

By turning disabilities into legal assets, the ADA encourages far more people to claim to be disabled. Anyone who is disabled acquires a right to request accommodations from employers and others, with the federal government and private lawyers waiting to sue anyone who fails to "accommodate." The ADA is essentially a federal command for people to treat certain other people "nice" — with harsh penalties for not being nice enough — and with *niceness* defined on a case-by-case basis through endless court cases and complaint settlements. Law professor Linda Krieger, a prominent disability rights activist, asserted that the ADA requires that the disabled "be treated differently, arguably better [than the nondisabled], to achieve an equal effect."[75]

"You snooze, you lose — you sue," was the *New York Post*'s summary of the latest ADA lawsuit trend for sleep apnea sufferers.[76] An obese New York hospital ex-employee sued her former employer for $10 million in 2018 because she was fired after twice falling asleep at her job as an ambulance dispatcher. Her lawyer told the *New York Post*: "Helen didn't have a job where it was critical that she be awake 100% of the time."[77] An Austin, Texas, police detective received a $240,000 award from a jury that concluded the police department violated the ADA by failing to accommodate the detective's narcolepsy. A Kansas policeman who repeatedly fell asleep in his patrol car due to sleep apnea received almost a million dollars in a jury verdict.[78]

The ADA provides "freedom" to some people by sacrificing other people's safety. A federal court ruled in 2016 that the Washington subway system violated the ADA by firing a mechanic who was twice caught drunk on the job.[79] (The D.C. subway is notorious for breakdowns.) The 2008 ADA amendments specifically overturned a Supreme Court decision rejecting an ADA claim from twin sisters with severely impaired vision who sought pilot jobs from United Airlines.

The ADA protects people with alcohol and illicit drug problems, as long as they claim to be recovering or seeking treatment, or offer any passable excuse for their behavior. An Oregon police officer who was fired after he crashed his undercover car while intoxicated sued for $6 million in damages, claiming the ADA protected him because of his alcoholism.[80] In 2018, an ex-policeman in suburban Chicago filed an ADA lawsuit (claiming he was mentally ill) seeking $75,000 in damages after he was fired for driving drunk, hitting and badly injuring a pedestrian, and leaving the scene of the accident.[81]

President Obama declared in 2015 that "thanks to the ADA, the places that comprise our shared American life — schools, workplaces, movie theaters, courthouses, buses, baseball stadiums, national parks — they truly belong to everyone." Workplaces do not "belong to everyone" — they are mostly privately owned — but the ADA entitles the feds to take command. The Justice Department issued a 275-page edict with byzantine ADA architectural mandates. As a 2013 analysis in the *American Interest* noted, federal officials forcibly redesigned

> virtually all of America's indoor and outdoor spaces, issuing mandates
> in head-spinning detail on the proper ways to design playgrounds,
> buses, trains, train stations, gym rooms, pools, spas, courtroom jury

stands, witness boxes, and even restaurant table arrangements and boat slips from sea to shining sea.[82]

The Justice Department dictated exactly how miniature golf courses must be configured and slanted, including mandating that 50% of the holes on new courses be playable by people confined to wheelchairs.

The ADA is known as "Attorney's Dreams Answered." As early as 1995, one federal judge denounced an ADA suit as "a blatant attempt to extort money" — something for which the law is now notorious. Lawyer Mark Pulliam, one of the most astute ADA critics, observed in 2018 that the ADA

> may be the most widely-abused law in our history… Nationwide, a cottage industry has developed among a bottom-feeding element of the plaintiffs' bar that specializes in bringing a high volume of cookie-cutter lawsuits against small businesses for technical violations of the ADA, and extorting quick settlements of several thousand dollars each.[83]

A California P.F. Chang restaurant was sued because the coat hook on the inside door of an accessible toilet stall was at an improper height. The *New York Times* reported that the ADA had unleashed a "flood of lawsuits" against New York City delis, bagel shops, flower shops and other businesses that many people considered nothing more than "ambulance chasing."[84] Hundreds of Florida businesses were hit with ADA lawsuits in 2016 and 2017 complaining that "the pipes in the bathrooms weren't properly wrapped" and similar deadly perils.[85] Lawyer Cris Vaughan noted that under California law, "plaintiffs can also claim up to $4,000 per visit [to stores with alleged ADA compliance problems]. And they can visit the same business multiple times."[86] One federal judge denounced a lawyer filing such lawsuits for behaving like "a parasite disguised as a social engineer."

The ADA is increasingly derailing the Internet. Law professor Richard Epstein observed: "The ability to work and shop online at one's own pace offers a set of dazzling technological improvements that have done more to help the disabled than the massive expenditures under the ADA." But lawyers are increasingly suing colleges, companies, and other targets because their websites are not accessible to the blind, claiming that webpages are "places of public accommodations." The University of California at Berkeley created a vast offering of free online lectures but shut it down after the Justice Department claimed it violated the ADA.[87]

The Justice Department promised to publish ADA compliance guidelines for online sites but abandoned the task in 2017 after muddying the issue. A tidal wave of litigation resulted, including more than two thousand federal lawsuits on the issue of Internet access in 2018 — three times as many as in 2017. Yaroslav Suris, a deaf man, sued Pornhub and similar websites for violating the ADA. Suris complained that, because of lack of closed captioning, he was unable to comprehend the action in *Hot Step Aunt Babysits Disobedient Nephew.*[88] Pornhub offered captions for more than a thousand videos, but apparently not enough to satisfy the plaintiff.

Domino's Pizza was sued by a blind person who claimed he was denied "full and equal enjoyment" of its pizza offerings on its website and app — even though Domino's offered 13 other ways to place an order for a pizza (including phone calls). Domino's claimed that it had made a good faith effort to serve all customers and that federal agencies failed to provide clear guidance on the ADA. But a federal appeals court dismissed that argument, declaring that "the Constitution only requires that Domino's receive fair notice of its legal duties, not a blueprint for compliance with its statutory obligations."[89] Domino's appealed to the Supreme Court, pointing out the chaotic online challenges:

> Each defendant must figure out how to make every image on its website or app sufficiently accessible to the blind, how to render every video or audio file sufficiently available to the deaf, or how to provide content to those who cannot operate a computer or mobile phone.[90]

Legal analysts pointed out that the website for the Supreme Court had the same purported defects used to convict Domino's. But the Supreme Court refused to take the case, thereby perpetuating the legal feeding frenzy.

Many of the most controversial ADA lawsuits and policies involve mental disability claims. The ADA is heavily influenced by the American Psychiatric Association's *Diagnostic and Statistical Manual of Mental Disorders* (*DSM*). The *DSM* now lists more than 300 mental illnesses, five times as many as it specified in the 1960s. The deluge of new labels is turning millions of healthy Americans into "mental patients," according to Dr. Allen Frances. Minor tweaks spur bogus epidemics: after the *DSM* redefined *autism* in the 1990s, the autism rate "quickly multiplied almost 100 fold."[91] Psychiatrist Laurent Mottron complained in 2023 that the latest version of the *DSM* "is full of vague and trivial definitions and ambiguous language that ensures more people fall into various, abnormal categories."[92]

Psychiatric and mental illnesses have spurred soaring numbers of ADA claims. In 2013, a federal court ruled that anxiety over potentially getting fired qualifies as a disability, thereby making the termination of an under-performing teacher an ADA violation. A 2018 *Dartmouth Law Journal* article[93] asserted that "approximately 1 in 5 current employees work with a psychiatric disability," based on data from the National Institutes of Health. Depression is the most common "mental disability" complaint. Employees who scream at their bosses or threaten their colleagues can invoke the "Disruptive Mood Dysregulation Disorder" excuse. Psychiatrists even christened "caffeine withdrawal" as a mental illness. Mental health disability claims skyrocketed when businesses required employees to return to the office after the COVID pandemic.

The ADA compels colleges and universities to provide "reasonable accommodation" to students who claim to have a disability. Even before the pandemic, up to 25% of students at top colleges were "classified as disabled, largely because of mental-health issues such as depression or anxiety, entitling them to a widening array of special accommodations like longer time to take exams," the *Wall Street Journal* reported in 2018.[94] Lawyer Miriam Kurtzig Freedman observed that giving extra testing time is "like lowering the basket from 10 feet to eight feet; you're changing the game." Between 2008 and 2019, the number of undergraduate students diagnosed with anxiety increased by 134%, 106% for depression, 57% for bipolar disorder, 72% for ADHD, 67% for schizophrenia, and 100% for anorexia, according to the National College Health Assessment.[95] Students' struggles skyrocketed after COVID shutdowns. A Boston University analysis of students on almost 400 campuses in 2022 found that "60% of the respondents met the qualifying criteria for 'one or more mental health problems, a nearly 50% increase from 2013.'"[96]

ADA's threat to freedom hit the front pages during the COVID pandemic. The Biden administration invoked the ADA to make wearing face masks compulsory for all public school and preschool attendees nationwide ages two years and above. Secretary of Education Miguel Cardona claimed that governors and state legislatures that failed to require students to wear masks violated federal law. In August 2021, the Department of Education launched civil rights investigations, claiming that five states that prohibited mask mandates "discriminate against students with disabilities who are at heightened risk for severe illness from COVID-19 by preventing them from safely accessing in-person education."[97]

Texas Governor Greg Abbott issued a ban on schools mandating masks for all students. In November 2021, a federal district court overturned his policy because "the use of masks *may* decrease the risk of COVID infection in group settings" (emphasis added). In July 2022, a federal appeals court overturned the lower court decision, noting "plaintiffs did nothing to… prove the relative efficacy of mask mandates" since most of the schools with mask mandates had similar or higher COVID transmission rates than schools with no mandate. The court noted that the plaintiffs' demands would effectively "require federal courts to enforce mobile mask mandates that go where plaintiffs go and require everyone around them to wear masks."[98] A Brown University analysis found no correlation between mask mandates and lower COVID case rates.[99]

President Obama declared in 2015: "The ADA offered millions of people the opportunity to earn a living and help support their families." But the ADA has actually been a disaster at helping the disabled find work and become financially self-reliant. A Massachusetts Institute of Technology study concluded that the ADA reduced employment "of disabled men of all working ages and all disabled women under age 40." A 2018 Brookings Institution analysis concluded that only four out of ten adults with disabilities were working — a decline of almost 20 percentage points compared to pre-ADA levels. A National Bureau of Economic Research analysis concluded: "This decline represents a clear break from past trends for both disabled and non-disabled workers, and therefore seems likely to have been caused by the ADA."[100] In 2019, the rate of people with disabilities aged 16 to 64 with a job was less than half the percentage of non-disabled adults.[101]

The ADA seeks "progress" via a legal regime that presumes average citizens and businesses must be endlessly scourged. But long before the ADA was enacted, Americans were becoming more accepting and compassionate towards the disabled (with plenty of ugly exceptions). The Florida *News-Press* reported that "some of the harshest critics of these [ADA] suits come from people who are disabled or advocate on behalf of people with disabilities." Kevin Berry, co-chairman of the Southwest Florida ADA Council, complained that the lawsuit surge "has the reverse effect. If someone comes in with a wheelchair or an obvious disability, the (business owner) is saying, 'Here comes a lawsuit.'"[102]

Conclusion: The Forgotten Peril of Arbitrary Power

Contemporary legislation often bestows bureaucratic blank checks. But "vague laws invite arbitrary power," warned Justice Gorsuch in 2018. Vague statutes leave "people in the dark about what the law demands and [allow] prosecutors and courts to... condemn all that [they] personally disapprove and for no better reason than [they] disapprove it," Gorsuch wrote.[103]

Politicians and bureaucrats have accumulated practically endless vetoes over private behavior with ever-changing and constantly growing edicts. Law professor Paul Bator observed in 1989: "Every day, Congress, the courts and [federal] agencies are manufacturing new law with an energy unparalleled either in our own history or that of any modern society."[104] Today, there is often scant difference between laws and arbitrary commands because few people recognize what convoluted laws and regulations actually require.

Vesting unchecked power in administrative agencies makes a mockery of representative government. People vote for politicians who go to Washington or state capitals and enact laws that entitle bureaucrats to vex whomever they please. Once government regulation passes the point where compliance is practically impossible, each additional regulation increases the subjugation of citizens to officialdom. The government will almost always come to court with overwhelming advantages over the citizen. The government has so much legal artillery and discretion that it can pulverize almost any target it chooses.

Arbitrary power converts bureaucrats into czars who can bedevil whomever they please. Government officials are presumed so superior to private citizens that they must be allowed to make up the rules as they go along — or to even change them retroactively. As French philosopher Benjamin Constant warned in 1815:

> Arbitrary power destroys morality, for there can be no morality without security... Arbitrariness is incompatible with the existence of any government considered as a set of institutions. For political institutions are simply contracts; and it is in the nature of contracts to establish fixed limits.[105]

Nowadays, as long as bureaucrats claim to have good intentions, their abuses are expunged or at least ignored. Arbitrary power is a non-issue because people have been taught that government is automatically benevolent. Pundits and professors have tacitly embraced the "Officer Friendly" notion of government almost across the board. And the biggest threat is not G-men off the leash, but people who distrust the government. But, as Hayek showed in his famous essay, "Why the Worst Get on Top," once government acquires great power, "the readiness to do bad things becomes a path to promotion."[106]

If government is not "under the law," citizens will be under the federal boot. Apathy over arbitrary power exemplifies the rising political illiteracy. If people don't recognize the peril of government violating its own laws, is American democracy beyond redemption?

8. Subsidies and Subjugation

Government programs increasingly domineer Americans' lives. Over the past hundred years, subsidies have proliferated for housing, farming, food, college, and many other activities. Politicians and bureaucrats have used tax dollars to commandeer one swath of American society and economy after another.

In a 1942 case involving a farmer who was harshly punished for growing wheat to feed his cattle, the Supreme Court decreed: "It is hardly lack of due process for the government to regulate that which it subsidizes."[1] It didn't matter that the farmer neither received nor wanted any subsidies. The Agriculture Department was entitled to unlimited power over his acreage simply because other farmers accepted subsidies. In 1971, the Supreme Court noted that government cash subsidies "have almost always been accompanied by varying measures of control and surveillance."[2]

Shortly after the United States invaded Iraq in 2003, pallets stacked high with newly printed $100 bills were flown into Baghdad. U.S. military officers tossed bundles of cash to local residents to buy influence and undermine resistance to the American occupation. The "Money as a Weapon System" program shoveled out $10 billion with little or no oversight. A 2012 Pentagon analysis stressed that the handouts demonstrated "positive intent or goodwill" and helped "gain access or influence."[3] In the same way, politicians rely on "money as a weapon system" to buy votes or undermine resistance to Washington. Presidents and congressmen are not formally carrying out a counterinsurgency campaign against the American people. But addicting citizens to government handouts is the easiest way to breed mass docility.

There are hundreds of programs gushing out tax dollars nowadays. We will examine a few areas where federal subsidies permeate American lives.

Wrecking Ball Benevolence

Politicians' aid to home buyers produced one of the biggest paternalist catastrophes of this century. Unfortunately, Washington learned nothing, and policymakers could be sending the nation back over the same cliff.

In the mid-1990s, 41% of black households owned their own homes, compared to over 70% of white households. The Clinton administration championed the idea that racism was to blame. Housing and Urban Development (HUD) Secretary Andrew Cuomo announced in 1998: "We will not tolerate a continued home ownership gap as wide as the Grand Canyon that divides Americans into two societies, separate and unequal."[4] Banks came under intense federal pressure to convert mortgages into an affirmative action program. The Clinton administration inflicted multibillion-dollar penalties on mortgage companies that failed to make more loans to minorities with shaky credit histories.

President George W. Bush hit the same theme: "The rate of homeownership amongst minorities is below 50%. And that's not right, and this country needs to do something about it."[5] Bush promised in 2002 to "use the mighty muscle of the federal government" to boost home ownership.[6] Bush was determined to end the bias against people who wanted to buy a home but had no money. Bush had plenty of support on Capitol Hill. Rep. Barney Frank (D-MA), the most influential congressman on housing policy, declared in 2003: "I want to roll the dice a little bit more in this situation toward subsidized housing."[7]

In 2003, Congress passed Bush's American Dream Downpayment Act, giving first-time home buyers up to either $10,000 or 6% of the home's purchase price, whichever was greater. Bush also swayed Congress to permit the Federal Housing Administration to make zero-downpayment loans to low-income Americans. Bush proclaimed: "Core American values of individuality, thrift, responsibility, and self-reliance are embodied in homeownership." In Bush's eyes, self-reliance was so wonderful that the government should subsidize it.[8] Bush's efforts evoked plenty of gratitude. The *New York Times* noted: "In the 2004 election cycle, mortgage bankers and brokers poured nearly $847,000 into Bush's re-election campaign, more than triple their contributions in 2000."[9]

Bush's 2004 re-election campaign trumpeted his downpayment giveaways as a triumph of "compassionate conservatism." Clinton-Bush policies resulted in a twentyfold increase in subprime lending to home buyers previously considered uncreditworthy. Fannie Mae and Freddie Mac, which profited from their quasi-federal status that allowed them to borrow more cheaply, bought up bundles of subprime loans created by other companies, deadening the incentive for mortgage lenders to avoid reckless behavior. Fannie and Freddie, along with the Federal Housing Administration (FHA), soon quasi-monopolized the market, holding half of all mortgages and most of the "27 million subprime and other low quality mortgages in the U.S. financial system."[10]

The tidal wave of subsidized lending helped send housing prices through the roof. Bush's top advisors ignored warnings that housing was heading for a crash.[11] When a recession began in 2007, home values skidded, and laid-off workers ceased paying mortgages. In mid-2008, Fannie and Freddie declared bankruptcy. Fannie and Freddie got away with perpetually irresponsible practices because they spent hundreds of millions of dollars on lobbying and campaign contributions to congressional candidates before their collapse.[12] This was crony capitalism at its worst — politicians making out like bandits while the economy was left in shambles.

"Affordable housing turned out to be the path to perdition for the U.S. mortgage market," Federal Judge Janice Rogers Brown lamented in a 2017 court opinion. Clinton-Bush policies succeeded in driving up the percentage of Americans living in their own homes to 69.2% — the highest rate on record. However, after housing prices collapsed, the rate fell to 62.3% in 2014. This is the equivalent of almost eight million families or individuals losing or otherwise exiting their homes. This was the biggest loss of home ownership in American history, a much sharper fall than occurred during the Great Depression, when the percentage of homeowners declined from 47.8% to 43.6%.[13]

The housing collapse ravaged the net worth of minority households. The black homeownership rate rose to almost 50% in 2005 but fell to a low of 41.7% by 2016. The *Washington Post* noted in 2012:

> The implosion of the subprime lending market has left a scar on the finances of black Americans — one that not only has wiped out a generation of economic progress but could leave them at a financial disadvantage for decades.[14]

Economist Mark Calabria, later appointed as chief of the Federal Housing Finance Agency, observed in 2016: "The racial homeownership gap is at a 100-year high" — even higher than it was prior to the 1968 Fair Housing Act which outlawed discrimination against blacks and other minorities.[15]

Hispanics took especially ruinous losses thanks to their purported friends in Washington. Subprime loans to Hispanics almost quadrupled between 2004 and 2006, a much faster growth rate than for any other group. Hispanic members of Congress championed low lending standards, resulting in a tidal wave of NINA — "no income, no assets" — and "no document" mortgages which relied solely on a borrower's asserted income.[16] The median net worth for Hispanic households declined by 66% between 2005 and 2009.[17]

Giving handouts that lead people to financial ruin is wrecking ball benevolence.[18] Even Rep. Frank admitted in August 2010 that "it was a great mistake to push lower-income people into housing they couldn't afford and couldn't really handle once they had it."[19] Since the housing market bottomed out, the partial rebound of home prices in subsequent years was no consolation to the millions of families who had lost their homes.

Despite the colossal losses from the 2007–08 housing crash, federal agencies began repeating the same follies within less than a decade. By 2019, Fannie, Freddie, and the FHA piled up almost $7 trillion in mortgage debt. The *Washington Post* noted in 2019 that the federal government had "dramatically expanded its exposure to risky mortgages, as federal officials over the past four years took steps that cleared the way for companies to issue loans that many borrowers might not be able to repay."[20]

Biden captured the presidency in part thanks to his promises to close racial gaps in homeownership, net worth, and other areas. Biden championed his own version of Bush's American Dream Downpayment Act, pushing Congress to spend $10 billion for downpayment assistance for "first-time, first-generation" home buyers.[21] Neither Biden nor any of his advisors admitted the role of government debacles in devastating minority net worth a dozen years earlier.

On May 1, 2023, the Biden administration launched a new mortgage policy that practically treated being creditworthy like a federal crime.[22] The new policy intentionally punished home buyers with good credit scores to subsidize people with shaky histories of paying their debts. The administration compelled adjusting mortgage calculations to penalize homebuyers with a FICO credit score of above 680 — almost two-thirds of the population. The windfall from this levy will be used to reduce costs for people with low credit scores — i.e., risky borrowers more likely to default on mortgages.

Federal regulations require that all charges and credits to buyers and sellers be explicitly listed in mortgage settlement statements. The new penalty for creditworthy borrowers should be explicitly listed on loan documents as a Social Justice Surtax. That surtax could amount to $60 or more per month — equivalent to more than $20,000 over a 30-year mortgage.

Federal Housing Finance Agency Director Sandra Thompson testified to Congress in 2022 that the racial homeownership gap "is higher today than when the Fair Housing Act [of 1968] was passed." The new compulsory cross-subsidy aimed to reduce that gap. "The average credit score in white communities was 727 in 2021, compared with 667 in Hispanic communities and 627 in Black communities," *Newsweek* noted.[23] But Thompson forgot to mention that much of the blame rests on politicians and bureaucrats who caused the 2007–08 housing crash.

The easiest way to ruin somebody's life is to give them a mortgage they can't afford. The Biden administration was pushing subsidized mortgages with little or no downpayment at the same time that housing prices were falling in much of the nation. That is a recipe for disaster for new homeowners with no equity in their dwellings.

Sowing Subsidized Havoc in Suburbia

Federal rental subsidies have spurred crime and chaos in neighborhoods across the land. HUD Secretary Shaun Donovan testified to Congress in 2010: "Living where we choose is one of our most treasured freedoms as Americans. We believe it's wrong for anyone not to have mobility." In reality, federal policies entitle government bureaucrats to determine who can live in residences they cannot afford. According to HUD, it is a social injustice if poor people have less mobility than rich people.

Through the Section 8 program, HUD now covers the rent for more than two million households nationwide. Tenants pay 30% of their income toward rent and utilities while the feds pay the rest. And if tenants claim to have zero income, they live rent-free. Section 8's budget has soared from $7 billion in 1994 to $27 billion in 2022. Section 8 "vouchers have come to be seen as a tool for promoting economic and racial/ethnic integration," as a HUD report noted.[24]

But the programs' lofty subsidies have always made a mockery of its stated goals. In 1980, six years after Section 8 was created, GAO warned that the program's goal of mixing the poor and the middle class was often not achieved because Section 8 "housing is often so costly that... even middle-income unassisted households cannot afford to live in it." GAO pointed out that "the high rents and quality of [Section 8] housing invite resentment on the part of the taxpaying public who see their subsidized neighbors living in better accommodations than they themselves can afford."[25]

Lavish subsidies allow Section 8 recipients to rent "boom-era showpieces, brimming with McMansion-like features" such as backyard barbecue grills and walk-in closets, the *Wall Street Journal* reported.[26] Section 8 renters in Florida moved into 6-bedroom mansions with swimming pools and three-car garages. Jacuzzis have also become a commonly-touted feature to attract Section 8 recipients and their federally guaranteed rent. In Chicago, HUD pays almost $5,000 a month for a spacious home in an affluent neighborhood, almost $4,000 for a fancy townhouse, and more than $3,500 for a bevy of lucky Section 8 recipients to live in new high-rises with glorious views of Lake Michigan.[27]

Section 8 applicants "sometimes celebrate almost like lottery winners" when they receive a voucher.[28] Qualifying can be like snaring a $100,000+ windfall, since the average recipient spends almost a decade collecting benefits. Receiving Section 8 benefits reduces subsequent earnings of able-bodied, working-age recipients by 10%.[29]

Any household with 80% of the median income in their locale can qualify for Section 8 subsidies. But the program is not an entitlement, and bureaucrats arbitrarily select recipients.[30] Bribery scandals involving Section 8 awards erupt as regularly as Old Faithful in Yellowstone Park. In 2014, when the Baltimore Housing Authority briefly allowed people to apply for 10,000 Section 8 vouchers, a third of the city's 240,000 households sought housing welfare.[31] (Almost 10% of Baltimoreans were already on the housing dole.) In Dallas, Texas, 5,000 people showed up to try to snare 100 Section 8 vouchers in 2011. Eight people were injured when the crowd rushed the opening doors.[32] In East Point, Georgia, 30,000 people turned out seeking to snare one of 455 vouchers. Sixty-two people were injured in the resulting melee. HUD profits from these commotions because it makes the agency appear to be responding to a grave social crisis.

Many Section 8 recipients previously lived in public housing projects with crime rates up to 20 times higher than the national average. HUD presumed that simply moving people out of the projects would solve that problem. However, "[c]rime, specifically homicide, became displaced to where the low-income residents were relocated. Homicide was simply moved to a new location, not eliminated," concluded a 2009 article in *Homicide Studies*.[33] In Louisville, Memphis, and other cities, violent crime skyrocketed in neighborhoods where Section 8 recipients resettled. The Steubenville, Ohio, police chief estimated that half that city's murders occurred at Section 8 addresses.[34] An Indianapolis Housing Authority investigation found that 80% of criminal homicides in Marion County, Indiana, were linked to individuals fraudulently obtaining federal assistance "in either the public housing program or the Section 8 program administered by the agency."[35] At least 30 people were killed at Section 8 residences in Chicago during the first half of 2016.[36] The *Chicago Sun-Times* and Chicago-based Better Government Association "matched the addresses of Section 8 housing in Chicago against the city's online crime database" and found that for the first six months of 2016, "police responded to reported crimes — from thefts to homicides — at 7,379 addresses where at least one voucher-holder lived." A HUD-financed study found that Section 8 relocations had "tripled the rate of arrests for property crimes" among boys who moved to new locales.[37]

In Houston, male Section 8 recipients are twice as likely to commit violent crimes as people with similar backgrounds and incomes who did not receive housing vouchers. A Texas A&M University analysis attributed the "increase in arrests for violent crime" to "the additional funds and leisure time available to voucher recipients that can be used to commit crimes."[38] The analysis noted: "Moving to a better neighborhood... could increase crime by providing easier and wealthier targets."

Because of the crime associated with the program, Section 8 renters have a bad reputation in many areas. Twelve states and more than a hundred localities "solved" this problem by compelling landlords to accept Section 8 applicants, banning so-called discrimination on "source of income." Since almost half of Section 8 recipients are black, landlords "saying they don't accept vouchers is... all very dog whistle racially coded," according to Christina Rosales of the advocacy organization Texas Housers.[39] But some of the most outspoken critics of Section 8 are black residents who see their middle- and working-class neighborhoods disrupted by freeloading new residents. "Chatham is a South Side neighborhood that has seen a dramatic rise in crime and drop in property values after a flood of Section 8 residents with housing vouchers moved into the area," the *Chicago City Wire* reported.[40] Keith Tate, the head of the local community association, complained that Section 8 "has been disastrous for Chatham. Never did we see individuals sitting on their cars drinking 40-ounce bottles of beer."[41]

Landlords who are conscripted into providing housing to Section 8 recipients can practically become serfs. Paul Arena of the Illinois Rental Property Owners Association complained:

> All of the control is in the hands of the housing authority. You
> operate on whatever terms they decide should exist at the beginning
> of the lease. And it says in the contract that they can change the terms
> in the middle of the lease.[42]

Landlords are also wary because HUD seems bent on creating a new civil right to raise hell in subsidized housing.[43] HUD forced the Cincinnati Metropolitan Housing Authority to cease enforcing noise violation and other nuisance laws because policing Section 8 tenant behavior was "an ineffective use of resources" that "could lead to inappropriate program terminations," according to a HUD spokeswoman.[44]

In 2021, Biden championed creating 200,000 new Section 8 vouchers, but Congress only approved 25,000 new vouchers — still the largest one-year increase since the start of the program. Biden also proposed to turn Section 8 into an entitlement, meaning that anyone whose income was below 80% of the local median income could automatically receive a voucher. But that would oblige the feds to pay rental subsidies for households with six-figure incomes. In San Francisco and San Mateo County, California, for example, households with annual incomes over $100,000 qualify for Section 8.[45]

The Right to Ravage Farmers

For a king, a prerogative is a right to do wrong, as Ambrose Bierce quipped. Similarly, bureaucracies have a prerogative to ruin whatever they claim to protect.

Farm subsidies have long exemplified paternalism run amok. In 1930, the *New York Times*, surveying the wreckage of agricultural markets after the federal government tried to drive up wheat prices, concluded: "It is perhaps fortunate for the country that its fingers were so badly burned at the very first trial of the scheme."[46] But that did not deter President Franklin Roosevelt and Congress from making the Secretary of Agriculture a farm dictator.[47]

Politicians first artificially raise crop prices, and then USDA forcibly reduces harvests. USDA's peanut program long combined the worst traits of feudalism and central economic planning. In 1949, to curb the cost of subsidies, Congress made it a federal crime to grow peanuts without a federal license. The feds closed off the peanut industry, distributing licenses to existing farmers and prohibiting anyone else from entering the business. The government also imposed draconian controls to prevent any unlicensed peanuts from entering Americans' stomachs, including aerial photography to determine whether farmers planted a few more square feet than they were permitted.[48] Though the program was purportedly created to help save family farms, the number of peanut growers plunged by more than 75% after licensing began. The program also sabotaged productivity because the licenses were locked into the same localities (peanuts are a soil-depleting crop). Many farmers sold their licenses to investors. The program sharply inflated the cost of production because, within a few decades, most farmers had to rent the license to raise their crop. Congress abolished the allotment regime in 2002, replacing it with a new program that proceeded to bombard peanut growers with much higher subsidies than other farmers received. By 2016, USDA was drowning in surplus peanuts that farmers dumped on Uncle Sam to collect hefty federal payments.[49]

Once politicians decide to benefit one group, they entitle themselves to sacrifice everyone else. For instance, the U.S. government has been heavily subsidizing sugar growers for 200 years. But sugar growers, unlike most American farmers, remain hopelessly uncompetitive with foreign producers. USDA perennially drives the U.S. price of sugar to double or triple the world sugar price, costing consumers $3 billion a year. Despite the aid, the number of sugar growers has declined by almost 50% in recent decades to less than six thousand.[50] The Government Accountability Office estimated that 1% of sugar growers captured almost half of all the benefits from the program.

Bankrolling sugar production in Florida makes as little sense as a subsidy program to grow bananas in Massachusetts. Because the U.S. mainland does not have a natural climate for sugar production, farmers have to compensate by dousing the land with fertilizer. Almost 500,000 acres of the Everglades have been converted from swampland to sugar fields, but phosphorus from the fertilizer has ravaged the region's ecosystem. Politicians have launched hugely expensive efforts to curb the environmental harm, but, as the *New York Times* reported, the United States Sugar Corporation, not the Everglades, was the prime beneficiary.

Thanks to the sugar program, food manufacturers are hostage to a byzantine combination of price supports and arbitrary import restrictions that make producing candy and many other foods far more expensive here than abroad. Nabisco shifted production of Oreo cookies to Mexico to capitalize on much lower sugar prices there. Since 1997, sugar policy has zapped more than 120,000 jobs in food manufacturing.[51] More than ten jobs have been lost in manufacturing for every remaining sugar grower in the United States.

New Deal-era agricultural marketing laws still empower federally authorized committees to commandeer much of a farmer's crop to drive up prices for the remainder of the harvest. The Raisin Administrative Committee commandeered up to half of a farmer's harvest as a "reserve" — purportedly to stabilize markets and prevent gluts. Sharecropping is apparently not a bad thing as long as the government is the master.

Marvin Horne, a 67-year-old raisin farmer in Fresno, California, was fined almost $700,000 for refusing to surrender 47% of his harvest in 2002 to the federal committee. Horne, who has been growing raisins for more than 40 years, described the regulatory regime as "involuntary servitude."[52]

The federal government has become so large and intrusive that few Washingtonians recognize how far its interventions reach. When Horne's case landed before the Supreme Court in 2013, Justices were amazed at the heavy-handed regulatory regime. During oral arguments, Justice Stephen Breyer stated: "I can't believe that Congress wanted the taxpayers to pay for a program that's going to mean they have to pay higher prices as consumers." Justice Elena Kagan suggested that the statute authorizing the raisin cartel could be "the world's most outdated law."[53] For USDA, "Does it make sense?" was trumped by "We have been doing this for a very long time."

The Obama administration and USDA insisted that, even though the government commandeers raisin farmers' harvest, there is no "taking" because the seizure drives up the price of the remaining raisins. But the Raisin Committee's sweeping powers failed to prevent vast swings in prices. Many California farmers capitulated, and the acreage devoted to raisin production fell by 75,000 acres after 2000.

The Obama administration told the Supreme Court that selling raisins in interstate commerce was a privilege which USDA could grant or withhold. It also asserted that the restrictions did not violate raisin farmers' rights because they could avoid the controls by "planting different crops." Chief Justice John Roberts, the author of an 8-to-1 ruling against USDA, scoffed: "'Let them sell wine' is probably not much more comforting to the raisin growers than similar retorts have been to others throughout history."[54]

Despite the Supreme Court ruling, USDA-authorized committees continue stifling the sale of cranberries, spearmint oil, and other crops, while "volume controls" are authorized but not currently in effect for walnuts, almonds, and other crops. The policies survived both judicial condemnations and widespread ridicule.

President Trump took a pause from his denunciations of socialism to deluge farmers with handouts after he wrecked their export markets. Trump boasted that "trade wars are good and easy to win."[55] China retaliated against Trump's tariffs by slashing their purchases of U.S. crop exports. Crop prices plummeted, and farmers were soon hit by the highest bankruptcy rate in decades. Trump responded with the Market Facilitation Program — a peculiar name for a program spurred by the destruction of export markets. In 2020, farm subsidies reached a record level of $46 billion a year — accounting for almost 40% of farm income. *Politico* reported in July 2020: "The massive payments have been a political boon to Trump in farm country — he tweeted in January that he hoped the money would be 'the thing they will most remember' — but risk creating a culture of dependency."[56] Trump policymakers jiggled accounts to evade federal law and provide up to $100 million in handouts to tobacco farmers, "easing some of the financial pain that has been felt particularly hard in the battleground state of North Carolina," the *New York Times* reported.[57]

Farm programs, like other federal aid programs, contained income limits on eligibility for handouts. But Congress designs the programs so that recipients can easily evade those limits. As the Environmental Working Group reported:

> Farmers can receive payments as long as their income is less than $900,000 a year, or $1.8 million for a farmer and spouse. There is a $125,000 annual payment limit, but a farm can have an unlimited number of "partners" that can each receive up to $125,000, allowing many people who do not live or work on the farm to get a check every year.[58]

Federal aid is skewed to acreage planted. The largest 1% of farms "received 13% of the federal payments, or more than $177,000 each. The bottom 80%, on the other hand, got an average payment of $5,136."[59]

Even without federal aid, farmers would be far more affluent than other Americans. According to USDA, the median farm household has a net worth of $827,307. However, this includes a vast number of recreational, gentlemen, and hobby farmers. The largest class of farmers — those who produce most farm products and harvest the largest share of the subsidies — have a median net worth of $2,586,000. In contrast, the median net worth for American households in 2022 was $121,700, according to the Federal

Reserve.[60] By any standard, the average farmer is worth at least six times as much as most American households. But that stark reality has failed to discredit policies based on myths of struggling farmers in a bygone era.

Food Aid Fiascos

In 1969, President Richard Nixon proclaimed: "The moment is at hand to put an end to hunger in America itself for all time." At that time, three million Americans received food stamps, a program that cost $228 million a year. By 2021, 41 million people collected $140 billion worth of food stamps. Thanks to an array of other subsidies, the federal government is now feeding more than 100 million people.[61] Despite a hundredfold increase in food stamp spending (in constant dollars) since Nixon's pledge, hunger is supposedly still widespread across the land.

So President Biden, speaking at the 2022 White House Summit on Hunger, Nutrition and Health, proclaimed a goal "to end hunger in this country by the year 2030."[62] Unfortunately, the perpetual failure of federal food assistance is a storyline that politicians and the media ignore.

Food stamps are simply a federal blank check to enable recipients to purchase whatever they please, regardless of nutritional content or lack thereof. The Congressional Budget Office warned in 1980 that "it still remains unclear if increased food purchases [via food stamps]... means improved nutritional status."[63]

In 2009, President Obama sharply boosted food stamp benefits and bankrolled recruiting campaigns to sway people to abandon self-reliance.[64] After the Obama administration canceled the program's work requirement, the number of able-bodied food stamp recipients doubled.[65] In most states, people could apply for benefits online — making it easier than going to a job interview. *Salon*, in an article titled "Hipsters on food stamps," noted that many recipients used their windfalls at Whole Foods to purchase artisanal bread, heirloom tomatoes, grass-fed beef, coconut milk, and organic asparagus.[66]

The Obama administration elbowed states to give food stamps to individuals who were far wealthier than average Americans. After 35 states abolished asset tests, millionaires became legally entitled to collect food stamps as long as they have little or no monthly income (good news for windfall lottery winners).[67] Millions of people with incomes above the eligibility cutoffs automatically qualified for food stamps after receiving one of a long list of other government handouts or services. In many states, simply receiving a brochure describing government benefits automatically qualified people for food stamps.[68]

Food stamps helped fuel a nationwide surge in obesity. Walter Willett, chair of Harvard University's Department of Nutrition, observed in 2015: "We've analyzed what [food-stamp] participants are eating, and it's horrible food. It's a diet designed to produce obesity and diabetes."[69] A 2017 study published in *BMC Public Health* found that food-stamp recipients were twice as likely to be obese as eligible non-recipients.[70] The *American Journal of Public Health* reported in 2017 that food stamp recipients had double the likelihood of cardio-related mortality and three times the rate of diabetes-related mortality than the general population, and sharply higher risks than eligible non-recipients of food stamps.[71] A 2011 National Institutes for Health report found that almost half of the women collecting food stamps are obese.[72]

Both Republican and Democratic governors and mayors requested permission to modify food stamps to prohibit using them for junk food. A Stanford University study concluded that prohibiting the use of food stamps for sugary drinks would prevent 141,000 kids from becoming fat and save a quarter million adults from Type 2 diabetes.[73] But the appearance of benevolence is worth more than the reality. The Obama administration portrayed food stamps as a nutrition program while blocking reforms to exclude purchases of unhealthy food. The Trump administration also prevented local and state governments from modifying the program to limit dietary damage. Food stamp revisions were defeated in 2018 by "corporate lobbying primarily by the beverage and food retail industries" and "a desire by liberals to defend SNAP as income support for the poor even if nutrition outcomes are sub-optimal," as Harvard professor Robert Paarlberg noted.[74]

Food stamps benefits are reduced by 30 cents for each dollar recipients earn. A *Journal of Public Economics* analysis concluded that receiving food stamps results in a nearly "50% reduction in total hours worked" by women,[75] while a Western Michigan University study found that each one-percent boost in food stamps "reduces work hours for families by about one half of one percent."

Those disincentives worsened after the Biden administration in 2021 canceled the work requirement (revived by the Trump administration) for able-bodied adults without children. Agriculture Secretary Tom Vilsack declared: "Groups with typically higher unemployment, including rural Americans, Black, Indigenous, Hispanic and People of Color, and those with less than a high school education would have been disproportionally harmed by this cruel policy."[76] At a time when employers were begging people to accept jobs, the Biden administration portrayed the necessity of working as a human rights violation — at least for those categories Vilsack cited. Rep. Jamaal Bowman (D-NY) portrayed the work requirement as genocidal: "Cutting SNAP will lead to homelessness, incarceration and death for 38 million Americans."[77]

In August 2021, the Biden administration tacitly invoked obesity to justify the biggest food stamp benefit hike in history. USDA revised its Thrifty Food Plan, which determines food stamp benefit levels, to "reflect current realities providing sufficient energy to support current weight status."[78] Angela Rachidi of the American Enterprise Institute noted: "Giving SNAP participants more money without restrictions will more than likely increase the consumption of unhealthy items, worsening the problems of obesity and disease caused by poor diet."[79] Secretary Vilsack justified the higher benefits to prevent beefy mobs from attacking USDA headquarters: "We may have a Constitution and a Declaration of Independence, but if we had 42 million Americans who were going hungry, really hungry, they wouldn't be happy and there would be political instability."[80] On the bright side, the Biden administration expanded "obesity counseling" for people who squander their food stamps.

Federally subsidized school meals also have a long record of undermining public health. GAO has lambasted the federal school lunch program for more than 40 years for its poor nutrient content. A 2010 University of Michigan study found that students who regularly eat school lunches were 29% more likely to be overweight, and that consumption of school lunches is the strongest single predictor of childhood obesity.[81]

In 2008, presidential candidate Barack Obama pledged to end child hunger by 2015. Thanks to the Healthy, Hunger-Free Kids Act of 2010, all schools with at least 40% low-income students were entitled to offer federally subsidized breakfasts and lunches free to all students. First Lady Michelle Obama, who spearheaded the effort, announced in 2010 that because children's nutrition is so important, "we can't just leave it up to the parents."[82]

But schools offered "carb loading" more appropriate for marathon runners than for schoolchildren. Homer Simpson is the patron saint of federal school breakfasts. Donuts, pastries, apple juice, and other high-sugar foods had starring roles in school breakfast menus across the nation.[83] USDA's 2012 School Nutrition Dietary Assessment Study found that the typical school breakfast included almost the entire maximum recommended *daily* intake for sugar and fat.[84]

To vastly expand the program, the feds reward schools that encourage all children to eat free breakfasts in the classroom. School officials scorned parents who protested schools feeding their kid a second breakfast (after they've eaten at home) and deluging them with sugary junk. A 2016 *Journal of the Academy of Nutrition and Dietetics* report found that "receiving school breakfasts more than doubled the odds of becoming obese for children from families below the federal poverty line compared with children of similar socioeconomic backgrounds who did not regularly receive school breakfasts."

At the 2022 White House Summit, Biden announced plans to "make at least 9 million more students eligible for free school meals — a major first step for free meals for every single student."[85] Despite promises of reform, almost all school systems continue to exceed dietary guidelines for sugar in breakfasts.[86] Among the most sugar-laden foods routinely now given to children are sweetened cereal, flavored milk, toaster pastries, cookies, cakes, and cinnamon buns. It is a federal crime for food manufacturers to sell products without nutritional labeling. But USDA does not require schools to disclose to parents how much sugar is being fed to their kids.

Biden asserted that "one in 10 American households still do not have enough access to enough food." The "one in 10" claim is a statistical charade based on federal surveys designed to create the illusion of mass hunger. USDA conducts an annual "food security" survey that mostly tabulates how many people voice concerns about missing meals at some future time or are unable to afford more expensive food which they prefer.[87] If someone fears running out of food on a single day (but didn't run out), that is considered an indicator of being "food insecure" for the entire year. If someone craves organic kale but can only afford conventional kale, they are "food insecure." Most of the households that USDA certifies as "food insecure" never ran out of food. While politicians portray hunger as the gravest peril for the poor, "seven times as many [low-income] children are obese as are underweight," the *Journal of the American Medical Association* noted in 2012.[88]

USDA has never cared enough to measure actual hunger in America. A National Academy of Sciences panel lamented in 2006 that there was little solid data on the problem and urged the government to develop reliable gauges of hunger.[89] Instead, USDA conducts an annual "food security" survey that politicians perennially misrepresent as a gauge of hunger.[90] Biden announced plans to boost federal outlays on "nutrition research" in 2022 — atop the $2-billion-a-year current spending. But there were no plans to devise a measurement for actual hunger. Instead, new research will focus on a "health equity lens" to expose "disparities" among different races and ethnic groups.

After the Biden administration maximized the number of kids relying on Uncle Sam, it sought to effectively decree: "Those who use incorrect pronouns shall not eat." It announced plans to withhold federal subsidies (including school meal funds) from any state or local agencies guilty of "discrimination based on gender identity or sexual orientation." That mandate would require 18 states to repeal laws that prohibited biological males from competing against female athletes in school sports, as well as permitting students to use the bathrooms and showers that they asserted aligned with their self-proclaimed gender identity. The mandate would also compel schools to use the pronouns that students preferred. Tennessee Attorney General Herbert Slatery complained: "This case is about a federal agency trying to change law, which is Congress's exclusive prerogative. The USDA simply does not have that authority."[91] On July 26, 2022, after a surge of lawsuits from state attorneys general, Federal Judge Charles Atchley blocked enforcement of the edict.[92]

Bad federal advice harmed the diets of Americans of all income groups. Beginning in 1977, federal guidelines identified fat as the greatest dietary peril and urged Americans to boost carbohydrate intake and curtail consumption of meat, eggs, and dairy products. In the 1980s, USDA Dietary Guidelines falsely declared that "too much sugar in your diet does not cause diabetes."[93] The Food and Drug Administration and Surgeon General also jumped on the "no sweat on sugar" bandwagon. Scores of millions of Americans responded by replacing fat in their diets with carbohydrates.

Since the guidelines were first issued, the percentage of Americans who are obese or afflicted with diabetes has soared. The guidelines were always on shaky scientific grounds. When major studies in the 1990s and later debunked the key dietary recommendations, the feds ignored the results. In 2015, the federal government grudgingly revised its guidelines, finally conceding that eggs, dairy products, and meat were not as toxic as previously portrayed. But the revised guidelines were muddled and confusing — in part because the Obama administration insisted on factoring in purported environmental sustainability into dietary advice. Congress sought to pass a law requiring a higher standard of evidence for official dietary recommendations, but the Obama administration thwarted the effort.

"Government feeds best" has been a disastrous recipe for America. Unfortunately, politicians can reap applause for fighting hunger regardless of the obesity, diabetes, and other problems caused by federal food programs. If federal spending could abolish hunger, the problem would have vanished long ago.

The Political Profits of College Debt

Student loans are now the second largest source of private debt, surpassed only by mortgage debt. Federal policies have helped turn young people into a debtor class perpetually clamoring for relief. Rather than seeing the federal government as a potential peril to their rights and liberties, many debt-burdened young adults view it as the Great Liberator.

Federal aid spurred tuition increases that make it far more difficult for unsubsidized students to afford higher education. The Higher Education Act of 1965 opened the floodgates for federal loans and grants to students. A student's financial "need" is defined largely by tuition fees. Every tuition increase means an increase in federal aid for students — and thus an increase in the federal aid for the college. In 1987, Education Secretary William Bennett asserted that "increases in financial aid in recent years have enabled colleges and universities blithely to raise their tuitions, confident that Federal loan subsidies would help cushion the increase." Between 1978 and 2012, the cost of college rose four times faster than the consumer price index.[94]

During his 2008 presidential campaign, Barack Obama promised: "I will make college affordable for every American. Period."[95] Obama boosted subsidies with predictable results. A 2012 study by the Center for College Affordability and Productivity concluded that financial aid "inevitably puts upward pressure on tuition. Higher tuition reduces college affordability, leading to calls for more financial aid, setting the vicious cycle in motion all over again."[96] A 2015 Federal Reserve analysis "found that for every new dollar made available in federally subsidized student loans, schools… rose their rates by 65 cents."[97]

The Obama administration created a byzantine system to exempt students from repaying their federal college debt and camouflaged the extent of loan defaults. By 2013, roughly 40% of "out-of-school borrowers… defaulted or delayed their payments."[98] In the final weeks of the Obama administration, the Education Department confessed to a "coding error" that vastly understated the defaults. More than half of students "have either defaulted, sought forbearance or enrolled in income-based repayment plans, which are causing many borrowers who are only making minimum payments to owe more debt due to accrued interest," the *Wall Street Journal* noted.[99]

Student debt helped Joe Biden win the 2020 presidential election. By 2020, federal student debt had reached almost $2 trillion — a fivefold increase since 2004[100] — owed by 46 million people. Biden promised to wipe out the student debt of anyone earning less than $125,000 a year who had attended a public university. Biden also promised to forgive at least $10,000 for every debtor. His promises enraptured zealots who portrayed every ex-student as an oppressed victim who should have all debts canceled. By 2022, the average student debt was $37,014.[101]

On August 24, 2022, Biden invoked an obscure provision in the post-9/11 Heroes Act to justify hundreds of billions of dollars of handouts to people who had taken out federal college loans. The Heroes Act permits the Education Department "to waive or modify student loan payments in times of national emergency" for members of the Armed Services during the War on Terror. Biden had previously admitted that the law would not justify blanket forgiveness of college loans, but he and his advisors decided to force Americans to pay any price for Democratic votes in the midterm congressional elections. The Department of Education justified Biden's decree as "a program of categorical debt cancellation… for borrowers who have been financially harmed because of the COVID-19 pandemic." When Congress enacted the 2003 law, it did not consider "working from home" as a sufficient hardship to absolve citizens' debts to the government. Former Education Department lawyer Hans Bader estimated that the total cost of Biden's student loan write-offs could exceed a trillion dollars.[102] Former Treasury Secretary Larry Summers objected: "Every dollar spent on student loan relief is a dollar that could have gone to support those who don't get the opportunity to go to college."[103] *Washington Post* columnist Catherine Rampell observed:

> Distributing debt forgiveness to Wall Streeters, Big Law associates and other white-collar professionals is a less equitable use of taxpayer dollars than giving that money to, say, the non-college-educated custodians who clean their bathrooms.[104]

Former Office of Management and Budget Director David Stockman observed: "Student debt is overwhelmingly an investment in professional credentialization that should never have been an obligation of the taxpayers in the first place."[105]

A few weeks after justifying loan forgiveness due to the COVID emergency, Biden told *60 Minutes* that "the pandemic is over." In October 2022, Biden declared that Congress had passed legislation to approve his student loan bailout: "I got it passed by a vote or two."[106]

Biden's student loan forgiveness decree skewed the 2022 midterm elections. Hopes for sweeping Republican victories were shattered by the 28% advantage that voters in the 18–29 age group delivered to Democratic candidates. Two days after the election, Biden tweeted, "I want to thank the young people of this nation" who voted for "student debt relief."[107]

But while the votes that 20- and 30-somethings delivered were irrevocable, Biden's student debt relief was contingent on federal court approval. Two days after the election, Federal Judge Mark Pittman struck down the bailout as an unconstitutional decree: "In this country, we are not ruled by an all-powerful executive with a pen and a phone. Instead, we are ruled by a Constitution that provides for three distinct and independent branches of government." Four days later, a federal appeals court in St. Louis unanimously voted to impose a nationwide "injunction considering the irreversible impact the Secretary's debt forgiveness action would have" on "Americans who pay taxes to finance the government." The Biden administration responded by closing the window for individuals to apply for student loan forgiveness. Twenty-six million applications had already been received, but their fate was in legal limbo.

Biden may have delayed the announcement of the student loan bailout so that it would not be overturned before the midterm elections. Some liberal activists believed Biden intentionally swindled young voters with a bait-and-switch scheme. Briahna Joy Gray, who was the press secretary for Bernie Sanders's 2020 presidential campaign, declared that the Biden administration "used the promise of student debt cancellation to induce young voter turnout — knowing it wasn't going anywhere [because] they relied on faulty legal authority. Hard to convince me the Biden admin didn't do this intentionally." Judicial Watch's Tom Fitton tweeted: "Was Biden's unlawful student debt scheme election interference?"

On June 30, 2023, the Supreme Court ruled as expected, voting 6 to 3 to nullify Biden's handout as an illegal power grab. When a reporter asked Biden about the decision later that day, Biden angrily retorted: "I didn't give any false hope!" But *Washington Post* columnist Rampell noted that Biden's action had caused "additional financial distress" for the borrowers who counted on his promises.[108] The Biden administration responded to the Court's decision by rushing to launch other initiatives to forgive as many billions of dollars of student loans as possible, regardless of legality.

Fairy Godmothers Bestowing Freedom

Subsidies have transmogrified into badges of freedom. On April 28, 2022, the Biden administration announced $33 billion in subsidies for the government of Ukraine. The White House Fact Sheet stated that the aid includes money for Ukrainian "journalists and independent media to defend freedom of expression."[109] The independence of Ukrainian journalists would be assured because U.S. government officials retained the receipt for their purchase. The State Department, the National Endowment for Democracy, and other agencies have long been avidly subsidizing "independent media" in foreign nations, assuring an "amen chorus" for U.S. intervention in their nations. The absurdity of the U.S. government financing "independent media" failed to register inside the Beltway.

The same "fairy godmother" notion of political power prevails among champions of handouts for U.S. media. Victor Pickard, a University of Pennsylvania professor, writing in the *Columbia Journalism Review*, called for hefty federal subsidies to assure that public media is "politically and economically independent" and reaches its "full democratic potential."[110] The notion that subsidies would obliterate media independence never arose in the article. Instead, the politicians and officials who controlled media purse strings were presumed benevolent guardians beyond corruption.

Media handouts are also favored by Professor Joshua Darr, writing for Harvard University's Nieman Lab.[111] After noting that 66% of Americans oppose federal subsidies for local news, Darr suggests that "it may be helpful to keep local news subsidies as one of many 'submerged' government policies that people benefit from without realizing it, if those policies can be big and bold enough to meet the moment." Americans' trust in the media collapsed in part because of perceived political bias. And the solution is for politicians to secretly bankroll the media? Darr did not mention the precursor for such subsidies — CIA's Operation Mockingbird, which lavished secret payments on American journalists for 30 years until it was exposed in the mid-1970s.

Conclusion: Subsidies as Damoclean Swords

As long as politicians can profit from giving away anything and everything, government programs will frantically scatter manna far and wide. Today's politicians redistribute to anyone they please — even sports stadium owners, who have received more than $4 billion in subsidies in recent decades.[112] Much of President George W. Bush's personal fortune stemmed from the subsidies and eminent domain seizures of private property tied to the stadium for the Texas Rangers baseball team he co-owned.[113]

Subsidy schemes often presume government agencies are damn near omniscient. But bureaucrats don't count what politicians don't want to know. In the same way that the Pentagon perennially denies the civilian death toll from bombing foreign nations, so federal agencies disregard the collateral damage from domestic interventions. Because the government doesn't pay the price of its mistakes, it has scant incentive to get the best information to guide its policies.

Politicians start by claiming to be generous but soon dictate terms and demand submission. Few politicians can resist the temptation to exploit "the mighty muscle of the federal government." Many government subsidy programs are worse than Faustian bargains. At least the Devil specified what Faust would get in return for his soul. Politicians perennially portray their handouts as "something for nothing." Then, when they decide to constrain or subjugate recipients, "nothing" becomes more expensive than what many people would have willingly paid.

Subsidies expand political power by determining who gets what. Speaking to an AFL-CIO convention in 2022, President Biden shouted: "I don't want to hear any more of these lies about reckless spending. We're changing people's lives!"[114] "Changing" routinely means controlling — but only for their own good, or at least for the re-election of their benefactors.

Subsidies mean politicians commandeering citizens' property to buy their submission. Each new benefit program extends political control over both the recipients and anyone forced to finance the handouts. Politicians cannot give one person a right to put his hand in other people's pockets without decreasing every person's right to their own paycheck. French philosopher Bertrand de Jouvenel wrote: "Redistribution is in effect far less a redistribution of free income from the richer to the poorer, than a redistribution of power from the individual to the state."[115]

Handouts provide cheap halos for politicians. The more aid government distributes, the more benevolent it appears. With enough largesse, political abuses will usually be forgiven — or, more accurately, ignored. Anything that sways people to view politicians as saviors imperils freedom. The more people who depend on Washington, the more unstoppable politicians become. For scores of millions of voters, the biggest peril from Washington is that politicians may curtail their handouts. The old saying "Don't bite the hand that feeds you" takes on new meaning when a hundred million Americans are government-fed.

The more subsidies government gives, the more votes politicians can buy. More than 150 years ago, British philosopher John Stuart Mill warned that "representative institutions... may be a mere instrument of tyranny" if citizens "sell [votes] for money."[116] Mill's observation was not controversial at the time but would be scandalous nowadays in progressive circles. But as economist Friedrich Hayek noted: "The conception that government should be guided by majority opinion makes sense only if that opinion is independent of government."[117]

But that stipulation was forgotten long before Hayek won the Nobel Prize in 1974. A century ago, H.L. Mencken quipped that "every election is a sort of advanced auction of stolen goods." Since Mencken's time, politicians have become more shameless. In 2020, Raphael Warnock, a Democratic candidate for U.S. Senate, distributed flyers declaring to Georgia voters: "Want a $2,000 Check? Vote Warnock."[118] When President-elect Joe Biden visited Georgia days before a run-off election, he assured people that if they voted Democratic, "those $2,000 [COVID 'stimulus'] checks will go out the door, restoring hope and decency and honor for so many people who are struggling right now... The power is literally in your hands."[119] Biden and Warnock presumed that politicians are entitled to spend unlimited tax dollars to snare power over taxpayers. The $2,000 bribe helped Warnock win a tight race, conferring control of the Senate on Biden and his Democratic allies, opening the floodgates to trillions of dollars of additional federal spending.

Politicians cannot undermine self-reliance without subverting self-government. The more politicians promise to some people, the more they entitle themselves to seize from everyone else. This has been a recipe for political ruin for thousands of years. Plutarch explained the downfall of the Roman Republic: "The people were at that time extremely corrupted by the gifts of those who sought office, and most made a constant trade of selling their voices."[120] French political philosopher Montesquieu warned in 1748:

> It is impossible to make great largesses to the people without great extortion... The greater the advantages citizens seem to derive from their liberty [of voting], the nearer they approach towards the critical moment of losing it.

Soaring government spending can become a Sword of Damocles over the entire political system. As economist Warren Nutter warned: "The more that government takes, the less likely that democracy will survive."[121] But the specter of collapse is doing nothing to deter contemporary political looting.

9. "Dominate. Intimidate. Control."

"Find out just what people will submit to, and you have found out the exact amount of injustice and wrong which will be imposed upon them."
– Frederick Douglass, 1857

Nothing has changed more radically for average Americans since 9/11 than air travel. The Transportation Security Administration, with checkpoint gauntlets at 400+ airports, is one of the most intrusive and inept federal agencies. For 20 years, every TSA boondoggle has been shielded by a bodyguard of bureaucratic lies.

The Supreme Court recognized in 1999 that the "'constitutional right to travel from one State to another' is firmly embedded in our jurisprudence." But a few years later, after the feds failed to stop hijackers, TSA commandeered sweeping power over anyone who bought an airline ticket. TSA prohibited anyone (except for wealthy Learjet passengers) from flying without undergoing a search by federal agents.

TSA then claimed that Americans effectively waived any right to privacy by "voluntarily" submitting to searches. A federal appeals court noted in 2019 that the Justice Department "contends that consent by passengers cancels the Fourth Amendment's effect," as far as prohibiting warrantless unreasonable searches.[1]

On its homepage, TSA pledges "to ensure freedom of movement for people and commerce." It fulfills this mission by badgering and accosting anyone who balks at TSA commands or intrusions. One of TSA's early mottoes was "Dominate. Intimidate. Control."[2] TSA's attitude towards the American public has never improved.

Keystone Kops on Amphetamines

The federal takeover of airport security was a knee-jerk reflex after 9/11. The Federal Aviation Administration (FAA) had left cockpits defenseless by prohibiting pilots from carrying pistols to stop hijackers. But that detail was quickly brushed aside in the stampede to vanquish all threats by unleashing federal agents on hapless travelers.

Transportation Secretary Norman Mineta pledged that TSA would "hire the best and the brightest" as screeners. To speed hiring, TSA minimized testing of its new screeners, many of whom proved comically inept. After

TSA used pizza box ads to recruit its workforce,[3] irate passengers groused that TSA stood for "Too Stupid for Arby's."

In New York, TSA job applicants were asked about smuggled bombs:

> Why is it important to screen bags for IEDs [Improvised Explosive Devices]?
>
>> a. The IED batteries could leak and damage other passenger bags.
>>
>> b. The wires in the IED could cause a short to the aircraft wires.
>>
>> c. IEDs can cause loss of lives, property, and aircraft.
>>
>> d. The ticking timer could worry other passengers.[4]

TSA did not reveal how many would-be screeners chose a wrong answer.

TSA spent billions of dollars buying unreliable minivan-sized machines and hand-held detectors to search for bombs in checked luggage. The new gizmos emitted false positives for almost a third of all luggage, which was then hand-searched by TSA screeners. Those forays spawned a nationwide looting epidemic.[5] TSA paid $1.5 million to 15,000 passengers who filed claims blaming TSA for stolen or damaged baggage.

TSA agents continued pilfering to their hearts' content, and more than 500 were eventually fired for robbing travelers. An Orlando TSA screener confessed to stealing 80 laptops from travelers, and another TSA agent in Florida filched $50,000 from travelers in six months and was only arrested after being caught with a passenger's iPad in his pants. TSA's image was not burnished by an ABC News report on "The Top 20 Airports for TSA Theft."

In 2003, TSA screeners failed to detect half of the weapons and fake bombs smuggled past them — even though testers were ordered not to "artfully conceal" their contraband. In 2005, the Department of Homeland Security (DHS) Inspector General told Congress that "the ability of TSA screeners to stop prohibited items... fared no better than the performance of screeners prior to Sept. 11, 2001."[6]

Regardless of its screeners' plundering and blundering, TSA demanded impeccable behavior from other Americans. In 2002, TSA covertly launched a program to punish bad attitudes. In a *Federal Register* notice that 99.9% of Americans never saw, TSA decreed that travelers could be fined or arrested if anything they said or did caused a screener to "turn away from his or her normal duties to deal with the disruptive individual."[7] Practically any comment or behavior that made a TSA agent "turn" could be a federal offense. Thousands of Americans were hit with fines of up to $1,500, weeks after their flights, for perturbing TSA employees.[8]

The Kosher Meal Magic Bullet

Prior to the 9/11 attacks, the FAA operated a Computer Assisted Passenger Prescreening System (CAPPS) which triggered alarms on 9 of the 19 hijackers on 9/11.[9] However, the FAA failed to notify airlines of the dangerous travelers despite numerous warnings inside the FBI and CIA of a potential hijacking conspiracy in the works.[10]

The feds' gross negligence entitled them to seize far more personal data. TSA commenced building CAPPS II, a database with more than a hundred million names, credit card numbers, addresses, and other details for every airline passenger, including everyone who requested a kosher meal, among many other terrorist warning signs. TSA sought to search every traveler's medical records but backed away after a public backlash.

CAPPS II aspired to snare any traveler wanted for any federal offense. Up to 2% of airline passengers "will be prohibited from boarding... and face police questioning and may be arrested," the *Washington Post* reported. Detaining 40,000 passengers each day could have required building new detention cells at scores of airports.

TSA violated federal privacy law by swaying JetBlue to secretly deliver 1.5 million passengers' records to an Army contractor for testing a CAPPS II prototype. After that switcheroo was exposed, TSA promised to hire a "privacy officer" and compel all TSA employees to participate in a "Respecting Privacy, Preserving Freedoms" program. The Electronic Frontier Foundation warned that CAPPS II could produce "the worst of both worlds: no real security against dedicated attackers, but a massive social surveillance system which will affect every American." TSA abandoned CAPPS II even before it was launched. The *New York Times* reported that the system was doomed because it was "expanded... to serve broader police purposes."[11]

Shortly after TSA capitulated on tracking meal preferences, a new twin peril was detected. After a Russian airliner was blown up by Chechen terrorists, TSA asserted (based on little or no evidence) that females had hidden bombs in their bras to destroy the plane. Accordingly, TSA screeners began groping busty American women's bosoms. The *New York Times* reported: "In dozens of interviews, women across the country say they were humiliated by the searches, often done in view of other passengers."[12] TSA relented, instructing screeners "not to touch women between their breasts unless they set off a hand-held metal detector in the chest area," the *Washington Post* reported. If only TSA policymakers had thought of that earlier! The Breast Bomb Brouhaha was a harbinger of far more aggressive TSA pat-downs.

Congress deluged TSA with money for one bogus anti-terrorist panacea after another. An Inspector General report slammed TSA for spending billions of dollars on equipment which was "ineffective, unreliable or too expensive to operate." Rep. Chris Cox (R-CA), chairman of the Homeland Security Committee, justified the profligacy: "After 9/11, we had to show how committed we were [to fighting terrorism] by spending hugely greater amounts of money than ever before, as rapidly as possible." Bonfires of tax dollars supposedly warded off all evil.

In 2006, TSA screeners at Newark Liberty International Airport missed 90% of concealed bombs and guns in a security test.[13] One airport security official confessed: "We just totally missed everything." In 2007, TSA screeners at Los Angeles International Airport failed to detect fake bombs 75% of the time.[14] TSA screeners belly-flopped even though TSA headquarters gave them advance warning and a physical description of one of the undercover testers.[15]

Nudie Scanners and Punitive Pat-Downs

In 2008, TSA began purchasing Whole Body Scanners that used radiation to take 360-degree unclad photos of every passenger. After TSA deployed the scanners at a few airports, the ACLU and 23 privacy groups formally protested that the new technology resulted in "unconstitutionally intrusive searches that are disproportionate and for which the TSA lacks any suspicion of wrongdoing."[16] TSA ignored the complaint.

On Christmas Day 2009, a young Nigerian man, Umar Farouk Abdulmutallab, sought to detonate 80 grams of plastic explosives in his underwear on a flight from Amsterdam to Detroit. His bomb misfired, and he was quickly subdued by vigilant Dutch passengers. Farouk boarded the plane thanks to multiple U.S. government pratfalls. His name was on a U.S. terrorist watchlist, and his father (one of the wealthiest men in Nigeria) had warned the U.S. embassy in Lagos that his son was "likely involved with terrorist groups."[17] He arrived in Amsterdam from Yemen with no baggage and paid cash for an expensive ticket. The State Department granted Farouk a visa even though he had lied about his connections to Islamic terrorists on a previous visa denial. [18] The only warning sign missing was a bright green "Al Qaeda Suicide Bomber" sash. President Obama interrupted his Hawaii vacation to condemn federal agencies' "mix of human and systemic failures that contributed to this potential catastrophic breach of security."

The Christmas bombing threat provided the pretext to deploy untested Whole Body Scanners everywhere. Rep. Collin Peterson (D-MN), a former airline pilot, slammed TSA's rush to deploy the new scanners: "I think a lot of what goes on at the airport is for show. It's almost like we're harassing passengers so they feel better." [19]

Many travelers objected to all-seeing scanners that could add birthday suit photos to federal dossiers. The Justice Department insisted that the new scanners are "designed to respect individual sensibilities regarding privacy, modesty and personal autonomy to the maximum extent possible." However, the scanners revealed hernias, implants, and whether guys were circumcised or potential porn stars. A former TSA agent revealed: "Women who'd had mastectomies were easy to discern — their chests showed up on our screens as dull, pixelated regions." [20] The Electronic Privacy Information Center labeled the scanners "one of the most sweeping, most invasive and most unaccountable suspicionless searches of American travelers in history."

TSA swore the scanners were safe, but a University of California biophysicist warned that their "effective dose [of radiation] could be 45 times as high as the TSA has estimated, equivalent to about 10% of a single chest X-ray." A ProPublica and PBS *NewsHour* investigation revealed that scanners could cause up to a hundred cancer cases per year among travelers. Citing health and privacy concerns, the European Union banned all body scanners that radiated travelers. The *New York Times* noted: "Most of what is known of the risks of radiation has been extrapolated from disease trends in Japan after World War II," when atomic bombs were dropped on Hiroshima and Nagasaki. [21] TSA neglected to decorate the scanners with smiley faces atop mushroom clouds.

Many travelers balked at passing through the new scanners, preferring to step through the magnetometers that TSA used since 2002. But anyone who "opted out" from the Whole Body Scanners received "enhanced pat-downs" — a term reminiscent of the Bush administration's "enhanced interrogation" euphemism for torture. As *USA Today* explained: "The new searches…

require screeners to touch passengers' breasts and genitals."[22] ABC News producer Carolyn Durand complained: "The [TSA] woman who checked me reached her hands inside my underwear and felt her way around. It was basically worse than going to the gynecologist." Cynics suggested that TSA now stood for "Total Sexual Assault."

After protests erupted, the media rushed to vindicate TSA. The *Los Angeles Times* weighed in with an editorial headlined: "Shut Up and Be Scanned."[23] *Washington Post* columnist Ruth Marcus, a prominent defender of Bush administration torture policies, derided the uproar as "overblown and immature" in a column headlined: "Grow up, America."[24] One columnist labeled the new procedures "freedom fondles" — as if citizens should be proud to be squeezed for the War on Terror.

TSA gave members of Congress "get out of grope free" cards to avoid checkpoint hassles. In 2011, Rep. James Clyburn (D-SC), then the number two-ranking Democrat in the House of Representatives, complained: "We've had some incidents where TSA authorities think that congresspeople should be treated like everybody else."[25] Clyburn warned: "I think we need to take a hard look at exactly how the TSA interact with members of Congress."[26] The ACLU complained that TSA was creating an "Air Travel Caste System" with "vast whitelists of individuals — including members of Congress, federal judges, and millions of Department of Defense personnel — who are automatically eligible for expedited screening at airports."[27]

The Whole Body Scanners were so inept that they could not distinguish human flesh from C-4 explosives. A New York engineer, Jonathan Corbett, posted a video on YouTube demonstrating how easy it was to smuggle potentially explosive contraband through the scanners. Rep. John L. Mica (R-FL), chairman of the House Transportation and Infrastructure Committee, conceded: "If we could reveal the [secret] failure rate [of the scanners], the American public would be outraged."[28] Former TSA agent Jason Harrington lamented in 2014: "The TSA was compelling toddlers, pregnant women, cancer survivors — everyone — to stand inside radiation-emitting machines that didn't work."

Intrusive scanners were supplemented by explosive detection tests that were so unreliable that glycerin in hand sanitizer triggered endless false alarms. TSA explosive tests never exposed anyone who intended to detonate a device on an airplane. But TSA screeners treated anyone who triggered a false explosive alarm to a far more aggressive pelvic-jamming "pat-down" than the Pentagon was permitted to use on accused enemy combatants at Guantanamo Bay.[29] Unfortunately, American travelers had no right to go unmolested.

In June 2015, a secret Inspector General report leaked out, revealing that TSA agents failed to detect 95% of the weapons and mock bombs smuggled past them by testers. The report destroyed TSA's bluster on Whole Body Scanners. TSA's acting administrator was quickly forced from his job.[30] Sen. Ben Sasse (R-NE), lamented: "The publicly available facts are disturbing, but the classified details are even worse."[31] Senate Homeland Security Committee Chairman Ron Johnson (R-WI), after seeing confidential data, suggested that TSA require passengers to go through old-fashioned metal detectors after passing through Whole Body Scanners.

Rather than repenting, TSA administrators decided that it was finally time to get tough with travelers. In early 2017, TSA announced new pat-down procedures mandating "more intimate contact than before," according to a TSA spokesman. Screeners were previously required to use the back of their hand to search passengers' intimate areas; the new policy entitled agents to grab passengers' private parts with the front of their hands. The new search policies were so intrusive that TSA preemptively notified local police to disregard complaints alleging TSA sexual assaults.[32]

But turbocharging groping failed to make flying safer. In June 2017, a covert testing team again succeeded 95% of the time in smuggling weapons and mock bombs past airport screeners in Minneapolis. In November 2017, the DHS Inspector General notified Congress that TSA screeners and equipment failed to detect mock threats in 80% in recent tests. TSA ignored the reports and the criticism and continued — accosting travelers. Massive airport travel delays spurred scoffing that TSA stood for "Thousands Standing Around."

Menstrual Malefactors

Menstruating women are frequently targeted for "enhanced pat-downs" after Whole Body Scanners detect sanitary napkins. In 2018, the ACLU charged that TSA agents took Zainab Merchant, a Harvard grad student and mother of three, to a private room and compelled her to pull down her pants and underwear and show her bloody menstrual pad after an enhanced pat-down. Merchant noted in a *Washington Post* op-ed that the TSA agents "hid their badges when I asked for their names."[33]

On Mother's Day 2019, Rhonda Mengert was flying out of Tulsa, Oklahoma, after visiting her son and grandchildren. Mengert notified TSA agents before passing through screening that she had a metal hip implant that often caused false alerts. After a pat-down detected a feminine hygiene product, she was marched to a private room by two female TSA agents. "I was told I needed to pull my pants and my underwear down to my knees and remove the item and show it to them for inspection," Mengert stated in a subsequent television interview.

After complying, she sued TSA for violating her constitutional rights. Justice Department lawyers scoffed that Mengert's "allegations amount to no more than indignities, annoyances, and *petty oppressions*... The intrusion on her privacy was no more severe than what could be routinely experienced in a women's locker room" (emphasis added).[34] But who entitled TSA agents to inflict "petty oppressions"? DOJ also pointed out that "nearly every woman in the country has worn many times in her life the same [menstrual pad] Plaintiff was wearing." Almost everyone wears underwear, but that doesn't mean that government agents have a right to stick their noses in every crotch. The Justice Department's attempt to absolve TSA's stripper squad by citing the "women's locker room" epitomized its contempt for consent in daily life. Perhaps those lawyers believed that Mengert had nothing to complain about as long as TSA agents did not strap her naked to a baggage cart and drive up and down the airport corridors with sirens blaring. Rather than admitting it blundered and settling Mengert's lawsuit, TSA and the Justice Department instead converted the abuse into a legal precedent to search any underwear, any time, and on any pretext.

TSA encourages passengers who feel abused to file customer complaints, but their grievances vanish into a bureaucratic black hole. TSA effectively exempted itself from the Freedom of Information Act (FOIA), which requires agencies to respond within 20 business days to requests for information. TSA delayed four years before releasing copies of passenger complaints about TSA to ProPublica investigators.[35] An Inspector General report slammed TSA for "'unjustifiable and inconsistent and arbitrary' use of the 'sensitive security information label'" to cover up its failures. Nitpickers scoffed that TSA stands for "Tactics to Suppress Accountability."

But TSA did not censor Twitter, where many aggrieved female travelers vent their rage:

- Emily White complained on August 26, 2019: "I was sexually assaulted by the @TSA on August 1 LaGuardia Airport's Marine Terminal at around 11:50 AM… If you don't want your vagina paddled multiple times, I recommend avoiding that crew."

- Liz Groeschen tweeted on July 10, 2019, that she almost missed her flight at JFK Airport thanks to "an invasive hand pat down that should be relabeled 'tsa hands in your vagina' to be completely accurate" and which was "an absolute embarrassment to America."

- Marina Modela complained on July 9, 2019: "At #seatac [Seattle Airport], 2 agents groped my labia in the name of 'security' and falsely accused me of having something in my pants. How does groping female genitalia promote security, especially when your agents are too incompetent to know the difference between labia and bombs?"

Women can get put on a secret TSA watchlist known as the "95 List" merely for pushing a TSA's screener's hands away from her breasts. TSA justified that watchlist because TSA screeners were allegedly assaulted 34 times in 2017. However, TSA's press office refused to release a list or any details of those assaults, including whether any alleged assailants were arrested. TSA also refused to disclose how it defined an "assault" on a TSA screener.[36]

TSA's official watchlist definition of *troublemaker* goes far beyond hooligans who slug screeners. Did someone "loiter" near a TSA checkpoint? Bingo. Any behavior which is "offensive [to the TSA] and without legal justification" can get a person secretly listed, according to a confidential TSA memo. TSA assistant administrator Darby LaJoye told Congress that any traveler who demonstrated "concerning" behavior can be secretly placed on the list.[37] "Concerning behavior" is vague enough to add 10,000 chumps a day to the watchlist.

TSA can put someone on the "95 list" solely because they are considered "publicly notorious." (Did getting publicly denounced by TSA chief John Pistole in 2014 for "maligning" and "disparaging" TSA agents qualify me for the list?[38]) The Brennan Center for Justice warned that TSA could add "pretty much anyone with even a modest public profile, such as journalists or activists," to the "95 list."[39] What happens to travelers put on that list? It's a secret. ACLU attorney Hugh Handeyside warned that the secret warning list permits TSA to "blacklist people arbitrarily and essentially punish them for asserting their rights."

Mindless Mind Readers

TSA has spent more than a billion dollars for thousands of TSA "Behavior Detection Officers," or BDOs, to roam America's airport terminals looking for "micro expressions" signaling trouble. BDOs also do "chat-downs" to select lucky travelers for further investigation and possible arrest.

TSA believes its elite force can detect dangerous travelers by a one-twentieth-of-a-second eyebrow rise. The *Washington Post* reported in 2007 that BDO teams

> are looking for people traveling without bags, sweating and constantly checking out every person passing by, especially those with badges and guns. People who avoid eye contact or veer away when police approach also draw their attention.

Those tripwires snared plenty of introverts and aging hippies.

In 2011, CNN revealed other BDO warning signs including yawning, gazing down, throat clearing, "exaggerated or repetitive grooming gestures," staring, whistling, or "wearing improper attire for location" (unlike the TSA agents' faux-military epaulets). TSA also targets anyone who seems "very arrogant and expresses contempt against airport passenger procedures." TSA is the only security agency in the world that believes would-be terrorists precede their attacks by taunting guards.

"Equal opportunity" is not in the BDO playbook. More than 30 TSA agents complained that the BDO program at Boston's Logan Airport was "a magnet for racial profiling, targeting not only Middle Easterners but also Blacks, Hispanics and other minorities," the *New York Times* reported.[40] Among the "terrorist" profiles TSA used: "Hispanics traveling to Miami or Blacks wearing baseball caps backward." TSA agents told the *Times* that the profiling occurred

> in response to pressure from managers to meet certain threshold numbers for referrals to the State Police, federal immigration officials or other agencies… The managers wanted to generate arrests so they could justify the program… Officers who made arrests were more likely to be promoted.[41]

The BDO squad at the Newark airport engaged in such blatant stereotyping that they were derided as "Mexican hunters" by other TSA agents.

GAO reported that TSA's mind readers were extremely subjective, with an 800% difference in their rates of referring suspicious passengers to law enforcement at different airports.[42] The National Academy of Science warned that the "scientific support" was "nonexistent" to determine the "behavioral and physiological markers" to recognize "when individuals hold terrorist intent and beliefs."

BDOs referred more than 100,000 travelers for additional interrogation or arrest, but TSA could not "cite any examples of how its behavior detection activities have thwarted threats to the nation's civil aviation system," GAO reported. GAO concluded in 2017 that 98% of the studies on "indicators" of terrorist intent that TSA invoked to justify the program failed to provide "valid evidence" to support TSA's claims. Bizarrely, almost 80% of the "sources" TSA cited were "news or opinion pieces," all of which GAO dismissed as invalid (even my articles).

TSA vindicated itself by stressing that its BDO agents keep an eye out for "unusual exposed wires or electrical switches on a person" seeking to board a plane. TSA is set to nab terrorists who learn all they know from Road Runner cartoons featuring Wile E. Coyote struggling to assemble Acme Bomb Kits.

First-Class Stalkers

TSA spends $800 million per year on thousands of air marshals who fly incognito to deter hijackers. TSA initially required air marshals to prove they could fire pistols accurately — a helpful skill for combat in airline cabins. But the marksmanship test was dropped after most recruits failed.

Though air marshals have never stopped a hijacking, they still produce headlines. One air marshal was "convicted of abducting a female escort during a July 2006 layover in the Washington, D.C., area," one was convicted of bank fraud for attempting to cash an $11 million bogus check, and one was sent to prison after soliciting someone to kill his ex-wife.[43] An air marshal was busted for taking up-skirt photos of women,[44] and numerous air marshals lost their guns on flights and in airports. House Oversight Committee Chairman Jason Chaffetz (R-UT) complained in 2015 about air marshals "disguising themselves as pornography producers, hiring prostitutes and using government-issued phones and other assets to film sexual encounters."[45] Rep. John Duncan (R-TN) groused that the air marshal program "has come to be a symbol of everything that's wrong with the DHS, when 4,000 bored cops fly around the country First Class, committing more crimes than they stop."[46]

In 2018, TSA ramped up a secret air marshal program that spied on or stalked thousands of Americans. TSA's Quiet Skies surveillance program, first revealed by the *Boston Globe*, hounds travelers on the flimsiest of pretexts. If you fall asleep or use the bathroom during your next flight, those incriminating facts could be added to your federal dossier. Likewise, if you look at noisy children seated nearby with a "cold, penetrating stare," that may be included on your permanent record. If you fidget, sweat, or have "strong body odor" — BOOM! the feds are onto you. Air marshals also zero in on "facial flushing," "gripping/white knuckling bags," "face touching," or "wide open, staring eyes," and "rapid eye blinking."[47]

What does it take to become a Quiet Skies target? "The criteria for surveillance appear fluid. Internal agency emails show some confusion about the program's parameters and implementation," the *Globe* noted. Anyone who recently traveled to Turkey was put on the list.[48] Passengers become suspects if they change clothes or shave while in the airport.

After a person makes the Quiet Skies list, a TSA air marshal team is placed on their next flight. Marshals receive "a file containing a photo and basic information" and carefully note whether the suspect's "appearance was different from information provided" — such as whether they have "gained weight," are "balding" or "graying," or have a beard or "visible tattoos." Marshals record and report any "significant derogatory information" on suspects.[49]

TSA air marshals follow targeted travelers, even writing down their license plate numbers. Marshals ascertain whether a "subject was abnormally aware of surroundings." Does that include noticing the federal agent stalking them in the parking lot? Dozens of air marshals told the *Globe* the program was "a waste of time and resources."[50] A TSA spokesman claimed that Quiet Skies had "robust oversight," but the agency had denied its existence until the *Globe* exposé — even keeping it secret from Congress. Sen. Edward Markey (D-MA) blasted the program as "the very definition of 'Big Brother.'"[51]

TSA claims that it places air marshals on flights which are considered high-risk for hijacking or terrorist attacks. But in 2021, insiders revealed that 900 air marshals — almost half the active total — were designated to stand by for flights taken by members of Congress. One veteran air marshal groused that the air marshal D.C. field office "was almost exclusively dedicated to VIP services for Congress."[52] The Air Marshal National Council formally complained that TSA had turned their program into a "concierge service" and "babysitting" for members of Congress, who exploited the program even for personal flights with no tie to official business.[53]

Absolute Power for Absolute Safety?

TSA does nothing to protect Americans against its own employees. The former TSA chief security director at the Jacksonville International Airport declared: "There is a culture at headquarters that we do what we want, no one holds us accountable to the rules."[54] The *New York Times* noted in 2016 that many TSA employees "had experienced a culture of fear and intimidation, where senior managers seemed more interested in targeting those who disclosed the agency's shortcomings rather than fixing problems." TSA employees consistently report the lowest job satisfaction of any federal agency.

TSA abuses proliferated because courts permit TSA to pretend that "it's not an assault when federal agents do it." Airline captain James Linlor sued after a TSA brutalizing in 2016 at Dulles International Airport that left him requiring surgery. A TSA video showed a TSA agent concluding a pat-down with a karate chop to Linlor's testicles. Linlor claimed that his rights were violated by an unconstitutional and unreasonable search. TSA asked a judge to dismiss Linlor's case because, instead of suing, he could have phoned in his complaint to the TSA Contact Center. TSA also insisted that its screener deserved legal immunity even if he did pummel Linlor's private parts. In a 2017 court hearing, a Justice Department lawyer stressed that there's no law "establishing a specific degree of permissible intrusiveness of a security screening pat down." Federal Judge James Cacheris scoffed at the government's "oratorical calisthenics" and rejected the inference that "a reasonable federal officer would be surprised to learn that gratuitously striking an individual in the groin while searching them violates the Fourth Amendment." (Linlor's case was later dismissed on procedural grounds.)

Federal courts have permitted TSA agents to lie and vilify travelers to get them wrongfully arrested. Architect Roger Vanderklok was selected for secondary screening at Philadelphia International Airport after a scan revealed a plastic tube with a heart monitoring watch he used while running marathons. Vanderklok believed a TSA agent was rude and abusive, and said he would file a complaint. A TSA supervisor retaliated by falsely claiming to police that Vanderklok made a bomb threat. Vanderklok was locked up overnight until his wife made a hefty deposit on his $40,000 bail. He went to trial a few months later for "threatening to place a bomb and making terroristic threats."[55] TSA's official blog stressed that Vanderklok was detected transporting "an unidentified organic mass" that raised suspicions of explosives.[56] The blog neglected to mention that the "organic mass" was Power Bars that Vanderklok intended to chomp during a race the following day. The TSA supervisor's testimony at Vanderklok's trial was so brazenly false (contradicted by TSA's video) that the judge dismissed the charges on the spot.

Vanderklok sued numerous TSA and other officials, claiming malicious prosecution, false arrest, and a violation of his freedom of speech. The U.S. government sought to torpedo the lawsuit by claiming sovereign immunity, but a few charges were permitted to move forward. In 2017, a federal appeals court dismissed Vanderklok's lawsuit because it could not proceed without implicating "the government's whole response to the Sept. 11 attacks, thus of necessity requiring an inquiry into sensitive issues of national security." Would pulling the curtain back on TSA Wizards of Oz obliterate any lingering faith in the War on Terror?

But federal judges are starting to crack TSA's inviolable legal shield. In June 2019, Michele Leuthauser was flying out of Las Vegas-McCarran International Airport when a Whole Body Scanner issued a false alert. She was wearing yoga pants that practically guaranteed that she was hiding nothing on that part of her body. Regardless, she was taken to a private room for a pelvic workover. A federal appeals court ruling noted, summarizing Leuthauser's allegations, that behind closed doors, a TSA officer

> conducted a pat-down during which [the officer] slid her hands along the inside of Leuthauser's thighs, touched her vulva and clitoris with the front of her fingers, and digitally penetrated her vagina. She asserts that she suffered symptoms of emotional distress, including shortness of breath, uncontrollable shaking, and nausea.[57]

After she sued TSA, the agency claimed it could not be sued regardless of what happened to Leuthauser. Justice Department lawyer Daniel Aguilar told a federal appeals court: "If there is any ambiguity that can support sovereign immunity, you must adopt it."[58] Judge Joseph Bataillon asked: "Does the general public have any remedy against a TSA agent who decides to grope?" Aguilar hemmed and hawed and said there might be cases where the feds refused to provide total immunity to a TSA screener on the job (excepting thieves), but that hasn't happened in TSA history. In June 2023, the appeals court rejected the TSA claims and sent the case back for trial at federal district court.

In April 2023, a different federal appeals court ruled that TSA could be sued after a TSA screener allegedly forced Erin Osmon, who was traveling out of the Asheville, North Carolina, airport, to spread her legs very wide and then "fondled her genitals twice."[59] The Justice Department sought to claim immunity because TSA agents were not "law enforcement officers" conducting a search. But TSA agents were applying federal law as they searched passengers at checkpoints. Federal Judge Stephanie Thacker was mystified by the denial that TSA agents conducted searches: "What are they doing? Just groping people?"[60]

COVID Conniptions

When the COVID pandemic broke out, TSA snared new power over travelers. In early 2021, TSA announced that it would fine travelers up to $1,500 for failing to wear a proper facemask or wearing a facemask improperly. TSA mandated: "Masks should fit snugly but comfortably against the side of the face." Would TSA checkpoint screeners run their fingers between the mask and the face to assure sufficient tightness like TSA agents test panty liners? TSA also prohibited "masks that do not fit properly (large gaps, too loose or too tight)." Was this a Goldilocks and the three bears' porridge "maybe so, maybe not" standard?

TSA agents were COVID propellants. Jay Brainard, TSA's top official in Kansas, publicly complained in June 2020 that TSA agents "became Typhoid Marys and contributed to the spread of that virus because TSA senior leadership did not make sure [screeners] were adequately protected."[61] Early in the pandemic, a top TSA official testified to Congress that TSA agents regularly changed their nitrile gloves after patting down passengers. However, several TSA federal security directors told National Public Radio that the policy had been that "gloves are changed between pat-downs only in the specific situation when an alarm is set off." After NPR's report, TSA announced that "passengers would now be allowed to request TSA screeners change their gloves." But would travelers get fined for a bad attitude for suggesting that TSA agents change their gloves? Any gynecologist who followed the same policy on changing gloves — only if patients requested a fresh pair — would have his license revoked.

After 20 years of TSA agents browbeating Americans to "show your papers," the Biden administration radically streamlined airport procedures. TSA permitted almost a thousand illegal aliens to board domestic flights in 2022 merely by showing as documentation the arrest warrants they received from the Department of Homeland Security. At a Senate hearing in July 2022, TSA chief David Pekoske insisted that federal agents had "verified" the personal information when they issued the arrest warrants. Sen. Josh Hawley (R-MO) complained:

> The point of an arrest warrant is for police to actively seek out and apprehend criminals… This dystopian inversion exceeds the point of absurdity where radical open-border policies attempt to accomplish the very opposite of DHS's core mission: apprehending those who cross our borders illegally.

In March 2023, senators introduced legislation to block the TSA policy. Sen. Jim Risch (R-ID) complained: "If an Idahoan gets a speeding ticket, they can't use the ticket to board a plane, so why does the president seem to think an illegal immigrant's arrest warrant is a valid form of identification to board a plane?"[62]

Smile for Your Dossier

TSA is running a pilot program in which travelers stand in photo kiosks that compare their faces with a federal database of photos from passport applications, drivers' licenses, and other sources. The new airport regime could roll out nationwide later this year. The *Washington Post* warned that airport facial recognition systems are "America's biggest step yet to normalize treating our faces as data that can be stored, tracked and, inevitably, stolen" (as happened to DHS facial records in 2019).[63] TSA initially promised that the new program would be voluntary. But the *Washington Post* reported in July 2023 that TSA agents at Reagan Washington National Airport threatened long delays for any passenger who refused to be photographed, including U.S. Sen. Jeff Merkley (D-OR).[64] Merkley noted that TSA falsely claimed that there were signs at National Airport notifying people that the facial scans are optional.

"Trust us" is the TSA mantra for the new program. But TSA has not disclosed any "hard data about how often its system falsely identifies people, through incorrect positive or negative matches."[65] TSA will be relying on photo identification systems with misidentification rates up to 100 times higher for blacks and Hispanics.[66]

TSA is already partnering with the Customs and Border Patrol agency to compel any American entering or leaving the nation to submit to being photographed for their database. That Trump administration initiative is named "Biometric Entry/Exit" — a euphemism for "Nobody Leaves Without Uncle Sam's Permission." Since the program will rely on computer databases and facial scans instead of a Berlin Wall, there is nothing to fear. "Biometric Entry/Exit" sets a precedent for federal controls over Americans' movement inside the U.S.

TSA will be capitalizing on vast federal poaching of state and local records, as well as online records. The FBI is regularly tapping into databases with more than 600 million facial photos. Mike Maharrey of the Tenth Amendment Center noted: "A 2019 report revealed that the federal government has turned state drivers' license photos into a giant facial recognition database, putting virtually every driver in America in a perpetual electronic police lineup." There are reports that the CIA and FBI "already want to leverage TSA checkpoints for law enforcement and intelligence purposes... pressure will build to expand it further and try to identify everyone from parole violators to deadbeat dads," according to an ACLU white paper.[67]

The Supreme Court ruled in a 2018 case: "A person does not surrender all Fourth Amendment protection by venturing in the public sphere."[68] But the proliferation of federal facial scanning makes a mockery of the Fourth Amendment's prohibition of warrantless unreasonable searches. As the ACLU's Jay Stanley wrote: "Travelers, including U.S. citizens, should not have to submit to invasive biometric scans simply as a condition of exercising their constitutional right to travel." Will the database TSA compiles be used to target anyone who attends a protest labeled seditious, extremist, or unpatriotic? Will the new facial recognition software automatically alert if travelers radiate disdain for TSA?

Conclusion

Federal officials sporadically admit that TSA procedures are absurd overkill for average Americans. TSA chief John Pistole admitted in 2014 that "the vast majority of people pose little to no threat to aviation."[69] A top DHS official told Congress: "The population base rate for high-risk travelers is extremely low. In other words, the vast majority of travelers pose no security risks." But TSA cannot admit that every grandmother in a wheelchair and every just-weaned toddler is not an imminent threat without forfeiting boundless sway over every traveler.

Instead, Washington pretends that TSA's punitive practices inflict zero collateral damage. A Cornell University study estimated that TSA's intrusive searches spurred more auto fatalities. As a Bloomberg Business analysis noted: "People switching from air to road transportation in the aftermath of the 9/11 attacks led to an increase of 242 driving fatalities per month."[70] A 2015 lawsuit by the Competitive Enterprise Institute proved that the number of lives lost from driving instead of flying continues to far exceed the number of lives TSA claimed to save with its intrusive Whole Body Scanners.[71] The Justice Department and TSA stonewalled and got the lawsuit dismissed.

TSA remains more devoted to polishing its image than to protecting travelers. In July 2023, three TSA agents at Miami International Airport were arrested because they pilfered property "while the passengers were distracted with their own screenings and not paying attention to their items," the *New York Post* reported.[72] A TSA agent admitted to partnering with another TSA employee to steal a thousand dollars a day from travelers, including grabbing cash from wallets sent through TSA x-ray systems. He was permitted to enroll in "a deferred prosecution program, and charges against him will be dropped if he meets the conditions of the program," *USA Today* reported.[73] TSA refused to disclose how many other TSA agents have recently been arrested or fired for plundering passengers, but the latest story evoked a torrent of online comments from other TSA theft victims. In lieu of transparency, officials recited the hollow pledge that TSA has "no tolerance" for its employees' misconduct.

The feds turned "consent" into a façade and then cite it to sanctify almost unlimited power. Rather than making Americans safe from terrorists, TSA makes them prey to federal agents. Other nations have far superior airport security systems. "More than 80% of Europe's commercial airports use private screening companies, including those in Britain, France, Germany, and Spain," according to the Cato Institute.[74] Canada also successfully privatized airport security and avoids the torrent of complaints and outrages that TSA regularly produces. A federal agency could set the safety standards and hire private companies to do the job, as currently happens around U.S. nuclear power plants. As federal agents, TSA staffers almost always receive legal immunity except in cases of grand larceny. There is no reason why the hirelings who paw baggage and travelers must wear epaulets and strut like prison guards hounding convicts into the showers.

TSA illustrates how "petty oppressions" proliferate when federal agents nullify constitutional rights. Airport security seems like a perpetual psycho-pathological experiment to determine how much degradation Americans will tolerate. TSA precedents could determine how federal agents treat American citizens across the board, not just at airports.

Despite squeezing millions of butts and boobs, TSA has never caught a real terrorist. By treating most Americans like suicide-bombers-in-waiting, TSA makes traveling vexing without making it safer. For 20 years, Washington bureaucrats and political appointees have promised to reform TSA so that it will cease being a farce and a menace. After pointlessly groping millions of Americans, TSA has no excuse for groping millions more.

10. Taxation and Tyranny

"The power to tax involves the power to destroy."

– Supreme Court, 1819[1]

Federal, state, and local tax burdens turn citizens into sharecroppers of their own lives. The average American is forced to labor for 20 years simply to support the government. Inflation is becoming the cruelest tax on millions of families struggling to afford necessities.

Tax policy empowers federal officials to punish whom they please. Sen. David Pryor (D-AR) warned in 1988: "The IRS operates a near totalitarian system… The taxpayer, meanwhile, is afforded hardly any rights during such proceedings other than to pay the alleged deficiency."[2] Former IRS district chief David Patnoe testified to Congress: "More tax is collected by fear and intimidation than by the law. People are afraid of the IRS."[3] The congressionally appointed Commission on Economic Growth and Tax Reform warned in 1996: "Twice as big as the CIA, and five times the size of the FBI, the IRS controls more information about individual Americans than any other agency… Without a trial, the IRS has the right to seize property from Americans." In subsequent decades, the IRS became more powerful and punitive.

Politicians boast of Americans' "voluntary tax compliance." That notion is another Orwellian triumph from inside the Beltway. As a 2022 IRS publication noted:

> The word "voluntary," as used… in IRS publications, refers to our system of allowing taxpayers initially to determine the correct amount of tax and complete the appropriate returns, rather than have the government determine tax for them from the outset.[4]

One tax analyst scoffed at the "voluntary" IRS: "You punch yourself, or we will punch you." Even the U.S. Tax Court derided that notion as "arrogant sophistry."[5]

As Henry David Thoreau observed: "If I deny the authority of the State when it presents its tax-bill, it will soon take and waste all my property, and so harass me and my children without end." The IRS perpetually subjugates workers so politicians can spend like royalty. Payroll withholding systems place politicians at the front of the line, and their "expenses" trump an individual's effort to support their own family. Federal revenues reached almost $5 trillion in fiscal year 2023, but politicians still ran a $2 trillion deficit.

Perpetually Scourging Political Enemies

The power to tax has long conferred the power to destroy political opponents. As author David Burnham noted in his 1990 masterpiece *A Law Unto Itself: The IRS and the Abuse of Power*: "In almost every administration since the IRS's inception the information and power of the tax agency have been mobilized for explicitly political purposes."[6]

President Franklin Roosevelt used the IRS to harass newspaper publishers who opposed the New Deal, including William Randolph Hearst. FDR dropped the IRS hammer on political rivals such as Louisiana Governor Huey Long and prominent Republicans such as former Treasury Secretary Andrew Mellon. In 1944, Roosevelt spiked an IRS audit of hefty illegal campaign contributions from a government contractor to U.S. Rep. Lyndon Johnson of Texas.[7] Johnson's career would have been destroyed if Texans learned of his dirty dealing. Instead, Johnson survived, and scores of thousands of Americans and hundreds of thousands of Vietnamese died as a result.

President John F. Kennedy raised the political exploitation of the IRS to an art form. Attorney General Robert Kennedy ordered IRS agents to install hundreds of illegal electronic bugging devices; the IRS even purchased telephone company trucks so its agents could pose as Ma Bell employees.[8] In 1961, President Kennedy denounced "the discordant voices of extremism" and derided people "who would sow the seeds of doubt and hate" to make Americans distrust their leaders. Kennedy's IRS launched the Ideological Organizations Audit Project, targeting the Christian Anti-Communist Crusade, the American Enterprise Institute, the Foundation for Economic Education, and many other conservative organizations.[9] Many civil rights activists in the South were targeted for abusive IRS audits.[10] A 1976 Senate report noted: "By directing tax audits at individuals and groups solely because of their political beliefs, the Ideological Organizations Audit Project established a precedent for a far more elaborate program of targeting 'dissidents.'"

After Kennedy's assassination, the IRS continued harassing presidential critics. In 1967, a federal appeals court overturned the conviction of an outspoken Oregon lawyer whose prosecution had been "outrageously unfair" and "contrary to law." The court declared: "The court will not place its stamp of approval upon a witch-hunt, a crusade to rid society of unorthodox thinkers and actors by using the federal income tax laws" to silence them.[11]

Neither that court decision nor the U.S. Constitution restrained the Nixon administration. The White House gave the IRS a list of targets to, in the words of presidential assistant John Dean, "use the available federal machinery to screw our political enemies." Nixon's henchmen created a Special Services Staff (SSS) to mastermind "all IRS activities involving ideological, militant, subversive, radical, and similar type organizations." More than 10,000 groups and individuals were targeted because of their political activism or slant between 1969 and 1973, including the John Birch Society and Nobel laureate Linus Pauling.

When the House Judiciary Committee recommended Nixon's impeachment in 1974, the second count charged him with seeking "to obtain from the Internal Revenue Service, in violation of the constitutional rights of citizens, confidential information contained in income tax returns for purposes not authorized by law." Congress enacted legislation to severely restrict political contacts between the White House and the IRS.

But the Clinton administration ignored that law. In 1995, the White House and the Democratic National Committee produced a 331-page report entitled "Communication Stream of Conspiracy Commerce" that attacked magazines, think tanks, and other entities and individuals who had criticized President Clinton. In the subsequent years, many organizations mentioned in the White House report were hit by IRS audits, including the Heritage Foundation and the *American Spectator* magazine. Almost a dozen individual high-profile Clinton accusers, such as Paula Jones and Gennifer Flowers, were also audited.

Capitol Hill also routinely exploited the IRS to send federal hitmen against their enemies. "Members of both parties in Congress have prompted hundreds of audits of political opponents in the 1990s," including "personal demands for audits from members of Congress," the Associated Press reported in 1999. Those audit requests were marked "expedite" or "hot politically," and IRS officials were obliged to respond within 15 days. Congressional staffers were also empowered to send IRS agents after specific individuals, organizations, or publications that riled their bosses. After controversy erupted, the IRS claimed that it could not find 114 key files relating to possible political manipulation of audits of tax-exempt organizations. As a *Wall Street Journal* editorial noted: "The IRS position is incredible. It says letters from politicians asking that someone be audited are confidential tax-return information."[12] Since the abuse was bipartisan, there was no enthusiasm on Capitol Hill for an investigation.

Shortly after he took office in 2009, President Barack Obama gave a commencement address at Arizona State University. After grousing about being refused an honorary degree, Obama "joked" that "[the university president Michael] Crowe and the Board of Regents will soon learn all about being audited by the IRS."[13] (Obama later joked during the White House Correspondents' Dinner about using predator drones to kill people he disliked.[14]) Obama's political "humor" set the tone for how the IRS enforced the law in the following years.

In 2010, IRS officials created a BOLO list — "Be on the Lookout" — for conservative organizations applying for nonprofit tax status. IRS officials subsequently stonewalled applications from 300 organizations seeking to get tax-exempt status for their donors. Among the BOLO target criteria: groups that "advocated education about the Constitution and the Bill of Rights." A 2013 Inspector General report concluded: "The IRS used inappropriate criteria that identified for review Tea Party and other organizations applying for tax-exempt status based upon their names or policy positions." The IRS demanded donor lists from 24 conservative nonprofits and proceeded to audit 10% of their donors — an audit rate ten times higher than average. House Majority Leader Eric Cantor in February 2014 denounced the IRS targeting of conservative nonprofit organizations as "the hallmark of authoritarian nations."[15] The investigation of the IRS abuses was stymied because the IRS claimed to have lost almost all the emails of the key players. In 2016, a federal appeals court ruled in favor of conservative groups suing the IRS, concluding that "it is absurd to suggest that the effect of the IRS's unlawful conduct... has been eradicated." The court concluded that the IRS had committed "unconstitutional acts against at least a portion of the plaintiffs."[16] The IRS later formally apologized to scores of conservative groups that it had wrongfully targeted in tax audits, including providing a payment of $3.5 million to some of the IRS victims.

Members of Congress continued treating the IRS as their personal financial hit squad. After Republicans captured control of the House of Representatives in 2010, Sen. Charles Schumer (D-NY) announced: "It's clear we're not going to pass anything legislatively... but there are many things that can be done by the IRS."[17] Schumer urged the IRS "to investigate various groups identified through reference to news articles." Sen. Carl Levin (D-MI) sent seven letters to the IRS ordering the agency to "investigate specific nonprofits" and "sought confidential nonprofit tax return information from the IRS, even after being warned, repeatedly... that such information could not be legally divulged," a *Wall Street Journal* op-ed noted. The Senate Ethics Committee justified the personal audit requests because senators "have broad discretion to comment on matters of public policy in communications with agencies." In other words, senators are entitled to "broad discretion" to persecute their critics and opponents.

The Trump administration issued new regulations prohibiting the IRS from targeting nonprofit applicants based on their political ideology. In 2021, the Biden administration pushed Congress to enact a law that would turbocharge IRS investigations of nonprofit applicants, including demanding access to their donor lists. Sen. Mike Braun (R-IN) complained that under Biden's favored bill, the "IRS would be empowered to block tax-exempt status and publicly expose a group's donors to harassment from liberal groups and the media if their beliefs are deemed to be politically unfavorable."

On March 9, 2023, journalist Matt Taibbi testified before a congressional committee on the vast federally funded "Censorship Industrial Complex" exposed by the "Twitter Files" revelations of FBI browbeating of social media. On the same day he testified, an IRS agent swooped down on his New Jersey home, ordering Taibbi to contact the agency regarding his tax returns from two prior years. Maybe the timing of that IRS visit was a coincidence, like someone who forgets to take off their ski mask before entering a bank.[18] The IRS House Judiciary Committee Chairman Jim Jordan (R-OH) was outraged and sent a letter demanding information from the Biden administration since "the IRS's action could be interpreted as an attempt to intimidate a witness before Congress."[19] The IRS later revealed that it began investigating Taibbi's taxes on Christmas Eve[20] 2022, shortly after he began exposing federal censorship abuses.[21]

Take the Money and Run

In 1997, IRS agent Jennifer Long testified to Congress that revenue agents are encouraged by IRS management to use "tactics... to extract unfairly assessed taxes from taxpayers, literally ruining families, lives, and businesses — all unnecessarily and sometimes illegally." Members of Congress were appalled by revelations from Long and other IRS officials. Congress eventually enacted the Internal Revenue Service Restructuring and Reform Act of 1998, and took a victory lap after promising the IRS would cease trampling Americans' rights.[22]

No such luck. Routine day-to-day outrages have continued unabated for decades.

Bank robbers steal roughly $30 million a year from the nation's banks. Guys wearing goofy masks and thrusting misspelled handwritten notes at bank tellers are pikers compared to the feds. The IRS seized a quarter billion dollars from banks between 2005 and 2012 because it disapproved of how businesses and individuals structured their bank deposits and withdrawals.[23] "Freedom under the law" became freedom to be fleeced by Uncle Sam.

In 1970, Congress enacted the Bank Secrecy Act, making it a crime for banks to keep secrets from the government. Banks were required to file a federal report for any cash transaction exceeding $10,000, a mandate that generated tens of millions of reports but few criminal convictions. The U.S. Sentencing Commission estimated in 1992 that almost 90% of money laundering convictions not involving drug money have been achieved via government sting operations. The Commission also warned that the law was ensnaring hapless business owners who inadvertently violated its provisions.

In 1994, the Supreme Court overturned a conviction of two gamblers who made a series of bank deposits under $10,000 to pay their blackjack debts in Reno, Nevada. The Justice Department insisted that it was irrelevant that the elderly couple were unaware of the federal law. Justice Ruth Bader Ginsburg wrote that the Court was "unpersuaded by the argument that structuring is so obviously 'evil' or inherently 'bad' that the 'willfulness' requirement is satisfied irrespective of the defendant's knowledge of the illegality of structuring." The Clinton administration responded by swaying Congress to speedily enact the Money Laundering Suppression Act, which removed the "willfulness" requirement from the statue. This made it easier to legally destroy citizens unaware they violated the law.[24]

In 2012, IRS agents confiscated the bank account of Carole Hinders, who had run a small restaurant named Mrs. Lady's Mexican Food in Arnolds Park, Iowa, for 40 years. She lost $33,000 because she deposited restaurant proceeds from her cash-only business into the local bank in amounts of less than $10,000. Banks are prohibited from warning customers that such deposits could trigger a federal seizure. Hinders was shocked: "Who takes your money before they prove that you've done anything wrong with it?"[25] When the feds offered to drop the case by refunding to her a portion of the seizure, she scoffed: "I would rather throw the money in the garbage than settle with the IRS."[26] (The IRS returned all her money after the case made the news.)

Randy Sowers, the owner of South Mountain Creamery in the distant Maryland suburbs of Washington, D.C., was hammered by a $63,000 "structuring seizure" in 2012. The *Washington Post* noted: "Sowers is a high-school-educated entrepreneur who describes himself as inspired by God to deliver local dairy products to busy locavores." A bank teller told his wife that deposits in excess of $10,000 from their farmers' markets sales and elsewhere required a special form, so they kept deposits below $10,000.[27] But after Sowers complained to local media, the feds played hardball with him. The feds caved and refunded his money a few years later after national papers picked up the story.[28]

In 2014, a flock of federal agents arrived at L&M Convenience Mart in the one-horse town of Fairmont, North Carolina, to notify its owner, Lyndon McLellan, that the IRS had confiscated $107,702.66 from his bank account. McLellan deposited his market's proceeds in amounts less than $10,000; the feds had no other evidence or allegations of his wrongdoing. After McLellan's case was discussed at a congressional hearing, a federal prosecutor warned his lawyer: "Publicity about it doesn't help. It just ratchets up feelings in the agency."[29] After the Institute for Justice came to McLellan's assistance, the IRS offered a partial refund of its unjustifiable seizure. Lawyer Robert Everett Johnson summarized the IRS's settlement offer: "We're not going to prosecute but we think you should give us half your money anyway."[30] After further toxic publicity, the IRS gave a full refund.

Between 2005 and 2012, the number of IRS seizures rose more than fivefold, but the vast majority of victims were never criminally prosecuted for structuring offenses. "One-third of those cases involved nothing more than making a series of sub-$10,000 cash transactions," the Institute for Justice reported. Such seizures can cost $20,000 or more in legal fees to fight — a prohibitive cost, especially since half the seizures were less than $35,000. (Some businesses have insurance policies that refuse to cover any loss above $10,000, spurring businesses to deposit amounts just below that threshold.)

In 2014, after a damning exposé in the *New York Times*, the IRS announced that it would cease seizing bank accounts from lawful businesses and individuals who inadvertently violated the deposit law. A 2017 Inspector General report found no evidence in 91% of the seizure cases that the money came from illegal activities. IRS criminal investigators simply looked at banking records and then confiscated private accounts. Most of the victims were "legal businesses such as jewelry stores, restaurant owners, gas station owners, scrap metal dealers, and others." The IRS targeted businesses with legal sources of income because, as the Inspector General reported:

> The Department of Justice had encouraged task forces to engage in "quick hits," where property was more quickly seized... rather than pursuing cases with other criminal activity (such as drug trafficking and money laundering), which are more time-consuming.[31]

The IRS chose to seize first, ask questions later. The IG noted further:

> Interviews with the property owners were conducted after the seizure to determine the reason for the pattern of banking transactions and if the property owner had knowledge of the banking law and had intent to structure.

Victims provided "realistic defenses" for their banking history in 54 cases, but there was "no evidence" the IRS considered their explanations in most cases. The IRS preferred to ruin the lives of people who failed to comply with unknown regulations.

The heavy-handed tactics used to plunder bank accounts were par for the IRS course. Between 2011 and 2014, hundreds of thousands of Americans were bushwhacked by a single arcane sentence in a 673-page law. The Food, Conservation and Energy Act of 2008 — known as the "Farm Bill" — contained more than 275,000 words shoveling out benefits far and wide. Section 14219 specified: "Notwithstanding any other provision of law, regulation, or administrative limitation, no limitation on the period within which an offset may be initiated or taken pursuant to this section shall be effective." Prior to that law, federal agencies had a 10-year statute of limitation for collecting debts allegedly due to them. According to the federal Consumer Financial Protection Bureau, most states impose a three- or six-year limitation on collecting private debts.[32]

The IRS exploited that 2008 provision to arbitrarily seize almost $5 billion from taxpayers. The IRS bushwhacked people for alleged Social Security overpayments their deceased parents received decades earlier. In 2013, an

NBC television affiliate in Chicago reported that, thanks to that sentence in the 2008 law, "anyone overpaid by a federal agency, at any time in their life, can now be tracked down and put on the hook for debts that are decades old." Federal agencies often had zero evidence of overpayments. But any accusation by any agency was sufficient for the IRS to confiscate people's tax refunds. CNBC noted that the seizure notification letters "the government sends to unsuspecting taxpayers are frightening, use accusatory language, and include other financial threats."

The Social Security Administration exploited the 2008 law to target 400,000 taxpayers who it claimed "collectively owe $714 million on debts more than 10 years old." One lawyer lamented: "It's really very sad: The class of people affected by this policy can be defined as people who lost a parent at an early age." The IRS snatched a Maryland tax refund owed to Ted Verbich, a federal employee, based on an alleged overpayment of benefits 37 years earlier to his kinfolk; the government "could provide no documents to back up the claim," the *Post* noted.[33] For alleged debts of deceased parents, "the government doesn't look into exactly who got the overpayment; the policy is to seek compensation from the oldest sibling and work down through the family until the debt is paid," the *Post* reported. Similar methods are favored by loan sharks, but automatically seizing tax refunds means the government doesn't need to break thumbs to snare money.

After controversy erupted, nobody in Congress would take credit or blame for crafting that sentence in the 2008 Farm Bill. Several senators publicly groused, but that provision of the law was not repealed. Instead, federal agencies promised to be more judicious in how they raided the graveyard (or at least to avoid spurring embarrassing newspaper headlines). It was predictable that nullifying the statute of limitation on government debt collection would lead to enforcement travesties. But most members of Congress care only about snaring more revenue to spend.

In 2015, Congress empowered the IRS to cancel the passports of Americans with alleged substantial tax delinquencies. Due process was not permitted to impede the IRS veto over Americans leaving the country. The IRS system of assessing tax delinquencies is notoriously inaccurate; penalties and interest can pile up hefty unjustified tax bills. The IRS can covertly revoke passports, and their targets might not recognize their plight until they arrive at the airport to depart. In 2018, the IRS announced that it had "started action to revoke the citizenship or residence rights of at least 260,000 U.S.

individuals due to significant tax debts," with another 100,000 people on the target list.[34] As *National Review*'s Kevin Williamson commented, Americans "who for whatever reason have an unmet obligation to the IRS are treated like East Germans locked behind the Checkpoint Charlie of the federal bureaucracy."[35] In a grudging concession, the IRS announced that it would not cancel passports of "tax-related identity theft" — including people whose IRS returns had been leaked to the media.

The Game Is Rigged

In ancient Rome, the Emperor Caligula posted "new tax laws in small print and hung them high atop pillars to entrap the people into unknowingly violating them."[36] The IRS would never do such a thing because IRS employees are members of government unions and cannot be required to climb up high pillars. However, tax law and regulations are so convoluted that most Americans are unaware of all their legal obligations to the revenooers.

Americans have no excuse for not paying all the taxes they owe, or all the taxes any IRS employee claims they owe. But compliance is tricky thanks to hellishly complex Internal Revenue Code regulations. The length of the federal tax code has more than tripled in recent decades, reaching four million words in 2012. As Chris Edwards of the Cato Institute observed: "Federal tax-code compliance overall consumes more than 6 billion hours of time each year, which is like having a 'tax army' of 3 million people just filling out tax returns year-round."[37] A 2013 study by the Mercatus Center at George Mason University estimated that "Americans face up to nearly $1 trillion annually in hidden tax-compliance costs."[38]

The complexity is compounded by constant changes. Tax law is not "law," but simply the latest whim of the U.S. Congress or the dweebs who write IRS regulations. Between 2000 and 2021, Congress enacted an average of "408 changes to the tax code each year," the National Taxpayers Union reported.[39] Because of the slowness of the rules-making process, IRS regulations are routinely retroactive, hitting people with tax liabilities they did not previously owe. The IRS scrambled for years to craft regulations to carry out Trump's Tax Cuts and Jobs Act (TCJA) that Congress passed on December 22, 2017, struggling to "write new regulations to administer provisions that are ambiguous and sometimes contradictory," the Tax Policy Center noted.[40]

Sen. Ben Cardin (D-MD) declared: "If you're not cheating on your taxes, you have nothing to worry about."[41] But byzantine complexity creates endless tax tripwires for befuddled citizens. Thomas Field, director of Tax Analysts and Advocates, wrote in 1974: "From the perspective of the IRS, the more ambiguous the law, the more powerful the enforcing agency."[42] One former high-ranking IRS attorney admitted in 1996: "There is the general view that the more mysterious tax enforcement is, the more likely taxpayers will voluntarily comply."[43] In a 1992 internal memo, IRS Commissioner Fred Goldberg asserted that IRS regulations "should make do with 'rough justice'" because providing "detailed rules" ends up "providing a road map for the few with larceny in their hearts."[44]

The IRS "roughs up" justice by refusing to explain how to comply with tax law. In 2016, the *Washington Post* exposed a "secret plan" showing that the IRS wanted to "get out of the business of talking with taxpayers," according to Nina Olson, the congressionally appointed National Taxpayer Advocate.[45] Olson warned that "traditional taxpayer services — telephone assistance and face-to-face assistance — will be scaled back dramatically." IRS Commissioner John Koskinen insisted his agency was bowing to popular preferences: "Our problem today is that we have a whole lot of people who would rather not see us at all, who want to go online, transact their business and move on."[46] But this blithely presumed that IRS employees would actually resolve issues citizens raised during online contacts.

The IRS's telephone service collapsed during the pandemic. In early 2021, the IRS answered fewer than 4% of taxpayers' phone calls seeking assistance. The 2022 Taxpayer Advocate reported on citizens' experience dealing with the IRS in 2021 and admitted that "from the perspective of tens of millions of taxpayers, it was horrendous… the most challenging year ever for taxpayers."[47] The official tally did not estimate how many billion hours Americans lost in "IRS voicemail hell."

During 2021, a huge backlog of unprocessed tax returns piled up, and legions of people did not receive expected tax refunds. IRS officials initially claimed that it was only a few million returns they had neglected. In February 2022, news leaked out that nearly 24 million returns from 2021 had not been processed. The *Washington Post* noted that information on the huge backlog came from "three people who spoke on the condition of anonymity because they were not approved to speak publicly," confirming that truth can be hazardous to bureaucratic careers.[48] The backlog occurred in part because

IRS employees were permitted to pretend to work from home for two years after the start of the pandemic.[49] Citizens faced harsh penalties for not filing their 1040s on time, but the IRS faced no penalty for making false statements about millions of tax returns it had failed to process.

In May 2022, an Inspector General report revealed that the IRS had destroyed 30 million tax information returns in 2021 without processing them because it was overwhelmed by the accumulating paper.[50] Bloomberg News noted: "The IRS explained the documents were destroyed because the agency's 'antiquated' information technology systems could no longer handle them." Texas CPA Brian Streig groused: "To see the IRS just destroy these [returns] is almost like the IRS admitting they don't really care."[51] Rep. Bill Pascrell (D-NJ) denounced the document destruction as a "scandal" and lamented that "all the American people see at the IRS is incompetence and catastrophe." Pascrell called for Biden to fire IRS chief Charles Rettig.[52] The IRS continued to "have a significant backlog of paper-filed individual and business tax returns that remain unprocessed."[53]

The Mirage of Confidentiality

The IRS has long scorned safeguarding the confidentiality of taxpayers' financial secrets. The National Research Council reported in 1993 that an ongoing multibillion-dollar overhaul of IRS computers could "lead to a wide range of potentially disastrous privacy and security problems for the IRS unless the IRS develops effective, integrated privacy and security policies."[54] IRS computer systems remain legendary for being backward, vulnerable, and unable to communicate with each other.

The Government Accountability Office reported in 2022 that there had been almost 500 confirmed cases of wrongful access to confidential tax return information by IRS employees in the prior decade, along with hundreds of allegations of wrongful disclosure of tax information.[55] In May 2015, the IRS announced that criminals had cracked its computer system "to pilfer nearly $50 million in refunds that belonged to more than 100,000 taxpayers."[56] An IRS spokesman explained: "These are extremely sophisticated criminals with access to a tremendous amount of data."[57] Since the culprits were "extremely sophisticated," the IRS was blameless. Eight months later, the IRS admitted that 700,000 taxpayers had been victimized, not a mere 100,000. The IRS never released any information on the identities of the transgressors who stole the personal information.

In June 2021, the tax returns of thousands of Americans were splayed on the front page of newspapers. ProPublica disclosed "a vast trove of Internal Revenue Service data on the tax returns of thousands of the nation's wealthiest people, covering more than 15 years."[58] The Biden administration assured Americans that the FBI was investigating the breach. The leaks supported the tax hikes that Biden championed and that Congress enacted in the summer of 2022. More than two years after the leak, the Justice Department announced that a former IRS contractor had downloaded tax returns of "thousands of the nation's wealthiest individuals and disclosed that information" to a news organization. The same individual had leaked Donald Trump's personal tax returns and leaked that information to various outlets including the *New York Times*, which disclosed Trump's tax payments shortly before the 2020 election. The former contractor was permitted to settle the charges by pleading guilty to a single count of unauthorized disclosure of tax returns. Shortly before the plea deal was announced, GAO reported that the IRS had ignored almost 80 recommendations for safeguarding taxpayer data and was especially at risk of exposure due to IRS contractors.[59]

Biden's Bigger Fist Panacea

President Biden is expanding the IRS budget and IRS power more than any American president in the preceding half-century. After announcing a wish list for new federal spending, Biden told Congress in 2021: "I've made clear that we can do it without increasing deficits." Biden believes he found a goose that will lay golden eggs for federal revenue — a new army of IRS agents to hound Americans and corporations to pay far more taxes. The *Washington Post* reported that "the single biggest source of new revenue in the plan comes from dramatically expanding the clout of the nation's tax agency."[60] *Slate* reported: "Biden wants to fund a massive upgrade to the American welfare state by making the IRS great at audits again."

The linchpin of Biden's proposal aimed to require reports to the IRS of anyone with more than $600 a year in financial transactions. But previous catch-all financial reporting requirements helped spur pervasive federal looting. Americans for Tax Reform protested that "the Biden administration wants to give the IRS new power to automatically access bank accounts, credit union accounts, and Venmo, PayPal, and CashApp account inflows and outflows for all business and personal accounts." Sen. Mike Crapo

(R-ID) denounced the Biden proposal as a "surveillance dragnet," a "huge violation of privacy," and "an egregious abuse of Americans' right to due process by inferring that all U.S. taxpayers are guilty of evading taxes until proven otherwise."[61] Paul Merski of the Independent Community Bankers of America warned that the Biden proposal would be "a historic invasion of financial privacy like we've never seen before... The IRS is absolutely incapable of handling or processing this massive amount of new data."[62]

What could possibly go wrong for average taxpayers? In U.S. Tax Court, IRS determinations of what citizens owe are "presumed correct," with taxpayers bearing the burden to prove the feds wrong. Corporations with hefty legal departments routinely defeat the IRS in court, but few citizens can afford to fight a federal agency that appears to hold all the cards. Tax expert Daniel Pilla estimates that the "IRS's audit results are incorrect between 60 and 90% of the time."[63] But most taxpayers acquiesce and pay whatever the IRS demands.

In 2022, Congress enacted the Inflation Reduction Act. This Biden-backed legislation boosted the agency's budget by $80 billion over a decade and authorized hiring 87,000 new IRS agents and employees. "Only 4% of the additional funding will be devoted to improving taxpayer service, while 58% will go to escalating enforcement efforts," the *New York Post* reported. Rep. Kevin Brady (R-TX), the ranking member of the House Ways and Means Committee, estimated that the law would result in more than a million new audits per year, including more than 700,000 targeting Americans earning less than $75,000 a year.[64]

The Biden administration and its media allies were outraged at suggestions that vastly expanding the number of IRS agents could result in bad things happening to innocent people. Rep. Thomas Massie (R-KY) observed: "The IRS has never pointed a gun at a billionaire or his employees, so why does the IRS need 87,000 new agents, AR-15s, and 5 million rounds of ammunition? They're not gunning for billionaires or their bank accounts."[65]

Controversy swirled about a film clip of an IRS recruiting program on college campuses. An IRS video showed Utah students putting on flak jackets and readying toy guns and handcuffs for "taking down a landscape business owner who failed to properly report how he paid for his vehicles." ("First they came for the tulip bulbs...") An IRS enforcement operation won't count as a raid unless agents shoot at least three people. And then it still won't matter because anyone who is gunned down will be labeled a suspected tax scofflaw.

Biden acquired new battalions of IRS enforcers at the same time the agency already obliterated unlucky taxpayers with deluges of penalties. The number of different penalties the IRS can inflict increased tenfold since the 1950s, and IRS liens and seizures have increased fivefold in this century. Penalties can quickly pile up and financially destroy hapless citizens and businesses.

The IRS can change its calculations of penalties at practically any point, levying financial ruin on its targets. In March 2023, the Supreme Court struck down an IRS policy that arbitrarily increased penalties fiftyfold. Alexandru Bittner, a Romanian-American businessman and dual citizen, failed to timely file five IRS annual forms listing his foreign bank accounts for five years he had lived back in Romania. The Bank Secrecy Act of 1970 required Americans to file a form notifying the IRS if they have foreign accounts above $10,000. Bittner was unaware of his obligation but voluntarily filed the forms after he returned to the U.S. Prior to 2015, the IRS did not levy fines for each separate account for each year, instead penalizing people for failing to file a catch-all form. Even though the IRS considered Bittner's offense to be "non-willful" (i.e., unintentional), the IRS compounded the fines and penalties and demanded $2.72 million by assessing the maximum penalty and interest for each bank account with his name. Penalties can easily exceed the total money in foreign accounts. A *Wall Street Journal* analysis noted:

> Roughly nine million U.S. citizens live abroad and another 45 million are foreign-born. Any of these Americans could hold foreign bank accounts for a variety of reasons: to send money back to their family, to give themselves easier access to funds when visiting or to hold the inheritance of a deceased family member.[66]

The Supreme Court opinion, written by Justice Gorsuch, declared: "We do not see any indication that Congress sought to maximize penalties for every nonwillful mistake."[67]

The IRS can impose a tax it doesn't even define. The Inflation Reduction Act of 2022 created a new corporate alternative minimum tax — a "15% minimum tax on a company's financial-statement income" — starting in 2023. In lieu of specifying how to comply with the new law, the Treasury Department webpage announced: "Treasury and the IRS continue to develop guidance on how corporations determine their tax owed." A *Wall*

Street Journal analysis noted: "The lack of clear tax rules allows the IRS to write new rules during audits. This dangerously expands the power of the IRS."[68]

The Biden revenue push is spurring some IRS agents to go above and beyond the call of duty. On April 25, 2023, an IRS investigator arrived unannounced at a home in Marion, Ohio. The agent told the female homeowner that his name was Bill Haus and he had questions about an estate for which she was listed as the fiduciary. She groused that she had received no prior IRS notifications. Didn't matter: Haus claimed she owed a "substantial amount." She produced proof of paying all the taxes, and then Haus revealed that he was actually there to demand payment for "several supposed delinquent tax returns related to the decedent of the estate."[69] The woman phoned her attorney who told Haus to leave her residence. Haus haughtily responded: "I am an IRS agent; I can be at and go into anyone's house at any time I want to be."[70] Haus threatened to freeze her assets and put a lien on her house if she didn't pay everything he demanded within a week.

The homeowner recorded Haus's license plate and called local police, fearing she was targeted by an IRS scam. The police verified that the license belonged to an IRS agent who had used an alias. After a Marion policeman warned "Haus" not to return to the woman's house, "Haus" filed a complaint against the policeman with the Treasury Department Inspector General. The IRS backed down from "Haus's" demands. The House Judiciary Committee launched an investigation into the incident.

"Fortunate Son" Tax Exemption

Author David Burnham noted: "The reality that so many are somehow in violation of a supremely murky law gives the agency and the individual agent an astonishingly free hand to pick and choose their targets."[71] This arbitrary power can be compounded when the feds choose to ignore or overlook brazen tax offenses by the politically connected.

President Biden's son Hunter is a tax dodger straight out of IRS Central Casting.[72] Between 2014 and 2019, he pocketed more than $8 million from shady foreign sources, triggering a bushel of Treasury Department Suspicious Activity Reports. Hunter failed to pay more than $1 million in taxes and was slapped by a tax lien of $112,805 for his 2015 taxes. The IRS even threatened to cancel his passport.

The IRS began formally investigating Hunter in 2018; by January 2020, a team of a dozen IRS employees were working on his case. The Justice Department failed to file any charges before the statute of limitation expired on Hunter's 2014 and 2015 tax violations. The IRS investigators were kept out of an October 2020 briefing on an alleged "criminal bribery scheme" investigation on Biden and his family. The IRS supervisor whistleblower notified his bosses in the summer of 2020 about the Justice Department's foot-dragging. If Hunter had been charged with tax violations prior to the 2020 election, his father might have lost the election because it would have bolstered Donald Trump's charges of Joe Biden's corruption. In 2022, a Hollywood mega-lawyer loaned Hunter $2 million to pay his IRS debt.

CNBC reported in April 2023 that federal prosecutors could charge Hunter with three tax crimes, including a felony charge for tax evasion. In May 2023, the Justice Department ordered the IRS to effectively fire its entire team that had spent years investigating Hunter Biden. John Fort, the former chief of the IRS's criminal division, said the purge of IRS investigators could be unprecedented. The loss of IRS investigative expertise could make it easier to bury the tawdry tax evasion details.

An IRS criminal supervisory special agent filed a whistleblower complaint in April 2023 asserting that the investigation of Hunter Biden's tax violations was being blocked by "preferential treatment and politics." In May 2023, a special agent in the IRS's international tax and financial crimes group who had spent five years investigating Hunter Biden also filed a whistleblower complaint. The House Ways and Means Committee complained that the IRS investigators probing Hunter's violations were met with a "'Delay, Divulge, and Deny' campaign that ultimately shielded the President's son by allowing the statute of limitations to expire on several tax crimes for… when Joe Biden was the Vice President of the United States."[73] Attorneys for Hunter Biden were tipped off ahead of time about searches, resulting in the removal or destruction of evidence. "Prosecutors instructed investigators not to ask witnesses questions about Joe Biden or references to the 'big guy,'" the congressional committee noted.

In the sweetheart deal that prosecutors delivered in June 2023, Hunter agreed to plead guilty to misdemeanor IRS offenses and pay a fine. The same offenses could result in two years in prison for other Americans. The plea bargain deal collapsed after a federal judge asked questions about the blanket immunity that prosecutors provided for Hunter's other possible criminal offenses.

Inflation: The Cruelest Tax?

On top of preemptive seizures of paychecks and bank accounts, the federal government is levying a brutal inflation tax. Inflation occurs when the government prints excessive currency, resulting in more money chasing the same amount of goods and services. Nobel Laureate economist Friedrich Hayek wrote: "Inflation is never an unavoidable natural disaster; it is always the result of the weakness or ignorance of those in charge of monetary policy."[74] As economist Per Bylund observed: "Inflation is money losing its purchasing power."[75] Government is the premier profiteer of inflation, providing politicians with "free" money to spend while systematically defaulting on any debts government promised to pay.

A century ago, Americans clearly recognized the moral implications of inflation. Vice President Calvin Coolidge bluntly declared in 1922: "Inflation is repudiation." But clear thinking on political swindles became scarce after Federal Reserve mismanagement of the currency thrust the nation into the Great Depression.

From the first years of the existence of the United States, the U.S. dollar was backed by both gold and silver. In 1933, President Franklin Roosevelt betrayed his campaign promises and seized gold owned by private citizens. FDR then announced a 59% devaluation in the gold value of the dollar, thereby allowing the government to profit from the confiscation.

From 1878 onwards, the U.S. Mint printed paper silver certificates that pledged: "This certifies that there is on deposit in the Treasury of the United States of America One Dollar in Silver Payable to the Bearer on Demand." But that promise became inconvenient, so the government canceled its pledge. In 1965, President Lyndon Johnson began eliminating the silver in new dimes and quarters. Rather than stopping deficit spending, Johnson debased the currency.

The final wooden stake in the heart of the dollar occurred on August 15, 1971. President Nixon announced that the U.S. government would cease paying gold to redeem the dollars held by foreign central banks. The dollar thus became a fiat currency — something which possessed value solely because politicians said so. Nixon simultaneously froze all prices and boosted the money supply to turbocharge the economy and boost his 1972 re-election campaign. Though Nixon assured the nation that "the effect of this action… will be to stabilize the dollar," the "Nixon Shock" led to "a decade of one of the worst inflations of American history and the most stagnant economy since the Great Depression. The price of gold rose to $800 from $35," as financial expert Lewis Lehrman noted.

After the high inflation of the late 1970s and early 1980s, President Reagan and the Federal Reserve hit the brakes, launching a long era of relatively low inflation. But all the lessons from the Reagan era were forgotten when the stock market and housing market began crashing in 2008. President George W. Bush announced: "I've abandoned free-market principles to save the free-market system."[76] The Federal Reserve announced a policy of "quantitative easing" (QE) — sharply increasing the money supply and massively purchasing private and government-backed securities. Matt Taibbi aptly described QE in 2010 as "dollar meth being injected into the financial bloodstream," declaring that "[a] more overtly anticapitalist and oligarchical pattern of behavior… could not possibly be imagined."[77] President Obama pirouetted as a champion of the downtrodden while the Fed fueled a bubble for assets owned by the richest Americans — a policy that continued off-and-on until early 2022. Former Treasury Secretary Larry Summers noted in 2021 that a key purpose behind QE is "to increase asset prices so that the private sector will spend more… That mechanism supports the wealthy who hold these assets, rather than the bulk of the population."[78]

The QE damage was compounded by the Fed's zero interest-rate policy. While the IRS policy of seizing bank accounts for violations of its $10,000 deposit/withdrawal rule had thousands of victims, the federal demolition of American savers had tens of millions of victims. To artificially stimulate the economy, the Fed effectively treated anyone with a savings account like a deadbeat who deserved punishment. Former Treasury Department analyst Alex Pollock, writing for the Mises Institute, estimated in 2021 that the Federal Reserve's zero-interest policy "since 2008 has cost American savers about $4 trillion."[79] Keeping interest rates at near-zero enabled "free" borrowing by corporations who bought back their stock and boosted its price. Big banks also received preferential almost-free access to money from the Fed, while average borrowers were hit by much higher interest rates.

Beginning in early 2020, the Federal Reserve responded to the COVID lockdowns by boosting the nation's money supply by 40% — the highest rate of money growth in U.S. history. In a May 13, 2020, interview with CBS

60 Minutes, Fed Chairman Jerome Powell agreed that the Fed "simply flooded the system with money" in response to the pandemic lockdowns.[80] But that was no problem because, as Powell told Congress in 2021, the link between inflation and the money supply "ended about 40 years ago."[81] "Everything is different this time" is the obligatory phrase before another financial crash.

In July 2021, Biden insisted: "There's nobody suggesting there's unchecked inflation on the way — no serious economist." Actually, there were plenty of dire warnings. Inflation rose more than sixfold after Biden took office, jumping from 1.4 to 9% — the highest rate in 40 years. In December 2021, Biden scoffed at inflation as a "bump in the road." But as fuel prices set one record after another, that "bump" became a hole in the gas tank for tens of millions of Americans who drive to work. Biden claimed inflation is a problem everywhere, but National Public Radio reported that "between 2019 and 2021, the U.S. saw one of the biggest inflation rate increases in the world, behind only Brazil and Turkey."

Experts kindly offered plenty of financial remedies to hard-pressed Americans. For Thanksgiving 2021, the Federal Reserve recommended that people rely on soybean-based dinners instead of turkey — saving 76 cents a serving.[82] Georgia Democratic Party leader Stacey Abrams touted abortion as a cure for inflation: "Having children is why you're worried about your price for gas. It's why you're concerned about how much food costs. For women, this is not a reductive issue."[83] Professor Teresa Ghilarducci, in a *Washington Post* op-ed, recommended that families with an income less than $289,000 per year "adjust" to inflation by eating lentils instead of meat, ditching their car and taking public transit, and maybe letting their pets die.[84] In October 2022, Biden implied that soaring food prices wouldn't be a real problem if Americans simply bought no-name, store-brand Raisin Bran instead of Kellogg's.

Pro-Biden media outlets painted inflation as practically a divine blessing that Biden is bestowing on Americans.[85] MSNBC tweeted, "Why the inflation we're seeing now is a good thing," while the *Intercept* went whole-hog on soaring milk prices: "Inflation is Good for You." The *Washington Post* editorial board rushed to absolve Biden: "The main reason inflation is at its highest level since 1982 [is that] people continue to spend a lot of time at home" and demand more goods. MSNBC anchor Joy Reid claimed in November 2022 that inflation was a word that Republicans "taught people… Most people [who] would have never used that word ever in their lives are using it now because they've been taught it."[86] That same month, Treasury Secretary Janet Yellen blamed inflation on citizens frustrated by lockdowns who "suddenly started splurging on goods."[87]

Actually, the problem is much worse than reported. Beginning in the 1980s, the formula for calculating inflation was revised dozens of times, almost always with a downward bias. Instead of comparing the price of the same basket of goods over time, federal officials concocted a gauge they claim measures a "constant level of satisfaction." In addition to that bureaucratic fairy dust, the inflation formula was changed to severely underweight rises in housing prices, instead relying on "the new concept of homeowners' equivalent rent, where the government would estimate how much it would cost to own your own house," John Williams, the founder of Shadow Stats, observed.[88] If the same gauge of inflation was used now as in the 1970s, the inflation rate in early 2022 would have been 14 or 15% — nearly the highest inflation rate in U.S. history. Understating inflation permits the government to deny much of the financial damage it is inflicting.

Biden portrayed himself as inflation's biggest victim. "Inflation is the bane of our existence," Biden lamented to a talk show host in June 2022.[89] Unfortunately, he was referring to inflation's effect on his approval ratings, not the plight of average Americans struggling to pay for gas and groceries. When Peter Doocy of Fox News asked about the impact of inflation in January, Biden called him "a stupid son of a bitch." The Biden administration presumed that giving more handouts to government dependents would ease the pain of self-reliant middle-class families — perhaps by osmosis.

Biden's policies are based on the "Magic Bean School of Political Economy." Biden's policymakers favor Modern Monetary Theory (MMT) — the notion that government spending almost never has an adverse effect on the economy. MMT advocates believe there is practically no problem that cannot supposedly be solved by bigger gushers of free government money. A *Washington Post* headline captured the administration's presumptions: "Biden's big bet: That he can remake economy with no bad side effects" such as "less incentive to work." But, as *USA Today* reported: "Many people have permanently stopped working, depressing labor force participation" by millions of people.

MMT champions are adamant that the flood of new money is irrelevant to rising price levels. In a March 2022 speech to Democratic members of Congress, Biden raged at being blamed for inflation: "I'm sick of this stuff!...

We have to talk about it because the American people think the reason for inflation is the government spending more money. Simply. Not. True."[90]

Biden sought to deflate the political peril by demagoguing against corporations for raising prices. After Russia invaded Ukraine, Biden found a new culprit: "Make no mistake, inflation is largely the fault of Putin."[91] But inflation was already at 7% before the invasion of Ukraine. Biden began denouncing the "Putin Price Hikes,"[92] but polls showed that few Americans swallowed that assertion. In June 2022, the *Washington Post* reported that Biden, blaming his staffers for his problem with inflation, "complained to aides that they were not doing a good job explaining the causes of inflation and what the administration is doing about it."

In the final weeks of the 2022 midterm congressional campaign, Biden boasted of the impact of inflation — at least on voters pocketing federal checks. He told senior citizens in Florida: "On my watch, for the first time in 10 years, seniors are getting an increase in their Social Security checks." In reality, Social Security benefits have increased every year since 2016. The White House tweeted: "Seniors are getting the biggest increase in their Social Security checks in 10 years through President Biden's leadership." Even CNN derided that comment, since Social Security benefits are linked to inflation by law. Actually, the benefit boost was the largest in 40 years.

Policymakers ignore the devastation they inflict. When asked during a January 2022 news conference about how "inflation affects different groups of Americans," Fed Chair Powell said he wasn't "aware of… inflation literally falling more on different socioeconomic groups… The point is some people are just really prone to suffer more." Inflation sounded like a problem that therapists must solve. In reality, lower-income households spend a far higher percentage of their income on food, gas, and heating their homes — three categories where prices have soared. A survey by Lending Club in early 2022 found that "61% of the U.S. population lived paycheck to paycheck, up seven percentage points since the first report in June 2021, including 77% of consumers earning less than $50,000." In October 2022, the Federal Reserve Bank of Dallas reported that most American workers had suffered the harshest fall in wages in 25 years, including a "median decline in real wages" of more than 8.5%.[93]

To purchase votes and buttress their own power, politicians subvert the currency and cripple citizens' ability to provide for themselves. By late 2023, Biden's inflation inflicted a 17% cut in the purchasing power of Americans' paychecks and savings accounts. Since President Roosevelt devalued the currency, the U.S. dollar has lost more than 95% of its purchasing power.

When politicians severed the dollar's link to gold, they opened the door to practically unlimited deficit spending. Thomas Jefferson declared more than two centuries ago: "To preserve their independence, we must not let our rulers load us with perpetual debt." But Jefferson's warning was ignored. The U.S. national debt hit a trillion dollars in 1982 and surpassed $33 trillion in 2023. The Biden administration budget is forecast to generate trillion-dollar deficits every year for a decade.[94] As interest rates rise in response to soaring inflation, debt service will be a crushing burden for taxpayers in the coming years, imposing a higher cost than almost anything else in the federal budget. Today's politicians claim a right to beggar posterity simply to buy votes and favors in our time.

Conclusion

"Good faith taxation" is almost as rare as an honest burglar. The charades used to label taxes "voluntary" epitomize how politicians define citizens into servitude. Politicians profiteer from revenue systems designed to preemptively confiscate the lion's share of citizens' paychecks.

Since late in the last century, Washington politicians have promised reforms to end IRS abuses of American taxpayers. It is an illusion that better statutes will redeem an agency renowned for trampling the law. It is a bigger delusion that citizens can remain independent when the government wrecks the financial system. How did politicians become entitled to plunder paychecks and decimate the currency's value to create a temporary illusion of prosperity to perpetuate their power?

Supreme Court Justice Sutherland declared in 1933: "The powers of taxation are broad, but the distinction between taxation and confiscation must still be observed."[95] Unfortunately, this distinction is increasingly lost on the average taxpayer facing the full force of tax collectors. There is no possible revenue system that would permit despised and distrusted politicians to snare $5+ trillion a year without pervasive threats and abuses.

11. No Place to Hide

"Few threats to liberty exist which are greater than that posed by the use of eavesdropping devices."

– Supreme Court, 1967[1]

Americans are in the federal crosshairs now more than ever before. Pervasive surveillance leaves citizens no place to hide from government prying. The Fourth Amendment recognizes Americans' right "to be secure... against unreasonable searches and seizures." But a different motto guides today's Washington: "Those who have nothing to hide have nothing to fear."[2]

The Biden administration is expanding the federal Enemies List faster than any time since the Nixon era. Federal intelligence agencies have a budget of roughly $75 billion and 200,000 employees — more than enough to target any American with bad attitudes. We will examine how political deceit, bureaucratic conniving, and technological developments are combining to practically exterminate privacy.

How Privacy Became an Endangered Species

Privacy was a revolutionary value for early Americans. In a 1974 ruling on illegal Nixon administration searches, Federal Judge Gerhard Gesell observed: "The American Revolution was sparked in part by the... unrestricted, indiscriminate searches of persons and homes" by British agents.[3] Colonists were outraged by "general warrants" that entitled British officials to pry into nooks or crannies of any private home. A century after the Revolution ended, the Supreme Court declared:

> It is not the breaking of his doors, and the rummaging of his drawers that constitutes the essence of the offense; but it is the invasion of his indefeasible right of personal security, personal liberty, and private property.[4]

The same spirit of defiance radiated in a 1934 Supreme Court decision warning against unleashing government agents to harass whomever they pleased: "A general, roving investigation... is unknown to our constitution and laws; and such an inquisition would be destructive of the rights of the citizen, and an intolerable tyranny."[5] But as government grew far larger and more intrusive, inquisitions became standard operating procedure.

In 1971, House Majority Leader Hale Boggs (D-LA) explained: "Freedom of speech, freedom of thought, freedom of action for men in public life can be compromised quite as effectively by the fear of surveillance as by the fact of surveillance."[6] During the Vietnam War, FBI agents were encouraged to conduct frequent interviews with antiwar activists to "enhance the paranoia endemic in such circles and… get the point across that there is an FBI agent behind every mailbox."[7] That effort was part of the COINTELPRO program spurring thousands of covert operations to incite street warfare between violent groups, get people fired, suppress free speech, and cripple or destroy activist groups that the FBI disapproved.[8] FBI agents forged "poison pen" letters to wreck activists' marriages, smeared innocent people by portraying them as government informants, and trashed the reputations of critics. A 1976 Senate report concluded: "The American people need to be assured that never again will an agency of the government be permitted to conduct a secret war against those citizens it considers threats to the established order."[9]

But flowery words failed to bind federal agencies. The Reagan administration ramped up a War on Drugs in the 1980s, leading to catch-all intrusions such as the "open fields" doctrine that permitted federal agents to conduct warrantless searches almost anywhere not walled off by high fences.[10] Drug testing mandates required students and employees to urinate on command. Judges acquiesced to the "plain feel" doctrine, allowing police to search practically anyone's pockets to see if they contained crack, marijuana, or illicit pills. Justice Thurgood Marshall protested in 1989 that there was "no drug exception" to the Constitution,[11] while Justice John Paul Stevens complained in 1991 that the Supreme Court "has become a loyal foot soldier" in the War on Drugs.[12]

Patriot Act: The Great Unleashing

On September 11, 2001, Arab terrorists crashed hijacked planes into the World Trade Center and the Pentagon, killing almost three thousand people. Even before the smoke ceased rising from the wreckage of the World Trade Center, President George W. Bush decided that privacy was a luxury Americans no longer deserved.

After 9/11, trampling the Constitution became a trifling matter. Congress speedily enacted the Provide Appropriate Tools Required to Intercept and Obstruct Terrorism Act. The Patriot Act treated every citizen like a suspected terrorist and every federal agent like a proven angel. The Bush administration carried off the biggest flimflam in U.S. constitutional history. Rather than targeting terrorists, Congress granted federal lawmen new powers to use against anyone suspected of violating any of the 4,000+ federal crimes on the books. The Patriot Act expanded surveillance while camouflaging how many innocent Americans were swept up in data dragnets.

The Patriot Act authorized life sentences in prison for computer hackers who maliciously spread viruses, but federal agents were exempt from the law. The FBI created a special program to send emails to individuals to infect their computers with malware that enabled keystroke monitoring and automatic detection of all passwords. Norton, McAfee, and other computer security firms secretly agreed to leave a backdoor for the FBI to exploit with no warning to computer users.[13] James Dempsey of the Center for Democracy and Technology observed: "In order for the government to seize your diary or read your letters, they have to knock on your door with a search warrant. But [FBI malware] would allow them to seize these without notice."[14] The FBI also developed malware permitting it to covertly turn on a computer's camcorder "without triggering the light that lets users know it is recording," as the *Washington Post* reported in 2013.[15]

The Patriot Act spurred the launch of Total Information Awareness (TIA). That program featured a spiffy logo with a giant green eye atop a pyramid, covering half the globe with a yellow haze along with the motto *Scientia est Potentia*, "Knowledge is Power." The ACLU's Jay Stanley labeled TIA "the mother of all privacy invasions. It would amount to a picture of your life so complete it's equivalent to somebody following you around all day with a video camera."[16] TIA even planned to vacuum up veterinary records. Columnist Ted Rall quipped: "The TIA believes that knowing if and when Fluffy got spayed — and whether your son stopped torturing Fluffy after you put him on Ritalin — will help the military stop terrorists before they strike."[17] TIA bankrolled research to achieve and "Gait Recognition" — so that no stride could go unrecognized — and "odor recognition" to identify people by their sweat or urine — creating new job opportunities for deviants.[18] TIA speedily dispersed dozens of research grants before Congress yanked in the reins after a public backlash.[19] The Pentagon changed the name of the program from Total Information Awareness to Terrorist Information Awareness, but they still needed unlimited information on everyone because you can't tell who might be a damn terrorist.

The Patriot Act made it far easier for FBI agents to snatch personal data via National Security Letters (NSLs). These subpoenas compel individuals, businesses, and other institutions to surrender confidential or proprietary information that the FBI claims is related to a national security investigation. As the *Washington Post* noted in 2005, NSLs enable the FBI to seize records that reveal

> where a person makes and spends money, with whom he lives and lived before, how much he gambles, what he buys online, what he pawns and borrows, where he travels, how he invests, what he searches for and reads on the Web, and who telephones or emails him at home and at work.[20]

The number of NSLs increased a hundredfold after 9/11.[21] There is no judicial oversight of this power, and each FBI field office is entitled to dictate its own NSLs. Almost every NSL is accompanied by a gag order — anyone who discloses that their data had been raided by the FBI could be sent to prison for five years.

By 2006, the FBI was issuing 50,000 NSLs a year.[22] A single NSL can lasso thousands of people's records. FBI agents compelled public libraries and bookstores to surrender records of what books people borrowed or bought. In 2004, the FBI used NSLs to snare personal data on almost a million people who visited Las Vegas around New Year's Eve.[23]

When the Patriot Act came up for renewal in 2006, the Bush administration deceived Congress by greatly understating the number of NSLs and denying that any abuses had occurred. The following year, an Inspector General report revealed that more than 10,000 NSLs may have violated federal law. Senate Majority Whip Richard Durbin (D-IL) asserted that the IG report "confirms the American people's worst fears about the Patriot Act."[24] Rather than arresting FBI agents who brazenly broke the law, FBI chief Robert Mueller created a new FBI Office of Integrity and Compliance. Federal Judge Victor Marrero castigated NSLs in 2007 as "the legislative equivalent of breaking and entering, with an ominous free pass to the hijacking of constitutional values."[25] But his decisions were overturned by federal appeals courts.

The J. Edgar Hoover Memorial Vacuum Cleaner

In 1972, the Supreme Court rebuked President Richard Nixon, declaring that our "Fourth Amendment freedoms cannot properly be guaranteed if domestic security surveillances may be conducted solely within the discretion of the Executive Branch."[26] In 1974, the House Judiciary Committee voted to impeach Nixon in part because of his illegal wiretapping.[27] In 1978, Congress passed the Foreign Intelligence Surveillance Act (FISA) to outlaw political spying on American citizens. FISA created a secret court to oversee federal surveillance of suspected foreign agents within the U.S., permitting a much more lenient standard for wiretaps than the Constitution permitted for American citizens.

The FISA Court, where judges hear only the government's accusations, rubberstamped almost all the 35,000 secret search warrant requests it received from federal agents between 1978 and 2001. FISA warrants authorize the FBI to

> conduct simultaneous telephone, microphone, cellphone, email and computer surveillance of the U.S. person target's home, workplace and vehicles. Similar breadth is accorded the FBI in physical searches of the target's residence, office, vehicles, computer, safe deposit box and U.S. mails.[28]

People surveilled under FISA orders rarely learn the feds have been intruding unless they are arrested as a result.

But the Bush administration ordained that neither federal law nor Supreme Court rulings limited the president's power to surveil Americans. Bush authorized the NSA to wiretap vast numbers of citizens who had no direct or suspected link to terrorism. During his 2004 re-election campaign, Bush falsely publicly proclaimed that the U.S. government was not wiretapping Americans without a warrant. The *New York Times* learned of the warrantless wiretaps in mid-2004 but delayed exposing the abuses until a year after Bush was re-elected. The *Times*'s James Risen revealed that the "NSA is now [illegally] eavesdropping on as many as five hundred people at any given time" in the U.S., while a secret presidential order entitled NSA to peruse "the email of millions of Americans."[29] One government official told the *Washington Post* that administration officials complained bitterly that the FISA process "demanded too much: to name a target... to put down a written justification for the wiretap. They couldn't dream one up."[30] The NSA program was quickly christened the "J. Edgar Hoover Memorial Vacuum Cleaner."[31]

Bush administration lawyers fought to re-establish wiretapping as a presidential prerogative. Attorney General Alberto Gonzales announced that "the president has the inherent authority under the Constitution, as commander in chief, to engage in this kind of activity."[32] The Justice Department asserted: "The use of signals intelligence to identify and pinpoint the enemy is a traditional component of wartime military operations."[33] Americans' phones and email were simply another battlefield on which George W. Bush had unlimited power. The administration never explained why it was entitled to treat all Americans as potential enemies. During the January 2006 State of the Union address, Republican members of Congress gave Bush a standing ovation after he announced that he was renaming his grand intrusion as the Terrorist Surveillance Program.

On May 10, 2006, *USA Today* revealed that the NSA was tracking the calls of tens of millions of Americans and constructing the "largest database ever assembled in the world."[34] The nation's largest telephone companies daily delivered masses of personal records to the feds. Under a 1986 federal law, companies faced penalties of a thousand dollars for each customer whose privacy was illegally violated. Bush responded to that exposé: "The intelligence activities I authorized are lawful" — but this was a "my lawyers told me so" version of legality.[35] Bush also declared: "We are not trolling through the personal lives of millions of innocent Americans."[36] But that was true only if almost all Americans are guilty — or at least guilty enough to spy on.

Two weeks later, the FISA Court swallowed one of the biggest legal howlers in U.S. history. The Patriot Act's Section 215 entitled the FBI to demand "business records" that are "relevant" to a terrorism or espionage investigation. The Bush administration bizarrely decided that the phone records of all Americans were "relevant" to terrorism investigations.[37] This "finding" was kept secret from the public and the vast majority of members of Congress — as well as from most of the federal judges who heard cases challenging the administration's surveillance regime. At the Bush administration and FBI's behest, the FISA Court compelled telephone companies to deliver all their calling records (including time, duration, and location of calls) each day to the NSA. A legal doctrine that could not withstand an hour's ridicule in the sunlight festered for years behind closed government doors.

Americans who believed they were being illegally wiretapped by the NSA filed lawsuits.[38] In August 2006, Federal Judge Anna Diggs Taylor scoffed that the administration's lawyers claimed "the inherent power" to violate federal laws and the Constitution.[39] Taylor summarized the issue: "There are no hereditary Kings in America and no power not created by the Constitution." The Justice Department speedily found a higher court to overturn Taylor's decision and refused to even consider the merits of the case because "the plaintiffs are ultimately prevented from establishing standing because of the State Secrets privilege." This was the judicial version of Frat Party Ethics: As long as the government blindfolded its victims, it could do as it pleases. The *Washington Post* applauded the contortions used to dismiss the case.

In the summer of 2007, the Bush administration railroaded the Protect America Act through Congress. That law temporarily entitled the feds to surveil any phone call or email by any Americans who they "reasonably believed" was contacting or being contacted by someone — anyone — outside the United States. That dragnet pulled in college students emailing their parents during a semester abroad as well as American soldiers phoning spouses from Baghdad. In July 2008, Congress awarded retroactive immunity to telephone companies who had betrayed their customers via the "Terrorist Surveillance Program" since 2001. Congress whitewashed the program without even knowing how many Americans' privacy had been obliterated. In the following years, the FISA Court approved 99.9% of all federal FISA warrant requests.[40]

"Hope and Change" Bait-and-Switch

Senator Barack Obama's denunciations of the Bush administration's warrantless wiretaps secured his stature as a champion of civil liberties. Campaigning for president, Obama pledged "no more illegal wiretapping of American citizens… No more ignoring the law when it is inconvenient."[41] However, after he clinched the Democratic Party presidential nomination, he reversed himself and voted for granting immunity to telecom companies. Obama appointees sharply expanded the NSA's seizures of Americans' personal data. The *Washington Post* characterized Obama's first term as "a period of exponential growth for the NSA's domestic collection."[42]

The acid drip of revelations of illicit surveillance continued regardless of "Hope and Change." In June 2009, the NSA admitted that it had collected the personal information of vast numbers of Americans; the *New York Times* reported that "the number of individual communications that were improperly collected could number in the millions."[43] But it wasn't a crime;

it was merely inadvertent "overcollection" of Americans' personal data which NSA would retain for five years. In 2010, the *Washington Post* reported that "every day, collection systems at the [NSA] intercept and store 1.7 billion emails, phone calls and other types of communications."[44] In 2011, NSA expanded a program to provide real-time location information of every American with a cellphone, acquiring more than a billion cellphone records each day from AT&T.[45]

Obama also perpetuated Bush-era legal doctrines to totally shield federal surveillance regimes from judicial scrutiny. After the Supreme Court accepted a case on warrantless wiretaps in 2012, the Obama administration urged the Justices to dismiss the case. A *New York Times* editorial labeled the administration's position "a particularly cynical Catch-22: Because the wiretaps are secret and no one can say for certain that their calls have been or will be monitored, no one has standing to bring suit over the surveillance."[46]

Cynical arguments sufficed for five Justices. Justice Samuel Alito, writing for the majority, declared that the Court was averse to granting standing to challenge the government based on "theories that require guesswork" and "no specific facts" and fears of "hypothetical future harm."[47] The Supreme Court insisted that the government already offered plenty of safeguards — such as the FISA Court — to protect Americans' rights. Law professor Stephen Vladeck responded to the decision: "The coffin is slamming shut on the ability of private citizens and civil liberties groups to challenge government counterterrorism policies."[48]

Three months later, newspapers around the world began publishing confidential documents leaked by former NSA analyst Edward Snowden. Americans learned that the NSA can tap almost any cellphone in the world, exploit computer games like *Angry Birds* to poach personal data, access anyone's email and web browsing history, remotely penetrate almost all computers, and crack the vast majority of computer encryption. The NSA used Facebook and Google apps to send malware to targeted individuals. NSA also filched almost 200,000,000 records a month from private computer cloud accounts.

Snowden revealed how the NSA had covertly carried out "the most significant change in the history of American espionage from the targeted surveillance of individuals to the mass surveillance of entire populations." The NSA created a "repository capable of taking in 20 billion 'record events' daily and making them available to NSA analysts within 60 minutes."[49] The NSA is able to snare and stockpile a billion times more information than did East Germany's Stasi secret police, one of the most odious agencies of the post-war era.

"Blame the messenger" was the response in official Washington. House Intelligence Committee Chairman Mike Rogers (R-MI) responded to Snowden's revelations: "You can't have your privacy violated if you don't know your privacy is violated."[50] Rogers was in charge of congressional oversight of federal surveillance, but he proffered the same excuse used by sleazeballs who use date rape drugs.

Top congressional leaders denounced Snowden as a "traitor," and some suggested the U.S. government hunt him down and kill him. Obama administration appointees insisted that NSA only targeted individuals linked to terrorism. But NSA's definition of *terrorist suspect* was ludicrously broad, including "someone searching the Web for suspicious stuff."[51] If someone used encryption for their emails, that alone justified wiretapping them. Snowden commented in 2014: "If I had wanted to pull a copy of a judge's or a senator's email, all I had to do was enter that selector into XKEYSCORE,"[52] an NSA program that required no warrant from FISA or any other court.[53]

President Obama boldly proclaimed: "There is no spying on Americans."[54] But Section 702 of the FISA Amendments Act of 2008 entitled the feds to vacuum up Americans' personal data for later perusal. The *Washington Post* analyzed a cache of 160,000 secret email conversations/threads (provided by Snowden) that the NSA intercepted and found that nine out of ten account holders were not the "intended surveillance targets but were caught in a net the agency had cast for somebody else."[55] Almost half of the individuals whose personal data was inadvertently commandeered were U.S. citizens. The files "tell stories of love and heartbreak, illicit sexual liaisons, mental-health crises, political and religious conversions, financial anxieties and disappointed hopes," the *Post* noted. If an American citizen wrote an email in a foreign language, NSA analysts assumed they were a foreigner who could be surveilled without a warrant.

Snowden also revealed that the FISA Court had "created a secret body of law giving the National Security Agency the power to amass vast collections of data on Americans," the *New York Times* reported in 2013.[56]

The classified rulings showed FISA judges rubberstamping stunning seizures of Americans' personal data, flagrantly contradicting Supreme Court rulings on the Fourth Amendment. The *Times* noted that the FISA Court had "become almost a parallel Supreme Court, serving as the ultimate arbiter on surveillance issues" — and almost always gave federal agencies all the power they sought. The vast majority of members of Congress were unaware that a secret court had secretly nullified much of the Bill of Rights. That did not deter Obama from proclaiming that the FISA Court was "transparent" — though only the White House could see.

Snowden's revelations outraged some judges. In December 2013, Federal Judge Richard Leon issued a ruling denouncing the NSA surveillance regime as "almost Orwellian": "I cannot imagine a more indiscriminate and arbitrary invasion than this systematic and high-tech collection and retention of personal data on virtually every single citizen... without prior judicial approval."[57] Obama sought to defuse the controversy by appointing an expert panel to vindicate his surveillance. But the panel reported that there was not a single case where the telephone data roundup had been necessary to stop a terrorist attack. The panel's report also warned: "Americans must never make the mistake of wholly trusting our public officials."[58]

Author and NSA expert James Bamford observed shortly before the 2016 election: "Over his two terms, Obama has created the most powerful surveillance state the world has ever seen."[59] Despite the uproars over Snowden's revelations, neither Congress nor federal courts fundamentally pulled in the reins.

Snowden's stunning disclosures also failed to curb the prerogative of federal agencies to meddle in presidential elections. (The FBI's abuse of FISA to target the 2016 Trump presidential campaign will be discussed in Chapter 14, "American Gestapo Run Amok.")

Non-Stop Courtly Kowtowing

The NSA continued stockpiling personal data but federal officials promised not to wrongfully peek. But in April 2021, a FISA Court report revealed that the FBI has pilfered that database for warrantless searches for "public corruption and bribery," "healthcare fraud," and other targets — including people who notified the FBI of crimes and even repairmen entering FBI offices.[60] Even people who volunteered for the FBI "Citizens Academy" program were illegally tracked by the FBI. An FBI agent conducted a database search "using the identifiers of about 16,000 people, even though only seven of them had connections to an investigation."[61] FISA Court Chief Judge James Boasberg lamented "apparent widespread violations" of the legal restrictions for FBI searches but shrugged them off and permitted FBI rummaging to continue.[62]

In June 2021, Fox News host Tucker Carlson charged that the NSA illegally spied on him and leaked his emails. Carlson explained that he went public with his charge "defensively... I don't have subpoena power. I can't arrest anybody. I can't make them answer questions."[63] The NSA responded with a statement declaring that "Carlson has never been an intelligence target of the Agency... With limited exceptions (e.g., an emergency), NSA may not target a U.S. citizen without a court order that explicitly authorizes the targeting."[64] But the vast majority of people whose emails and other data are dragged into NSA dragnets are not NSA's actual targets. Axios reported that "Carlson was talking to U.S.-based Kremlin intermediaries about setting up an interview with Vladimir Putin shortly" before he accused the NSA of spying on him.[65] U.S. government officials allegedly became aware of Carlson's effort to interview Putin, but leaking his emails would still be a federal crime.

In 2022, for the first time, the FISA Court revealed the number of warrantless searches the FBI conducted on Americans using Section 702. The report stated that "fewer than 3,394,053" Americans' privacy had been zapped by FBI warrantless searches.[66] It was surprising that the feds did not use this alternative headline for the press release: "More than 320,974,609 Americans not illegally searched by the FBI." That report was issued from the Office of Civil Liberties, Privacy, and Transparency of the Office of the Director of National Intelligence. But there was scant transparency aside from a raw number that raised far more questions than it answered. Almost two million of those searches involved an investigation of Russian hacking. But there aren't that many hackers in the United States. The State Department's Global Engagement Center presumed that anyone whose tweets agreed with a position of the Russian government should be banned by Twitter for being a Russian agent. Did the FBI use a similar "catch-all" standard to justify seizing two million Americans' email and other online data?

In May 2023, a heavily redacted FISA Court decision revealed that the FBI continued exempting itself from the Constitution.[67] For each American that the FISA Court authorized the FBI to target, the FBI illicitly surveilled almost 1,000 additional Americans. The FBI admitted to conducting 278,000 illicit searches of Americans in 2020 and early 2021 (the period covered by the FISA Court ruling released in May 2023).

The FBI presumed that any American suspected of supporting the January 6, 2021, protests forfeited his constitutional rights.[68] An FBI whistleblower revealed in congressional testimony in May 2023 that FBI headquarters pressured FBI agents to treat anyone who attended the January 6 protests as a criminal suspect.[69] Roughly 2,000 pro-Trump protestors (including an unknown number of undercover agents and informants) entered the Capitol that day. But an FBI analyst exploited FISA to unjustifiably conduct searches on 23,132 Americans citizens "to find evidence of possible foreign influence, although the analyst conducting the queries had no indications of foreign influence," according to FISA Chief Judge Rudolph Contreras.

The FBI exploited FISA to target 19,000 campaign donors to a candidate who challenged an incumbent member of Congress. An FBI analyst justified the warrantless searches by claiming that "the campaign was a target of foreign influence," but the Justice Department concluded that almost all of those searches violated FISA rules. (In March, Rep. Darin LaHood [R-IL] revealed that he had been wrongly targeted by the FBI in numerous FISA 702 searches.)

The FBI conducted secret searches of the emails and other data of 133 people arrested during the protests after the killing of George Floyd in 2020. The FBI also conducted 656 warrantless searches to see whether they could find any derogatory information on people they planned to use as informants. The FBI routinely conducted warrantless searches on "individuals listed in police homicide reports, including victims, next-of-kin, witnesses, and suspects." Even the Justice Department complained those searches were improper.

FISA Chief Judge Contreras lamented that FBI "compliance problems… have proven to be persistent and widespread." But the FISA Court treats the FBI like sap-headed judges treat serial shoplifters. FISA Court rulings have complained for 20 years about FBI agents lying to the court. As long as the FBI periodically promises to repent, the FISA Court entitles them to continue decimating the Fourth Amendment. FISA should be renamed the "Trust Me, Chumps!" Surveillance Act.

You Might Be a Terrorist If...

Surveillance also exploded at the street level after 9/11. In a 2003 terrorist advisory, the Department of Homeland Security warned local law enforcement agencies to keep an eye on anyone who "expressed dislike of attitudes and decisions of the U.S. government."[70] DHS officials urged local lawmen to be on alert for potential suicide bombers who "may appear to be in a 'trance'" or whose "eyes appear to be focused and vigilant," as well as people whose "clothing is out of sync with the weather" or whose "clothing is loose." Federal experts were especially fretful of malcontents for whom "waiting in a grocery store line becomes intolerable." A 2015 Air Force publication characterized Muslim women wearing hijabs as a form of "passive terrorism,"[71] while a 2009 Pentagon document categorized antiwar protests as "low level terrorism."[72] As Techdirt.com quipped: "The price of freedom may be eternal vigilance, but the price of security is endless paranoia."[73]

Wacky warnings spewed out of federally funded state Homeland Security departments. In 2012, the New Jersey Office of Homeland Security and Preparedness published a terrorist warning list including "signs of nervousness," "exaggerated yawning when engaged in conversation," "rigid posture," "goose bumps," and "glances" (which are more suspicious in Jersey City than anywhere else in the nation).[74]

DHS bankrolls roughly 70 fusion centers that serve as hubs for cooperation between federal, state, and local agencies. Fusion centers deluge federal counterterrorism centers with Suspicious Activity Reports assembled by law enforcement. The Los Angeles Police Department encourages people to notify the authorities if they see "individuals who stay at bus or train stops for extended periods while buses and trains come and go," "joggers who stand and stretch for an inordinate amount of time," and people "using binoculars."[75] The Kentucky Office of Homeland Security encourages citizens to report "people avoiding eye contact" or homes or apartments that have numerous visitors "arriving and leaving at unusual hours."[76] Colorado's fusion center "produced a fearmongering public-service announcement asking the public to report innocuous behaviors such as photography, note-taking, drawing, and collecting money for charity as 'warning signs' of terrorism," the ACLU reported.[77] The Jacksonville Urban Area Security Initiative used a federal grant to produce an 8-minute film entitled "Domestic Terrorism: The First Line of Defense," which urged viewers to be especially wary of people "of average or above-average intelligence" (unlike the wizards who made the film).

Fusion centers target political opinions. A Texas fusion center warned that Muslim lobbying groups were "providing an environment for terrorist organizations to flourish" and urged local law enforcement to report Muslim "hip hop bands," chat forums, and blogs.[78] Utah's fusion center warned in 2016 that anyone displaying the Revolutionary War-era Gadsden flag ("Don't Tread on Me") might be an "extremist." A 2010 DHS report went even further, warning that being "reverent of individual liberty" is a trait of potential right-wing terrorists.[79] The Missouri Information Analysis Center warned about people who "display Constitutional Party, Campaign for Liberty, or Libertarian material" and who were supporters of "former Libertarian presidential candidate Ron Paul."[80] Such catch-all standards help explain why the federal terrorist watchlist now contains more than a million names. In 2014, the Electronic Frontier Foundation warned that "fusion centers have been used to record and share information about First Amendment-protected activities in a way that aids repressive police activity and chills freedom of association."[81]

A Senate investigation found that no evidence the fusion centers ever detected or disrupted a terrorist plot. But it would be unfair to expect fusion centers to discover terrorists when the feds cannot even locate the centers. A DHS internal report found that 4 of 72 fusion centers did not actually exist. The Senate investigation found that the federal estimates of spending on fusion centers varied by more than 400% — ranging from $289 million to $1.4 billion. The *Washington Post* highlighted a few of the dubious findings: "More than $2 million was spent on a center for Philadelphia that never opened. In Ohio, officials used the money to buy rugged laptop computers and then gave them to a local morgue."[82]

But the FBI made fusion center reports look like paragons of prudence. The FBI cranked out loony warning lists for dozens of businesses and industries. In its "Potential Indicators of Terrorist Activities Related to Internet Cafés," the FBI sounded the alarm about customers who "are overly concerned about privacy, attempts to shield the screen from view of others," "always pay cash," or "travel illogical distance to use Internet Café."[83] The FBI did not include a mileage formula for "logical distances." Anyone who worked at an Internet café was urged to contact law enforcement on such dangerous customers: "Gather information about individuals without drawing attention to yourself. Identify license plates, vehicle description, names used, languages spoken, ethnicity, etc." After gathering the incriminating information, Internet café employees or managers were instructed to call the Joint Regional Intelligence Center (JRIC) and say the word "Tripwire." The FBI pamphlet did not specify whether callers should hide in a bomb shelter after muttering "Tripwire."

Tattoo shops were instructed to watch for terrorist traits including people who "have missing fingers" or anyone who "significantly alters appearance from visit to visit (shaving beard, changing hair color, style of dress, etc.)." So shops that dye skin should freak out if customers dye their hair?[84]

The terrorist warning list for hotel guests includes "using payphones for outgoing calls," using "Do Not Disturb" signs, and "not using a credit card to settle a hotel bill." In 2016, DHS issued a "Safe Action Project" alert urging hotel staff to notify police or the FBI if guests used too many condoms.[85]

The Obama administration also created a set of warning signs to target families. In 2014, the National Counterterrorism Center issued a report "to alert government officials to individuals at risk of turning to radical violence, and to families or communities at risk of incubating extremist ideologies." That report recommended that "police, social workers and educators rate individuals on a scale of one to five in categories such as 'Expressions of Hopelessness, Futility'... and 'Connection to Group Identity (Race, Nationality, Religion, Ethnicity),'" as the *Intercept* reported.[86] Low scores signaled "susceptibility to engage in violent extremism." The report recommended judging families by their level of "Parent-Child Bonding" and rating localities on the basis in part of the "presence of ideologues or recruiters." Would copies of Ayn Rand's *Atlas Shrugged* or Marx's *Das Kapital* on the living room bookshelf trigger a warning of incipient extremism?

Biden Bonanza of Paranoia

In early 2021, the Biden administration's National Strategy for Countering Domestic Terrorism revealed that guys who can't get laid could be terrorist threats due to "involuntary celibate violent extremism."[87] Administration officials did not disclose whether self-abuse was the latest terrorist warning sign.[88] The FBI's guide to Involuntary Celibate Violent Extremism lists phrases signaling potential violent extremism including "baldcel" (someone who is bald), "Red Pill" (the awakening to the pervasive deceit of the current society and regime), and "Ascension" (a term for when an incel finally miraculously gets laid).[89]

The Biden administration is narrowing the boundaries of respectable thought. Policymakers launched a "legal workaround" to spy on and potentially entrap Americans who are "perpetuating the 'narratives' of concern," CNN reported.[90] The DHS plan would "allow the department to circumvent [constitutional and legal] limits" on surveillance of private citizens and groups. Federal agencies are prohibited from targeting individuals solely for First Amendment-protected speech and activities. But federal hirelings would be under no such restraint. Private informants could create false identities, which would be problematic if done by federal agents.

One DHS official wailed to CNN: "Domestic violent extremists are really adaptive and innovative. We see them... couching their language so they don't trigger any kind of red flag on any platforms."[91] Certain groups of people are apparently guilty regardless of what they say ("couching their language"). Many of the targets simply have a bad attitude towards Washington.[92]

In a February 7, 2022, Terrorist Alert, DHS warned of a "heightened threat environment" fueled by "false or misleading narratives."[93] DHS fretted about online agitators who seek to "sow discord and undermine public trust in government institutions to encourage unrest." The feds were especially spooked by "widespread online proliferation of false or misleading narratives regarding unsubstantiated widespread election fraud and COVID-19." But many of the claims on COVID by federal agencies in early 2022 were later exposed as false. As journalist Alex Berenson noted: "These [DHS] public statements are not merely wallpaper. They can reflect secret government decisions about what police or intelligence tactics are acceptable against targeted groups."

On November 30, 2022, DHS issued a "heightened threat" warning:

> Perceptions of government overreach continue to drive individuals to attempt to commit violence targeting government officials... Some domestic violent extremists have expressed grievances based on perceptions that the government is overstepping its Constitutional authorities.

Fear of "government overreach" justified viewing people as potential terrorists, regardless of how far the feds were reaching.

The terrorist threat was exploited for political profit. In a May 2023 speech at Howard University, President Biden declared: "White supremacy... is the single most dangerous terrorist threat in our homeland."[94] Former FBI agent Steve Friend lamented in 2023 the broad brush of suspicion being used by the FBI and federal intelligence agencies:

> There is this belief that half the country are domestic terrorists and we can't have a conversation with [them]. There is a fundamental belief that unless you are voicing what we agree, there is an understanding that you are the enemy.[95]

In 2022, a senior government official told *Newsweek*'s William Arkin, one of the best investigative journalists in D.C.: "Washington is obsessed with threats to Washington itself. We've become too prone to labeling anything we don't like as extremism, and then any extremist as a terrorist."[96]

Current and former FBI officials told the *Washington Times* that "the demand for White supremacy" from FBI headquarters "vastly outstrips the supply of White supremacy. We have more people assigned to investigate White supremacists than we can actually find." In 2023, FBI Special Agent Garret O'Boyle notified congressional investigators that the FBI was multiplying domestic terrorism cases by breaking individual cases into multiple investigators. O'Boyle observed: "I was working on one case. But, the FBI can then say, well, he actually had four, and so we need you to give us more money because look at how big of a threat all this domestic terrorism is."[97]

One FBI agent groused:

> We are sort of the lapdogs... trying to find a crime to fit otherwise First Amendment-protected activities. If they have a Gadsden flag and they own guns and they are mean at school board meetings, that's probably a domestic terrorist.

Buck Naked at the Border

Federal agencies exploit any flimsy legal pretext to obliterate citizens' privacy. In 2008, DHS formally entitled Customs agents to "detain" Americans' phones, laptops, and private papers "for a reasonable period of time" to "review and analyze information" when they return from abroad. Customs agents became entitled to seize "'any device capable of storing information,' including hard drives, flash drives, cellphones, iPods, pagers, beepers, and video and audio tapes," the *Washington Post* reported.[98] Agents are also entitled to commandeer "all papers and other written documentation," including books, pamphlets, and "written materials commonly referred to as 'pocket trash' or 'pocket litter.'" Federal agents are authorized to photocopy any papers and electronic records a person possessed.

"Absent individualized suspicion" is the "open-sez-me" legal phrase entitling the feds to unlimited power at the border. Bureaucrats have the right to vacuum up your life simply because they are the government and you are a lowly private citizen. A federal appeals court ruled in 2015 that copying traveler's hard drives was "essentially a computer strip search" and said officials' concerns about crime did "not justify unfettered crime-fighting searches or an unregulated assault on citizens' private information." But other courts upheld the searches, and the pilfering continues.

In September 2022, the *Washington Post* reported that the Customs and Border Protection agency was adding "data from as many as 10,000 electronic devices each year to a massive database they've compiled from cellphones, iPads and computers."[99] Once that data is in a federal depository, it is retained for 15 years (for "long-term review") and can be searched for any reason (depravity? sheer curiosity?) by thousands of Customs and Border Patrol agents and perhaps also by legions of other federal agents.

Wherever You Go, We Know

Geysers of federal funding are propelling local and state surveillance. License plate readers are proliferating across the nation thanks to grants from DHS. Maryland used federal grants to equip hundreds of police cars with license plate scanners that create almost 100 million records per year detailing exactly where and when each vehicle travels. The grants also paid for stationary cameras that recorded license plates passing on nearby roads. The vast databank has been almost a total failure at nailing violent criminals or car thieves or terrorists.[100]

License plate readers are creating a federal database of gun show attendees.[101] Immigration and Customs Enforcement (ICE) arranged for local police to scan license plates of attendees at a Southern California gun show.[102] A 2015 ACLU investigation concluded that DEA and ATF also used license plate readers to round up information about gun show attendees. Anyone who attended gun shows in recent years could have a federal dossier which could justify further investigations and targeting.

In 2018, Americans learned that the radar speed signs scattered across the nation's roads were often actually covert DEA license trackers.[103] DEA is secretly constructing a nationwide network of license plate readers "to track in real time the movement of vehicles around the U.S., a secret domestic intelligence-gathering program that scans and stores hundreds of millions of records."[104] The ACLU revealed that DEA was also stockpiling photos of anyone traveling in the cars. Devlin Barrett of the *Wall Street Journal* observed that internal DEA documents made "repeated references to the primary goal of this program being asset forfeiture."[105] As Chapter 2 noted, DEA agents deployed in the nation's airports are notorious for pilfering travelers' cash on any flimsy pretext.

Dragnet-style surveillance on America's roads enables government agencies to know far too much about private citizens. As a federal appeals court ruled:

> A person who knows all of another's travels can deduce whether he is a weekly church goer, a heavy drinker, a regular at the gym, an unfaithful husband, an outpatient receiving medical treatment, an associate of particular individuals or political groups — and not just one such fact about a person, but all such facts.[106]

The Biggest "Workaround" of the Constitution

The feds are snaring more personal information on Americans than ever before.[107] The Supreme Court ruled in 2018 that police need a search warrant to seize tracking data on a person's car. But government agencies can poach the same information now by purchasing commercially available information (CAI) that private companies vacuum up from smartphones, computers, and other digital devices and trackers. A June 2023 report by the Office of the Director of National Intelligence noted:

> The government would never have been permitted to compel billions of people to carry location tracking devices on their persons at all times, to log and track most of their social interactions, or to keep flawless records of all their reading habits.

Federal agencies have always been permitted to use publicly available information for investigations. But the contrast between that data and the new data is the difference between "a ride on horseback" and "a flight to the moon," as a federal court declared in 2014. The feds could use CAI "to identify every person who attended a protest or rally based on their smartphone location or ad-tracking records," the report warned.

The Centers for Disease Control and Prevention bought private data from tens of millions of cellphones to check obedience to COVID lockdown and curfew decrees.[108] A California county paid for information revealing how many people attended each church during COVID lockdowns. The Internal Revenue Service purchased location and tracking data from a private firm that sells data harvested from dating apps. Thanks to CAI, the feds can learn about any website you visited, any tweet you liked, anywhere you drove, and almost anything you purchased with a credit card. The potential abuses are so sweeping that even Biden's Director of National Intelligence waved a caution flag.

CAI is child's play compared to illicit surveillance technology that the Biden administration recently banned. Foreign companies are marketing powerful surveillance technology that provides "near-effortless remote infection of devices" including cellphones. In late 2021, the Biden administration banned U.S. companies from purchasing potential spyware from specific foreign companies in part because of concern about targeting of U.S. government officials. However, U.S. government agencies continued to patronize one of the banned companies, and most U.S. cabinet departments purchased foreign software to enable warrantless tracking of individuals and other intrusions.[109] Albert Fox Cahn of the Surveillance Technology Oversight Project warned: "We can't allow every federal department to turn into its own spy agency." More scandals are pending.

Conclusion: How Spying Subverts Freedom

Federal intelligence agencies refuse to estimate how many Americans' lives have been snared in government databases. There is no reason to presume that the feds have come clean. Prior to Edward Snowden's leaks, the feds probably admitted to less than 1% of their dubious surveillance abuses. Not to worry: the NSA recently ordered its staff to use "dignity and respect" when spying on its targets.[110]

Tracking illicit surveillance schemes is a never-ending Whack-a-Mole game. But a program occasionally pops up that showcases Washington's shamelessness. Because some drug dealers use money-counting machines, DEA absurdly decided to treat all purchasers like suspected drug dealers. DEA commenced compelling companies to report the name and address of anyone who purchased a money-counting machine, and many customers were subsequently hounded. One DEA official assured his colleagues:

"Unless a federal court tells us we can't do this, I think we can continue this project." The program was "legal" simply because it was secret and DEA denied its existence. DEA agents complained about wasting time targeting people "without any connection to illicit activity." After the Inspector General exposed the bureaucratic crime spree in 2019, DEA responded by issuing a press statement "pledging fealty to the rule of law," the *New York Times* noted.[111] But no DEA official was held responsible for the illegal searches, and DEA marched merrily on to larger budgets.

"Secrecy in lieu of legality" is D.C.'s favorite template. Illegal surveillance regimes are buttressed by bodyguards of lies. When one set of false claims is exposed, it doesn't torpedo a conniving federal agency. Instead, there is a brief pause, some administrative tweakings, and a new bureaucratic shroud. Surveillance programs should include a Miranda warning: any information the feds capture can be used against you.

Government surveillance is almost always more extensive than politicians admit. The scams used to protect programs from disclosure also quickly shield them from the law, the Constitution, and Congress. Americans rarely learn of the vast majority of outrages because regimes are designed for deniability. Judges presume surveillance regimes are innocuous as long as the names of victims are hidden. The government is irrevocably innocent unless it publicly confesses its crimes. Ludicrous denials of wrongdoing are the only safeguard Americans' rights and liberties need — or deserve. The new definition of *paranoia* is suspecting the feds are up to no good when they break the law.

Spying regimes can go berserk after being unleashed. A 2011 PowerPoint slide show captured NSA's pursuit of omniscience: "Know It All, Collect It All, Process It All, Exploit It All, Partner It All."[112] But the U.S. government already overdosed on trivia. Prior to 9/11, U.S. intelligence agencies "wanted to know everything about everything all the time," according to a 2002 congressional analysis.[113] As a result, the CIA, NSA, and FBI failed to focus on the gravest terrorist threats.

Once vast surveillance regimes are created, bureaucratic momentum continually discovers new enemies. Nixon White House aide Tom Charles Huston testified to Congress in 1973 that the FBI's COINTELPRO program continually stretched its target list "from the kid with a bomb to the kid with a picket sign, and from the kid with the picket sign to the kid with the bumper sticker of the opposing candidate."[114] Nowadays, suspicion

extends to ever wackier targets, including anyone paying cash to surf the
Internet, tourists photographing landmarks, and three-fingered tattoo parlor
customers.

The further government intrudes, the easier it becomes to frighten people
into submission. Sen. Sam Ervin (D-NC) observed shortly before the
Watergate scandal: "When people fear surveillance, whether it exists or not,
when they grow afraid to speak their minds and hearts freely to their
Government or to anyone else, then we shall cease to be a free society."[115]
Permitting the feds to cannibalize personal data means that "we have the
government controlling us instead of us controlling the government," as Sen.
Patrick Leahy (D-VT) said in 2014.[116] Almost 40 years earlier, Sen. Frank
Church (D-ID) warned that the NSA's surveillance "capability at any time
could be turned around on the American people and no American would
have any privacy left… There would be no place to hide."[117]

The NSA's surveillance power became far greater in the subsequent
decades with the rise of the Internet and the digitization of records. The NSA
has already used its colossal database of Americans' phone and email records
to "create sophisticated graphs of some Americans' social connections that
can identify their associates, their locations at certain times, their traveling
companions and other personal information."[118] As a 1976 Senate report
warned: "The mere existence of the additional information gained through
the investigative programs inevitably demonstrated those particular
organizational or personal weaknesses which were vulnerable to
disruption."[119] A leaked 2012 NSA document exposed how the agency
exploits "personal vulnerabilities" by tracking their targets "viewing sexually
explicit material online."[120]

Pervasive surveillance undermines one of the most effective checks on
government abuses. Supreme Court Justice Robert Jackson declared in a
1949 dissent: "Uncontrolled search and seizure is one of the first and most
effective weapons in the arsenal of every arbitrary government."[121] Jackson,
who had been the chief prosecutor at the Nuremberg war crimes trials, had
seen the effects of the Nazi regime's total surveillance and ruthless searches.
Jackson warned that no other government attack on the rights of citizens
was "so effective in cowing a population, crushing the spirit of the individual
and putting terror in every heart."

It is an illusion that privacy can survive like Guam in the middle of the
Pacific Ocean despite federal dragnets. Boundless spying fundamentally

changes the relation of the government to the American people. Shortly after Snowden's revelations, PEN — the world's leading literary and human rights organization — released a survey showing that American writers "deliberately avoided certain topics in phone or email conversations" and "avoided writing or speaking about a particular topic" because of the NSA. Journalist Glenn Greenwald asserted that governments "crave surveillance... precisely because the possibility of being monitored radically changes individual and collective behavior," spurring "fear and collective conformity."[122] Security expert Bruce Schneier observed: "The fact that you won't do things, that you will self-censor, are the worst effects of pervasive surveillance."[123]

Is America defaulting into a "Don't-Hurt-Me Democracy"? Are people acquiescing to systemic lawbreaking while clinging to hope that they will not be placed on the target list? Citizens cannot submit to endless illicit intrusions without forfeiting their right to any remaining privacy.

12. "See No Evil" Democracy

"The road to tyranny… begins with the destruction of the truth."
— President Bill Clinton, 1995[1]

Secrecy and lying are two sides of the same political coin. The Supreme Court declared in 1936: "An informed public is the most potent of all restraints upon misgovernment."[2] Thus, conniving politicians have no choice but to drop an Iron Curtain around Washington.

Politicians guarantee that Americans are left clueless on the most controversial or dangerous federal policies. The government is creating trillions of pages of new secrets every year.[3] The total is equivalent to "20 million four-drawer filing cabinets filled with double-spaced text on paper."[4] If those cabinets were laid end to end, they would stretch almost to the moon. The feds have accumulated the equivalent of hundreds of pages of secrets for each American, blighting any hope for citizens to learn of their rulers' rascality.

Politicians and federal agencies recognize that "what people don't know won't hurt the government." James Madison, the Father of the Constitution, in 1798 described "the right of freely examining public characters and measures" as "the only effectual guardian of every other right." But as Daniel Ellsberg, who risked life in prison to leak the *Pentagon Papers*, observed in 2002, "The overwhelming majority of secrets do not leak to the American public."[5]

Secrecy is justified for narrow swaths of foreign policy, some aspects of national defense (such as new weapons systems), and a smattering of other official procedures. But in the decades after World War II, government secrecy mushroomed even faster than federal spending.

Throughout history, regimes have used secrecy and deceit to start wars, oppress citizens, and unleash havoc. "How do we make government and politicians honest?" is a quixotic question. Instead, the issue is: "How do we curtail the damage from official deceit?" The first step is to understand how secrecy proliferated, the damage it inflicts, and why secrecy is a grave peril to the survival of both liberty and democracy.

Secrecy and Mass Carnage

In 1961, President John F. Kennedy affirmed: "The very word 'secrecy' is repugnant in a free and open society; and we are as a people inherently and historically opposed to secret societies, to secret oaths, and to secret proceedings."[6] But such rhetorical flourishes did nothing to prevent the federal government from becoming a covert operation.

In the years after JFK's 1963 assassination, secrecy delivered a death warrant for tens of thousands of Americans and hundreds of thousands of Vietnamese. President Johnson fabricated claims about an alleged North Vietnamese attack in the Gulf of Tonkin to sway Congress to give him unlimited authority to attack North Vietnam.[7] Johnson assumed he was entitled to deceive Americans to vastly expand the war he decided to fight. When Assistant Defense Secretary Arthur Sylvester visited Saigon in 1965, he hectored American correspondents covering the Vietnam War: "Look, if you think any American official is going to tell you the truth, then you're stupid. Did you hear that? Stupid!" Sylvester declared that he expected the American press to be "the handmaidens of government."[8]

As the Vietnam War turned into a quagmire, the Pentagon ordered experts to analyze where the war had gone wrong. The resulting 47-volume study was labeled secret, but that did not stop the *New York Times* from commencing to publish it in 1971. After the Nixon administration got an injunction to block, the Court ruled 6 to 3 that the newspapers had the right to publish the classified documents. Justice Hugo Black wrote:

> The Government's power to censor the press was abolished so that the press would remain forever free to censure the Government. The press was protected so that it could bare the secrets of government and inform the people. Only a free and unrestrained press can effectively expose deception in government.[9]

Unfortunately, Americans' awareness of the perils of official deceit faded as the decades passed, and the U.S. government became far more aggressive abroad and at home.

Secrecy and the Divine Right to Deceive

"All rulers in all ages have tried to impose a false view of the world upon their followers," George Orwell wrote in his novel *1984*. This is where government classification — i.e., secrecy — comes in handy. The more information government classifies, the easier it becomes for politicians to dupe the American people. In Washington, deniability is better than the truth.

In March 1972, President Richard Nixon, as part of his "pledge to create an open Administration," announced that the classification system "failed to meet the standards of an open and democratic society, allowing too many papers to be classified for too long a time." He promised "to lift the veil of secrecy which now enshrouds" federal documents. Nixon's campaign against secrecy faltered after the Watergate coverup destroyed his presidency.

In 1991, former National Security Council official Rodney McDaniel estimated "that only 10% of classification was for 'legitimate protection of secrets.'"[10] In 1997, a federal commission headed by Sen. Daniel Patrick Moynihan (D-NY) lamented that "secrets in the federal government are whatever anyone with a stamp decides to stamp secret."[11]

In the weeks after the 9/11 attacks, the percentage of Americans who trusted the federal government doubled. The Bush administration exploited the new credulity to boost the number of classified government documents almost tenfold. The more secretive the government became, the safer citizens would supposedly be.

But secrecy again signed a death warrant for thousands of Americans. President George W. Bush persuaded Americans to support invading Iraq by blaming Saddam Hussein for the 9/11 attacks, among other pretexts.[12] Bush could vilify Iraq thanks to a coverup. In late 2002, a joint House-Senate investigation into the 9/11 terrorist attacks completed an 838-page report, but the Bush administration suppressed the section of the report on the Saudi government's role. Sen. Richard Shelby (R-AL), the vice chairman of the joint inquiry, urged declassifying that section because "the American people are crying out to know more about who funds, aids, and abets terrorist activities in the world." In 2016, those 28 pages were finally declassified by the Obama administration, revealing how Saudi government officials directly financed and provided diplomatic cover for several of the hijackers in the U.S. shortly before they unleashed havoc.

Excessive secrecy was sporadically criticized as some Bush deceptions were exposed. William Leonard, former chief of the federal Information Security Oversight Office, complained of seeing information "classified that I've also seen published in third-grade textbooks."[13] The *New York Times* reported in 2005 that federal agencies were "classifying documents at the rate of 125 a minute as they create new categories of semi-secrets bearing vague labels like 'sensitive security information.'"[14]

In his 2008 presidential campaign, Obama promised to "turn the page on a growing empire of classified information." But he "turned the page" by multiplying the number of secret documents. In 2012, for the first time, agencies issued almost 100 million decisions to classify federal documents. Regardless of his own record, Obama promised that the era of "too much secrecy... is now over."[15]

Obama's Justice Department launched almost three times as many Espionage Act prosecutions as all previous administrations combined. The Obama Justice Department proclaimed in 2011 that government officials who "elected to disclose the classified information publicly through the mass media" were "posing an even greater threat to society" than do foreign spies.[16] Obama administration officials compared former NSA analyst Thomas Drake to mass killers and terrorists after Drake was accused of leaking information on NSA boondoggles to the *Baltimore Sun*. Drake and his lawyers heroically whipped the Justice Department in federal court.

According to the Obama administration, even federal judges must bow to classification labels. "We don't think there is a First Amendment right to classified documents," Justice Department lawyer Catherine Dorsey told a federal judge in 2015.[17] *New York Times*'s James Risen spent almost a decade in the federal crosshairs after his 2006 book *State of War* exposed the NSA's illegal warrantless wiretapping and other federal crimes. Robert Litt, general counsel for the Director of National Intelligence, compared journalism to drunk driving to justify punishing any journalist who published confidential information. But the Justice Department could not prove Risen's disclosures harmed anything except federal credibility. Risen labeled the Obama administration as the "greatest enemy of press freedom" in our time. Risen declared: "The attorney general of the U.S. has been turned into the nation's chief censorship officer."[18]

Secrecy epitomizes Washington elitism. Almost 3 million federal employees are approved to access "confidential" or "secret" information, while almost 1.5 million have been approved to view "top-secret" information.[19] All other Americans are presumed unfit or unworthy to know or judge government policies. Any breach of those restrictions turns the perpetrator into the legal equivalent of Benedict Arnold.

Classification prohibits millions of government employees from exposing government crimes or failures. Former government officials, contractors, and military personnel are prohibited "from publishing a book or blog post about [their] experience in government without first submitting it to official censors."[20] Mark Fallon, a veteran counterintelligence officer and counterterrorism expert, wrote a book entitled *Unjustifiable Means: The Inside Story of How the CIA, Pentagon and U.S. Government Conspired to Torture*. But his account of the torture regime was interminably delayed and heavily censored. Fallon asserted that much faster, friendlier treatment was given to books by the architects and apologists for CIA torture, including former CIA Director George Tenet, Acting General Counsel John Rizzo, and former Counterterrorism Center Chief Jose Rodriguez.[21] Similarly, when former FBI counterterrorism agent Ali Soufan wrote a book on CIA torture abuses, the CIA demanded that Soufan — who was on-site for brutal interrogations — remove the pronouns "I" and "me" from his narrative. In contrast, the feds took only seven weeks to approve Hillary Clinton's memoir and only eight weeks to approve former FBI chief James Comey's memoir, *A Higher Loyalty*.[22]

State Secrets as the Highest Truth

After the 9/11 attacks, a California consulting company owned by Dennis Montgomery became a superstar after creating software revealing hidden messages of pending terrorist attacks in Al Jazeera broadcasts. Federal agencies swooned. National Public Radio reported that "starting in the fall of 2003, Montgomery's analysis led directly to national code orange security alerts and cancelled flights. The only problem: he was making it all up." Thanks to the bogus software, top Bush administration officials "talked about shooting down [passenger] planes identified as targets because they feared that supposed hijackers would use the planes to attack the United States," the *New York Times* reported.[23] French intelligence officials, exasperated after flights from Paris were disrupted, exposed the hoax. But, as author James Risen noted: "The CIA buried the whole insane episode and acted like it never happened."[24] U.S. government agencies continued bankrolling Montgomery's company for six more years, plowing another $20 million into the company's coffers.

And this is where State Secrets came in handy. Both the Bush and Obama administrations invoked the State Secrets legal doctrine to stifle lawsuits seeking to expose one of the biggest farces of the War on Terror.

The federal government first formally asserted the State Secrets doctrine in a 1953 Supreme Court case involving a B-29 bomber crash. The Air Force claimed that the report on the crash contained national security secrets, thereby torpedoing a lawsuit by the widows of the crash victims. The Supreme Court took the bait and created a new privilege for federal agencies. Half a century later, the government declassified the report which contained no vital national security information but proved that negligence caused the crash. Suppressing the truth for almost half a century allowed the State Secrets doctrine to become sacrosanct.

The State Secrets doctrine was rarely invoked until this century. The George W. Bush administration invoked State Secrets in almost 50 cases, almost three times as often as all prior administrations combined. Bush's lawyers played the State Secrets card to seek "blanket dismissal of every case challenging the constitutionality of specific, ongoing government programs," according to a study by the bipartisan Constitution Project. When illegal NSA wiretapping was challenged in federal appeals court, Judge Harry Pregerson groused that the "bottom line... is [whether] the government declares something is a state secret, that's the end of it. The king can do no wrong."[25] The Bush team invoked State Secrets to prohibit torture victims from disclosing to their defense attorneys the specific interrogation methods they suffered.

As a presidential candidate, Obama slammed the Bush administration for abusing the State Secrets privilege.[26] But Obama perpetuated State Secrets claims in all the Bush-era cases still percolating in federal court. A federal appeals court derided the Obama administration in April 2009: "According to the government's theory, the judiciary should effectively cordon off all secret government actions from judicial scrutiny, immunizing the CIA and its partners from the demands and the limits of the law."[27] Obama administration lawyers invoked State Secrets to veto revelations on how interrogators used scalpels to sexually mutilate a detainee.

State Secrets shielded Obama's newfound presidential prerogative to assassinate Americans who were terrorist suspects. When the ACLU sought the Obama administration's secret memos and policy guidelines justifying the killing of an American citizen in Yemen, the administration refused to disclose any information. A Justice Department attorney asserted in federal court that no judge has authority to be "looking over the shoulder" of the Obama administration's targeted-killing program.[28] In 2013, Federal Judge Colleen McMahon bewailed the "veritable Catch-22" of secrecy rules governing the case but, characterizing her own ruling as an "Alice-in-Wonderland pronouncement," upheld the administration's claim to secrecy.

The Biden administration invoked State Secrets to shroud one of the CIA's best-known atrocities. In 2002, the CIA captured Abu Zubaydah, a Palestinian radical, and falsely believed he was a kingpin with al Qaeda. The CIA took him to Thailand and Poland and "waterboarded Zubaydah at least 80 times, simulated live burials in coffins for hundreds of hours," and brutalized him to keep him awake for six days in a row. The CIA admitted some of the details, and Zubaydah's name was mentioned a thousand times in the 683-page executive summary released in 2014 as part of a much longer secret Senate report on the CIA torture regime.

But the Supreme Court upheld a State Secrets claim to block Zubaydah's lawyers from serving subpoenas on the American psychologists who crafted the CIA torture program. The Court's ruling also blocked Polish investigators seeking information about the crimes committed at a CIA torture site on their turf. As the 6-to-3 ruling written by Justice Stephen Breyer declared, the Court "should exercise its traditional reluctance to intrude upon the authority of the Executive in military and national security affairs" after the State Secret privilege is invoked.

Two years earlier, Federal Judge Richard Paez rejected the CIA's argument because "in order to be a 'state secret,' a fact must first be a 'secret.'" Even the president of Poland admitted that crimes were committed at that CIA torture site. But the Supreme Court proclaimed that "sometimes information that has entered the public domain may nonetheless fall within the scope of the State Secrets privilege." According to the Court, "truth" is only what federal officials have publicly confessed.

The Court upheld State Secrets to assist the CIA in "maintaining the trust" with foreign spy agencies. Justice Breyer warned: "To confirm publicly the existence of a CIA [torture] site in Country A, can diminish the extent to which the intelligence services of Countries A, B, C, D, etc., will prove willing to cooperate with our own." The Court acted as if it was merely smoothing the path for a Girl Scout cookie sale at a shopping center instead of shrouding a "crime against humanity" (the UN's verdict on torture).

Breyer stressed: "Obviously, the Court condones neither terrorism nor torture, but in this case, we are required to decide only a narrow evidentiary dispute." But the Supreme Court condones any crime it cloaks. The Court's sweeping rulings on State Secrets and sovereign immunity provided a get-out-of-jail-free card for Bush-era torturers and torture policymakers. No victim of Bush-era torture has received justice in federal courts.

Justice Neil Gorsuch dissented, warning that granting "utmost deference" to the CIA would "invite more claims of secrecy in more doubtful circumstances — and facilitate the loss of liberty and due process history shows very often follows." Gorsuch noted that the Supreme Court decision was granting the same type of "crown prerogatives" to federal agencies that the Declaration of Independence described as evil.

Shielding State Secrets makes the Supreme Court the guardian of Leviathan Democracy. A State Secrets claim is the equivalent of a political command to a judge to shut down a case. The State Secrets doctrine presumes that "government knows best, and no one else is entitled to know." Not only are the feds above the law; they don't have to explain why they are above the law. Eventually, instead of a good excuse for breaking the law, all that is necessary is to claim that an excuse exists — even if the excuse is secret.

The Freedom from Information Act

The best-known antidote to federal secrecy is also one of Washington's greatest frauds. After long and fierce disputes, Congress formally recognized Americans' right to federal records when it enacted the Freedom of Information Act (FOIA) in 1966. On July 4, 1966, a White House press release attributed the following quote to President Johnson: "I signed this measure with a deep sense of pride that the United States is an open society in which the people's right to know is cherished and guarded." But Johnson privately railed to his staff: "The Justice Department tells me this goddamn bill will screw the Johnson Administration." Johnson's White House Press Secretary Bill Moyers recalled that "LBJ had to be dragged kicking and screaming to the signing... He hated the very idea of the Freedom of Information Act; hated the thought of journalists rummaging in government closets and opening government files; hated them challenging the official view of reality."[29]

LBJ's public praise and private loathing set the paradigm for FOIA. The FOIA law was quickly bureaucratically sandbagged, resulting in almost no disclosures. J. Edgar Hoover ordered the FBI to totally refuse to comply with the law.[30] That 1966 law specified that if federal FOIA staffers failed to obey judicial orders for disclosure, federal courts "may punish the responsible officers for contempt." But in more than 50 years, no federal FOIA official has ever been jailed for violating the law by refusing to disclose information.

In 1978, the Supreme Court declared that "the basic purpose of FOIA is to ensure an informed citizenry… and to hold the governors accountable to the governed."[31] In 1993, President Bill Clinton asserted that FOIA "has played a unique role in strengthening our democratic form of government" and was "based upon the fundamental principle that an informed citizen is essential to the democratic process."[32] But his appointees perennially blocked the release of damaging political information.

By 2001, the FOIA process in many agencies had practically collapsed. Though federal agencies were legally obliged to reply within 20 business days to requests, the FBI took an average of almost three years to fulfill FOIA requests while the Energy Department averaged more than five years.

Attorney General John Ashcroft recognized that the real problem was excessive transparency. On October 12, 2001, Ashcroft formally encouraged federal agencies to block FOIA requests on any plausible pretext and assured them that "the Department of Justice will defend your decisions" to deny FOIA requests.[33] The world's largest law firm took its place at the bulwarks blocking the entrances to every federal agency.

FOIA provided zero relief after the Bush administration suppressed the names of the 1,200 Arabs, Muslims, and others arrested as "suspected terrorists" after the 9/11 attacks. The Justice Department insisted on secret court hearings for all arrestees and on secret immigration hearings for subsequent deportations. Even though not one of the arrestees was connected to the 9/11 attacks, the Bush administration claimed that disclosure of any of their names would provide a "mosaic" that aided terrorists. Federal Judge Gladys Kessler trounced the Bush policy: "Secret arrests are a concept odious to a democratic society… The public's interest in learning the identity of those arrested and detained is essential to verifying whether the government is operating within the bounds of law." The Supreme Court refused to hear the case, and the policy continued.

The Justice Department denied almost all FOIA requests on the Patriot Act. When Congress considered legislation to renew that law in 2006, Attorney General Alberto Gonzales testified: "There has not been one verified case of civil liberties abuse" in the War on Terror. In reality, the feds had already discovered thousands of abuses by FBI agents, but they were covered up until after Congress renewed the Patriot Act.

On President Obama's second day in office in 2009, he pledged to strengthen FOIA, "the most prominent expression of a profound national commitment to ensuring an open government."[34] He promised that the law would "be administered with a clear presumption: In the face of doubt, openness prevails."

Unless, of course, a White House official objected. Three months after Obama took office, White House Counsel Gregory Craig quietly notified all federal agencies that "all documents and records that implicate the White House in any way are said to have 'White House equities' and must receive an extra layer of review, not by agency FOIA experts, but by the White House itself," as a 2016 congressional report noted. Obama staffers apparently believed that anything that could tarnish the administration's image violated its "equities." *Politico* noted in 2016 that, in some cases, White House FOIA "referrals have led to years of delay."[35]

Obama's Justice Department formally proposed to entitle federal agencies to falsely claim that FOIA-requested documents did not exist. Such deceitful responses would deter citizens from filing pesky lawsuits to compel disclosure. The ACLU and other activist organizations complained that the proposal allowed "a law designed to provide public access to government information to be twisted to permit federal law enforcement agencies to actively lie to the American people."[36]

The Obama administration formally withdrew the proposal but continued stonewalling. In 2015, the Obama administration "set a record again for censoring government files or outright denying access to them" under FOIA.[37] A 2016 congressional report titled "FOIA Is Broken" noted that journalists had completely abandoned "the FOIA request as a tool because delays and redactions made the request process wholly useless for reporting." The Pentagon responded to a request for a simple list of titles of its reports by offering a partial disclosure if the journalist promised never to file another FOIA request. DEA torpedoed a FOIA request regarding a notorious Mexican drug lord by charging $1.4 million to prepare a response.

DEA also denied a FOIA request by someone seeking "information about his own kidnappers… because he did not have a signed waiver from the men who had held him hostage," the *Washington Examiner* reported.[38] A federal judge slammed the FBI in 2017 for claiming it needed 17 years to fulfill a FOIA request on surveillance of antiwar activists in the 1960s.[39] FBI FOIA were blighted by frenzies of redactions, including deleting the names of Clark Kent and Lois Lane from a theatrical adaptation of *Superman* because disclosing them would "constitute a clearly unwarranted invasion of personal privacy."[40] Some federal agencies routinely and unjustifiably denied almost all FOIA requests, presuming that people are not seriously seeking information until they file a lawsuit. The media gave a hundred times more coverage to Obama's ludicrous boast of "the most transparent administration" than it gave to the Obama administration's subversion of FOIA.

FOIA furors helped elect Donald Trump to the presidency. Federal law requires the government to preserve the emails of top officials. Secretary of State Hillary Clinton evaded FOIA's mandate by setting up a private server in her own house and refusing to turn over her emails once she left office in 2013. Clinton also violated federal law by handling top-secret information on an unsecure communications system. The State Department rejected more than a dozen FOIA requests for Hillary Clinton's official emails, paving the way for clashes and leaks that roiled the 2016 election campaign. When a congressional committee subpoenaed her emails in 2015, her staffers destroyed more than 30,000 messages with BleachBit software. Critics suggested that undisclosed emails could reveal decisions that provided windfalls to the Clinton Foundation and up to $50 million in speaking fees to her husband, among other controversies. Federal Judge Royce Lamberth labeled the Clinton email affair "one of the gravest modern offenses to government transparency."[41]

The State Department declared that it would require 75 years to comply with its FOIA request for emails from Hillary's top aides. The State Department also delayed for more than five years answering a simple request from the Associated Press for a list of Secretary Clinton's schedules and meetings. Federal judges and the State Department Inspector General slammed the FOIA stonewalling and foot-dragging on the Clinton case.

But the Clinton controversies spurred zero FOIA reform. Bureaucratic and judicial incorrigibility shone through in controversies about money and weapons sent to "moderate" Syrian rebels seeking to overthrow the government of Bashar Assad. The U.S. intervention was so boneheaded that CIA-backed Syrian rebels ended up fighting Pentagon-backed rebels. Much of the U.S. aid ended up in the hands of terrorist groups, some of whom were allied with al Qaeda. Providing material support to terrorist organizations is a federal crime, except when done by U.S. government agencies.

In 2018, President Trump tweeted a denunciation of the "massive, dangerous, and wasteful payments to Syrian rebels fighting Assad." Trump's outburst spurred a FOIA request by the *New York Times* for CIA records on payments to Syrian rebel groups. The CIA denied the request, and the case ended up in court.[42] CIA officer Antoinette Shiner warned the court that forcing the CIA to admit that it possessed any records of aiding Syrian rebels would "confirm the existence and the focus of sensitive Agency activity that is by definition kept hidden to protect U.S. government policy objectives." But the CIA had been bragging to journalists about the program for years.

Federal judges, unlike Syrian civilians slaughtered by U.S.-funded terrorist groups, had the luxury of pretending the program did not exist. In 2020, a federal appeals court stressed that affidavits from CIA officials are "accorded a presumption of good faith" and stressed "the appropriate deference owed" to the CIA. Since Trump's tweet did not specifically state that the program he sought to terminate actually existed, the CIA was entitled to pretend it was still secret. Judge Robert Katzmann dissented, declaring that the court's decision put its "imprimatur to a fiction of deniability that no reasonable person would regard as plausible."

The Trump and Biden administrations stonewalled FOIA requests from the *Washington Post* that exposed "more than 500 retired U.S. military personnel — including scores of generals and admirals" taking "lucrative jobs since 2015 working for foreign governments, mostly in countries known for human rights abuses and political repression."[43] A *Post* exposé noted that the Pentagon and State Department "withheld virtually all information" about retired U.S. generals working for foreign regimes even though the Pentagon specifically approved almost every such gig. The U.S. government claimed that releasing the names would "violate former service members' privacy and could subject them to 'embarrassment and harassment' and 'unfairly harm their public reputation.'" But those generals and admirals were not conscripted to serve Saudi tyrants. Some of the retired top military officers regularly testify before Congress "and appear on television to debate national security, but rarely divulge whether they are on a foreign government's payroll."

FOIA shielded the Biden COVID storyline. Under White House pressure (as discussed in Chapter 5, "COVID Crackdown Catastrophes"), the Food and Drug Administration rushed to grant final approval in 2021 to the Pfizer COVID vaccine application in only 108 days — far faster than usual. Biden touted the FDA decision to "prove" vaccines were safe and to justify mandating COVID vaccines for more than a hundred million American adults. However, when a coalition of professors and scientists sought a copy of Pfizer's vaccine application, FDA claimed it would need 75 years to fully disclose the data. In its FOIA lawsuit, the coalition noted that FDA had 18,000 employees and a budget of $6 billion — more than adequate resources to process disclosures regarding the most important vaccine in this century.[44] Federal Judge Mark Pittman rebuffed FDA in 2022, declaring that "this FOIA request is of paramount public importance," and ordered FDA to disclose 55,000 pages a month until the process was completed.[45]

"Truth delayed is truth defused" is FOIA's tacit motto. No wonder that journalists deride FOIA as the "Freedom from Information Act." Should we presume that the feds are obeying every law except the statute enacted to expose government wrongdoing?

Protecting Presidents from History

The Presidential Records Act of 1978 was enacted after former President Richard Nixon claimed that his secret Oval Office tapes and other records were his personal property. The 1978 law declared that "the United States shall reserve and retain complete ownership, possession, and control of Presidential records." Archivist of the United States David Ferriero announced in 2022: "The Presidential Records Act is critical to our democracy, in which the government is held accountable by the people." But this law has more loopholes than a congressional ethics reform bill.[46]

From the beginning, the Presidential Records Act was often ignored or subverted. Aside from the tapes, Nixon fought ferocious legal battles to control 42 million pages of documents from his presidency. Historian Bruce Montgomery noted in 1993 that Nixon's lawsuits against the National Archives "managed to block releasing the majority of his White House records." Suppressing those records assured that Nixon had a better reputation than he deserved when he died in 1994. The Nixon Library did not release the final batch of his secret tapes until 2013 — 39 years after Nixon was driven from office.[47] The Lyndon B. Johnson Library did not release the final batch of his secret tapes of presidential conversations until 2016 — 43 years after his death and 47 years after he left office.[48]

Under the law, unclassified papers of a president must be routinely released 12 years after the end of a president's term. But in 2001, President George W. Bush "effectively rewrote the Presidential Records Act, converting it from a measure guaranteeing public access to one that blocks it," as law professor Jonathan Turley noted. Bush's executive order reversed the law's burden of proof. Historians and others were required to prove "a demonstrated, specific need" for documents to overcome any assertion of privilege, however spurious or self-serving, by a former president. Bush gave the current president veto power over any release of documents from former presidents, thus permitting each new president to blockade history. Bush's edict also permitted vice presidents, former presidents, or their designated representatives to block public release of records in perpetuity.[49]

President Barack Obama partially reversed Bush's order in 2009 but retained plenty of veto powers for himself over American history. Obama White House lawyers repeatedly invoked procedures to "delay the release of thousands of pages of records from President Bill Clinton's White House," *Politico* reported. Congress passed a law in 2014 to curb White House prerogatives over presidential papers, but the system remained rigged.[50]

Rather than blanket disclosures of past records, citizens must file a FOIA request for specific documents — which former presidents and their minions can often endlessly delay. *Politico* reported in March 2022: "At many presidential libraries, the queues for processing FOIAs stretch for years," and requests "involving classified information can take more than a decade."[51]

At the end of the Obama administration, 30 million pages of documents from his presidency were shipped to a vast empty furniture store near Chicago.[52] The Obama Foundation, a private nonprofit organization, promised to scan the documents for the National Archives and Records Administration, which administers all other presidential libraries. Pulitzer Prize-winning historian David Garrow warned: "The absence of a true Obama presidential library will have the effect of discouraging serious and potentially critical research into the Obama presidency."[53] The Obama Foundation estimated that "95 percent" of Obama administration records were "born digital." They could be easily placed online — if disclosure was the goal. After several delays, the Obama Foundation lateraled the entire project back to the National Archives.

The Presidential Records Act is a propellant for windfall profits. Former President Bill Clinton received a $15 million advance for his memoir, George W. Bush received a $10 million advance, and Barack Obama and his wife Michelle received $60 million for a two-book memoir deal. Presidents can practically use any information they please to write their memoirs with expedited clearance of classified information. By keeping the vast majority of their records secret, former presidents prevent investigators from exposing more of their fabrications and abuses of power. Former presidents should forfeit any right to confidentiality of their papers on the day they sign a contract to write a memoir.

On August 8, 2022, a phalanx of FBI agents conducted a heavily televised raid on former President Trump's Mar-a-Lago home in Palm Beach, Florida, and seized 33 boxes of evidence and documents. In January 2023, the Justice Department announced that investigators had also discovered numerous classified documents wrongfully stored in President Biden's home and offices. Attorney General Merrick Garland appointed Special Counsels to investigate both the current president and former president. In June 2023, Special Counsel Jack Smith raced to indict Trump on 37 federal charges tied to his possession and mishandling of classified documents.[54] In contrast, Special Counsel Robert Hur did not interview Biden on his wrongfully possessed documents until October 2023, long after Trump had been indicted.[55]

Press Corps to the Barricades

The federal blindfold slipped momentarily in the Spring of 2023 when a stash of confidential documents on U.S. military and foreign policy leaked out.[56] On April 13, 2023, the FBI arrested Jack Teixeira, a 21-year-old Massachusetts Air National Guard member, and charged him with retention and transmission of national defense information and willful retention of classified documents. A *Washington Post* editorial noted that the alleged culprit had "complained of government overreach," so obviously he was up to no good.[57]

It wasn't clear whether Teixeria intended to leak the documents or whether people in the Discord gaming group where the documents were allegedly posted made them public on their own. The documents were practically the only honest U.S. information disclosed in early 2023 on the Russia-Ukraine War. They revealed that the Ukrainian military was in far worse shape than the Biden administration claimed. The documents predicted that a pending offensive by the Ukrainian army would be a flop if not a disaster. The documents also contained embarrassing information on Israel's Mossad, the Russian government, and U.S. spying on South Korea.

White House National Security spokesman John Kirby warned the media that the leaked documents are "not intended for public consumption… This is information that has no business in the public domain."[58] Unfortunately, that is Washington's verdict for almost all the information regarding U.S. foreign policy. Congress joined the "know nothing" stampede by refusing to appoint an Inspector General to expose waste, fraud, and abuse of the $100+ billion in aid pledged to Ukraine.

The Washington media responded like a mob of peasants hankering to burn a heretic. *New York Times* military correspondent David Philipps tweeted: "The NYT worked feverishly to find the identity of the guy leaking [Top Secret] docs on Discord. Ironically, if [the] same guy had leaked to the NYT, we'd be working feverishly to conceal it."[59] (Philipps wasn't endorsing that fever.) At a Pentagon press conference, journalists showed far more indignation about the breach of federal secrecy than about the official lies the documents exposed. The press corps preen as "the handmaidens of government" just as Assistant Defense Secretary Sylvester demanded in 1965.

Media docility is also epitomized by the apathy regarding the bombing of the Nord Stream pipeline, the biggest act of environmental terrorism in history. The *Washington Post* reported that the message from the U.S. and Western European governments is "Don't talk about Nord Stream."[60] Almost all reporters and editors were "good boys" and moved along as if there was nothing to see. If American media investigations discovered and exposed a U.S. government role in the pipeline attack, it could have severely undermined the Biden administration's bellicosity and endless aid for the Ukraine government.

Conclusion: Secrecy versus Self-Government

Federal secrecy is spawning a caste system that betrays democracy. When only 1 percent of the populace can access federal dirt, the vast majority of

Americans have been classified as unfit to judge their own government. The flipside of the 1 percent's "need to know" is that 99 percent of the populace "need to not know." By endlessly restricting information, a regime can usually guide public sentiment (and elections) as it pleases. If government policymakers can withhold potential bombshell information from almost everyone, then democracy is doomed.

Eminent Washingtonians who condemn leaks of confidential information offer no alternative for Americans to learn what "their" government is doing. As long as average citizens stay in their place, paying and obeying, everything will work out fine — at least for Washington real estate values. If democracy is now little more than a system where insiders deceive people for their own good, how does it differ from all the other regimes that conned people throughout history?

Secrecy places the most dishonorable profession on the honor system. The more secrets politicians keep, the less trust they deserve. Secretary of State Hillary Clinton declared in 2012: "Lack of transparency eats away like a cancer at the trust people should have in their government."[61] Even Biden's Director of National Intelligence, Avril Haines, lamented to Congress in 2022 that the current excessive federal secrecy "erodes the basic trust that our citizens have in their government."[62]

Politico reported in August 2022 that the Biden White House is launching a "new war on secrecy" and is especially concerned about "potentially illegal [government] activities that have been shielded from the public for decades."[63] A Biden administration official said that it is in the "nation's best interest to be as transparent as possible with the American public." (He insisted on anonymity to avoid ruining his career by endorsing transparency.) Sen. Elizabeth Warren (D-MA) recently commented: "We spend $18 billion protecting the classification system and only about $102 million… on declassification efforts… That ratio feels off in a democracy." But inside the Beltway, rigging the game 176-to-1 is "close enough for government work" for transparency.

Secrecy is not a technical glitch in administrative regimes. The whole point of secrecy is to prevent citizens from controlling the government. To expect bureaucracies to "correct" excessive secrecy is like expecting kings to abdicate their thrones. There is no reason for citizens to trust secretive federal programs more than Washington trusts American citizens.

Americans cannot passively await presidents to announce when the law and Constitution have been trampled. Sweeping secrecy is inherently authoritarian. It means that the political system, regardless of its external forms, is based on blind trust in officialdom — the same as most regimes in history. Pervasive secrecy defines down democracy: people merely select their Supreme Deceivers. If trillions of pages of new secrets a year is not a perversion of democracy, why not simply keep secret everything that the government does?

Attorney General Ramsey Clark warned in 1967: "Nothing so diminishes democracy as secrecy." Yet Americans are still told that they are governing themselves because they are permitted to vote for presidents who appoint bureaucrats who drop a cloak around federal machinations. This is like claiming that people who attach their own blindfold still enjoy perfect vision. Self-government is a sham if citizens are prohibited from knowing what elected officials are doing in their name.

Secrecy is perhaps the ultimate incumbent protection policy. Secrecy makes political deceit irrefutable. The United States enjoys the Rule of Law because the feds will prosecute any official who reveals otherwise. Leakers are hated because they revoke sovereign immunity from the truth.

The growth of government secrecy sparks an arms race by citizens seeking to learn what politicians are doing before it is too late to stop them. Lies subvert democracy by crippling citizens' ability to rein in government. In his 1971 opinion on the *Pentagon Papers* case, Supreme Court Justice Hugo Black declared that a free press has "the duty to prevent any part of the government from deceiving the people and sending them off to distant lands to die of foreign fevers and foreign shot and shell." Unfortunately, the media's acquiescence to near-total secrecy has long betrayed that duty. If Americans had speedy access to the actual information in government files, far more citizens would recognize the falsehoods exploited to plunge the nation into one foreign debacle after another. As WikiLeaks's Julian Assange observed: "If wars can be started by lies, they can be stopped by truth."

Government secrecy deludes people as effectively as federal marshals smashing newspaper printing presses with axes and sledgehammers. If democracy depends on transparency, and government transparency is an illusion, then what is our democracy? We can either have vast secrecy, or we can have "government under the law." How many official lies and crimes can democracy survive? Unfortunately, the answer is a secret.

13. Mindless Ministry of Truth

Americans' freedom of speech is increasingly targeted by a vast Censorship-Industrial Complex. Federal agencies are massively and covertly intervening to protect America's "cognitive infrastructure."[1] And the most important cognitive fix is to train Americans to never doubt Uncle Sam.

On July 4, 2023, Federal Judge Terry Doughty condemned the Biden censorship regime for potentially "the most massive attack against free speech in United States history."[2] Doughty issued an injunction banning federal agencies and the White House from browbeating social media companies into suppressing Americans' online posts and comments. On September 8, 2023, a federal appeals court ratified part of the injunction, prohibiting federal officials from acting "to coerce or significantly encourage social-media companies to remove, delete, suppress, or reduce, including through altering their algorithms, posted social-media content containing protected free speech." The Supreme Court announced in October 2023 that it would hear the case, potentially the biggest First Amendment landmark since the 1971 *Pentagon Papers* case.

Mary Poppins Tossed Overboard

On April 28, 2022, Americans learned that they lived under the sway of a Disinformation Governance Board. The Department of Homeland Security created the board two months earlier to combat any person or group seeking to "undermine public trust in government institutions," among other sins. DHS promised that the board would also "protect privacy, civil rights, and civil liberties" — presumably as long as no one used their liberties to endanger trust in government.[3]

Nina Jankowicz, a 33-year-old Bryn Mawr College graduate, was America's new Disinformation Czar. She was hailed as an "information warfare expert" but that honorific did not indicate which side of the barricades she would take.[4] Jankowicz previously worked for an arm of the National Endowment for Democracy, a federal agency which perennially interfered in foreign elections. She also worked for StopFake, a federally funded media-influence operation "aggressively whitewashing two Ukrainian neo-Nazi groups with a long track record of violence, including war crimes."[5] She won laurels from Team Biden from joining the chorus in October 2020 condemning Hunter Biden's laptop as a Russian disinformation ploy. She gained further credibility after caterwauling on National Public Radio about rumors that Elon Musk might buy Twitter: "I shudder to think about if free speech absolutists were taking over more platforms."

That line was the Rosetta Stone for understanding the Disinformation Governance Board. The goal was not "truth" — which could arise from the clash of competing opinions. Instead, political overlords sought power to domineer Americans by suppressing disapproved opinions.

Critics denounced the new board as an Orwellian "Ministry of Truth." But the scheme quickly became a laughingstock. Before appointing Jankowicz, Biden staffers forgot to ask, "Does she sing?" Her greatest performances were quickly discovered online, including her TikTok version of a "Mary Poppins" song warning: "Information laundering is really quite ferocious." More surprising was her YouTube Christmas parody song performance, "Who do I fuck to be famous and powerful?"[6]

The Board quickly became a political lightning rod. As controversy snowballed, the *Washington Post* quoted an unnamed DHS spokesperson: "The Board's purpose has been grossly mischaracterized; it will not police speech... Its focus is to ensure that freedom of speech is protected."[7] Why didn't the Founding Fathers think of adding a clause to the First Amendment creating a nefarious-sounding government agency to ride shotgun alongside the nation's media?

The Disinformation Board would not have been created unless policymakers felt entitled to bamboozle Americans. Jankowicz believed that "trustworthy experts" such as herself (she boasted that she was "verified" by Twitter) should be empowered to "edit" other people's tweets to "add context."[8] Jankowicz's arrogance was invisible in Washington because Biden policymakers shared the hubris. In the 1960s, the "best and the brightest" claimed the right to lie Americans into the Vietnam War. Nowadays, swaggering Washingtonians believe they have the right to blindfold 330 million Americans. In a city that already had hundreds of full-time political appointees whose task is to lie to the American public, why was another board needed? Admittedly, Disinformation Governance Board was a more palatable name than the Keep Damn Federal Lies Sacrosanct Panel.

"My country, right or wrong" is the motto for patriots who automatically place their nation on a pedestal. "My government, right or wrong" is the motto of Disinformation Warriors determined to quash dissent.

"Disinformation" is often simply the lag time between the pronouncement and the debunking of government falsehoods.

On May 18, 2022, the Biden administration announced that it was suspending the Disinformation Board.[9] After Jankowicz was dethroned as Disinformation Czar, she formally registered as a foreign agent.[10] Some conservatives took a victory lap, as if their work was done. But that board was not even the tip of the iceberg of federal suppression efforts.

Five months later, billionaire Elon Musk finalized his purchase of Twitter.[11] The following week, President Biden went ballistic at a Democratic fundraiser: "Elon Musk goes out and buys an outfit that spews lies all across the world… There's no editors anymore in America."[12] At another fundraiser a few weeks earlier, Biden played Pontius Pilate: "How do people know the truth? How do they make a distinction between fact and fiction?"[13] Biden didn't mention that DHS and FBI had been "editing" Twitter for years.

Musk was aghast when he learned how the feds had secretly domineered his new company. "Twitter is both a social media company and a crime scene," he tweeted on December 10.[14] A few weeks later, after the exposure of more Washington meddling, Musk lamented: "To be totally frank, almost every conspiracy theory that people had about Twitter turned out to be true."[15] Musk opened Twitter's archives to expose the vast extent of federal censorship. Some of the examples in the following sections are drawn from reports detailing federal interventions in Twitter's files. Lawsuits, court decrees, and congressional investigations revealed that other social media companies were even more submissive to Washington.

Carpet-Bombing Wayward Americans

Have you ever tweeted about Russia? You could be tarred as an "unwitting proliferator of Russian narratives" by U.S. government scorekeepers.[16]

Did you support the French "yellow vest" anti-lockdown protests? You are "Russia-aligned," according to Uncle Sam.[17]

Are you a Cuban immigrant to America? A federal contractor might try to get you banned on Twitter because you're a Hindu nationalist.

In 2016, President Barack Obama issued Executive Order 13721 to establish the Global Engagement Center (GEC) to "counter the messaging and diminish the influence of international terrorist organizations." Congressional legislation mandated that GEC take the lead in exposing and countering "foreign state and non-state propaganda and disinformation efforts aimed at undermining United States national security interests."

GEC is based in the State Department but also partners with the FBI, CIA, DHS, NSA, and the Pentagon. Disinformation is so perfidious that GEC tries to keep its operations secret. The center has a budget of roughly $74 million and "reportedly gave [grants] to at least 39 different organizations, whose names were redacted" in an Inspector General report.[18] GEC "funded a secret list of subcontractors and helped pioneer an insidious — and idiotic — new form of blacklisting," journalist Matt Taibbi revealed.[19]

GEC seeks to silence vast numbers of innocent Twitter users in hopes of hitting some bad guys. "GEC has doubled its budget by aggressively overstating threats through unverified accusations," according to a top Twitter official. Twitter owner Elon Musk labeled GEC as "the worst offender in U.S. government censorship & media manipulation."[20]

In early 2020, GEC issued a histrionic report titled "Russian Disinformation Apparatus Taking Advantage of Coronavirus Concerns." GEC castigated social media companies for failing to totally suppress any suggestions that the COVID-19 virus originated in a lab at the Wuhan Institute, secretly funded by the U.S. government.[21] Even references to "research conducted at the Wuhan institute" supposedly justified banishment from social media. The State Department produced a list of 250,000 Twitter accounts it wanted suppressed, including American journalists, foreign diplomats, and the Canadian military. The U.S. government swayed Twitter to suspend ZeroHedge, one of the most popular news accounts, for its postings on the Wuhan lab. (The FBI and U.S. Department of Energy subsequently concluded the virus likely originated in that lab.)

GEC followed up by sending Twitter a target list of 5,500 names it wanted suppressed because it believed they were "Chinese... accounts" engaged in "state-backed coordinated manipulation."[22] The list was so sloppy that it "included multiple Western government accounts and at least three CNN employees based abroad." Twitter Trust and Safety chief Yoel Roth scoffed at the list in an internal message: "What a total crock."

In June 2021, a GEC contractor sent Twitter a list of "around 40k Twitter accounts that our researchers suspect are engaging in inauthentic behavior... and Hindu nationalism more broadly." But the list was full of hapless Americans with no ties to India or its politics.[23]

Any Twitter accounts that posted opinions concurring with Russian government positions could be presumed to be "Moscow-controlled." One Twitter executive scorned the presumption that "If you retweet a news source linked to Russia, you become Russia-linked." Twitter rebuffed many of GEC's requests to cancel accounts, but many innocent Americans were likely either silenced or suppressed in the process.

"Guilt by intellectual association" suffices to suppress anyone suspected of being part of foreign "ecosystems." A GEC chart on "Pillars of Russia's Disinformation and Propaganda Ecosystem" asserts that "weaponization of social media" includes "standing campaigns to undermine faith in institutions" or "amplification of protests or civil discord."[24] Any organization that agreed, partly or wholly, with a Russian position was presumed guilty. A 2020 GEC report asserted that independent outlets "muddy the waters of the information environment in order to confuse those trying to discern the truth."[25] In other words, being independent was simply another perfidious ploy to dupe federal disinformation warriors.

GEC views political skepticism as a pox that must be suppressed. "In 2021, the GEC spent $275,000 producing a 'counter-disinformation video game' that programmed audiences to associate citizen critiques of government waste, fraud, and abuse with a social media disinformation campaign," the House Foreign Affairs Committee reported in 2023. Will the feds indoctrinate Americans to respond to the word *boondoggle* like Americans in the 1950s were taught to react to *communist?*

Swinging the 2020 Election?

In 2016, top FBI officials, the Obama administration, and their media allies fueled a conspiracy that the Trump presidential campaign was colluding with the Russian government. FBI falsehoods spurred a total surveillance wiretapping operation approved by the FISA Court, accompanied by leaks of misleading information that spurred media firestorms.[26] (See Chapter 14, "American Gestapo Run Amok.") Those allegations led to the appointment of Special Counsel Robert Mueller, who dragged out an investigation for almost two years before admitting that no evidence existed to prosecute Trump or his 2016 campaign officials for colluding with Russia. By that point, Trump had been irredeemably tainted and Democrats had exploited the controversy to capture control of the U.S. House of Representatives in 2018.

Twitter fell under federal sway thanks to demagoguery and selective xenophobia. In 2017, fueled by leaks from the FBI and other sources, the media stirred fears of widespread Russian covert propaganda disrupting American politics. Twitter investigated and identified only a few hundred accounts that it suspended because of "suspected Russian origin." Congressional committees vilified Twitter for not suppressing far more accounts, and the company continually sought to placate Washington to avoid punitive legislation.[27] Twitter assured the U.S. government that it would delete the account of "any user 'identified by the U.S. intelligence community' as a state-sponsored entity committing cyber operations."[28] And "fact-checkers need not apply" when the feds passed judgment.

Federal bureaucrats exploited the controversy over alleged Russian interference in the 2016 election to appoint themselves as overseers of Americans' thoughts. In 2018, Congress created a new federal agency — the Cybersecurity Infrastructure Security Agency (CISA) — in DHS.

CISA realized that it would be politically and legally perilous to directly muzzle Americans, so it relied on "censorship by surrogate." The feds evaded the Constitution by subcontracting the destruction of freedom. CISA partnered with federal grantees to form the Election Integrity Partnership a hundred days before the 2020 presidential election.[29] That project, along with the efforts of other federal agencies, created an "unrelenting pressure" with "the intended result of suppressing millions of protected free speech postings by American citizens," according to Judge Doughty.

During the 2020 election, CISA targeted for suppression assertions such as "mail-in voting is insecure" — despite the long history of absentee ballot fraud. Democrats exploited the COVID pandemic to finagle electoral changes that opened the floodgates to unverified mail-in ballots. A report by the Foundation for Freedom Online noted: "Pre-censoring U.S. citizen debate about mail-in ballots five months before an election has the impact of devastating the ability of concerned citizens to pressure their state representatives to take legal action on changing voting procedures." Some states sent absentee ballots to all voters, violating the Election Clause of the Constitution (which specifies that state legislatures make the rules for federal elections). Rather than the traditional scrutiny for mail-in ballots (and a ballot reject rate up to 20%), many locales accepted practically any piece of paper with a mark. Trump received more votes on Election Day, but 43,000 mail-in ballots in three states sealed Biden's victory — a minuscule portion of the 65 million mail-in and absentee votes that Biden received.

CISA established a "Rumor Control" webpage to deal with threats to the election — including rumors that the feds were censoring Americans. CISA quickly began targeting American citizens who complained about elections, and any criticism tacitly became a threat to the nation's election infrastructure. Contractors composing the Election Integrity Partnership filed endless objections to Americans' online posts with social media firms. Most of the censorship during the 2020 election cycle targeted posts "related to delegitimizing the election results," the court decision noted. Once the government began censoring, the definition of *misinformation* mushroomed. The Election Integrity Partnership bragged about targeting social media posts merely for being "out of context" or "exaggerating issues." Many of those alleged factual infractions were piddling compared to the sweeping falsehoods proclaimed by both Trump and Biden.

The FBI pressured Twitter to suspend accounts for posting "possible civic misinformation" (not including FBI press releases). The FBI hammered Twitter to torpedo parody accounts that only idiots or federal agents would not recognize as humor. Twitter had plenty of tricks to make disfavored users practically vanish. "Visibility filtering" tools minimized the number of people who saw disapproved tweets or accounts — all without leaving fingerprints. Ill-fated users were often unaware they tweeted into a void that no one saw.

Federal agencies also directly pressured social media companies to ramp up their censorship before the 2020 election. Taibbi noted: "Requests [to suppress accounts] poured in from FBI offices all over the country, day after day, hour after hour. If Twitter didn't act quickly, questions came: 'Was action taken?'"[30] Requests to suppress accounts and tweets "arrived and were escalated from all over: from Treasury, the NSA, virtually every state, the HHS, from the FBI and DHS, and more," including "an astonishing variety of requests from officials asking for individuals they didn't like to be banned."[31] "The FBI [acted] as doorman to a vast program of social media surveillance and censorship, encompassing agencies across the federal government — from the State Department to the Pentagon to the CIA."[32] Judge Doughty noted that "virtually all of the free speech suppressed was 'conservative' free speech. Using the 2016 election and the COVID-19 pandemic, the Government apparently engaged in a massive effort to suppress disfavored conservative speech."

The most brazen federal intervention in the 2020 election rescued the favorite candidate of the Washington establishment. In December 2019, FBI agents commandeered a laptop computer that Hunter Biden, the drug-addicted son of Democratic presidential candidate Joe Biden, had abandoned at a Delaware computer repair shop. That laptop was a treasure trove of possible crimes, including evidence that Hunter and other Bidens had collected millions in payments from foreign sources for providing access and/or fixes in Washington. Journalist Michael Shellenberger reported in the Twitter Files: "It likely would have taken a few hours for the FBI to confirm that the laptop had belonged to Hunter Biden." But that confirmation could have doomed Biden's presidential candidacy. FBI agents were prohibited from examining the laptop because their bosses told them that the FBI is "not going to change the outcome of the election again," according to an FBI whistleblower complaint.[33] Sen. Charles Grassley (R-IA) reported that FBI agents revealed that certain FBI officials had schemed "to undermine derogatory information connected to Hunter Biden by falsely suggesting it was disinformation."[34] The Justice Department commenced a criminal investigation of Hunter Biden in 2019, but that potential bombshell was not disclosed until after the 2020 election.

The Delaware computer store owner, John Paul Mac Isaac, made a copy of the hard drive before the FBI seized it. In August 2020, he gave the copy to Rudy Giuliani, who was aiding the Trump re-election campaign, who passed the copy to the *New York Post*. When Hunter Biden's lawyer heard that the *New York Post* was getting ready to expose the laptop weeks before the presidential election, strings were pulled in Washington. "Two hours later, an FBI Special Agent in San Francisco named Elvis Chan sends 10 documents to Twitter's Trust and Safety chief Yoel Roth, through Teleporter, a one-way communications channel from the FBI to Twitter," Shellenberger reported. James Baker, Twitter's general counsel, who was previously the FBI's top lawyer, led the push at Twitter to ban information on the laptop. After perusing Twitter's internal files, journalist Matt Taibbi noted:

> Twitter took extraordinary steps to suppress the [laptop] story, removing links and posting warnings that it may be "unsafe." They

even blocked its transmission via direct message, a tool hitherto reserved for extreme cases, e.g., child pornography.[35]

The FBI swayed news media executives, Twitter, and other social media companies to suppress the laptop story. The FBI had repeatedly warned social media companies of a Russian "hack-and-leak" operation to impact the election. Facebook CEO Mark Zuckerberg told podcast host Joe Rogan: "The FBI basically came to us [and] was like, 'Hey… you should be on high alert. We thought that there was a lot of Russian propaganda in the 2016 election. There's about to be some kind of dump similar to that.'" Twitter's Yoel Roth stated in December 2020 that during weekly meetings in mid-to-late 2020: "Federal law enforcement agencies communicated that they expected 'hack-and-leak operations' by state actors" that "would involve Hunter Biden."[36] Once the laptop story appeared, Biden advisor Anthony Blinken reportedly orchestrated the writing of a letter signed by 51 former senior intelligence officials asserting that the Hunter Biden laptop story "has all the classic earmarks of a Russian information operation."[37] That effort was directly assisted by at least one current CIA official — part of a concerted effort to provide a "talking point" for Biden in the final presidential debate. The FBI had long since verified that the laptop was authentic and belonged to Hunter but said nothing, enabling former spooks to torpedo the story. In the final presidential candidate debate, Biden touted that absolution: "There are 50 [sic] former national intelligence folks who said that what he's accusing me of is a Russian plant. Five former heads of the CIA… say what he's saying is a bunch of garbage. Nobody believes it."[38]

The Justice Department investigated Hunter Biden for more than five years before announcing in June 2023 that he had accepted a wrist-slap plea bargain with no jail time. If Hunter Biden had been charged with federal crimes before the 2020 election, his father would likely have lost.

As Judge Doughty observed, thanks to federal string-pulling on the laptop allegations, "millions of U.S. citizens did not hear the story prior to the November 3, 2020, election." The efforts by the FBI, social media companies, and mainstream media outlets to suppress the laptop story may have changed the election outcome. A pro-Trump pollster asserted that "4.6% of Biden voters would have changed their minds if they had known about it, easily enough to flip results in key states."[39] That estimate may have sharply exaggerated the potential impact of the laptop story. But changing the election outcome didn't require a landslide.

A few weeks after the 2020 election, Twitter's "Baker and his colleagues even sent a note of thanks to the FBI for its work," Shellenberger noted. Baker boasted to Twitter associates that "we made money" because the FBI paid Twitter $3.4 million for aiding and abetting federal suppression efforts. Elon Musk scoffed: "Government paid Twitter millions of dollars to censor info from the public."[40]

The Great COVID Blindfold

Did you complain to anyone that vaccine passports violated your liberty? You were deluded, if not depraved, and guilty of propelling a deceptive "anti-vaccination narrative about the loss of rights and freedoms," according to federal censorship contractors.[41]

Did you make any "worrisome jokes" about COVID vaccines? Then you were a public enemy guilty of spreading dangerous disinformation.

Did you ask questions about COVID policy? You were guilty of a tactic "commonly used by spreaders of misinformation to deflect culpability."

Once FDA gave emergency approval for new COVID vaccines, the Biden administration tacitly decreed that it was heresy to disparage them. Because federal bureaucrats rubberstamped claims from Pfizer and other companies that the vaccines were almost 100% effective, any dissent became disinformation that would cause people to die.

The Biden White House preemptively attacked critics of the new COVID vaccine:

• On March 21, 2021, White House Director of Digital Strategy Rob Flaherty notified Facebook that suppressing false information on COVID was not enough. A Facebook official assured the White House that Facebook was also suppressing "often-true content" that might discourage people from getting vaccinated.[42]

• On March 26, 2021, Flaherty explained to Facebook officials that "intellectually my bias is to kick people off" of social media — presumably for anything that the administration disapproved.[43]

• Biden White House Senior COVID Advisor Andy Slavitt was "outraged" that Facebook did not speedily delete a humorous meme: "10 years from now you will be watching TV & hear… 'Did you or a loved one take the COVID vaccine? You may be entitled…'"[44]

• On April 9, 2021, Flaherty emailed Facebook that he cared only about how its "interventions" were "increasing vaccine interest within hesitant communities."[45] He called for a crackdown on WhatsApp exchanges [private messages] between individuals, especially a "reduction in forwarding" of messages that would undermine mass vaccination.[46]

• On April 14, 2021, Flaherty complained to Facebook that a Tucker Carlson video had not been suppressed. "How was that not violative? The second half of the segment is raising conspiracy theories about the government hiding that [COVID] vaccines aren't effective." Facebook speedily assured Flaherty that the Carlson video was "being demoted" and "we still do not allow categorical claims that it or other vaccines are unsafe or ineffective."

• On April 22, 2021, Flaherty complained to Google that its YouTube site was "'funneling' people into hesitance and intensifying people's hesitancy" about getting vaxxed.[47] Flaherty bewailed "hesitance inducing content" as if he were a frustrated heroin pusher at a school playground. Flaherty warned that if the feds had "trouble getting people to get vaccinated," bad things could happen.[48]

• On May 12, 2021, the White House sought total suppression of any content that raised doubts on the vaccine. Flaherty hectored a Facebook official: "'Removing bad information from search' is one of the easy, low-bar things you guys do to make people like me think you're taking action… Pinterest doesn't even show you any results other than official information when you search for 'vaccines.' I don't know why you guys can't figure this out."[49]

The Biden White House sought across-the-board suppression of news and commentary from conservative or unapproved sources. Flaherty suggested to Facebook that it "change the algorithm so that people were more likely to see NYT [New York Times], WSJ [Wall Street Journal], any authoritative news source over Daily Wire, Tomi Lahren, polarizing people."[50] The White House specifically targeted the *New York Post* for suppression. The White House made no effort to reconcile that arm-twisting with the First Amendment. Instead, it was simply exploiting its clout.

The Biden administration sought to maximize fear to maximize vaccinations. After perusing the barrage of federal messages to Twitter, journalist David Zweig summarized the Biden agenda: "Be very afraid of

COVID and do exactly what we say to stay safe."[51] Biden administration fearmongering worsened the pandemic's mental health collateral damage, with a surge of suicides and deaths from alcohol and drug abuse.

The Biden administration vilified social media companies that failed to grovel. On July 15, 2021, U.S. Surgeon General Vivek Murthy publicly moaned: "Modern technology companies have enabled misinformation to poison our information environment... We can't wait longer for them to take aggressive action." Murthy called for social media platforms to "prioritize early detection of misinformation 'super-spreaders.'"[52] If Washington edicts could not vanquish the virus, at least forbidden thoughts could be eradicated. Murthy dropped the velvet cover from the iron fist, calling for exploring "appropriate legal and regulatory measures that address health misinformation." At the same press briefing, White House Press Secretary Jen Psaki stated that "decisions to regulate or hold to account any platform [spreading misinformation] would certainly be a policy decision."[53]

The following day, Biden proclaimed that Facebook and other social media companies were "killing people" by failing to suppress misinformation.[54] Biden added: "The only pandemic we have is among the unvaccinated." A few days later, Biden promised in a CNN town hall that people who were vaccinated were immune from COVID infections. That assertion became the highest profile misinformation of the entire pandemic. Ironically, the Biden administration threatened social media companies for misinformation at the same time the CDC suppressed information on COVID vaccines' failure to prevent infection and transmission. (See Chapter 5, "COVID Crackdown Catastrophes.")

Following Biden's murder accusation, Twitter bowed to White House pressure and banned thousands of critics of Biden's COVID policies including former *New York Times* science reporter Alex Berenson. Any statement that differed from CDC guidelines could be labeled "misinformation" and lead to banishment or blacklisting. Doctors were suspended for tweeting "demonstrably true information."[55] Twitter aggressively suppressed individuals who mentioned how CDC data proved COVID was far less of a threat to children than other illnesses. Anything that deterred parents from getting their kids injected was objectively false, at least according to the Biden cheat sheet. Twitter suppressed an Israeli scientific study linking COVID vaccines to cardiac arrests. A Rhode Island physician was permanently suspended for a tweet that cited a peer-reviewed study that "found a deterioration in sperm concentration and total motile count in sperm donors following mRNA vaccination."[56]

On March 3, 2022, the Biden White House threatened antitrust investigations against social media companies that failed to suppress "disinformation" about COVID vaccines. On March 3, Surgeon General Murthy demanded that social media companies provide the feds with lists of individuals who spread COVID "misinformation."[57] Companies had 60 days to submit data on "exactly how many users saw or may have been exposed to instances of COVID-19 misinformation."[58] The White House was still tacitly defining as misinformation any assertion that COVID vaccines failed to protect against infection or transmission.

Federal censorship contractors rushed to squelch dissent on COVID decrees.[59] Missouri Attorney General Andrew Bailey observed that the Surgeon General's Office, the Centers for Disease Control, and the Department of Health and Human Services collaborated in a "censorship enterprise called the Virality Project, which procures the censorship of enormous quantities of First Amendment-protected speech." The feds paid Stanford University's Virality Project for "detecting and mitigating the impact of false and misleading narratives related to COVID-19 vaccines."[60] Partnering with other federal contractors, the Virality Project sent weekly "anti-vax disinformation" reports to Twitter and other social media companies. Louisiana Attorney General Jeff Landry summarized the White House COVID playbook in early 2023: "If it goes against the political orthodoxy of the moment, it must be subjected to the cancel-culture campaign stemming directly from the White House."[61]

Federally funded disinformation warriors suppressed "false" claims about COVID vaccine side effects, especially the *true* claims. Since FDA approved COVID vaccines, any reports of side effects were automatically disinformation. The Virality Project recommended that social media companies suppress "stories of true vaccine side effects" and "true posts which could fuel [vaccine] hesitancy."[62] The Virality Project derided as "misinformation" claims that the vaccines failed to prevent COVID transmission even after the CDC conceded the vaccines' failure on that score.

In June 2021, Fauci emails revealing his flip-flops on masks and his kowtowing to the Chinese government were disclosed thanks to a FOIA request. The Virality Project warned Twitter that the official emails were being exploited "to foment increased distrust in Fauci's guidance and in American public health officials and institutions." But it wasn't cynics' fault that Fauci flip-flopped on key COVID policy issues. Regardless, Americans were doomed if they doubted their federal masters. A Virality Project report warned: "This continual process of seeding doubt and uncertainty in authoritative voices leads to a society that finds it too challenging to identify what's true or false."[63] Federal falsehoods were irrelevant — or at least picayune — compared to the peril of the peasantry losing faith.

Federal censorship contractors trumpeted the same menace that White House Chief of Staff H.R. Haldeman evoked to President Nixon 50 years earlier, after the publication of the *Pentagon Papers*. Haldeman warned that exposing official lies on the Vietnam War would teach Americans: "You can't trust the government; you can't believe what they say… and the implicit infallibility of presidents… is badly hurt by this."[64] Hard times continue for government infallibility.

COVID censorship controversies failed to curb the megalomania of federal officials. "Misinformation" remained an incantation magically entitling federal agencies to supreme power. FDA Commissioner Robert Califf announced in 2022 that "misinformation is now our leading cause of death."[65] FDA officials were unable to provide journalists with any data to support Califf's claim. A year later, Califf backtracked: "I want to modify my statement. And I'll keep working on this, to try to get it right. I would say I actually believe it is the leading cause of premature death."[66] Califf did not specify how many more swings at the issue he would need to "get it right."[67] Former FDA regulatory review analyst Jessica Adams scoffed: "It's unbelievable for him to make these assertions with no scientific backing."[68]

Facebook deleted at least 18 million posts with alleged COVID misinformation. In June 2023, Facebook chief Mark Zuckerberg complained of censorship pressure on COVID issues on which "there hadn't been time to fully vet a bunch of the scientific assumptions" and the feds "asked for a bunch of things to be censored that, in retrospect, ended up being more debatable or true. That stuff… really undermines trust."[69] But when was it not folly to trust censors?

The Biden Censorship Stampede

After the 2020 election, CISA raced to expand its control over Americans' thoughts. According to CISA chief Jen Easterly: "The most critical infrastructure is our cognitive infrastructure, so building that resilience to misinformation and disinformation... is incredibly important."[70] The best way to build resilience is to maximize docility.

On November 21, 2021, Easterly declared: "We live in a world where people talk about alternative facts, post-truth, which I think is really, really dangerous if people get to pick their own facts." Judge Doughty retorted: "The Free Speech Clause was enacted to prohibit just what Director Easterly is wanting to do: allow the government to pick what is true and what is false." As former State Department official Mike Benz warned: "DHS is carrying out an official state policy that if public trust is not earned, it must be installed... The U.S. government, in effect, censored the ability to 'cast doubt' on the U.S. government."[71]

Prior to Biden taking office, CISA had a "Countering Foreign Influence Task Force." But in 2021, that was renamed the "Mis, Dis and Malinformation Team" ("MDM Team"). But almost all the targets of federal censorship during the Biden era have been Americans.

CISA was purportedly intended to fight foreign threats to election security and U.S. infrastructure. A CISA advisory committee issued a 2022 report which "broadened 'infrastructure' to include 'the spread of false and misleading information because it poses a significant risk to critical function, like elections, public health, financial services and emergency responses,'" Judge Doughty noted. Thus, any idea that government officials label as "misleading" could be a "significant risk" that the feds can suppress.

The Biden administration pressured social media companies "to censor misinformation regarding climate change, gender discussions, abortion, and economic policy," Judge Doughty noted. A confidential 2022 DHS document detailed pending crackdowns on "inaccurate" information on "the efficacy of COVID-19 vaccines, racial justice, U.S. withdrawal from Afghanistan, and the nature of U.S. support to Ukraine."[72] Any facts that embarrassed the Biden administration were presumed inaccurate.

Cynicism was the ultimate Biden target. His 2021 National Strategy for Countering Domestic Terrorism explicitly proclaimed a "broader priority" of "enhancing faith in government."[73] In a March 2022 meeting with top Twitter executives, FBI agent Laura Dehmlow "warned that the threat of subversive information on social media could undermine support for the U.S. government." Dehmlow was the chief of the Foreign Influence Task Force which strong-armed social media companies into suppressing any claims or opinions it labeled suspicious. The FBI has 80 agents on a task force to curb "subversive data utilized to drive a wedge between the populace and the government."[74]

Prior to the 2022 midterm elections, the FBI ramped up its pressure on Twitter. On November 5, 2022, the FBI's National Election Command Post emailed the FBI San Francisco field office (which dealt directly with Twitter) "a long list of accounts that 'may warrant additional action'" — i.e., suppression.[75] Taibbi wrote: "The master-canine quality of the FBI's relationship to Twitter comes through in this November 2022 email, in which 'FBI San Francisco is notifying you' it wants action on four accounts."[76] The vast majority of federal censorship of the 2022 election has likely not yet been revealed.

Biden's congressional allies sought to destroy critics of his censorship regime at a March 10, 2023, House hearing.[77] Though Twitter Files' Matt Taibbi was a bestselling author and respected reporter, House Democrats pounded him as a "so-called journalist," a hypocrite, a profiteer, a threat to the peace, and a lackey for Twitter owner Elon Musk. Democratic members portrayed the Twitter Files as nothing but a slur on benevolent bureaucrats. After the hearing, Del. Stacey Plaskett (D-VI) threatened Taibbi with perjury charges and a five-year prison sentence after she claimed that he had made a minor misstatement in his testimony.[78] The Federal Trade Commission demanded "all internal communications by, from or about Musk — and telling him to name reporters he's shared info with."[79] Does the FTC now consider exposing federal abuses an unfair trade practice? Musk denounced the federal demand as "a shameful case of weaponization of a government agency for political purposes and suppression of the truth!"[80]

There was scant concern on Capitol Hill because some congressmen had long since jumped on the censorship bandwagon. House Intelligence Committee Chairman Adam Schiff (D-CA) successfully pressured Twitter to ban one of his critics, journalist Paul Sperry, and sought blanket suppression of Twitter critics of his congressional staff.[81] Sen. Angus King (I-ME) pressured Facebook to cancel "suspected accounts" for crimes such as sharing the image or comments praising his political opponent.[82] Taibbi commented on the Angus King target list: "If Dick Nixon sniffed glue, this is what his enemies list might have looked like."[83]

Governor Katie Hobbs of Arizona requested Twitter censor her critics. In August 2017, when she was in the state legislature, Hobbs tweeted that

Trump supporters were a "neo-Nazi base." After Hobbs became Arizona Secretary of State, overseeing the state's elections, she exploited her position to contact Twitter in 2020, asking them to suppress criticisms of her neo-Nazi tweet.[84]

The Biden administration received plenty of tacit help in sweeping the scandal under the rug. The mainstream media have less interest in exposing federal censorship than a 1920s Mississippi sheriff had in solving a Klan lynching. Pundits know disinformation is a grave peril because the government tells them so — making it a Beltway Revealed Truth.

Defining Censorship Down

In his July 4, 2023, decision, Judge Doughty concluded that the White House "engaged in coercion of social media companies to such extent that the decisions of the social media companies should be deemed that of the Government." That issue was the crux in August 2023 when three judges on a federal appeals court heard the government's challenge to Doughty's decision.

In its briefs to the court, the Justice Department declared, "There is a categorical, well-settled distinction between persuasion and coercion," and castigated Judge Doughty for having "equated legitimate efforts at persuasion with illicit efforts to coerce." Instead of coercion, federal agencies merely made requests for "content moderation." Actually, there were tens of thousands of "requests" that resulted in the suppression of millions of posts and comments by Americans. Justice Department lawyer Daniel Tenny told the judges: "There was a back-and-forth sometimes it was more friendly sometimes people got more testy um there there were circumstances in which um the everyone saw eye-to-eye there were circumstances in which they disagreed [sic]."[85]

Judge Don Willett said he had no problem with federal agencies publicly criticizing what they judged false or dangerous ideas. But that wasn't how Team Biden compelled submission: "Here you have government in secret, in private, out of the public eye, relying on… subtle strong-arming and veiled or not-so-veiled threats."[86] Willett vivified how the feds played the game: "That's a really nice social media platform you've got there; it would be a shame if something happened to it." Judge Jennifer Elrod compared the Biden censorship regime to the Mafia: "We see with the mob… They have these ongoing relationships. They never actually say, 'Go do this or else you're going to have this consequence.' But everybody just knows."

Yet the Biden administration was supposedly innocent because the feds never explicitly spelled out "or else," according to the Justice Department lawyer. The Biden administration champions a "no corpse, no delicta" definition of censorship. Since federal SWAT teams did not assail the headquarters of social media companies, the feds are blameless. But as economist Joseph Schumpeter aptly observed: "Power wins, not by being used, but by being there."

On September 8, the appeals court unanimously ruled that the White House, FBI, Centers for Disease Control and Prevention (CDC), and Office of the Surgeon General had trampled the First Amendment and that Biden administration "officials have engaged in a broad pressure campaign designed to coerce social-media companies into suppressing speakers, viewpoints, and content disfavored by the government."[87] The court declared that "beyond express threats, there was *always* an unspoken 'or else.' The officials made clear that the platforms *would* suffer adverse consequences if they failed to comply, through express or implied threats, and thus the requests were not optional" (emphasis in original). The appeals court also took a "real world" view of the nation's most feared law enforcement agency: "Although the FBI's communications did not plainly reference adverse consequences, an actor need not express a threat aloud so long as, given the circumstances, the message *intimates* that some form of punishment will follow noncompliance" (emphasis in original). The appeals court narrowed the scope of the injunction that Judge Doughty imposed, but the Biden administration quickly appealed the partial injunction to the Supreme Court.

Pentagon's Shameless Satrap, Etc.

Twitter has boasted for years that it takes extraordinary efforts to protect users from government covert propaganda. But Twitter has behaved like a Pentagon satrap when it came to gift-wrapping U.S. propaganda for foreign audiences.

In 2017, the Pentagon provided Twitter with a list of hundreds of its own Arabic-language accounts that sought to "amplify certain messages" to foreign audiences. Journalist Lee Fang noted: "Twitter verification would have bestowed a number of advantages, such as invulnerability to algorithmic bots that flag accounts for spam or abuse, as well as other strikes that lead to decreased visibility or suspension."[88] Twitter approved the accounts because they were clearly identified as U.S. government entities. The Pentagon then double-crossed Twitter by deleting any evidence of a tie to the U.S. government, pretending the accounts were independent foreign activists. Some Twitter accounts were burnished with "deep fake" pictures of "photorealistic human faces generated by artificial intelligence." Fang noted that "an authentic-looking Persian-language news portal or a local Afghan woman would have greater organic influence than an official Pentagon press release."

Twitter recognized the switcheroo but still permits the U.S. government to continue deceiving Twitter users around the world. The U.S. government has been harshly criticized around the globe since 2009 for drone strikes in Yemen and elsewhere that resulted in the deaths of countless innocent civilians. But Twitter approved a covert U.S. account whose tweets "emphasized that U.S. drone strikes were 'accurate' and killed terrorists, not civilians, and promoted the U.S.- and Saudi-backed assault on Houthi rebels in that country." Twitter also sanctioned covert Pentagon accounts trumpeting "U.S.-supported militias in Syria," even though those militias have been linked to perennial atrocities against Syrian women and children. The Twitter-protected U.S. propaganda accounts "relentlessly pushed narratives against Russia, China, and other foreign countries. They accused Iran of 'threatening Iraq's water security and flooding the country with crystal meth,' and of harvesting the organs of Afghan refugees," Fang noted. After Twitter complained to the Pentagon about its duplicity, a top Twitter attorney emailed colleagues warning that "the Pentagon may want to retroactively classify its social media activities 'to obfuscate their activity in this space, and that this may represent an overclassification to avoid embarrassment."[89]

At the same time it kowtowed to the Pentagon, Twitter and other social media companies censored criticism of U.S. foreign policy. After the CIA finagled its way into the Twitter censorship regime, Twitter came under heavy pressure to suppress tweets asserting that Joe Biden had "put his son on the board of Burisma," a corrupt Ukrainian company which added Hunter Biden to its board in 2014 while Biden was Vice President overseeing U.S. Ukraine policy.[90] Taibbi noted that some of the targets the CIA wanted suppressed were "just long lists of newspapers, tweets or YouTube videos guilty of 'anti-Ukraine narratives.'" Twitter routinely but not always obeyed.

In July 2023, the House Judiciary Committee revealed that the FBI routinely colluded with Ukraine's spy agency which sought help to suppress social media accounts that criticized the Ukraine government or "inaccurately reflects events in Ukraine" (including accurate battlefield reports of Ukrainian military defeats). The House report revealed that the FBI "routinely relayed these lists [of accounts] to the relevant social media platforms" and sought their suppression. The House report noted that "authentic accounts of Americans, including a verified U.S. State Department account and those belonging to American journalists, were ensnared in the censorship effort and flagged for social media companies to take down."[91]

American media coverage of the war was profoundly slanted by the endless emissions from U.S. government-funded propaganda operations in Ukraine and beyond. The U.S. funds foreign propaganda operations that echo in American newspapers and cable news, and the White House exploits those stories to drag this nation further into the East European war. American social media companies propagated one brazen Ukrainian propaganda scheme after another — such as the imaginary "Ghost of Kyiv" shooting down 40 Russian warplanes.[92] But increased censorship was supposedly the remedy for battlefield defeats. At the start of Biden's Summit for Democracy, eight governments, including Ukraine and Poland, issued a call in March 2023 for social media companies to further suppress posts that "weaken our support to Ukraine amid Russia's war of aggression."[93]

Conclusion: Censorship and the Death of Democracy

Censorship could cast the deciding vote in the 2024 presidential election. Judge Doughty issued his injunction in part because federal agencies "could use their power over millions of people to suppress alternative views or moderate content they do not agree with in the upcoming 2024 national election." Will a Supreme Court ruling prevent the feds from rigging the next election?

The patron saint of the War on Disinformation is the authoritarian German philosopher G.W.F. Hegel. Hegel deified government and gushed about "the truth which lies in power." Contemporary censors rarely invoke Hegel, but their schemes often tacitly presume that political power is divine — if not in origin, at least in its effect. CISA, for instance, settled controversies by simply asking government officials and "apparently always assumed the government official was a reliable source," the court decision noted. Any assertion by officialdom was enough for CISA to "debunk postings" by private citizens. But when did government I.D. badges become the Oracle of Delphi?

"Truth" is whatever the government proclaims. "Disinformation" is whatever contradicts the latest government pronouncements. It is irrelevant how many false statements politicians or bureaucrats make. Government retains a monopoly on truth and on the right to deceive.

Censorship rests on the presumed moral and intellectual superiority of the ruling class. But as Thomas Macaulay wrote almost two centuries ago: "None of the modes by which a magistrate is appointed, popular election, the accident of the lot, or the accident of birth, affords… much security for his being wiser than any of his neighbors." The illusion of omniscience can be maintained only as long as governments suppress news of their finance and frauds.

The presumption that politicians are benevolent underlies the latest schemes to save humanity via censorship. Supposedly, government would only lie to people for their own good. And what is the proof? It is secret. Why would political censorship be more honest than politicians?

Should we replace the First Amendment with a simple censorship-friendly disclaimer: "For your own good"? Unfortunately, any such revision would likely be done clandestinely, and Americans wouldn't learn about the alteration until long after the perversion was codified.

Censorship is not merely a question of stifling heartfelt expressions. There can be scant freedom of thought without freedom of speech and press. Censorship seeks to force each person to live in mental isolation, with no sparks for their thoughts from fellow citizens. As German philosopher Immanuel Kant wrote, "The external power that deprives man of the freedom to communicate his thoughts publicly, deprives him at the same time of his freedom to think."[94] By barricading individuals from each other, censors create millions of intellectual Robinson Crusoes stranded on islands and trying to figure out everything for themselves. Prohibiting citizens from sharing facts of government abuses spawns a bastardized form of sovereign immunity. As Hannah Arendt warned, "The chances of factual truth surviving the onslaught of power are very slim indeed; it is always in danger of being maneuvered out of the world not only for a time but, potentially, forever."[95]

The key to the new censorship is that it is not an isolated attack on the Constitution or Bill of Rights. Instead, it epitomizes an across-the-board assault on freedom. Washingtonians take it as a self-evident truth that the feds must be in charge of practically everything, including truth.

Unfortunately, many Americans suffer the same deferential delusion. Fifty-five percent of American adults support government suppression of "false information," even though only 20% trust the government.[96] Relying on dishonest officials to eradicate "false information" is not the height of prudence. A September 2023 poll revealed that almost half of Democrats believed that free speech should be legal "only under certain circumstances" (perhaps excluding criticism of their party's elected officials).[97] Support for censorship is stronger among young folks whose schooling perhaps smote their natural love of freedom.

If the Biden administration can destroy freedom of speech by renaming censorship as "content moderation," what other freedoms can be zapped with rhetorical scams? If endless threats by the FBI and other agencies don't amount to "coercion," the feds will never admit how they are bludgeoning Americans' rights and liberties. If the feds can censor their online critics, their deceits become almost irrefutable.

Nullifying freedom of speech turns citizens into political pawns who will be sacrificed as their rulers please. The doctrines which justify censorship obliterate the moral and philosophical foundations for contemporary democracy. In the Declaration of Independence, Thomas Jefferson invoked "the consent of the governed" as a test for legitimacy. But "informed consent" by voters is a mirage if federal agencies can pervert plain facts as they please.

Should polling booths have signs formally notifying voters: "Enjoy your last informed choice"? With the current extent of government censorship, "informed consent" ends after Election Day as winning politicians become entitled to deceive citizens for their entire term of office. At best, citizens can only choose their censors once — since every subsequent election is tainted by censorship. Does winning an election automatically convert tinhorn politicians into minor deities entitled to control the thoughts of all the voters?

14. American Gestapo Run Amok

"You should not trust me."
— FBI chief James Comey congressional testimony, 2015[1]

In 1945, President Harry Truman wrote in his diary: "We want no Gestapo or Secret Police. FBI is tending in that direction."[2] But Truman and subsequent presidents failed to restrain the nation's most feared G-men. For more than a hundred years, the Federal Bureau of Investigation has been trampling the law and the Constitution.

The FBI's prerogative to enforce more than 5,000 federal criminal laws gives it sway over almost every part of American life. The FBI has always used its "good guy" image to keep a lid on its crimes and fiascos. Despite perennial scandals, politicians and media allies have shielded the FBI's power, backstopped by federal judges happy to grant impunity to the agency.

In 2018, former FBI director James Comey described himself as the "guardian" of the FBI's role "as an independent force in American life."[3] But the Founding Fathers never intended a secret police force to be an independent fourth branch of the federal government akin to the Senate or Supreme Court. As James Madison warned in 1788: "Wherever the real power in a Government lies, there is the danger of oppression."[4] Unfortunately, many Americans and most of the media forgot that lesson as the FBI accumulated vast power over the past century. Agents have been taught at the FBI Academy that targets of investigations "have forfeited their right to the truth."[5] But zealous FBI leaders presumed that Congress and the citizens also forfeited their right to truth about the Bureau.

Specific FBI abuses have been covered in prior chapters of this book. Here are some of the lesser known or most outrageous FBI scandals in this century.

Sniper SNAFU: Famous But Incompetent

On September 9, 2001, the *New York Times* reported that the FBI was in the "worst crisis in a generation." Thanks to a series of "debacles," only 24% of Americans had a favorable view of the agency — far lower than in previous eras.[6] Within 48 hours, far worse FBI blunders would contribute to the toppling of the World Trade Center.

But the FBI's reputation was rescued by the tidal wave of pro-government sentiment that politicians and the media spurred after 9/11. In the weeks after the attacks, the percentage of Americans who "trust the government in Washington to do what is right" either "just about always" or "most of the time" more than doubled, reaching 64%.[7]

Prior to the 9/11 attacks, the FBI's pervasive failures "contributed to the United States becoming, in effect, a sanctuary for radical terrorists," according to a 2002 congressional investigation.[8] In 1997, FBI Director Louis Freeh promised Congress that he would "double the 'shoe leather'" for counterterrorism investigations. But walking was no substitute for thinking. The FBI's profound aversion toward modern technology left it blindfolded to al Qaeda and other threats. Despite almost $2 billion spent for computer upgrades, many FBI agents on 9/11 had eight-year-old machines that were incapable of searching the Web or sending email. One FBI agent observed that the Bureau ethos is that "real men don't type. The only thing a real agent needs is a notebook, a pen and gun, and with those three things you can conquer the world... The computer revolution just passed us by."[9] The Bush administration deceived the nation by refusing to publicly admit until May 2002 that FBI agents had sent clear warnings of Arab hijackers to FBI headquarters that Washington disregarded.

Regardless of the Bureau's failures, Congress responded to 9/11 by sharply boosting the FBI budget. The FBI also captured vast new power over Americans thanks to the Patriot Act.

The new, improved FBI had the chance to strut in late 2002 when two snipers went on a rampage that left ten people dead in the Washington, D.C., area. President George W. Bush proclaimed that the sniper attacks were "a form of terrorism" and boasted of "lending all the resources of the Federal Government" to the investigation.[10] But the killings continued for 23 days.

Prior to the start of the rampage, the FBI and ATF received reports from five different people in Washington State (where John Muhammed, the lead sniper, lived) warning about his comments about killing police, his interest in buying silencers for his rifle, and his visit to a gunsmith to inquire about modifying the rifle to make it more easily concealed.[11] The feds never bothered to pursue any of those leads.

Once the killings began, more than seven hundred FBI agents were involved in the investigation. FBI trainees staffed the telephone tip lines at the Montgomery County, Maryland, police headquarters, where the first shootings occurred. The FBI, scorning the technological revolutions of the prior half-century, relied on the same methods used to pursue John Dillinger in the 1930s. Instead of entering tips from the public into a computer database, FBI trainees would write out the information by hand and stack the reports into piles marked "immediate," "priority," or "routine." FBI agents would then drive the stacks of reports to other locales where the snipers attacked, including Fairfax County and Richmond, Virginia. Numerous lawmen complained to the *Washington Post* that "the FBI's problems handling thousands of phone tips are slowing and hampering the probe." After 9/11, the FBI had created a new system called "Rapid Start" to handle a huge volume of leads. But local police derided it as "Rapid Stop."

When the FBI recruits were not laboriously scrawling the latest tip, they were busy hanging up on the snipers. In a note attached to a tree after the ninth shooting, the snipers complained that operators at the tip line hung up on them five times. The note denounced police "incompitence" [sic] and declared: "We have tried to contact you to start negotiation. These people took [our] calls for a hoax or a joke, so your failure to respond has cost you five lives."[12] At the scene of an Ashland, Virginia, shooting, the killers left a note with a demand for money in a Ziploc bag.[13] But no law enforcement official bothered to read the note before it was shipped off to check for fingerprints. The FBI ignored the bevy of clues in the note and in the other material in the Ziploc bag. If the note had been publicized — like the Unabomber's manifesto — savvy citizens might have fingered the culprits much sooner.

Instead of exploiting excellent leads, the feds unleashed Pentagon spy planes to track all vehicles in the entire Washington area.[14] The spy planes may have violated the Posse Comitatus Act (which prohibits using the military for domestic law enforcement) but provided no useful information.

Shortly after the arrest of the two suspects, Washington, D.C., Police Chief Charles Ramsey publicly confessed: "We were looking for a white van with white people, and we ended up with a blue car with black people." The only "evidence" that the killers were white was the dogma of FBI and other serial killer profilers. Police spotted the snipers' blue car and recorded its out-of-state license plates at least ten different times during the month of the killings; the vehicle was reported to have been stopped or seen five times at roadblocks established immediately after shootings.[15] Because they were searching for a white van or truck, police disregarded the suspects again and again. One federal investigator later complained: "The car was screaming, 'Stop me.' It's dilapidated. It's got Jersey tags. It's got a homemade window tint."[16]

Rather than FBI heroics, it was a leak of key information that nailed the snipers. News media had been listening to police scanners, and, on October 23, MSNBC and CNN broadcast the snipers' license plate and car description. Within hours, an alert citizen phoned in a tip that the suspects' car was at an interstate rest stop in Frederick County, Maryland. A SWAT team quickly swarmed to arrest the suspects, and the FBI claimed victory by boasting that it had some agents in the posse making the arrest that night.

FBI = Full-Blown Idiot

On May 7, 2004, the FBI arrested Brandon Mayfield, an Oregon lawyer, for his ties to train bombings in Madrid, Spain, that killed 191 and left 2,000 wounded.[17] A federal official told *Newsweek* that Mayfield's fingerprint was an "absolutely incontrovertible match" to a copy of the fingerprint found on a bag of bomb detonators near the scene of the Madrid attack. Mayfield's arrest ramped up the fear index since he was the first American directly linked to mass slaughter abroad. Mayfield was informed that he could face the death penalty for his crimes.

Mayfield was one of 20 Americans whose fingerprints resembled the print that Spanish authorities retrieved from a bomb bag after the train attack. The FBI did not have sufficient evidence to get a search warrant from a federal judge to target Mayfield. However, thanks to the Patriot Act, the FBI went to the Foreign Intelligence Surveillance Court and secured a warrant with far less evidence by claiming Mayfield was tied to a foreign terrorist group. The FBI conducted secret searches of Mayfield's home and tapped his phone and email.

Mayfield was arrested as a "material witness," thereby permitting the feds to hold him as long as they pleased without charging him with a specific crime and to interrogate him without a lawyer present. "Material witness" charges became standard practice after 9/11 as the FBI and other law enforcement agencies conducted hundreds of secret arrests. The Justice Department refused to disclose how many people were being held as "material witnesses" in prisons around the country. A week before Mayfield's arrest, a federal judge warned that Bush material witness policy could make "detention the norm and liberty the exception" in America.[18]

FBI agents raided Mayfield's home and office and carted off boxes of his papers and his family's belongings. Among the items seized were "miscellaneous Spanish documents," according to an FBI statement to the federal court. These supposedly incriminating papers turned out to be the Spanish homework of Mayfield's son. Perhaps FBI investigators suspected that "Hola, Paco. ¿Como estas?" was a secret code.

The FBI also froze Mayfield's bank accounts. The FBI's arrest affidavit revealed that its agents had "observed Mayfield drive to the Bilal Mosque located at 415 160th Ave., Beaverton, Oregon, on several different occasions." Another incriminating detail in the arrest warrant: Mayfield advertised his legal service in the Muslim Yellow Pages. Mayfield, a former Army lieutenant, converted to Islam and had an Egyptian wife. In early April, the Spanish police described Mayfield as "a U.S. military veteran who was already under investigation by U.S. authorities for alleged ties to Islamic terrorism."[19]

Yet the crux of the FBI's case — the fingerprint — was more dubious than a late-night TV herbal supplement commercial. FBI officials made a deluge of false claims in federal court to secure absolute power over their target. The arrest warrant wrongly claimed the Spaniards were "satisfied" with the FBI's match. The FBI informed a federal judge: "It is believed that Mayfield may have traveled under a false or fictitious name." But Mayfield, whose passport expired the previous year, had not left the country in the prior decade. The FBI apparently never bothered to check whether Mayfield had been absent from the U.S. before making one of the most high-profile terrorism arrests of the year.

The FBI's victory parade ended on May 20 when Spanish authorities arrested an Algerian whose fingerprint perfectly matched those on the bomb bag. A few weeks later, Attorney General Ashcroft informed the Senate Judiciary Committee that the Mayfield case vindicated the FBI and the American system of justice: "As a matter of fact, the pride of our system is that people are found innocent because we adjudicate these things."[20] But there was no adjudication in this case because Mayfield was classified as a "material witness" — which meant he could be detained indefinitely. Ashcroft also testified: "When we learned that the reservations of the Spanish were so substantial, we went to the court [and] asked for the release of Mr. Mayfield." In reality, the Justice Department ended its vendetta only after the Spanish government effectively closed the case. An internal FBI investigation concluded that the fiasco occurred in part "because the FBI culture discouraged fingerprint examiners from disagreeing with their superiors."[21]

In late 2006, after Republicans lost control of Congress, the Justice Department agreed to pay $2 million to settle Mayfield's suit on his wrongful jailing and other violations of his rights.[22] In 2007, Federal Judge Ann Aiken ruled that the Patriot Act provision that the FBI used to target Mayfield was unconstitutional because it "permits the executive branch of government to conduct surveillance and searches of American citizens without satisfying the probable cause requirements of the Fourth Amendment."[23]

The Mayfield episode was one of a long series of FBI evidence tampering disasters. A 1997 Inspector General report found that FBI lab experts provided court testimony "that appeared tailored to the most incriminating result" involving "speculation beyond [their] scientific expertise." A 2004 National Academy of Sciences report concluded that decades of FBI court testimony matching bullets to specific firearms in thousands of homicide cases was "unreliable" and "misleading under federal rules of evidence."[24] An elite FBI forensic unit gave misleading court testimony in 95% of the cases reviewed, including 32 cases that sentenced defendants to death (including 14 cases where the convicted were executed or died in prison).[25] The FBI helped convict a teenager for murder based on a DNA match to a single hair at the crime scene. After the supposed offender served 28 years in prison, his conviction was overturned and a re-examination revealed that it was a hair of a dog.[26]

Entrapment Gold Rush

FBI counterterrorism training teaches agents that "the FBI has the ability to bend or suspend the law to impinge on the freedom of others."[27] This doctrine has helped the FBI manufacture more terrorists than any foreign entity could hope to recruit in America. For 20 years, the Bureau has profited mightily from ginning up bogus plots to generate lurid headlines.

Trevor Aaronson, the author of *The Terror Factory: Inside the FBI's Manufactured War on Terrorism*, estimated that only about 1% of the 500 people charged with international terrorism offenses in the decade after 9/11 were bona fide terrorists.[28] Thirty times as many were induced by FBI informants to behave in ways that prompted their arrest. In one high-profile case, a judge concluded that the government "came up with the crime, provided the means, and removed all relevant obstacles" and made a terrorist out of a man "whose buffoonery is positively Shakespearean in scope" and who was involved in a "fantasy terror operation."

On June 23, 2006, the Bush administration whipped up hysteria by announcing the arrest of seven plotters who planned to ravage Miami and Chicago. At a time when Bush's war in Iraq had become a quagmire, and shortly before the 2006 midterm elections, top officials greeted the arrests like manna from heaven. Attorney General Alberto Gonzales asserted that the plotters promised a "full ground war against the United States"[29] and represented "a new brand of terrorism" created by "the convergence of globalization and technology." FBI chief Robert Mueller called the arrestees a "homegrown terrorist cell... self-recruited, self-trained, and self-executing."[30]

Except that the entire plot was fabricated by the FBI. FBI informants had targeted a group of poor mostly Haitian-Americans who became known as the "Liberty City Seven" after the arrests. The FBI lavished money on an informant who offered plenty of goodies to this gang of misfits. The informant suggested the idea of blowing up government buildings and then tape-recorded the subsequent discussions to incriminate his targets. The plotters were so knuckle-headed that they asked the FBI informant for terrorist uniforms and wanted to conduct a parade in their low-rent neighborhood. At one point, the lead plotter talked about blowing up the Sears Tower in Chicago, the nation's tallest building, "so that it would fall into Lake Michigan and create a tsunami" — thereby allowing the plotters to free all the Muslims detained in Chicago jails. That guy later admitted he got that brilliant idea "from watching the movies."[31]

The plotters were so poor that they asked one of the FBI informants (who were paid $140,000 in total) for free shoes, specifying the shoe sizes of the members of the group. The informant coached the men into reciting a goofily-worded pledge of allegiance to al Qaeda, which was secretly videotaped.

The FBI gave the plotters a digital video camera and rented them a car so they could visit downtown Miami and photograph the FBI building and other federal targets they were encouraged to attack. The videotape was one of the few pieces of concrete evidence offered at the subsequent trial. One of the informants kept dangling the prospect of giving $50,000 to the plotters if they moved forward with their scheme. When the feds raided the warehouse that the government provided for the plotters' headquarters (complete with a fully stocked refrigerator), they found no weapons or plans for attacks.[32] After the arrests were announced, a local activist told *Democracy Now*: "Everyone in Liberty City is joking that the guys were going to kick down the FBI building with their new boots, because they didn't have any devices which could have been used to explode" the target.[33] One commentator suggested that the "Liberty City Seven" would be incapable of robbing a 7-Eleven, much less overthrowing the U.S. government. A top FBI official admitted that the plot was "more aspirational than operational," but it sufficed for an FBI victory lap.

The federal case went downhill after the initial "shock and awe" headlines. As National Public Radio noted: "The Liberty City Seven saga is the first major counterterrorism sting by the FBI that became highly visible because the people who were arrested, the defendants, chose to go to trial… because they thought they were innocent."[34] But federal judges prevented their lawyers from informing the juries of the sordid past of the informants the FBI used to nail them.

The prosecution of the highest-profile domestic terrorist plot went awry from the start. The first jury refused to convict, deadlocking on charges except for one defendant found not guilty. The Justice Department claimed the verdict entitled the feds to try again, but a second jury also deadlocked. In a shameless abuse of power, the feds tried the accused again and finally got a conviction in 2009 for five of the six accused. The feds spent up to $10 million prosecuting the case. Trevor Aaronson observed regarding the FBI's conclusion from the Liberty City Seven: "If they can convict these guys in Miami, they convict just about anybody."[35] The feds happily destroyed a half-dozen lives to give a booster shot of fear for Bush's War on Terror.

The Liberty City Seven was one of a list of targets of the FBI's cadre of 15,000 informants who are paid more than $40 million per year.[36] Prosecutors bolstered informants' claims by introducing secret evidence at trials to secure jury convictions. The post-9/11 hysteria that politicians and government agencies fueled often subverted the chance for fair trials by government targets.

In 2010, prosecutors convicted four black Muslims in a wild-eyed plot to use a Stinger missile (which they never possessed) to attack a U.S. Air Force Base and synagogues in New York. On July 27, 2023, Federal Judge Colleen McMahon overturned convictions of three defendants and condemned the

FBI for sending a "villain" to "troll among the poorest and weakest of men for 'terrorists' who might prove susceptible to an offer of much-needed cash in exchange for committing a faux crime." McMahon declared that "the real lead conspirator was the United States."[37]

The government's star witness, Shaheed Hussain, pirouetted for a decade as an FBI "superinformant." He had previously been arrested for murder in Pakistan but escaped after someone bribed police. After coming to America, he was caught helping people cheat on DMV tests. The FBI recruited him, and his lies delivered court victories that burnished the Bureau's halo. The FBI also provided luxury cars to Hussain to jump-start his limousine business.[38] His vehicles endlessly failed safety inspections, he racked up vast numbers of traffic tickets, and the company was caught falsifying reports, but his business was never shut down. In 2018, the brakes on one of his malfunctioning limousines failed, and it crashed while going 118 miles per hour. Twenty people were killed. The role of the FBI in providing impunity for Hussain and his killer limousine was a key topic at a 2023 trial in Albany.

FBI informants have helped fan fears of extremism since long before 9/11. In 2006, an FBI informant organized and led a neo-Nazi march in Florida.[39] It bankrolled an extremist right-wing New Jersey blogger and radio host for five years before his 2009 arrest for threatening federal judges. In 2017, a long-term violent FBI informant spearheaded a Ku Klux Klan rally in Charlottesville, Virginia.[40] In August 2021, court filings revealed that the FBI had provided more than $100,000 to the publisher of neo-Nazi books since 2013.[41] How many bloggers, talk-show hosts, or activists is the FBI currently financing?

How far will the FBI go to spur havoc? In 2015, an undercover FBI agent urged two ISIS supporters to "tear up Texas" by attacking people at an anti-Muslim cartoon event in Garland. The undercover G-man arrived with two ISIS supporters at the event and used his cellphone to film a security guard whom the ISIS zealots quickly gunned down. Those two ISIS supporters were quickly killed by on-scene police and irate Texans. The FBI agent fled the scene after the shooting started and was briefly arrested by local police (until he showed his FBI badge, presumably). The FBI blocked investigations into its full role in the killings. But the casualties that day were politically profitable. As *Salon* noted in 2017: "The Garland shooting has been used to justify a vast array of anti-Muslim policies and measures."[42]

FBI = Forever Burying Investigations

In 2014, 71-year-old Nevada rancher Cliven Bundy and his sons were involved in an armed standoff with the FBI and the Bureau of Land Management (BLM) stemming from decades of disputed cattle grazing fees. BLM controls 48 million acres in Nevada, equal to 63% of the state's land. Cattlemen and BLM have perpetually clashed due to the federal agency's arbitrary and capricious treatment of Nevadans.

The Bundys summoned supporters to help defend them, asserting that FBI snipers had encircled their house. The Bundys were spooked by the specter of Ruby Ridge, where FBI snipers surrounded an Idaho cabin in 1992 and gunned down all the adults even though they never fired a shot at the FBI.[43] Though both the feds and the Bundy supporters were heavily armed in 2014, no gunfire was exchanged. After the feds backed down, the FBI went to astounding lengths to nail their critics. The FBI assembled a bogus "independent" documentary film crew who spent almost a year hounding the Bundy family and their supporters, seeking to gather incriminating evidence during interviews.[44]

In 2016, Cliven and his two sons were arrested and charged with conspiracy, assaults, threats against the government, and obstruction of justice during the 2014 standoff. Federal prosecutors stressed that the Bundys used "deceit and deception" to sway friends and supporters to defend them by making false accusations against the FBI.

But a Nevada jury smelled a federal rat. In August 2017, in what the Associated Press labeled a "stunning setback to federal prosecutors," the jury found four supporters of Cliven Bundy not guilty for their role in the 2014 confrontation. Even though Federal Judge Gloria Navarro muzzled defendants and prohibited them from invoking their constitutional rights, jurors scorned federal claims that the men were part of a conspiracy against the government.[45] The defendants claimed to be exercising their constitutional right to free speech and peacefully carrying weapons — common practice in rural parts of the West.

Cliven Bundy and his sons went on trial in late 2017. Shortly before the trial began, BLM special agent Larry Wooten charged that BLM chose "the most intrusive, oppressive, large scale and militaristic trespass cattle [seizure] possible" against Bundy's herd. He cited a "widespread pattern of bad judgment, lack of discipline, incredible bias, unprofessionalism and misconduct, as well as likely policy, ethical and legal violations" by BLM officials in the case. BLM agents even "bragged about roughing up Dave Bundy [Cliven's son], grinding his face into the ground, and Dave Bundy having little bits of gravel stuck in his face" while he was videotaping federal agents.[46] As the Portland *Oregonian* noted:

> Wooten said he learned from other agency supervisors that Love had a "Kill Book" as a "trophy," in which he essentially bragged about "getting three individuals in Utah to commit suicide," following a joint FBI-BLM investigation into the alleged trafficking of stolen artifacts.[47]

Steven Myhre, the lead federal attorney, cast "the 2014 standoff as an armed uprising, not a peaceful protest over federal control of vast stretches of land in the U.S. West, as the Bundys claim," the Associated Press reported. Myhre's opening statement of the Bundy trial stressed "that the case centered on the need to respect the rule of law." But the government exempted itself from the law and the Constitution in its crusade against the Bundys.

As the trial progressed, the judge forced the Justice Department to turn over thousands of pages of evidence that had been wrongfully concealed from the Bundys' lawyers. The feds belatedly disclosed multiple threat assessments revealing that the Bundys were not violent or dangerous, including an FBI analysis that concluded that BLM was "trying to provoke a conflict" with the Bundys.

As their case began unraveling, federal prosecutors insisted that the judge must prohibit the Bundys from claiming the feds provoked the confrontation or that the Bundys acted in self-defense. Myhre declared: "The Court needs to put a stop to these illegal theories and defenses in order for the government to receive a fair trial. The government, too, is entitled to a fair trial." Fairness had been in short supply since the start of the case, but better late than never. Justice Department lawyers complained that allowing the jury to see too much evidence meant "putting the *victims* [federal officials and prosecutors] in this case in the position of having to justify their every move when no force was used" (emphasis added).[48] According to the Justice Department, jurors had no right to pass judgment on federal conduct.

The remnants of federal credibility vanished when it was revealed that the FBI actually had snipers around the Bundy home — despite three years of denials by the FBI and the Justice Department. On December 20, 2017, Federal Judge Gloria Navarro declared a mistrial and condemned the "grossly shocking" withholding of evidence from defense counsel. Two weeks later, she dismissed all charges against Bundy and his sons. Navarro slammed the FBI and Justice Department prosecutors for "outrageous" abuses and "flagrant misconduct" and said that "a universal sense of justice has been violated" by federal misconduct in the Bundy trial.

Cliven Bundy walked free after 700 days in jail. After the case was dismissed, his son, Ammon Bundy, told a television interviewer: "They basically came to kill our family; they surrounded us with snipers. And then they wanted to lie about it all like none of it happened. And they were caught." The mission of the federal snipers around the ranch was unclear, but it is understandable that their targets did not presume benign intent. As the left-leaning *Intercept* observed, federal missteps "fueled long-standing perceptions among the right-wing groups and militias that the federal government is an underhanded institution that will stop at nothing to crush the little guy and cover up its own misdeeds."[49]

Orlando: FBI = Federal Bureau of Illusions

On June 12, 2016, Omar Mateen killed 49 people and wounded 53 at Orlando's Pulse nightclub — the worst terrorist attack in the U.S. since 9/11. Police loitered outside the club for several hours while Mateen continued his killing spree.

On the day after the carnage, FBI chief James Comey promised: "We will leave no stone unturned, and we will work all day and all night to understand the path to that terrible night... We'll look at it in an open and honest way and be transparent about it."[50] But Comey fastidiously avoided overturning any stones exposing the FBI's role in the calamity. Comey complained of the difficulty of investigating lone wolf terrorists like Mateen: "We are looking for needles in a nationwide haystack." Comey also declared on Mateen: "There is confusion about his motives."

But any confusion was solely the result of FBI deceit. During his night-long rampage, Mateen made several phone calls to 911 and talked at length to police negotiators. The FBI redacted the transcript of those calls to expunge Mateen's motivation. He pledged allegiance to the Islamic State — radicals who were on a beheading spree in the Mideast — and expressed solidarity with Muslim terrorists that had attacked in the U.S. and abroad. He proclaimed: "You have to tell America to stop bombing Syria and Iraq. They're killing a lot of innocent people. So what am I to do here when my people are getting killed over there?" Republican leaders condemned the

Obama administration for seeking to "downplay the shooting's connection to radical extremism."[51]

The FBI was reticent about admitting that it had placed Mateen on a terrorist watchlist after interviewing him in 2013. At some point prior to his attack, his name was removed. Comey claimed that a "confidential witness" had assured the FBI that after Mateen "got married, and had a child, and got a job as a security guard," he was "no longer concerned about" [Mateen's] radical tendencies.[52]

But prior to his attack, Omar Mateen was practically walking around Florida wearing a sandwich board announcing: "FUTURE MASS KILLER."[53] He had boasted of his ties to terrorists, threatened to have al Qaeda kill a co-worker's family, and talked of wanting to be a martyr — when he was not vocally vilifying African-Americans. Even his mosque warned authorities that he could be a threat to public safety. When FBI officials investigated him in 2013, he repeatedly lied to them. But the FBI swayed the local sheriff's department to drop its investigation because a "confidential informant" assured FBI agents that Omar Mateen was not a terrorist and would not "go postal or anything like that." That "confidential informant" was probably Mateen's father.

The Obama administration and FBI chief Comey rushed to exploit the Pulse nightclub massacre to extend federal power. Democrats seized upon the death toll to push new gun control legislation. Comey said Omar Mateen had been "radicalized at least in part through the Internet"[54] — very convenient for Comey's campaign to sway Congress to give the FBI new power to seize Internet records of Americans without a search warrant, the FBI's "top legislative priority" for 2016.[55] Sen. John McCain (R-AZ) led the charge, assuring fellow senators that if the FBI could "more easily determine Internet activity of those suspected of radicalization," the Orlando carnage might not have happened.

Rather than admitting that Mateen's rage was sparked by U.S. government killings of Muslims abroad, the Obama administration fabricated a storyline about anti-gay bias. The Pulse nightclub was a hotspot for Hispanic gays and lesbians in the Orlando area. Attorney General Loretta Lynch announced: "This was clearly an act of terror and an act of hate."[56] President Obama visited Orlando, praised the nightclub as a place where people could "be who you truly are," and declared: "Hatred toward people because of sexual orientation, regardless of where it comes from, is a betrayal of what's best in us." But Mateen was unaware that it was a gay nightclub. Instead, he chose it because of proximity after his efforts to launch a mass killing at a nearby shopping and entertainment complex were doomed by heavy security. The Pulse nightclub had already become canonized as an anti-gay hate crime at that point. For the 2023 anniversary of the shooting, President Biden issued a proclamation that portrayed the killings as spurred by anti-gay bias.[57] A few weeks later, Supreme Court Justice Sonia Sotomayor cited in a dissenting opinion the "Pulse nightclub massacre" as an example of deadly anti-gay bias.

In 2018, Noor Salman, Omar Mateen's widow, was put on trial, charged with material support of a foreign terrorist organization and lying to the FBI about knowing about her husband's plan to attack the nightclub. Eleven days after the trial began, the Justice Department belatedly admitted that the killer's father, Seddique Mateen, had been a paid FBI informant for 11 years, starting in 2005. Seddique Mateen, who came to America from Afghanistan, produced a pro-Taliban, anti-American Dari language television program. On the day after the massacre, when asked if the FBI was investigating Seddique Mateen, Comey replied, "No comment." The FBI had continued relying on Seddique Mateen even after hearing allegations that he sought to finance terrorist attacks on the Pakistani government.[58]

The FBI vigorously interrogated Noor Salman for 18 hours without a lawyer and with no video recording. FBI agents threatened that she would lose custody of her infant son unless she signed a confession.[59] Salman, who reportedly had an IQ of only 84, initially denied any knowledge of her husband's plans but relented and signed a lengthy statement composed by an FBI agent.

Federal prosecutors at the trial flourished Salman's confession as the ultimate proof of her perfidy. But the memo contained false statements and contradictions which even the government could not sweep away, spurring a not guilty verdict and a huge black eye for the Justice Department.[60]

FBI agents, unlike most local and state police departments, almost always refuse to record interrogations or suspects' confessions.[61] Instead, after talking to a target, FBI agents later write up a memo purportedly summarizing the conversation (known as Form 302). Most judges treat Form 302s as gospel truth. Federal agents have the right to lie to you and to put you in prison if you lie to them.[62] Any citizen who makes even a single-word ("no" or "yes") false utterance to a federal agent faces up to five years in prison and a $250,000 fine. By not videotaping interviews, FBI agents can fabricate the words used to convict citizens of lying. Boston defense attorney Harvey Silverglate derided the FBI's refusal to record interviews as foul play that allows "the FBI to manipulate witnesses, manufacture convictions, and destroy justice as we once knew it."[63]

Rigging the 2016 Presidential Election?

The FBI has long tampered with elections. In the 1948 presidential campaign, J. Edgar Hoover brazenly championed Republican candidate Thomas Dewey, leaking allegations that Truman was part of a corrupt Kansas City political machine.[64] In 1952, Hoover sought to undermine Democratic presidential candidate Adlai Stevenson by spreading rumors that he was a closet homosexual. In 1964, the FBI illegally wiretapped Republican presidential candidate Barry Goldwater's presidential headquarters and plane[65] and conducted background checks on his campaign staff seeking evidence of homosexual activity. In 1972, acting FBI chief Patrick Gray burned incriminating evidence from the White House in his fireplace shortly after the Watergate break-in by Nixon "plumbers"; he was forced to resign in 1973 for that ignition. FBI Deputy Director Mark Felt leaked damning information about Nixon's re-election campaign to *Washington Post* reporters, spurring the Watergate scandal and Nixon's resignation.

But those interventions were chump change compared to the FBI's role in the 2016 election. Hillary Clinton, the Democratic Party frontrunner, had used an insecure private email server to handle top-secret documents while she was Secretary of State from 2009 to 2013. The server in a bathroom of Clinton's Chappaqua, New York, mansion exposed emails with classified information to detection by foreign sources, household servants, and others.

Clinton's private email server was not publicly disclosed until she received a congressional subpoena in 2015. A few months later, the FBI Counterintelligence Division opened a criminal investigation examining the "potential unauthorized storage of classified information on an unauthorized system." Attorney General Lynch swayed FBI chief Comey to mislead the public by denying the existence of a criminal investigation; instead, it was referred to simply as a "matter."

The FBI treated Clinton and her coterie like royalty worthy of endless deference, according to a 2018 report by the Justice Department Inspector General. The FBI agreed to destroy the laptops of top Clinton aides after a limited examination of their contents (including a promise not to examine any post-January 31, 2015, emails or content).[66] When Clinton aides used BleachBit software and hammers to destroy email evidence under congressional subpoena, the FBI treated it as a harmless error.[67] The Inspector General criticized FBI investigators for relying on "rapport building" with Team Hillary instead of using subpoenas to compel the disclosure of key evidence.

FBI investigators shrugged off every skullduggery they encountered from Hillary's staffers. The Inspector General report revealed that key FBI agents in the investigations were raving partisans. "We'll stop" Trump from becoming president, lead FBI investigator Peter Strzok texted his mistress/girlfriend, FBI lawyer Lisa Page, in August 2016. One FBI agent labeled Trump supporters as "retarded" and declared, "I'm with her" [Hillary Clinton]. Another FBI employee texted that "Trump's supporters are all poor to middle class, uneducated, lazy POS."[68]

The FBI delayed interviewing Clinton until the end of the investigation, after she had clinched the Democratic presidential nomination, and just before the Democratic National Convention. FBI agents at that interview found Clinton's answers "strained credulity"; one agent put her responses in the "bucket of hard to impossible to believe." The FBI planned to absolve her "absent a confession from Clinton," the Inspector General noted. There was no recording or transcript of that final interview. Minimizing the evidence maximized the discretion of FBI officials in a landmark political case.

Shortly after that interview, FBI chief James Comey publicly announced that "no charges are appropriate" because Hillary didn't intend to violate federal law. But that law is a strict liability statute; "intent" is irrelevant to the criminal violation. After his actions outraged supporters of both Trump and Clinton, Comey blamed Twitter "demagoguery" for the widespread belief that the FBI was not "honest" or "competent."[69]

In May 2023, Special Counsel John Durham issued his report documenting how the FBI's 2016 favoritism repeatedly rescued Hillary Clinton.[70] The Clinton Foundation raked in hundreds of millions of dollars in squirrely foreign contributions while she was Secretary of State and readying her presidential campaign. The Durham report found that "senior FBI and Department officials placed restrictions on how [the Clinton Foundation investigation was] handled such that essentially no investigative activities occurred for months leading up to the election." On top of that dereliction,

> the FBI appears to have made no effort to investigate… the Clinton campaign's purported acceptance of a[n illegal] campaign contribution that was made by the FBI's own long-term [confidential human source] on behalf of Insider 1 and, ultimately, Foreign Government.

Shortly after Comey publicly exonerated Hillary, "Clinton allegedly approved a proposal from one of her foreign policy advisors to tie Trump to Russia as a means of distracting the public from her use of a private email server," according to the Durham report. CIA chief John Brennan briefed President Obama, Vice President Joe Biden, and other top officials on "alleged approval by Hillary Clinton on July 26, 2016, of a proposal… to vilify Donald Trump by stirring up a scandal claiming interference by Russian security services." There is no evidence that Obama and his policymakers had any objections to Hillary's vilification proposal (referred to as the "Clinton Plan" in Durham's report). FBI officials relied on the "Clinton Plan" to target the Trump campaign even though "[n]o FBI personnel… [took] any action to vet the Clinton Plan intelligence," the report noted.

The Democratic National Committee and the Clinton campaign paid former British agent Christopher Steele to create a dossier — known as the "Steele dossier" — with lurid, unverified accusations against Trump. The FBI was willing to pay any price to defeat Trump and offered Steele $1 million in cash if he could prove the charges in the dossier before the 2016 election.[71] Steele could not do so. Steele was already on the FBI payroll, though he was terminated in November 2016 for dishing allegations to the media. "The FBI discounted or willfully ignored material information that did not support the narrative of a collusive relationship between Trump and Russia," the Durham report noted. As FBI analysts recognized that the Steele dossier was a hoax, FBI bosses ordered "no more memorandums were to be written" analyzing its claims.

The FBI relied on the Steele dossier to get warrants to spy on Trump campaign officials from the Foreign Intelligence Surveillance Court. Even after the Steele dossier was discredited, the FBI paid Igor Danchenko, the primary Russian source for the dossier, as a "confidential human source for more than three years until the fall of 2020 when he was terminated for lying to agents."[72] The Federal Election Commission fined the Democratic

National Committee and the Hillary Clinton campaign $113,000 in 2022 for their deceptive funding to cover up their role in spawning the Steele dossier.[73]

After the 2016 election, FBI officials sought to cripple Trump's presidency with fabricated evidence of connections to Russia. A 2019 Inspector General report concluded that FBI officials made 17 "significant inaccuracies and omissions" in its application to the FISA Court to spy on former Trump advisor Carter Page.[74] The FBI withheld details from the court that would have crippled the credibility of the warrant request.

Kevin Clinesmith, a top FBI lawyer, was convicted for falsifying evidence to secure a FISA warrant to target Trump campaign officials. A federal prosecutor declared that the "resulting harm is immeasurable" from Clinesmith's action. But Federal Judge James Boasberg conducted a "pity party" at the sentencing, noting that Clinesmith "went from being an obscure government lawyer to standing in the eye of a media hurricane... Clinesmith has lost his job in government service — what has given his life much of its meaning." Scorning the prosecutor's recommendation for jail time, the judge gave Clinesmith a wrist-slap — 400 hours of community service and 12 months of probation.[75]

After he was fired in May 2017, FBI chief James Comey leaked official memos with confidential information to a lawyer who delivered them to the *New York Times*, a disclosure that was later condemned by the Inspector General.[76] Comey's leak triggered the appointment of Special Counsel Robert Mueller to investigate Trump. Mueller's investigation generated endless allegations and controversies and helped Democrats capture control of the House of Representatives in 2018. In April 2019, after two years of media frenzies, Mueller finally admitted he found no evidence to prosecute Trump or his campaign officials for colluding with Russia in the 2016 campaign.

The Trump era saw the greatest surge in support for the FBI since the days when Hollywood shamelessly pandered to J. Edgar Hoover. A 2018 poll showed that 77% of Democrats had a positive view of the FBI.[77] Partisan rage against Trump expunged all memories of FBI's misdeeds.

FBI = Following Biden's Instructions

It is as yet unclear how many favors Joe Biden owed the FBI before he became president. In 2011 and 2012, FBI sources reported foreign bribery efforts targeting Vice President Biden. The FBI did not pursue the matter. In 2015, 2016, and 2017, the FBI received reports that Biden's son Hunter was collecting payoffs from corrupt foreign sources. The FBI did not pursue the matter. In 2020, FBI agents sought to interview Hunter during an investigation into his tax evasion and illicit foreign influence peddling. Top officials at either the FBI or Justice Department sabotaged the interview shortly before it was to occur.

Congressional investigations are revealing new details of FBI favors for Biden and his family. New FBI whistleblowers are coming forward — or at least going to congressional committees — practically every month. The FBI is also currying Biden's favor by propping up the White House storyline on the January 6 "insurrection."[78] After that ruckus in the weeks preceding Biden's inauguration, the FBI's Washington Field Office pressured the FBI Boston office to open investigations on 138 bus passengers who traveled to D.C. in the days before January 6, 2021. They were all labeled worthy of official hounding merely because "two individuals [on the buses] entered restricted areas of the Capitol that day." Boston FBI officials responded by asking for video showing the wrongdoing, especially since there was no evidence the passengers had even entered the Capitol. FBI headquarters replied that it couldn't supply video because it might disclose undercover agents or confidential human sources in the crowd. In lieu of providing evidence, FBI bosses wanted agents across the nation to presume anyone who was suspected was automatically guilty.

The Biden campaign to concoct more terrorist hobgoblins got a turbo shot from the FBI's vilification of traditional Catholics. A January 2023 FBI intelligence analysis from its Richmond, Virginia, office called for targeting conservative Catholics as potential extremists. The analysis declared that the Bureau could "distinguish the bad Catholics from the good ones" based on their "preference for 'the Traditional Latin Mass and pre-Vatican II teachings.'" The FBI analysis relied on "evidence" such as an *Atlantic* article "How the Rosary Became an Extremist Symbol," which "slammed Catholic rosary beads for increasingly being associated with right-wing Christians, especially those who are gun owners."[79] The FBI analysis also suggested using "mainline Catholic parishes" to "serve as suspicious activity tripwires" for Catholics whose beliefs perhaps differed too much from the Bidens'. Twenty-two Republican state attorneys general sent a protest to the FBI: "We are particularly alarmed by the memorandum's suggestion that FBI operatives should be developing 'sources with access,' including in 'places of worship,' to identify the bad Catholics." FBI chief Christopher Wray claimed that the analysis represented the effort of a single FBI district office, but a congressional subpoena compelled the Bureau to admit that California, Virginia, and Oregon were involved in the Catholic witch-hunt.

As the 2024 election season heated up, the FBI placed Donald Trump's supporters in the terrorist investigation crosshairs. *Newsweek* reported in October 2023 that the FBI has created "a new category of extremists that it seeks to track and counter: Donald Trump's army of MAGA followers."[80]

FBI bureaucrats heaved together a bunch of letters to contrive an ominous new acronym for the latest peril to domestic tranquility. The result: AGAAVE — "anti-government, anti-authority violent extremism" — which looks like an overheated typo for a sugar substitute. The great majority of the FBI's "current 'anti-government' investigations are of Trump supporters," William Arkin reported in *Newsweek*.

The FBI vastly expanded the supposed AGAAVE peril by broadening suspicion from "furtherance of ideological agendas" to "furtherance of political and/or social agendas." Anyone who has an agenda different from Team Biden's could be AGAAVE'd for his own good.

The FBI is required to have (or claim to have) solid information before launching a criminal investigation. But the Bureau needs almost zero information to open an "assessment." The FBI conducted more than 5,500 domestic-terrorism "assessments" in 2021, a tenfold increase since 2017 and a fiftyfold increase since 2013. "Assessments are the closest thing to domestic spying that exists in America and generally not talked about by the Bureau," Arkin noted. The House Weaponization Subcommittee warned that "the FBI appears to be complicit in artificially supporting the Administration's political narrative" that domestic violent extremism is "the 'greatest threat' facing the United States."[81]

Biden's war on extremism could become a self-fulfilling prophecy that destroys American political legitimacy. An official in the Office of Director of National Intelligence lamented: "So we have the president increasing his own inflammatory rhetoric which leads Donald Trump and the Republicans to do the same" — and the media follow suit.[82] Biden is exempt from official suspicion even when he denounced Republicans as fascists who want to destroy democracy. Yet if Republicans sound equally overheated, Biden's FBI has pretexts to target and take them down.

Conclusion

Will the FBI's interventions in the 2024 presidential election be even more brazen than its 2016 and 2020 stunts? Will the agency exploit its "assessments" to recruit knuckleheads to engage in another pre-election Keystone Kops plot to kidnap a governor, as it did in Michigan in 2020?

Congress has been perennially prone to cower before the nation's most powerful law enforcement agency. In 1971, House Majority Leader Hale Boggs declared that Capitol Hill was terrified of the FBI: "Our very fear of speaking out [against the FBI] has watered the roots and hastened the growth of a vine of tyranny... Our society... cannot survive a planned and programmed fear of its own government bureaus and agencies."[83] It has been nearly 50 years since a Senate committee had the gumption to reveal the stunning details of FBI misconduct.

It is folly to permit a federal agency to capture boundless power when there is scant courage in the legislative and judicial branches of government to leash the agency. The Bureau's vast power and pervasive secrecy guarantee that more FBI scandals are just around the bend. It is time to cease venerating a federal agency whose abuses have perennially menaced Americans' constitutional rights.

15. Last Chance for Liberty?

"For the saddest epitaph which can be carved in memory of a vanished liberty is that it was lost because its possessors failed to stretch forth a saving hand while yet there was time."

– Supreme Court Justice George Sutherland, 1937[1]

Citizens must cease tolerating regimes that increasingly shackle and defraud them. The worse politicians have blundered, the more dominant they have become.

Democracy cannot survive power worship. It is time to cease pretending politicians' iron fists are magic wands that solve all problems. Governments rely on coercion regardless of whether they are supported by 1% or 99% of the populace. The *Federal Register* is backstopped by federal prisons. The statute book is enforced by the world's largest law firm — the U.S. Justice Department and its 6,000 prosecutors. Even the most arbitrary executive orders are quickly enforced by an army of FBI, DEA, ATF, and other federal agents. Presidential promises are piffle compared to the total force and threats deployed to compel submission. There is no magic crowbar to transform government repression into an uplifting force.

Americans must never forget that the most dangerous inequality is that between the rulers and the ruled. No private citizen has a prerogative to forcibly accost, wrongly shoot, and wantonly plunder their neighbors. Laws against torturing pets are better enforced than laws prohibiting government agents from tormenting private citizens. Once government is irrevocably presumed benevolent, curbing politicians' power is almost impossible. The endless appeals to government as a "force for good" camouflage the evils that politicians regularly commit. We cannot legislatively flog humanity to utopia.

We have a faux constitutional system where the nation's founding document is retained largely for decorative purposes. American democracy today often means the enforcement of the secret commands of the Supreme Leader. In a 1952 decision nullifying President Truman's confiscation of steel mills, the Supreme Court declared: "With all its defects, delays and inconveniences, men have discovered no technique for long preserving free government except that the Executive be under the law."[2] But the Supreme

Court often overlooks that technicality when presidents behave like Elective Dictators.

Leashing politicians determines whether government is servant or master. There will be no rebirth of liberty as long as politicians have impunity for their crimes. Political life is now largely a scramble for power and plunder. In a 1973 ruling on Nixon's secret White House tapes, a federal appeals court ruled: "Sovereignty remains at all times with the people, and they do not forfeit through elections the right to have the law construed against and applied to every citizen."[3] That axiom did not deter subsequent presidents from concocting prerogatives to seize ever greater sway over citizens' lives. As Senator John Taylor wrote 200 years ago, "If the people are sovereign, their governments cannot also be sovereign."[4] Politicians must be dethroned so that citizens can reclaim control over their own lives.

Each lost freedom becomes a domino falling against all the remaining rights and liberties. Secrecy and censorship spur a deadly political spiral. If the media is cowed into silence or turned into political accomplices, citizens are unlikely to learn of proliferating abuses. If there is no freedom of information, government officials can fabricate perils to frighten people into ever greater submission. It then becomes easier to justify expanding surveillance, thereby deterring people from voicing criticism or even expressing wayward thoughts in emails. Once dissent is stifled, rulers can contrive pretexts to restrict or prohibit protests. Suppressing evidence of rising discontent enables politicians to further aggrandize their power. Citizens may not recognize the totality of their oppression until it is too late to resist.

Democracy perishes if there is no antidote to government lies. There is no such thing as retroactive self-government after political coverups collapse. We are one whistleblower away from the total destruction of federal credibility. Deceiving the American people should no longer be treated as a victimless crime. To idealize political power is to scorn political history. As Thomas Jefferson warned in 1798, blind confidence in rulers "is everywhere the parent of despotism."[5] There will always be psychological bootlickers who believe anything that the authorities proclaim. But people who take their values and "facts" from their rulers are already half-subjugated. "Clear thinking requires courage rather than intelligence," wrote Hungarian psychiatrist and philosopher Thomas Szasz. How many laws must be violated before citizens recognize that a government is fundamentally lawless?

Winning votes doesn't make scoundrels trustworthy. Promising reforms is the easiest way to perpetuate abuses. A political system must offer more than imaginary remedies to uphold illusory rights. America has seen too many elections that merely hammered more coffin nails into democracy. Voting is no substitute for the self-government of one's own life. As the Supreme Court ruled in 1943: "The very purpose of a Bill of Rights was to withdraw certain subjects... beyond the reach of majorities and officials."[6] Liberty is invaluable regardless of how many politicians seek to destroy it or how many fools fail to cherish it.

Americans cannot presume that the alternative to freedom are warm-hearted rulers cosseting them around the clock. Politicians won't finally become benevolent after they eradicate all opposition. British political philosopher John Locke declared in 1690: "He who attempts to get another man into his Absolute Power, does thereby put himself into a State of War with him."[7] The American republic was forged by individuals who vanquished the most powerful empire in the world. Politicians who continue assailing our rights and liberties forget that lesson at their peril.

Citizens cannot shrug off political onslaughts until a neon "Here Comes Tyranny!" sign flashes in Times Square. Will people continue submitting until reckless rulers utterly destroy their lives? Abolitionist Frederick Douglass summed up his journey from slavery to freedom: "I prayed for twenty years but received no answer until I prayed with my legs." Those who expect to be perpetually rescued by their rulers have already forfeited the dignity of independent citizens.

In the decades after the 9/11 attacks, politicians commandeered one swath of Americans' lives after another. Many stalwart Americans are appalled at the passive obedience of their fellow citizens. But prospects looked worse in earlier eras. The arrogance of power remains the best hope for the survival of liberty. As historian Thomas Macaulay observed on England's Glorious Revolution of 1688: "Oppression speedily did what philosophy and eloquence... failed to do."[8] Rome was not built in a day, but plenty of emperors saw their power collapse within hours. Once legitimacy is lost, governments can collapse like overheated souffles. Obedience can vanish after one decree too far, or after one government muzzle flash too many.

It is time to void the blank check that the ruling class wrote itself to domineer humanity. There will be no peace as long as politicians can subjugate and fleece whomever they please. It is time to extol what each person can achieve in their own life. Vast bounties of liberty are waiting to be harvested.

Endnotes

Chapter 1

[1] Quin Hillyer, "Justice Gorsuch: Too many laws make 'criminals' of well-meaning citizens," *Washington Examiner*, February 26, 2021.

[2] Christopher Ingraham, "Law enforcement took more stuff from people than burglars did last year," *Washington Post*, November 23, 2015.

[3] *Byrd v. Lamb*, 990 F.3d 879 (2021).

[4] "Justice Alito calls Covid restrictions 'previously unimaginable,' cites danger to religious freedom." Associated Press, November 13, 2020.

[5] James Bovard, "Perform Criminal Background Checks at Your Peril," *Wall Street Journal*, February 14, 2013.

[6] James Bovard, "The feds are buying mountains of your personal data and one day could use it against you," *New York Post*, June 19, 2023.

[7] *Memorandum Ruling on Request for Preliminary Injunction, Missouri et al. v. Biden et al.*, July 4, 2023.

[8] *James Brogan v. U.S.*, 522 U.S. 398 (1998).

[9] "'I have impeached myself' — Edited transcript of David Frost's interview with Richard Nixon broadcast in May 1977," *The Guardian*, September 7, 2007.

[10] James Bovard, "Assassination nation: Are there any limits on President Obama's license to kill?" *Christian Science Monitor*, May 17, 2011.

[11] Charlie Savage, "Trump and His Lawyers Embrace a Vision of Vast Executive Power," *New York Times*, June 4, 2018.

[12] "Remarks by President Biden to Military Families on Independence Day," White House Briefing Room, July 4, 2022.

[13] Grayson Quay, "Poll: Over 50 percent of Americans expect a civil war 'in the next few years,'" *The Week*, July 20, 2022.

[14] James Bovard, "Free-Speech Zone," *American Conservative*, December 15, 2003.

[15] Emily Ekins and Jordan Gygi, "Nearly a Third of Gen Z Favors the Government Installing Surveillance Cameras in Homes," Cato Institute, June 1, 2023.

Chapter 2

[1] James Ely, *The Guardian of Every Other Right: A Constitutional History of Property Rights* (New York: Oxford University Press, 1992), p. 14.

[2] C.J. Ciaramella, "Indiana Is Still Arguing That It's Constitutional to Seize Your Car for Driving 5 MPH Over the Speed Limit," *Reason*, July 3, 2019.

[3] Statement by Justice Department attorney Irving Gornstein, Oral hearings before the Supreme Court, *U.S. v. Bajakajian*, no. 96-1487, November 4, 1997.

[4] Patrick Richardson, "Institute for Justice report cites abuses of civil asset forfeiture," *The Sentinel*, September 24, 2022.

[5] Eugene Volokh, "Justice Thomas sharply criticizes civil forfeiture laws," *Washington Post*, March 6, 2017.

[6] Glenn Harlan Reynolds, "Forget Russia. I'd fire Jeff Sessions over civil forfeiture," *USA Today*, July 24, 2017.

[7] *U.S. v. All Assets of Statewide Auto Parts, Inc.*, 971 F.2d 896 (1992).
[8] *U.S. v. $12,390.00*, 956 F.2d 807 (1993).
[9] James Bovard, "Blown Away," *Playboy*, August 1996.
[10] *Bennis v. Michigan*, 517 U.S. 1163 (1996).
[11] Tim Cushing, "National Police Union President Says Asset Forfeiture Abuse Is a 'Fake Issue' Generated by the Media," Techdirt, January 9, 2017.
[12] Christopher Ingraham, "Trump jokes with sheriffs about destroying a Texas legislator's career over asset forfeiture," *Washington Post*, February 7, 2017.
[13] Kelly Cohen, "Jeff Sessions says new asset forfeiture rules coming this week," *Washington Examiner*, July 17, 2017.
[14] Pam Dempsey and Karen Liu, "Taken: Despite Reforms, Burden Still Heavy on Owners of Seized Property," *St. Louis Post-Dispatch*, MidWest Center for Investigative Reporting, IowaWatch, Iowa Public Radio, June 11, 2019.
[15] Daryl James, "The Police Dog Who Cried Drugs at Every Traffic Stop," *Reason*, May 13, 2021.
[16] Radley Balko, "The Supreme Court's 'alternative facts' about drug-sniffing dogs," *Washington Post*, February 5, 2019.
[17] Eric Boehm, "Federal Agents Had No Authority to Seize Contents of Safe Deposit Boxes, Newly Unsealed Warrant Confirms," *Reason*, August 6, 2021.
[18] Michael Finnegan, "FBI misled judge on Beverly Hills seizure warrant," *Los Angeles Times*, September 23, 2022.
[19] Ian Spiegelman, "The FBI Is Trying to Keep More Cash Seized from a Beverly Hills Vault," *Los Angeles Times*, September 20, 2021.
[20] Michael Finnegan, "FBI misled judge on Beverly Hills seizure warrant," *Los Angeles Times*, September 23, 2022.
[21] Michael Sallah, Robert O'Harrow, Jr., Steven Rich, and Gabe Silverman, "Stop and Seize," *Washington Post*, September 6, 2014.
[22] Kevin Drum, "'Forfeiture Corridors' Are the New Speed Traps," *Mother Jones*, April 2, 2012.
[23] Author interview with Gerard Arenberg, September 10, 1996.
[24] Michael Sallah, Robert O'Harrow, Jr., Steven Rich, and Gabe Silverman, "Stop and Seize," *Washington Post*, September 6, 2014.
[25] Edgar Walters and Jolie McCullough, "Texas police made more than $50 million in 2017 from seizing people's property," *Texas Tribune*, December 7, 2018.
[26] Sarah Stillman, "Taken," *New Yorker*, August 12, 2013.
[27] Elora Mukherjee, "Settlement Means No More Highway Robbery in Tenaha, Texas," American Civil Liberties Union, August 9, 2012.
[28] Sarah Stillman, "Taken," *New Yorker*, August 12, 2013.
[29] Ibid.
[30] Eric Dexheimer and St. John Barned-Smith, "Cash seized by tainted HPD unit isn't always being returned," *Houston Chronicle*, November 4, 2022.
[31] William H. Freivogel, "For Phelps County, Seizing Suspects' Assets Is 'Like Pennies from Heaven,'" St. Louis Public Radio, February 20, 2019.
[32] Anna Lee, Nathaniel Cary, and Mike Ellis, "TAKEN: How police departments make millions by seizing property," *Greenville News*, January 27, 2019.
[33] William H. Freivogel, "For Phelps County, Seizing Suspects' Assets Is 'Like Pennies from Heaven,'" St. Louis Public Radio, February 20, 2019.
[34] Ibid.

[35] Michael Finnegan, "Armored car marijuana cash seizure called illegal," *Los Angeles Times*, January 28, 2022.

[36] Andrew Wimer, "Sheriffs Team Up with the Feds to Hold Up Armored Car Company, Civil Forfeiture Makes It Possible," *Forbes*, February 2, 2022.

[37] Michael Finnegan, "FBI abandons $1 million marijuana cash seizure in California," *Los Angeles Times*, May 10, 2022.

[38] Editorial, "Acting like Robbers under color of Law," *Press-Enterprise* (Riverside, California), May 13, 2022.

[39] Nick Sibilla, "Federal Audit: Confidential Sources Received Millions in Forfeiture Funds for Helping DEA Seize Cash," *Forbes*, November 10, 2016.

[40] Brad Heath, "DEA regularly mines Americans' travel records to seize millions in cash," *USA Today*, August 10, 2016.

[41] Ibid.

[42] Matt Zapotosky, "Inspector general faults DEA for seizing money without any connection to a larger criminal investigation," *Washington Post*, March 29, 2017.

[43] Brad Heath, "DEA regularly mines Americans' travel records to seize millions in cash," *USA Today*, August 10, 2016.

[44] "Call Kurtis: The Government Seized $29K of Mine When I Did Nothing Wrong," CBS News, July 26, 2018.

[45] Justin Jouvenal, "The DEA seized her father's life savings at an airport without alleging any crime occurred, lawsuit says," *Washington Post*, January 15, 2020.

[46] Gary Fields, "'Robbery with a Badge' in the nation's Capital," *USA Today*, May 18, 1992.

[47] Sarah Stillman, "Taken," *New Yorker*, August 12, 2013.

[48] Max Rivlin-Nadler, "When cops just take your cash and car," *New York Daily News*, November 8, 2015.

[49] Max Rivlin-Nadler, "The NYPD's Civil Forfeiture System Has Taken Millions from Low-Income New Yorkers," *Village Voice*, August 9, 2016.

[50] Max Rivlin-Nadler, "NYPD: Revealing the Truth About the Millions We Seize Would 'Lead to Systems Crashes,'" *Village Voice*, September 16, 2016.

[51] Kevin Rector, "Baltimore council panel calls for more transparency around police seizures of guns, drugs, cash and dirt bikes," *Baltimore Sun*, January 10, 2018.

[52] James Bovard, "An End to Federal Plundering?" *American Spectator*, April 2001.

[53] Kristan Trugman, "Police Put Brakes on Car Seizures," *Washington Times*, October 23, 1997.

[54] Jessica Jaglois and Mike Baker, "In Memphis, Car Seizures Are a Lucrative and Punishing Police Tactic," *New York Times*, March 23, 2023.

[55] Ryan Boetel, "Albuquerque won't seize cars in DWI cases until conviction," *Albuquerque Journal*, April 9, 2018.

[56] C.J. Ciaramella, "Michigan May Stop Police from Seizing Property without Getting a Conviction First," *Reason*, February 26, 2019.

[57] George Hunter, "Class-action suit challenges civil forfeitures," *Detroit News*, July 16, 2018.

[58] Elliott Ramos, "Chicago Police Impounded 250,000 Vehicles Since 2010," WBEZ.org, July 13, 2020.

[59] C.J. Ciaramella, "Chicago Is Trying to Pay Down Its Debt by Impounding Innocent People's Cars," *Reason*, April 25, 2018.

[60] C.J. Ciaramella, "Chicago Impounded This Grandmother's Car for a Pot Offense She Didn't Commit," *Reason*, October 3, 2019.

[61] This case was settled thanks to the intervention of the Institute for Justice. Their press releases and court filings on the case are here: ij.org/case/eagle-pass-civil-forfeiture.

[62] Joe Davidson, "Another federal law enforcement agency is hit for losing track of weapons, ammunition," *Washington Post*, October 9, 2018.

[63] Chris Ingraham, "Customs agents seized a lawful gun owner's truck over five bullets," *Washington Post*, October 20, 2017.

[64] Chris Palmer, "Philly agrees to overhaul civil forfeiture program to settle lawsuit," *Philadelphia Inquirer*, September 18, 2018.

[65] Sarah Stillman, "Taken," *New Yorker*, August 12, 2013.

[66] Christopher Ingraham, "How Philadelphia seizes millions in 'pocket change' from some of the city's poorest residents," *Washington Post*, June 10, 2015.

[67] "Philadelphia's Civil Forfeiture Machine Facts and Figures," Institute for Justice, ij.org/philadelphia-facts-and-figures.

[68] Mike Ellis, "For years, a SC city tried to seize a widow's home. It still might," *Greenville News*, January 27, 2019.

[69] Ross Jones, "Highland Park seized their building; the price to get it back was 2 new police cars," WXYZ, May 18, 2022.

[70] Cory Doctorow, "Leaked ICE forfeiture manual instructs agents to seize houses if they contain a phone implicated in crime," Boing Boing, October 18, 2017.

[71] Ryan Devereaux, "Leaked ICE Guide Offers Unprecedented View of Agency's Asset Forfeiture Tactics," *The Intercept*, October 13, 2017.

[72] Ibid.

[73] Nick Sibilla, "'IF IN DOUBT… TAKE IT!' Behind Closed Doors, Government Officials Make Shocking Comments about Civil Forfeiture," BuzzFeed News, November 10, 2014.

[74] Scott Shackford, "Forfeiture News: New York's Program a Mess; Lawmakers Want to End Federal Asset Sharing Program," *Reason*, January 12, 2015.

[75] Jacob Ryan, "Seized: Few Kentucky Police Agencies Report What They Take Through Asset Forfeiture," Kentucky Center for Investigative Reporting, 89.3 WFPL, November 29, 2018.

[76] Edgar Walters and Jolie McCullough, "Texas police made more than $50 million in 2017 from seizing people's property," *Texas Tribune*, December 7, 2018.

[77] *Amended Answer, Affirmative Defenses, and Counterclaims, City of Albuquerque, ex rel., Albuquerque Police Department, v. One (1) 2014 Nissan 4dr Silver V.I.N. 3n1cn7ap4el842551, New Mexico License No. 116SM2*, August 31, 2016.

[78] Stewart M. Powell, "Asset forfeiture both an effective tool, civil-liberties nightmare," *Houston Chronicle*, May 26, 2013.

[79] Richard Brenneman, "Librarians Win Battle Against Ashcroft's Edict to Censor Statute," *Berkeley Daily Planet*, August 13, 2004.

[80] Scott Shackford, "The FBI Hopes These Cute Puppies Will Distract You from Unconstitutional Civil Asset Forfeitures," *Reason*, July 1, 2019.

[81] James Bovard, "No halo for Holder on forfeiture fix," *Washington Times*, January 20, 2015.

[82] Robert O'Harrow, Jr., and Steven Rich, "D.C. police plan for future seizure proceeds years in advance in city budget documents," *Washington Post*, November 15, 2014.

[83] C.J. Ciaramella, "Manhattan D.A. Spent $250K in Asset Forfeiture Funds on Fine Dining and Luxurious Travel," *Reason*, April 4, 2019.

[84] Richard D. Emery, "Civil Forfeiture and Accountability," *New York Times*, December 10, 2014.

[85] Eric Dexheimer and St. John Barned-Smith, "Cash seized by tainted HPD unit isn't always being returned," *Houston Chronicle*, November 4, 2022.

[86] Chris Joyner and Bill Rankin, "'Like a slush fund': Revenue agents bought pricey perks with seized assets," *Atlanta Journal-Constitution*, March 12, 2020.

[87] Joel Handley, Jennifer Helsby, and Freddy Martinez, "Inside the Chicago Police Department's secret budget," *Chicago Reader*, September 29, 2016.

[88] Tom Schuba and Frank Main, "CPD launched drone program with off-the-books cash," *Chicago Sun-Times*, May 12, 2021.

[89] John Yoder and Brad Cates, "Government self-interest corrupted a crime-fighting tool into an evil," *Washington Post*, September 18, 2014.

[90] Eugene Volokh, "Justice Thomas sharply criticizes civil forfeiture laws," *Washington Post*, March 6, 2017.

[91] Editorial, "Texas' asset forfeiture laws require changes," *Dallas Morning News*, December 30, 2014.

[92] *Timbs v. Indiana*, 139 S. Ct. 682 (2019)

[93] Christopher Ingraham, "How the IRS seized a man's life savings without ever charging him with a crime," *Washington Post*, May 15, 2015.

[94] Nick Sibilla, "Cops Taking Property from the Innocent Is 'Legitimate,' South Carolina Supreme Court Rules," *Forbes*, September 20, 2022.

Chapter 3

[1] *Brief for the United States, Staples v. U.S.*, No. 92-1441, August 9, 1993.

[2] Joel Gehrke, "In '95, Holder called for anti-gun info campaign: 'Brainwash people into thinking about guns in a vastly different way,'" *Washington Examiner*, December 17, 2012.

[3] Phoebe Maltz Bovy, "It's Time to Ban Guns. Yes, All of Them," *New Republic*, December 10, 2015.

[4] Lindsay Kornick, "Highland Park shooting blamed on Americans being 'slaves' to an 'ancient document': MSNBC guest," Fox News, July 5, 2022.

[5] Kelly Bostian, "'Wait and see': Showdown likely over firearms as Oklahoma medical marijuana users would run afoul of federal law," *Tulsa World*, June 28, 2018.

[6] Jacob Sullum, "A Judge Accepts the Biden Administration's Dubious Argument for Banning Gun Possession by Marijuana Users," *Reason*, November 9, 2022.

[7] Betty Adams, "Five central Maine men indicted on federal firearms charges," *Kennebec Journal*, April 27, 2018.

[8] Kristen Consillio, "Medical Marijuana Users 'Have 30 Days' to Turn In Their Guns, Honolulu Police Say," *Honolulu Star-Advertiser*, December 2, 2017.

[9] Kevin Krause, "Do you use drugs? If you own a gun, the feds could put you in prison, which worries cannabis advocates," *Dallas Morning News*, June 12, 2021.

[10] Rebekah Allen and James Barragán, "Will Texans give up gun rights to get medical marijuana? Federal government says they have to," *Dallas Morning News*, June 17, 2019.

[11] Jacob Sullum, "DOJ Says Letting Pot Users Own Guns Is Like Okaying Drunk Gun Use," *Reason*, March 22, 2023.

[12] Nate Raymond, "Ban on marijuana users owning guns is unconstitutional, U.S. judge rules," Reuters, February 6, 2023.

[13] Jacob Sullum, "DOJ Says Letting Pot Users Own Guns Is Like Okaying Drunk Gun Use," *Reason*, March 22, 2023.

[14] "Highlights for the 2021 National Survey on Drug Use and Health," Substance Abuse and Mental Health Services Administration, January 31, 2023.

[15] Tara Palmeri and Ben Schreckinger, "Sources: Secret Service inserted itself into case of Hunter Biden's gun," Politico, March 25, 2021.

[16] David Codrea, "ATF Claims FOIA Request on Hunter Biden Gun Violates His Privacy," Ammoland, Inc., May 25, 2021.

[17] "Rapper Kodak Black gets prison sentence in weapons case," Associated Press, November 13, 2019.

[18] "Hunter Biden's Plea Reveals DOJ Has Double Standard on Gun Charges," Gun Owners of America, June 26, 2023.

[19] Steven Nelson and Priscilla DeGregory, "Hunter Biden indicted over lies about drug addiction while buying gun," *New York Post*, September 14, 2023.

[20] Frank Murray, "Clinton Aides Back Away from Gun-Ban Statement," *Washington Times*, March 14, 1994.

[21] Editorial, "Hyping the Crime Bill," *Washington Post*, September 15, 1994.

[22] Charles Krauthammer, "Disarm the Citizenry but Not Yet," *Washington Post*, April 5, 1996.

[23] "Assault Weapons Ban of 2013," Press Release from Sen. Dianne Feinstein, 2013 (undated web posting).

[24] "Number of murder victims in the United States in 2020, by weapon used," Statista.com, 2021.

[25] James Hohmann, "The newest purity test for Democrats is whether to mandate assault weapons buybacks," *Washington Post*, August 16, 2019.

[26] Holmes Lybrand, "Fact check: Joe Biden's comments on gun control," CNN, March 21, 2020.

[27] Bradford Betz, "Biden calls 9mm 'high-caliber weapons,' suggests banning them," Fox News, May 30, 2022.

[28] "Biden Pushes 9mm Handgun Ban, Harris Wants to Ban Common Semi-Autos," National Rifle Association, Institute for Legislative Action, June 2, 2022.

[29] "Remarks by President Biden After Visiting with Local Firefighters," White House Briefing Room, November 24, 2022.

[30] twitter.com/HouseDemocrats/status/1534681434409115649

[31] Lindsay Kornick, "ATF director lambasted for not defining 'assault weapon': 'Why is he leading the agency?'" Fox News, April 19, 2023.

[32] Brad Polumbo, "Biden Repeats False Attack on the 2nd Amendment that Even WaPo Debunked," *Based Politics*, February 3, 2022.

[33] J.D. Tuccille, "Biden's False Gun Claims Are a Lousy Basis for Law," *Reason*, February 7, 2022.

[34] "In the matter of the March 12, 2020, police-involved shooting in Potomac, Maryland," Montgomery County Maryland State Attorney's Office, December 31, 2020.

[35] Michael Ollove, "States Tackle Mental Illness and Gun Ownership," Stateline, March 21, 2013.

[36] Jacob Sullum, "If You Want to Keep Your Guns in New York, Avoid Mental Health Professionals," *Reason*, October 20, 2014.

[37] James Jacobs and Zoe Fuhr, "New York Disarms the 'Mentally Ill,'" Marshall Project, December 2, 2015.

38 Ibid.

39 Anemona Hartocollis, "Mental Health Issues Put 34,500 on New York's No-Guns List," *New York Times*, October 19, 2014.

40 Ilya Shapiro, Josh Blackman, and Randal John Meyer, "The Social Security Administration Shouldn't Be Deciding Who's Too 'Mentally Defective' to Own a Gun," Cato Institute, July 5, 2016.

41 James Bovard, "Should Gun Owners Fear the Deep State?" *America's 1st Freedom*, National Rifle Association, August 10, 2018.

42 "Grandma Got Run Over by Obama: SSA Finalizes New Gun Prohibition Rule," National Rifle Association, Institute for Legislative Action, December 23, 2016.

43 Jesse O'Neill, "Feds pay $128M to families after FBI bungled tips about Parkland school shooter," *New York Post*, March 16, 2022.

44 Brett Samuels, "Trump: 'Take the guns first, go through due process second,'" *The Hill*, February 28, 2018.

45 Jacob Sullum, "States Are Depriving Innocent People of Their Second Amendment Rights," *Reason*, November 2019.

46 Walter Olson, "'Red flag' laws can have deadly consequences," *Washington Post*, August 13, 2019.

47 Jacob Sullum, "States Are Depriving Innocent People of Their Second Amendment Rights," *Reason*, November 2019.

48 Nick Sibilla, "Supreme Court Closes Fourth Amendment Loophole that Let Cops Seize Guns without Warrants," *Forbes*, May 17, 2021.

49 *Payton v. New York*, 445 U.S. 573 (1980).

50 James Bovard, "Will Supremes Unleash Biden Red Flag Gun Raids?" *American Conservative*, April 9, 2021.

51 Nick Sibilla, "Supreme Court Closes Fourth Amendment Loophole that Let Cops Seize Guns without Warrants," *Forbes*, May 17, 2021.

52 Hannah Cox, "This Democrat Governor Just Proved Why Red Flag Laws WILL Be Abused," *Based Politics*, June 17, 2022.

53 Chris Pandolfo, "Justice Department 'weaponized' bipartisan gun safety law to 'illegally fund' red flag laws, Republicans say," Fox News, July 25, 2023.

54 "Letter from Congress to the DOJ on BSCA Funding and the Misuse of Grants," July 25, 2023.

55 "DOJ Releases Biden Gun Confiscation Order Legislation," NRA-ILA, June 9, 2021.

56 "Guns and Congress: The proposals lawmakers are talking about," CBS News, March 1, 2018.

57 Jacob Sullum, "Joe Biden Learns to Love Gun Control by Presidential Fiat," *Reason*, April 8, 2021.

58 Devlin Barrett, "Justice Department will ban bump-stock devices that turn rifles into fully automatic weapons," *Washington Post*, December 18, 2018.

59 Brooke Singman, "Trump administration to ban bump stocks, 'all devices' that turn 'legal' weapons into machine guns," Fox News, March 23, 2018.

60 Joanna Allhands, "Federal bump stock ban could make you a criminal. What you need to know," *Arizona Republic*, March 26, 2019

61 Ibid.

62 twitter.com/GunOwners/status/1631142286519140356

[63] Damon Root, "Trump's Bump Stock Ban Just Lost Big in Federal Court," *Reason*, March 26, 2021.

[64] Megan Hadley, "Bump stock ban remains intact as U.S. appeals court deadlocks," *U.S. News*, December 3, 2021.

[65] Chad D. Baus, "Military court rules Trump ATF was wrong: bump stocks are not machineguns," Buckeye Firearms, September 22, 2021.

[66] Congressional Research Service, "Handguns, Stabilizing Braces, and Related Components," April 19, 2021.

[67] Scott Weiser, "Mountain States Legal Foundation files comments on ATF pistol-brace ban," *Denver Gazette*, September 9, 2021.

[68] Daniel Dale, "Fact check: Biden makes 5 false claims about guns, plus some about other subjects," CNN, June 21, 2023.

[69] Chris Pandolfo, "NRA, 25 states sue Biden ATF to stop 'arbitrary' and 'unlawful' pistol brace rule," Fox News, February 9, 2023.

[70] James Bovard, "The Wreckers of New York and Their Bitter Rivalry," American Institute for Economic Research, March 2, 2021.

[71] *Pena v. Lindley*, 898 F.3d at 984 (2018).

[72] S.H. Blannelberry, "California Supreme Court Upholds Ban on New Handguns," GunsAmerica.com, July 3, 2018.

[73] Chris Cillizza, "President Obama's amazingly emotional speech on gun control," *Washington Post*, January 5, 2016.

[74] "Brady Handgun Violence Prevention Act," U.S. Congress, House Committee on the Judiciary, March 21, 1991.

[75] *Caleb Barnett et al. v. Kwame Raoul et al.*, Case 3:23-cv-00209-SPM, Southern District of Illinois, April 28, 2023.

[76] Ibid.

[77] "Priorities for Research to Reduce the Threat of Firearm-Related Violence," National Academies Press, 2013.

[78] Don Thompson, "COVID gun store shutdowns in Los Angeles, Ventura Counties ruled illegal," Associated Press, January 22, 2022.

[79] Miriam Berger, "Pittsburgh paper accused of barring black reporters from covering protests, censoring stories," *Washington Post*, June 6, 2020.

[80] Joe Concha, "CNN ridiculed for 'Fiery But Mostly Peaceful' caption with video of burning building in Kenosha," *The Hill*, August 27, 2020.

[81] David E. Bernstein, "The Right to Armed Self-Defense in Light of Law Enforcement Abdication," *Georgetown Journal of Law & Public Policy*, Winter 2021.

[82] Ibid.

[83] Willis L. Krumholz, "Progressive politicians watch as Minneapolis burns," *City Journal*, May 29, 2020.

[84] Julia Marsh, "De Blasio backs George Floyd protests despite coronavirus gathering ban," *New York Post*, May 29, 2020.

[85] Miranda Devine, "Lefty pols have put cops everywhere in peril," *New York Post*, June 3, 2020.

[86] John Bolger, "NYPD Took Hours to Respond to Mass Looting, Despite Quickly Cracking Down on Protests," *The Intercept*, June 1, 2021.

[87] Editorial, "Goodbye, Summer of Love," *Wall Street Journal*, December 13, 2020.

[88] Lia Eustachewich, "Seattle sees 525 percent spike in crime thanks to CHOP: Mayor Durkan," *New York Post*, July 2, 2020.

[89] Sydney Brownstone and Ashley Hiruko, "Seattle police stopped investigating new adult sexual assaults this year, memo shows," *Seattle Times*, June 1, 2022.

[90] Peter Nickeas, "'Rudderless' city government faulted for Minneapolis protest response after George Floyd's murder," CNN, March 14, 2022.

[91] Tom Schuba, Sam Charles, and Matthew Hendrickson, "18 murders in 24 hours: Inside the most violent day in 60 years in Chicago," *Chicago Sun-Times*, June 8, 2020.

[92] Matt Rosenberg, "New 2021 Chicago data shows 400,000 high-priority incidents where dispatchers had no police available to send," Wirepoints, June 30, 2022.

[93] Douglas Belkin, Rob Copeland and Elizabeth Findell, "Uvalde Shooter Fired Outside School for 12 Minutes Before Entering," *Wall Street Journal*, May 26, 2022.

[94] Timothy Bella, "Police slow to engage with gunman because 'they could've been shot,' official says," *Washington Post*, May 27, 2022.

[95] Arelis R. Hernández, Timothy Bella, and Mark Berman, "Armed Uvalde officers waited for key to unlocked door, official says," *Washington Post*, June 21, 2022.

[96] *Bowers v. DeVito*, 686 F.2d 616, 618 (1982).

[97] Don Feder, "Five Myths of Gun Control," *Washington Times*, February 10, 2022.

[98] Maya Eling, "'It's my constitutional freaking right': Black Americans arm themselves in response to pandemic, protests," Politico, July 26, 2020.

[99] Seth Barron, "New York's Supreme Gun Distraction," *City Journal*, Summer 2022.

[100] Damon Root, "In Landmark 2nd Amendment Ruling, SCOTUS Affirms Right 'To Carry a Handgun for Self-Defense Outside the Home,'" *Reason*, June 23, 2022.

[101] "Gun Controllers: Ban Firearms for 'Radicals' (and Designate Political Opposition Under that Category)," National Rifle Association, September 6, 2022.

[102] twitter.com/GunOwners/status/1565476694319927297/photo/1

[103] Ryan McMaken, "Rising 'Constitutional Carry' Is a Sign of Failing Trust in Government," Mises Institute, August 4, 2022.

[104] "Remarks by President Biden on Gun Violence in America," White House Briefing Room, June 2, 2022.

[105] twitter.com/RepSwalwell/status/1063527635114852352

[106] Sinéad Baker, "Biden mocked gun-rights advocates who say they need assault weapons to fight the government: 'You need F-15s and maybe some nuclear weapons,'" *Business Insider*, June 24, 2021.

[107] George Lardner, Jr., and Richard Lei, "Government Witnesses Cause Case to Collapse," *Washington Post*, September 5, 1995.

[108] Sam Verhovek, "11 in Texas Sect Are Acquitted of Key Charges," *New York Times*, February 27, 1994.

[109] Richard Leiby, "FBI Reverses Its Stand on Waco," *Washington Post*, August 26, 1999.

[110] *U.S. v. Emerson*, 46 F. Supp. 2d 598, N.D. Tex. (1999).

[111] Joyce Lee Malcolm, *To Keep and Bear Arms: The Origins of an Anglo-American Right* (Cambridge: Harvard University Press, 1994), p. 130.

[112] Ibid., p. 141.

[113] Ibid., p. 161.

[114] Huey Newton, "In Defense of Self-Defense," June 20, 1967.

[115] twitter.com/blkgunsmattr/status/1166839724792844288

[116] twitter.com/RepSwalwell/status/1063531633771339781

[117] Kerri Breen, "New Zealand's ban on semi-automatic weapons is now fully in effect," GlobalNews.ca, December 20, 2019.

[118] twitter.com/SallyMayweather/status/1322354744892006401. Quoted in James Bovard, "Lockdowns Wrecked Democracy around the World," American Institute for Economic Research, March 10, 2021.

[119] Steven Nelson, "'Better than people': Biden hugs baby as WH scrambles to clean up latest gaffe," *New York Post*, March 23, 2023.

[120] Daniel Dale, "Fact check: Biden falsely claims he has 'been to every mass shooting,'" CNN, September 22, 2023.

Chapter 4

[1] Joanna Schwartz, "How the Supreme Court Protects Police Officers," *The Atlantic*, January 31, 2023.

[2] Fox Butterfield, "Ideas & Trends: Bookkeeping; When the Police Shoot, Who's Counting?" *New York Times*, April 29, 2001.

[3] Lucy McCalmont, "Holder 'concerned' over Ferguson," Politico, August 14, 2014.

[4] Rob Barry and Coulter Jones, "Hundreds of Police Killings Are Uncounted in Federal Statistics," *Wall Street Journal*, December 3, 2014.

[5] Ciara McCarthy, "Loretta Lynch: government shouldn't require reports of people killed by police," *The Guardian*, October 2, 2015.

[6] Ibid.

[7] Matt Apuzzo and Adam Liptak, "At Supreme Court, Eric Holder's Justice Dept. Routinely Backs Officers' Use of Force," *New York Times*, April 21, 2015.

[8] Kimberly Kindy, "Fatal police shootings in 2015 approaching 400 nationwide," *Washington Post*, May 30, 2015.

[9] Jon Swaine, Oliver Laughland, Jamiles Lartey, and Ciara McCarthy, "The Counted," *The Guardian*, December 31, 2015.

[10] Patrick Ball, "Police Homicides in the United States," *Granta*, March 4, 2016.

[11] Christal Hayes, "Half of Police Killings Aren't Documented, and Many of the Dead Are Black, Young," *Newsweek*, October 11, 2017.

[12] Jamiles Lartey, "US police killings undercounted by half, study using Guardian data finds," *The Guardian*, October 11, 2017.

[13] Tim Arango and Shaila Dewan, "More Than Half of Police Killings Are Mislabeled, New Study Says," *New York Times*, September 30, 2021.

[14] U.S. General Accounting Office, "LAW ENFORCEMENT: DOJ Can Improve Publication of Use of Force Data and Oversight of Excessive Force Allegations," December 2021.

[15] Tom Jackman, "FBI may shut down police use-of-force database due to lack of police participation," *Washington Post*, December 9, 2021.

[16] Editorial, "We now have a better count of nonfatal police shootings," *Washington Post*, November 8, 2022.

[17] American Civil Liberties Union, "War Comes Home: The Excessive Militarization of American Policing," June 2014.

[18] Kevin Sack, "Door-Busting Drug Raids Leave a Trail of Blood," *New York Times*, March 18, 2017.

[19] Ibid.

[20] Ibid.

[21] George Joseph, "NEMLEC SWAT Documents Give Ugly Snapshot of Police Militarization," *The Intercept*, July 7, 2015.

[22] *Richards v. Wisconsin*, 520 U.S. 385 (1997).

23 Kevin Sack, "Door-Busting Drug Raids Leave a Trail of Blood," *New York Times*, March 18, 2017.

24 Ibid.

25 James Bovard, "Arresting Someone for Laughing May Sound Funny, but It Is No Joke," *Washington Post*, May 3, 2017.

26 Marvin Mack, "How did local police acquire surplus military weapons?" *Business Insider*, April 28, 2021.

27 Christi Parsons, "Obama bars some military equipment from going to local police," *Los Angeles Times*, May 18, 2015.

28 Kevin Sack, "Door-Busting Drug Raids Leave a Trail of Blood," *New York Times*, March 18, 2017.

29 Charlotte Lawrence and Cyrus J. O'Brien, "Federal Militarization of Law Enforcement Must End," American Civil Liberties Union, May 12, 2021.

30 Chris Joyner and Nick Thieme, "Police killings more likely in agencies that get military gear, data shows," *Atlanta Journal-Constitution*, October 8, 2020.

31 Casey Delehanty, Jack Mewhirter, and Jason Wilks, "Militarization and Police Violence: The Case of the 1033 Program," *Research & Politics*, June 14, 2017.

32 Julia Angwin and Abbie Nehring, "Hotter than Lava," ProPublica, January 12, 2015.

33 Ibid.

34 Radley Balko, "Flashbangs Under Fire," *Reason*, February 17, 2010.

35 Kevin Sack, "Door-Busting Drug Raids Leave a Trail of Blood," *New York Times*, March 18, 2017.

36 Anne-Marie O'Connor, "Bereft Family Disputes Police Shooting Report," *Los Angeles Times*, August 26, 1999.

37 Radley Balko, "Federal appeals court criticizes SWAT teams who 'flash-bang first, ask questions later,'" *Washington Post*, July 30, 2019.

38 Tim Cushing, "Court: No Immunity for SWAT Team that Hurled a Flash-Bang Grenade in the General Direction of a Two-Year-Old Child," Techdirt, July 29, 2019.

39 Zach Benoit, "Grenade burns sleeping girl as SWAT team raids Billings home," *Billings Gazette*, October 12, 2012.

40 "Feature: Children and Swat Raids: An Unintended Consequence," *Worcester Magazine*, March 1, 2018.

41 Nicole Dungca and Jenn Abelson, "No-knock raids have led to fatal encounters and small drug seizures," *Washington Post*, April 15, 2022.

42 Dara Lind, "Cops do 20,000 no-knock raids a year. Civilians often pay the price when they go wrong," *Vox*, May 15, 2015.

43 Kevin Sack, "Door-Busting Drug Raids Leave a Trail of Blood," *New York Times*, March 18, 2017.

44 Tim Cushing, "After No-Knock Raid Goes Horribly Wrong, Police Union Boss Steps Up to Threaten PD's Critics," Techdirt, February 8, 2019.

45 Jacob Sullum, "'No One Will Hurt You,' a SWAT Officer Promised an Hour After Houston Cops Killed a Couple Falsely Accused of Selling Heroin," *Reason*, July 26, 2019.

46 Lucio Vasquez, "Former Houston Police Officer Pleads Guilty to Falsifying Records in Harding Street Raid Case," *Houston Chronicle*, June 1, 2021.

47 "War Comes Home: The Excessive Militarization of American Police," American Civil Liberties Union, June 2014.

48 Kevin Sack, "Door-Busting Drug Raids Leave a Trail of Blood," *New York Times*, March 18, 2017.
49 Jon Swaine, Oliver Laughland, Jamiles Lartey, and Ciara McCarthy, "The Counted," *The Guardian*, December 31, 2015.
50 George Joseph, "New SWAT Documents Give Snapshot of Ugly Militarization of U.S. Police," *The Intercept*, July 7, 2015.
51 American Civil Liberties Union, "War Comes Home: The Excessive Militarization of American Policing," June 2014.
52 Kevin Sack, "Door-Busting Drug Raids Leave a Trail of Blood," *New York Times*, March 18, 2017.
53 "Report in the matter of the March 12, 2020, police-involved shooting in Potomac, Maryland," Montgomery County State's Attorney's Office.
54 James Bovard, "The Official Whitewash of the Killing of Duncan Lemp," *American Conservative*, January 1, 2021.
55 Author interview with Rene Sandler, December 31, 2020.
56 James Bovard, "Death of Maryland man shows continued out-of-control nature of SWAT, no-knock raids," *USA Today*, February 2, 2021.
57 *Harlow v. Fitzgerald*, 457 U.S. 800, 818 (1982).
58 Joanna C. Schwartz, "The Case Against Qualified Immunity," *Notre Dame Law Review*, 2018.
59 Lynn Adelman, "The Supreme Court's Quiet Assault on Civil Rights," *Dissent*, Fall 2017.
60 Lawrence Hurley, "U.S. Supreme Court rules for Texas trooper in fatal shooting," Reuters, November 9, 2015.
61 Mark Joseph Stern, "The Conservatives vs. Sonia Sotomayor," *Slate*, April 2, 2018.
62 William Baude, "Is Qualified Immunity Unlawful?" *California Law Review*, February 2018.
63 *Filarsky v. Delia*, 566 U.S. 377 (2012).
64 Jacob Sullum, "A License for Outrageous Police Conduct," *Reason*, September 25, 2019.
65 Andrew Wimer, "New Supreme Court Appeal Asks: 'Can Police Arrest and Prosecute You for Making Fun of Them?'" Institute for Justice, September 27, 2022.
66 "Yet another federal judge tears into qualified immunity, citing Cato Institute & Will Baude," Unlawful Shield, Cato Institute, September 21, 2018.
67 Irving Younger, "The Perjury Routine," *The Nation*, May 3, 1967.
68 *Briscoe v. LaHue*, 460 U.S. 325 (1983).
69 Stuart Taylor, Jr., "For the Record," *American Lawyer*, Oct. 1995.
70 Joseph D. McNamara, "Has the Drug War Created an Officer Liars' Club?" *Los Angeles Times*, February 11, 1996.
71 Jennifer Gonnerman, "Tulia Blues," *Village Voice*, August 1, 2001.
72 "Department Probes Texas Drug Bust," Associated Press, October 26, 2000.
73 Phil Magers, "Analysis: Are there more Tulias out there?" United Press International, June 16, 2003.
74 "Texas undercover cop convicted of perjury," Associated Press, January 14, 2005.
75 Joseph Goldstein, "'Testilying' by Police: A Stubborn Problem," *New York Times*, March 18, 2018.

[76] Michael Sisitzky and Simon McCormack, "This Law Makes It Nearly Impossible to Police the Police in New York," New York Civil Liberties Union, April 19, 2018.

[77] Sue Anne Pressley, "Miami Police Arrested in Shootings Scandal; 13 Current, Former Officers Accused of Planting Guns, Making Up Evidence," *Washington Post*, September 8, 2001.

[78] "The price of Baltimore police misconduct — $24.5 million and rising," *Baltimore Brew*, September 18, 2019.

[79] Kevin Rector, "Baltimore Police officer found guilty of fabricating evidence in case where his own body camera captured the act," *Baltimore Sun*, November 9, 2018.

[80] C.J. Ciaramella, "Florida Sheriff Deputy Arrested After Planting Drugs on Innocent People," *Reason*, July 11, 2019.

[81] Karl Etters, "Former deputy Zachary Wester sentenced to more than 12 years in prison for drug planting," *Tallahassee Democrat*, July 13, 2021.

[82] Paul Solotaroff, "Did Falsified Drug Tests Lead to Thousands of Wrongful Convictions?" *Rolling Stone*, January 3, 2018.

[83] Shawn Musgrave, "The Chemists and the Cover-Up," *Reason*, February 9, 2019.

[84] Kevin Underhill, "Crime-Lab Chemist Was High While Testifying in Drug Cases," *Legal Humor. Seriously.*, May 9, 2016.

[85] Tom Jackman, "Prosecutors slammed for 'lack of moral compass,' withholding evidence in widening Mass. drug lab scandal," *Washington Post*, October 4, 2017.

[86] Dahlia Lithwick, "Crime Lab Scandals Just Keep Getting Worse," *Slate*, October 29, 2015.

[87] Jess Bidgood, "Misconduct by Chemist Will Nullify Drug Cases," *New York Times*, April 19, 2017.

[88] Ibid.

[89] Dahlia Lithwick, "Crime Lab Scandals Just Keep Getting Worse," *Slate*, October 29, 2015.

[90] Kim Barker, Michael H. Keller, and Steve Eder, "How Cities Lost Control of Police Discipline," *New York Times*, December 22, 2020.

[91] Ibid.

[92] Ibid.

[93] Lawrence Mower, "Inquests undercut by prosecutorial inaction, deference to police," *Las Vegas Review Journal*, November 30, 2011.

[94] James Bovard, "Killer Cops," *Playboy*, December 2001.

[95] Yanet Amanuel, "Maryland police reform is far from over," *Washington Post*, September 2, 2022.

[96] Dhammika Dharmapala, Richard H. McAdams, and John Rappaport, "Collective Bargaining Rights and Police Misconduct: Evidence from Florida," *Chicago Unbound*, University of Chicago Law School, August 2019.

[97] Stephen Rushin and Atticus DeProspo, "Interrogating Police Officers," *George Washington Law Review*, 2019.

[98] Samantha Max, "NYPD officers accused of wrongdoing can now watch all relevant video of an incident before speaking to investigators," Gothamist, July 14, 2023.

[99] Dhammika Dharmapala, Richard H. McAdams, and John Rappaport, "Collective Bargaining Rights and Police Misconduct: Evidence from Florida," *Chicago Unbound*, University of Chicago Law School, August 2019.

[100] "Police Unions and Civilian Deaths," National Public Radio, June 3, 2020.

[101] George Joseph, "Leaked police files contain guarantees disciplinary records will be kept secret," *The Guardian*, February 7, 2016.

[102] John Sullivan, Derek Hawkins, Kate McCormick, and Ashley Balcerzak, "In fatal shootings by police, 1 in 5 officers' names go undisclosed," *Washington Post*, March 31, 2016.

[103] Adeshina Emmanuel, "How Union Contracts Shield Police Departments from DOJ Reforms," *In These Times*, June 21, 2016.

[104] John Sullivan, Derek Hawkins, Kate McCormick, and Ashley Balcerzak, "In fatal shootings by police, 1 in 5 officers' names go undisclosed," *Washington Post*, March 31, 2016.

[105] "Pennsylvania House Passes Bill to Hide Cops Who Kill," ACLU of Pennsylvania, March 20, 2017.

[106] David Simon, "In Baltimore, No One Left to Press the Police," *Washington Post*, March 1, 2009.

[107] Mark Puente, "Price of legal action: silence; Baltimore stands out in restrictive policy on brutality settlements," *Baltimore Sun*, December 28, 2014.

[108] "ACLU Files Two Lawsuits Challenging Gag Orders that Silence Victims of Police Abuse," ACLU of Maryland, June 29, 2017.

[109] Tim Ryan, "News Outlet Fights Baltimore Police's Standing Gag Order," Courthouse News Service, June 30, 2017.

[110] Edward Ericson, Jr., "Baltimore Police Cannot Condition Brutality Settlements on Gag Orders," Courthouse News Service, July 12, 2019.

[111] Eugene Volokh, "City May Not Bargain for Certain Speech Restrictions When Settling Lawsuits Against Police Department," Volokh Conspiracy, July 15, 2019.

[112] Ben Poston and Maya Lau, "Here are the stories about police misconduct uncovered so far by a new media partnership," *Los Angeles Times*, March 19, 2019.

[113] Robert Lewis and Jason Paladino, "California keeps a secret list of criminal cops, but says you can't have it," *Mercury News* (San Jose, California), February 26, 2019.

[114] Jenny Weng, "Berkeley-based journalists face government backlash over confidential police data," *Daily Californian*, March 5, 2019.

[115] Sophia Bollag, "Thousands of California cops could be decertified under new law," *San Francisco Chronicle*, June 14, 2023.

[116] Trân Nguy, "California governor proposes rolling back access to police misconduct records," *San Diego Union-Tribune*, June 17, 2023.

[117] Keith L. Alexander, Steven Rich, and Hannah Thacker, "Repeated police misconduct cost taxpayers $1.5 billion in settlements," *Washington Post*, March 9, 2022.

[118] Akela Lacy, "NYPD 'Transparency' Site Leaves Out Misconduct Lawsuits Settled for Millions," *The Intercept*, September 25, 2023.

[119] James Bovard, "Mayor Pete Buttigieg's Friendly Police Fantasy," *American Conservative*, July 5, 2019.

[120] Timothy M. Maher, "Police Chiefs' Views on the Nature, Extent, and Causes of Police Sexual Misconduct," University of Missouri-St. Louis, 2008.

[121] Nancy Phillips and Craig R. McCoy, "Extorting sex with a badge," *Philadelphia Inquirer*, March 29, 2007.

[122] Conor Friedersdorf, "Police Have a Much Bigger Domestic-Abuse Problem Than the NFL Does," *The Atlantic*, September 19, 2014.

123 Sarah Cohen, Rebecca R. Ruiz, and Sarah Childress, "Departments Are Slow to Police Their Own Abusers," *New York Times*, November 23, 2013.
124 Philip Matthew Stinson, John Liederbach, Steven P. Lab, and Steven L. Brewer, Jr., "Police Integrity Lost: A Study of Law Enforcement Arrested," National Institute for Justice, 2016.
125 Matt Sedensky, "Hundreds of officers lose licenses over sex misconduct," Associated Press, November 1, 2015.
126 Casey Quinlan, "Police sexual abuse isn't just the case of a few 'bad apples,'" ThinkProgress.org, December 4, 2017. Quote is from Andrea Richie, author of book about police sex crimes against women.
127 Kimbriell Kelly, Wesley Lowery, and Steven Rich, "Fired/Rehired: Police chiefs are often forced to put officers fired for misconduct back on the streets," *Washington Post*, August 3, 2017.
128 Casey Quinlan, "Police sexual abuse isn't just the case of a few 'bad apples,'" ThinkProgress.org, December 4, 2017. Quote is from Andrea Richie, author of book about police sex crimes against women.
129 Albert Samaha, "An 18-Year-Old Said She Was Raped While in Police Custody The Officers Say She Consented," BuzzFeed, February 7, 2018.
130 Editorial, "Close the Police Rape Loophole," *New York Times*, February 12, 2018.
131 Albert Samaha, "New York Just Passed a Bill Banning Cops from Having Sex with People in Custody," BuzzFeed, March 30, 2018.
132 Andrew Denney, "Judge explains no-jail deal for ex-NYPD cops who had sex with suspect," *New York Post*, August 29, 2019.
133 Ellie Bufkin, "'Zero tolerance for resisting police': Barr slams law enforcement protesters," *Washington Examiner*, August 14, 2019.
134 James Bovard, "William Barr's Connection to Ruby Ridge, Defending FBI Snipers," *American Conservative*, January 16, 2019.
135 Taylor's line was the abridged version of Chief Justice John Marshall's opinion in *Marbury v. Madison* (1803): "The government of the United States has been emphatically termed a government of laws, and not of men. It will certainly cease to deserve this high appellation, if the laws furnish no remedy for the violation of a vested legal right."

Chapter 5

1 Amy Sherman, "Joe Biden exaggerates efficacy of COVID-19 vaccines," PolitiFact, July 22, 2021.
2 Ruth Simon, "Covid-19's Toll on U.S. Business? 200,000 Extra Closures in Pandemic's First Year," *Wall Street Journal*, April 16, 2021.
3 Kevin M. Esvelt, "Manipulating viruses and risking pandemics is too dangerous. It's time to stop," *Washington Post*, October 7, 2021.
4 Press Release, "Wenstrup Reveals Explosive Emails from Fauci Ally, Requests Additional Communications," House Oversight Committee, June 29, 2023.
5 Jonathan Turley, "COVID lab leak is a scandal of media and government censorship," *New York Post*, February 26, 2023.
6 Jon Cohen, "CIA bribed its own COVID-19 origin team to reject lab leak theory, anonymous whistleblower claims," *Science*, September 12, 2023.
7 Myah Ward, "15 times Trump praised China as coronavirus was spreading across the globe," Politico, April 15, 2020.

[8] Jeffrey Tucker, "The Day Anthony Fauci Wrecked American Freedom," Brownstone Institute, July 26, 2022.

[9] Jeffrey Tucker, "The Small Print That Destroyed America," *Epoch Times*, July 26, 2022.

[10] Philip Bump, "The self-anointed 'wartime president' finds a new, more exciting war," *Washington Post*, June 1, 2020.

[11] Sonam Sheth, "Trump falsely claims that 'when somebody is the president of the United States, the authority is total'" *Business Insider*, April 13, 2020.

[12] "WHO Director-General's opening remarks at the media briefing on COVID-19," World Health Organization, March 3, 2020.

[13] twitter.com/LauraPowellEsq/status/1694947315650548028

[14] Jeffrey Tucker, "Don't Cry for Donald McNeil," American Institute for Economic Research, February 8, 2021.

[15] Sheila Kaplan, "C.D.C. Labs Were Contaminated, Delaying Coronavirus Testing, Officials Say," *New York Times*, April 20, 2020.

[16] Suzy Khimm, Laura Strickler, and Brenda Breslauer, "Many private labs want to do coronavirus tests," NBC News, March 11, 2020.

[17] Jeff Cox, "Nearly 40% of the poorest households hit with a job loss during pandemic, Fed study shows," CNBC, May 14, 2020.

[18] Noah Higgins-Dunn, "Coronavirus crisis creates 'perfect storm' for suicide risk as job losses soar and people are isolated at home," CNBC, May 12, 2020.

[19] Larry Elder, "Experts expect rise in 'deaths from despair' during coronavirus recession," *Boston Herald*, May 18, 2020.

[20] Harriet Alexander, "'You can have cocaine and heroin, but not turkey?' Oregon Gov. Brown is slammed," *Daily Mail*, November 23, 2020.

[21] Brie Stimson and Travis Fedschun, "Michigan stay-at-home order now bans visits to friends, relatives, governor says," Fox News, April 11, 2020.

[22] "Gov. Whitmer is attempting to sidestep the Michigan Supreme Court," Mackinac Center, October 6, 2020.

[23] Michael Tracey, "New Documents Show Police Charged Thousands of People For Petty COVID Violations," Michael Tracey's Substack, May 12, 2021.

[24] "How '15 Days to Slow the Spread' Turned into a Constitutional Battle for Religious Freedom," FirstLiberty.org, March 12, 2021.

[25] Brianna Lyman, "LA Mayor Bans Unnecessary Walking as Part of New COVID-19 Restrictions," *Daily Caller*, December 3, 2020.

[26] twitter.com/lhfang/status/1334389792113475590

[27] Nick Paumgarten, "Andrew Cuomo, the King of New York," *New Yorker*, October 19, 2020.

[28] Ben Smith, "Andrew Cuomo Is the Control Freak We Need Right Now," *New York Times*, March 16, 2020.

[29] Joseph Choi, "Cuomo calls a sheriff who won't enforce mask mandate a 'dictator,'" *The Hill*, November 23, 2020.

[30] Tim Graham, "Cuomo Revelations Should Embarrass Media," *Daily Signal*, February 18, 2021.

[31] Editorial, "New emails highlight a Team Cuomo COVID priority: promoting Andrew," *New York Post*, May 31, 2023.

[32] James Bovard, "How $600 billion was stolen from the American people," *New York Post*, October 2, 2022.

[33] Jonathan O'Connell, Emma Brown, Steven Rich, and Aaron Gregg, "Faulty data collection raises questions about Trump's claims on PPP program," *Washington Post*, July 14, 2020.

[34] Ken Dilanian and Laura Strickler, "Biggest fraud in a generation," NBC News, March 28, 2022.

[35] "Police: Inmates got out of Illinois jail with pandemic loans," *Washington Post*, September 22, 2022.

[36] Ryan Nelson, "Documents Reveal Murder-for Hire-Plot, PPP Fraud Behind Killing of TSA Agent in Naranja," NBC 6, February 15, 2022.

[37] Ken Dilanian and Laura Strickler, "Biggest fraud in a generation," NBC News, March 28, 2022.

[38] James Bovard, "Deceit and Demagoguery in Montgomery County, Maryland," American Institute for Economic Research, August 7, 2020.

[39] twitter.com/DrLeanaWen/status/1328168114949910529

[40] Ryan Carter, "Lancaster calls special meeting to call no-confidence vote in Ferrer and consider own public health department," *Los Angeles Daily News*, November 27, 2020.

[41] James Bovard, "County Puts Bag Recycling Before Grocery Workers' Health," *American Conservative*, April 25, 2020.

[42] John Tierney, "The Failed Covid Policy of Mask Mandates — Maskaholics," *City Journal*, April 18, 2022.

[43] Dionne Searcey and Reid J. Epstein, "Social Distancing Informants Have Their Eyes on You," *New York Times*, May 4, 2020.

[44] Joe Dwinell and Erin Tiernan, "Massachusetts residents burning up the COVID-19 snitch line," *Boston Herald*, October 5, 2020.

[45] Lena H. Sun and Joel Achenbach, "CDC chief says coronavirus cases may be 10 times higher than reported," *Washington Post*, June 25, 2020.

[46] Bruce Y. Lee, "WHO Warning About Covid-19 Coronavirus Lockdowns Is Taken Out of Context," *Forbes*, October 13, 2020.

[47] Kevin Kiley, "How Gov Gavin Newsom Abuses Shutdowns to 'Reshape' California for 'Equity,'" *Daily Caller*, October 8, 2020.

[48] Jon Guze, "There is no world in which the Constitution permits Nevada to favor Caesars Palace over Calvary Chapel," John Locke Foundation, July 25, 2020.

[49] "TRANSCRIPT: Joe Biden, Kamala Harris' first joint interview with ABC's David Muir," ABC News, August 23, 2020.

[50] "Pennsylvania Covid Restrictions Unconstitutional, Judge Says," Bloomberg Law, September 14, 2020.

[51] Charles "Cully" Stimson and GianCarlo Canaparo, "In COVID-19 Restrictions Ruling, Judge Holds Pennsylvania Governor to the Constitution," Heritage Foundation, September 25, 2020.

[52] Aaron Blake, "Mark Meadows tries to clean up his disclosure of Trump's positive coronavirus test — poorly," *Washington Post*, December 2, 2021.

[53] Nusaiba Mizan, "Fact check: Yes, Biden botched stats on COVID-19 and gun deaths," *USA Today*, July 18, 2020.

[54] Yaron Steinbuch, "Joe Biden mistakenly says 200 million people have died from COVID-19 in US," *New York Post*, September 21, 2020

[55] Anna Palmer and Jake Sherman, "It's the pandemic, stupid," Politico, October 30, 2020.

[56] Jonathan Rothwell and Sonal Desai, "How misinformation is distorting COVID policies and behaviors," Brookings Institution, December 22, 2020.

[57] "Exit Polls," CNN, November 2020.

[58] twitter.com/tribelaw/status/1339300875253264389

[59] *Brief of Attorney General of Texas — Motion for Leave to File Bill of Complaint, Texas v. Pennsylvania, Georgia, Michigan, Wisconsin*, December 7, 2020.

[60] Ibid.

[61] Mary Margaret Olohan, "SCOTUS Calls New York's COVID Restrictions 'Discriminatory,' Sides with Religious Organizations," *The Stream*, November 26, 2020.

[62] Jesse McKinley and Liam Stack, "Cuomo Attacks Supreme Court, but Virus Ruling Is Warning to Governors," *New York Times*, November 26, 2020.

[63] Ben Cost, "Dr. Fauci endorses Tinder hookups 'if you're willing to take a risk,'" *New York Post*, April 15, 2020.

[64] Tara Parker-Pope, "Masks, No Kissing and 'a Little Kinky': Dating and Sex in a Pandemic," *New York Times*, June 11, 2020.

[65] "Safer Sex and COVID-19," Pennsylvania Department of Health, October 7, 2020.

[66] Ariel Zilber, "Nate Silver: 'Liberal elites' pressured Pfizer to delay vaccine until after 2020 election," *New York Post*, August 25, 2022.

[67] MacKenzie Sigalos, "You can't sue Pfizer or Moderna if you have severe Covid vaccine side effects," CNBC, December 17, 2020.

[68] "Executive Order on Protecting the Federal Workforce and Requiring Mask-Wearing," White House Briefing Room, January 20, 2021.

[69] twitter.com/dailycaller/status/1352374482753658880

[70] James Bovard, "We're Fed Up with Covid Edicts and Hypocrisy," *USA Today*, February 8, 2022.

[71] James Bovard, "Masking America's Greatest Natural Monuments," American Institute for Economic Research, February 6, 2021.

[72] "Justice Neil Gorsuch Speaks Out Against Lockdowns and Mandates," Brownstone Institute, May 18, 2023.

[73] "Remarks by President Biden on the Anniversary of the COVID-19 Shutdown," White House Briefing Room, March 11, 2021.

[74] Libby Cathey, "Biden announces 'all-of-America sprint' to get more vaccinated by July Fourth," ABC News, June 2, 2021.

[75] Kate Sullivan, Kate Bennett, and Paul LeBlanc, "Biden touts US coronavirus progress at July 4 White House event: 'America is coming back together,'" CNN, July 4, 2021.

[76] Amy Sherman, "Joe Biden exaggerates efficacy of COVID-19 vaccines," PolitiFact, July 22, 2021.

[77] Rachel Roubein and David Lim, "CDC under fire for decision to limit tracking of Covid-19 cases in vaccinated people," Politico, July 30, 2021.

[78] twitter.com/nytimes/status/1420972977005412354

[79] Samuel Chamberlain, "White House slams NYT, Washington Post over tweets on CDC COVID data," *New York Post*, July 30, 2021.

[80] "CDC Says 100,000-Plus New COVID Cases Recorded Wednesday," *The Situation Room*, CNN, August 5, 2021.

[81] Anders Hagstrom, "Psaki Confirms White House 'Breakthrough' Infections After Vaccinated Aide Tests Positive For COVID-19," *Daily Caller*, July 20, 2021.

82 Caitlin Owens, "New data on coronavirus vaccine effectiveness may be 'a wakeup call,'" Axios, August 11, 2021.

83 "Press Briefing by Press Secretary Jen Psaki and Surgeon General Dr. Vivek H. Murthy," White House Briefing Room, July 15, 2021.

84 David Hogberg, "NIH director forced to clarify statement that parents should wear masks around unvaccinated children," *Washington Examiner*, August 3, 2021.

85 Yasmeen Abutaleb and Lena H. Sun, "How CDC data problems put the U.S. behind on the delta variant," *Washington Post*, August 19, 2021.

86 Bernard Condon, Matt Sedensky, and Meghan Hoyer, "New York's true nursing home death toll cloaked in secrecy," Associated Press, August 11, 2020.

87 Jesse McKinley, Danny Hakim, and Alexandra Alters, "Cuomo Sought $4 Million Book Deal, Aides Hid Damaging Death Toll," *New York Times*, March 31, 2021.

88 Marina Villeneuve, "Gov. Andrew Cuomo resigns over sexual harassment allegations," Associated Press, August 10, 2021.

89 Savannah Rychcik, "Maryland Governor on the Unvaccinated: 'Threatening the Freedoms of All the Rest of Us,'" *Independent Journal Review*, August 5, 2021.

90 twitter.com/ASlavitt/status/1436856483094745093

91 Zeke Miller, "Biden eyes tougher vaccine rules without provoking backlash," Associated Press, August 13, 2021.

92 "Remarks by President Biden on the COVID-19 Response and the Vaccination Program," White House Briefing Room, August 23, 2021.

93 Sarah Owermohle, "Biden's top-down booster plan sparks anger at FDA," Politico, August 31, 2021.

94 Katie Camero, "Why did CDC change its definition for 'vaccine'? Agency explains move as skeptics lurk," *Miami Herald*, September 27, 2021.

95 twitter.com/RepThomasMassie/status/1435606845926871041

96 Tom Porter, "Video shows President-elect Biden saying 10 months ago he wouldn't make vaccines mandatory," *Business Insider*, September 10, 2021.

97 "Biden's Speech on Vaccine Mandates and the Delta Variant: Full Transcript," *New York Times*, September 9, 2021.

98 Ibid.

99 "Remarks by President Biden on the Importance of COVID-19 Vaccine Requirements," White House Briefing Room, October 7, 2021.

100 Daniel Villarreal, "Biden Mocks Vaccine Skeptics: 'I Have the Freedom to Kill You with My COVID,'" *Newsweek*, October 21, 2021.

101 "Medicare and Medicaid Programs; Omnibus COVID-19 Health Care Staff Vaccination," *Federal Register*, November 5, 2021, p. 61555.

102 Editorial, "Vaccines offer an exit from the pandemic. Mandates work," *Washington Post*, November 8, 2021.

103 David Cole and Daniel Mach, "We Work at the A.C.L.U. Here's What We Think About Vaccine Mandates," *New York Times*, September 2, 2021.

104 "Transcript: Mayor de Blasio Holds Media Availability," New York City Office of the Mayor, August 2, 2021.

105 Emily Guskin and Michael Brice-Saddler, "About 3 in 4 D.C. residents support vaccine rules Bowser just rescinded, poll finds," *Washington Post*, February 15, 2022.

106 James Bovard, "There Is No Cure for Washington's Arrogance," Brownstone Institute, March 16, 2023.

107 twitter.com/stinchfield1776/status/1426536668115374085

108 twitter.com/emilymiller/status/1431739953197768707

109 "Remarks by President Biden on the 100 Million Shot Goal," White House Briefing Room, March 18, 2021.

110 Meredith Wadman, "Having SARS-CoV-2 once confers much greater immunity than a vaccine — but vaccination remains vital," *Science*, August 26, 2021.

111 "'Estimated Covid Burden' – Data & Science – COVID Data Tracker," CDC.gov, Centers for Disease Control and Prevention. Accessed November 16, 2021.

112 Jessica Chasmar, "Biden's 'pandemic of the unvaccinated' narrative falls apart as omicron cases skyrocket," Fox News, January 4, 2022.

113 Allie Malloy and Maegan Vazquez, "Biden warns of winter of 'severe illness and death' for unvaccinated due to Omicron," CNN, December 16, 2021.

114 "Remarks by President Biden on the Fight Against COVID-19," White House Briefing Room, December 21, 2021.

115 Apoorva Mandavilli, "The C.D.C. Isn't Publishing Large Portions of the Covid Data It Collects," *New York Times*, February 20, 2022.

116 twitter.com/mtracey/status/1473564356747145219

117 "Vermont's October infections break pandemic record," WCAX, October 29, 2021.

118 Javier E. David, "Omicron prompts rethink of vaccine impact, COVID-19 mandates," *Yahoo News*, December 29, 2021.

119 Nate Rattner, "U.S. Covid cases rise to pandemic high as delta and omicron circulate at same time," CNBC, December 29, 2021.

120 Lisa Shumaker, "U.S. reports 1.35 million COVID-19 cases in a day, shattering global record," Reuters, January 11, 2022.

121 Rebecca Tan and Jenna Portnoy, "Maryland covid deaths have hit a monthly record amid omicron," *Washington Post*, January 25, 2022.

122 James Bovard, "Who screwed up COVID-19 testing? Blame Trump, Biden and our health care bureaucracy," *USA Today*, January 27, 2022.

123 Yasmeen Abutaleb, Lena H. Sun, Laurie McGinley, Dan Diamond, and Tyler Pager, "Rapid coronavirus tests are still hard to find in many places, despite Biden vows," *Washington Post*, December 9, 2021.

124 "Remarks by President Biden on the Anniversary of the COVID-19 Shutdown," White House Briefing Room, March 11, 2021.

125 Annie Linskey, "Inside the administration's failure to avert a covid testing shortfall," *Washington Post*, December 23, 2021.

126 "Remarks by President Biden on Fighting the COVID-19 Pandemic," White House Briefing Room, September 9, 2021.

127 Katherine Eban, "The Biden Administration Rejected an October Proposal for 'Free Rapid Tests for the Holidays,'" *Vanity Fair*, December 23, 2021.

128 Annie Linskey, "Inside the administration's failure to avert a covid testing shortfall," *Washington Post*, December 23, 2021.

129 Yasmeen Abutaleb, Lena H. Sun, Laurie McGinley, Dan Diamond, and Tyler Pager, "Rapid coronavirus tests are still hard to find in many places, despite Biden vows," *Washington Post*, December 9, 2021.

130 Christopher Miller, "This Scientist Created a Rapid Test Just Weeks into the Pandemic," ProPublica, December 21, 2021.

131 Scott Lincicome, "Why Federal Promises to Boost Covid Testing Keep Failing," *Barron's*, January 20, 2022.

132 "Remarks by President Biden at COVID-19 Response Team's Regular Call with the National Governors Association," White House Press Office, December 27, 2021.
133 Luc Montagnier and Jed Rubenfeld, "Omicron Makes Biden's Vaccine Mandates Obsolete," *Wall Street Journal*, January 10, 2022.
134 Amber Randel, "AAO–HNS Guidelines for Tonsillectomy in Children and Adolescents," American Family Physician, 2011.
135 Samuel Chamberlain, "Supreme Court's liberal justices slammed over vax mandate statements," *New York Post*, January 7, 2022.
136 James Bovard, "COVID-positive nurses are in our hospitals. But Biden's mandate forbids unvaccinated ones," *USA Today*, January 7, 2022.
137 "Medicare and Medicaid Programs; Omnibus COVID-19 Health Care Staff Vaccination," *Federal Register*, November 5, 2021, p. 61555.
138 Jaclyn Diaz, "A N.Y. Hospital Will Stop Delivering Babies As Workers Quit Over A Vaccine Mandate," National Public Radio, September 13, 2021.
139 Amy Neff Roth, "More patients, fewer workers: Mohawk Valley Health System limits services amid staffing shortage," USA Today, November 24, 2021.
140 "CDC cuts quarantine time for healthcare workers amid Omicron surge," Reuters, December 23, 2021.
141 Allana Akhtar and Aria Bendix, "COVID-positive nurses say they're being pressured to work while sick, and they're petrified of infecting patients," *Business Insider*, January 6, 2022.
142 Ibid.
143 Eli Sherman and Ted Nesi, "COVID positive health care workers called into work in Rhode Island," WPRI.com, January 3, 2022.
144 "CDC cuts quarantine time for healthcare workers amid Omicron surge," Reuters, December 23, 2021.
145 Lena Sun, "Booster effectiveness wanes after 4 months, but showed sturdy protection against hospitalization, CDC study shows," *Washington Post*, February 11, 2022.
146 Luc Montagnier and Jed Rubenfeld, "Omicron Makes Biden's Vaccine Mandates Obsolete," *Wall Street Journal*, January 10, 2022.
147 Fenit Nirappil and Dan Keating, "Covid deaths no longer overwhelmingly among the unvaccinated as toll on elderly grows," *Washington Post*, April 29, 2022.
148 Aaron Blake, "'Most people are going to get covid': A momentous warning at a Senate hearing," *Washington Post*, January 11, 2022.
149 Jacob Fischler, "Supreme Court blocks Biden workplace vaccine rule, allows health care workers mandate," *Wisconsin Examiner*, January 13, 2022.
150 "Remarks by President Biden at Virtual Meeting on Military Deployments Supporting Hospitals for the COVID-19 Response," White House Briefing Room, January 13, 2022.
151 Brian Myers, "The false 'pandemic of the unvaccinated' motto did lasting harm," *Des Moines Register*, April 17, 2022.
152 Editorial, "Utah leaders have surrendered to COVID pandemic," *Salt Lake City Tribune*, January 15, 2022.
153 James Bovard, "Justin Trudeau's Canadian injustice is just a naked grab for power," *New York Post*, February 15, 2022.
154 "Why the word 'freedom' is such a useful rallying cry for protesters," CBC Radio, February 13, 2022.

[155] "Remarks of President Joe Biden — State of the Union Address," White House Briefing Room, March 1, 2022.

[156] Jamie Ducharme, "Almost 60% of Americans Have Had COVID-19, CDC Says," *Time*, April 26, 2022.

[157] Sharon Otterman, "Why a Covid Vaccine Mandate for N.Y.C. Schoolchildren Is Unlikely Soon," *New York Times*, May 10, 2022.

[158] "Remarks by President Biden on the Continued Battle for the Soul of the Nation," White House Briefing Room, September 1, 2022.

[159] Spencer Kimball, "U.S. extends Covid public health emergency even though Biden says pandemic is over," CNBC, October 13, 2022.

[160] twitter.com/potus/status/1612519798184763413

[161] Allysia Finley, "The Deceptive Campaign for Bivalent Covid Boosters," *Wall Street Journal*, January 23, 2023.

[162] Rob Stein, "What's behind the FDA's controversial strategy for evaluating new COVID boosters," National Public Radio, August 18, 2022.

[163] Alexander Tin, "More than 9 in 10 kids have survived at least one bout with COVID, the CDC estimates," CBS News, December 15, 2022.

[164] Leana S. Wen, "A compromise on the military covid vaccine mandate," *Washington Post*, December 18, 2022.

[165] Roni Caryn Rabin, "Alcohol-Related Deaths Spiked During the Pandemic, a Study Shows," *New York Times*, March 22, 2022.

[166] Casey B. Mulligan and Robert D. Arnott, "Non-COVID Excess Deaths, 2020–21: Collateral Damage of Policy Choices?" National Bureau of Economic Research, June 2022.

[167] Daniel E. Slotnik, "E.R. visits following suspected suicide attempts rose among U.S. teen girls during the pandemic," *New York Times*, June 11, 2021.

[168] Brianna Hoge, "Study shows greater increase in depression and anxiety in minorities during the pandemic," UAB News, May 9, 2022.

[169] Gianna Melillo, "Youth type 2 diabetes diagnoses jumped 77 percent during COVID-19," *The Hill*, August 25, 2022.

[170] Sabrina Tavernise and Abby Goodnough, "American life expectancy fell by one year, to 77.8 years, in the first half of 2020," *New York Times*, July 21, 2021. The decline continued in 2021: Deidre McPhillips, "US life expectancy continues historic decline with another drop in 2021, study finds," CNN, April 8, 2022.

[171] J.D. Tuccille, "At High Cost, COVID-19 Lockdowns Saved Few Lives," *Reason*, February 4, 2022.

[172] John Tierney, "Lockdowns: The Self-Inflicted Disaster," *City Journal*, July 6, 2023.

[173] Raymond Palmer, "Covid 19 vaccines and the misinterpretation of perceived side effects clarity on the safety of vaccines," *Biomedicine*, September 1, 2022.

[174] "Understanding mRNA COVID-19 Vaccines," CDC.gov, Centers for Disease Control and Prevention, July 15, 2022. Archived at: archive.ph/kDUCP#selection-1653.11-1653.32.

[175] Clayton Fox, "The Feds Pile Up Vaccine 'Adverse Event' Reports as They Decry Scaremongering Elsewhere," Real Clear Investigations, July 14, 2022.

[176] Sarah Sloat, "Menstrual changes after Covid vaccines may be far more common than previously known," NBC News, July 15, 2022.

[177] Marty Makary, "10 myths told by COVID experts — and now debunked," *New York Post*, February 27, 2023.

178 Adam Sabes, "CDC investigating whether Pfizer COVID vaccine increases stroke risk for people over 65," *New York Post*, January 14, 2023.
179 Katherine Donlevy, "Biden says 'over 100' Americans have died from COVID in latest blunder," *New York Post*, July 25, 2023.
180 Melissa Healy, "Fauci's warning to America: 'We're living in a progressively anti-science era and that's a very dangerous thing,'" *Yahoo News*, December 22, 2022.
181 "Scientific Integrity: HHS Agencies Need to Develop Procedures and Train Staff on Reporting and Addressing Political Interference," Government Accountability Office, April 2022.
182 Brianna Herlihy, "Fauci emailed friend saying masks were 'ineffective,' pushed for mandates anyway, Missouri AG says," Fox News, November 25, 2022.
183 Josh Christenson, "HHS bars Wuhan Institute of Virology from receiving US funding for next 10 years," *New York Post*, September 20, 2023.
184 John Stuart Mill, *A System of Logic: Ratiocinative and Inductive* (London: 1843).
185 twitter.com/jeffreyatucker/status/1315265693223452672
186 John Kopp and Bob McGovern, "100 years ago, 'Spanish flu' shut down Philadelphia — and wiped out thousands," *Philadelphia Inquirer*, September 27, 2018.

Chapter 6

1 Edward B. Fiske, "Commission on Education Warns 'Tide of Mediocrity' Imperils U.S.," *New York Times*, April 27, 1983.
2 Laurel Shaper, "Goals 2000 Act Broadens Federal Role," *Christian Science Monitor*, April 11, 1994.
3 Lawrence A. Uzzell, "Education Reform Fails the Test," *Wall Street Journal*, May 10, 1989.
4 James Bovard, "Corrupt Federal Statistics Mask Government Cons," American Institute for Economic Research, April 7, 2022.
5 "Nevada's minority students more likely to be left behind in test scores," *Nevada Appeal*, April 16, 2006.
6 "Nebraska tossed 25 percent of No Child Left Behind tests," Associated Press, April 19, 2006.
7 "Transcript: George W. Bush's Speech to the NAACP," *Washington Post*, July 10, 2000.
8 David Kirp, "The Widest Achievement Gap," *National Affairs*, Fall 2010.
9 Trip Gabriel, "Proficiency of Black Students Is Found to Be Far Lower than Expected," *New York Times*, November 9, 2010.
10 "Secretary of Education Arne Duncan Interviewed on Bloomberg TV," Analyst Wire, November 21, 2013.
11 Michele McNeil, "States Punch Reset Button with NCLB Waivers; Many revise subgroup goals," *Education Week*, October 15, 2012.
12 James Bovard, "Education goals are getting resegregated," *USA Today*, May 9, 2014.
13 Emma Brown, "D.C. schools set new achievement targets for students by race and income," *Washington Post*, September 18, 2012.
14 Michele McNeil, "States Punch Reset Button with NCLB Waivers; Many revise subgroup goals," *Education Week*, October 15, 2012.
15 Jamon Smith, "New education standards factor in student race, economic status," *Tuscaloosa News*, June 30, 2013.

[16] Roger Chesley, "Lowering state test standards leads students to lower theirs," *Virginian-Pilot*, August 23, 2012.

[17] Emily Richmond, "Are Schools Setting Achievement Goals Based on a Student's Race?" *National Journal*, November 20, 2012.

[18] Dana Goldstein, "After 10 Years of Hopes and Setbacks, What Happened to the Common Core?" *New York Times*, December 6, 2019.

[19] Tamar Lewin, "Many States Adopt National Standards for Their Schools," *New York Times*, July 21, 2010.

[20] Dana Goldstein, "After 10 Years of Hopes and Setbacks, What Happened to the Common Core?" *New York Times*, December 6, 2019.

[21] Liz Bowie, "Teachers complain about access to new curriculum," *Baltimore Sun*, September 23, 2013.

[22] Saliqa A. Khan, "Former BCPS superintendent Dallas Dance sentenced," WBAL TV, April 20, 2018.

[23] Charles Chieppo and Jamie Gass, "Why states are backing out on common standards and tests," *Hechinger Report*, August 15, 2013.

[24] Sandra Stotsky, "Common Core's Cloudy Vision of College Readiness in Math," Pioneer Institute, July 1, 2013.

[25] Valerie Strauss, "Actually, Louis C.K. was right about Common Core — Ravitch," *Washington Post*, May 3, 2014.

[26] Lance Izumi, "Common Core Has Failed America's Students," *Daily Caller*, May 22, 2019.

[27] James Bovard, "How Teachers Teach Selfishness," *Washington Monthly*, June 1981.

[28] Peter Applebome, "GOP Efforts Put Teachers' Unions on the Defensive," *New York Times*, September 4, 1995.

[29] Ovie Carter, *Chicago Schools: Worst in America* (Chicago: *Chicago Tribune*, 1988), p. 77.

[30] Larry Sand, "Our Failing Schools Are a National Crisis," *City Journal*, July 14, 2023.

[31] Editorial, "Fresh evidence that COVID school closures led to dramatic setbacks in learning for America's kids," *New York Post*, October 24, 2022.

[32] Tawnell D. Hobbs and Lee Hawkins, "The Results Are In for Remote Learning: It Didn't Work," *Wall Street Journal*, June 5, 2020.

[33] Barnini Chakraborty, "Teachers unions' unprecedented power grab during Biden administration, COVID-19 could be here to stay," *Washington Examiner*, January 3, 2022.

[34] Jon Miltimore, "'Our Fight Is Against Capitalism' and 'the Patriarchy,' Says Union Boss Leading Teachers Strike," Foundation for Economic Education, March 12, 2022.

[35] James Bovard, "Teachers Unions Have Always Been Terrible," *American Conservative*, February 15, 2021.

[36] "Teachers' union apologizes for using coffin props at protest," Associated Press, October 9, 2020.

[37] Dimitri A. Christakis, Wil Van Cleve, and Frederick J. Zimmerman, "Estimation of US Children's Educational Attainment and Years of Life Lost Associated with Primary School Closures During the Coronavirus Disease 2019 Pandemic," *JAMA Network*, November 12, 2020.

38 Jude Schwalbach, "How Teacher Unions Failed Students During the Pandemic," *Public Discourse*, April 4, 2022.
39 Megan Kuhfeld, Jim Soland, Karyn Lewis, and Emily Morton, "The pandemic has had devastating impacts on learning. What will it take to help students catch up?" Brookings Institution, March 3, 2022.
40 Joseph G. Allen, "We Learned Our Lesson Last Year: Do Not Close Schools," *New York Times*, December 20, 2021.
41 Donna St. George, "Failing grades double and triple — some rising sixfold — amid pandemic learning," *Washington Post*, December 3, 2020.
42 Kayla Gaskins, "Congress debates causes of Covid-19 learning loss," WSBT.com, July 28, 2023.
43 Cory Turner, "6 things we've learned about how the pandemic disrupted learning," National Public Radio, June 22, 2022.
44 Michael J. Petrilli, "Teacher unions, which forced long lockdowns, now outrageously claim student learning loss is no big deal," *New York Post*, October 24, 2022.
45 Kathleen Moore, "NYS changes minimum scores for student proficiency in math, English," *Times-Union* (Albany, New York), March 16, 2023.
46 Jessica Chasmar, "Robert Redfield, CDC director: School 'one of the safest places' kids can be," *Washington Times*, November 20, 2020.
47 twitter.com/TPCarney/status/1398387723963076622
48 "Results From the NAEP 2021 School Survey for Private Schools," National Assessment of Educational Progress (Federal Department of Education), Summer/Fall 2021.
49 James Bovard, "How Teachers Teach Selfishness," *Washington Monthly*, June 1981.
50 Misty Severi, "Randi Weingarten blames politicians for turning teachers into 'social justice warriors,'" *Washington Examiner*, September 2, 2022.
51 Position Statement, "Media Education in English Language Arts," National Council of Teachers of English, April 12, 2022.
52 Chris Papst, "Leaked documents show Baltimore high schoolers perform math, reading at grade school level," WBFF Fox 45, June 2, 2021.
53 Chester Finn, "Whole Language Lives On: The Illusion of Balanced Reading Instruction," Thomas B. Fordham Foundation, October 2000.
54 twitter.com/HansFBader/status/1558963962745610248
55 David Boaz, "Phonics, Failure, and the Public Schools," Cato Institute, August 11, 2022.
56 Jessica Lee, "Did Oregon Officials Say 'Showing Work' in Math Class Is White Supremacism?" *Snopes*, February 22, 2021.
57 Diane Ravitch, "Ethnomathematics," Brookings Institution, June 20, 2005.
58 Williamson M. Evers, "California Leftists Try to Cancel Math Class," *Wall Street Journal*, May 18, 2021.
59 Faith Bottum, "California's Weapons of Math Destruction," *Wall Street Journal*, August 18, 2023.
60 Williamson M. Evers, "California Math Framework: Proven Methods vs. Political Ideology," Independent Institute, July 22, 2023.
61 Brian Stieglitz, "US educators slam math workbook that claims it's racist to ask students to get the right answer," *Daily Mail*, June 23, 2021.

[62] Randi Weingarten, "Remarks to the AFT TEACH Conference," American Federation of Teachers, July 6, 2021.
[63] Betsy Russell, "Sandra Day O'Connor decries state of U.S. civic ed, says nation needs to 'get busy' and improve it," *Spokesman-Review* (Boise, Idaho), September 11, 2014.
[64] Kayla Jimenez, "US history, civics scores drop for nation's 8th graders. What experts say is to blame," *USA Today*, May 3, 2023.
[65] Sam Long, Lewis Steller, and River Suh, "Gender-Inclusive Biology: A framework in action," *The Science Teacher*, September/October 2021.
[66] Spencer Lindquist, "National Science Teachers Association's 'Gender-Inclusive Biology' Calls Women 'People with Ovaries,'" Breitbart News, May 20, 2022.
[67] Erika Sanzi, "Parents are sounding the alarm on woke education for good reason," *Washington Examiner*, April 25, 2022.
[68] Christopher Rufo, "In Portland, the Sexual Revolution Starts in Kindergarten," *City Journal*, July 27, 2022.
[69] Christopher Rufo, "San Francisco Unified School District facilitates secret child sexual transitions and allows students to identify as 'it,'" *City Journal*, September 22, 2022.
[70] Christopher Rufo, "Concealing Radicalism — Michigan's Department of Education encourages teachers to facilitate child sexual transitions without parental consent," *City Journal*, September 14, 2022.
[71] Reagan Reese, "'Person Who Produces Sperm': Vermont School District Will No Longer Use Gendered Terms in Sex Ed Classes," *Daily Caller*, April 26, 2023.
[72] Christopher Rufo, "Sexual Liberation in Public Schools," Manhattan Institute, July 20, 2022.
[73] Jack Phillips, "'Let Them Die': Top NAACP, PTA Official Attacks Anti-Critical Race Theory Protesters," *Epoch Times*, July 16, 2021.
[74] Laura Meckler, "National school board group says it wrongly took sides in political debate," *Washington Post*, May 21, 2022.
[75] Callie Patteson, "School board org wanted Biden to send National Guard to districts: report," *New York Post*, May 23, 2022.
[76] "Justice Department Addresses Violent Threats Against School Officials and Teachers," Justice Department Office of Public Affairs, October 4, 2021.
[77] Susan Ferrechio, "FBI comes calling, terrifies mom of three who spoke out at school board meeting," *Washington Times*, May 12, 2022.
[78] Jeremiah Poff, "FBI opened multiple investigations into protesting parents, GOP lawmakers say," *Washington Examiner*, May 12, 2022.
[79] Laura Meckler, "National School Boards Association stumbles into politics and is blasted apart," *Washington Post*, January 13, 2022.
[80] Nicole Goodkind, "Democrats have wanted to spend billions on pre-K for years," *Fortune*, January 29, 2022.
[81] Peter Gray, "Research Reveals Long-Term Harm of State Pre-K Program," *Psychology Today*, 2021.
[82] "A Proclamation on American Education Week 2022," White House Briefing Room, November 10, 2022.
[83] twitter.com/POTUS/status/1676650904655634448
[84] Lydia Saad, "Private Schools First, Public Schools Last in K-12 Ratings," Gallup News, August 21, 2017.

85 J.D. Tuccille, "McAuliffe vs. Youngkin Is a Glimpse at Education Battles to Come," *Reason*, November 1, 2021.
86 George Will, "Taking Back Education," *Washington Post*, August 26, 1993.
87 Dale Russakoff, "Book Review: 'The Death of Public School,' by Cara Fitzpatrick," *New York Times*, September 11, 2023.
88 Laura Williams, "Take the Money and Run: Taxpayers in AZ Will Fund Students, not Schools," American Institute for Economic Research, July 26, 2022.
89 J.D. Tuccille, "North Carolina Governor Declares a 'State of Emergency' Over Education Debate," *Reason*, May 26, 2023.
90 Kevin Huffman, "Homeschooling during the coronavirus will set back a generation of children," *Washington Post*, March 27, 2020.
91 Erin O'Donnell, "The Risks of Homeschooling," *Harvard Magazine*, May/June 2020.
92 Elizabeth Bartholet, "Homeschooling: Parent Rights Absolutism vs. Child Rights to Education & Protection," *Arizona Law Review*, 2020.
93 Carolyn Thompson, "Homeschooling surged during the pandemic. As schools reopen, many parents continue to educate their children," *Fortune*, April 14, 2022.
94 Eric Boehm, "The Pandemic Set Off a Homeschooling Boom," *Reason*, January 28, 2022.
95 Vivian Jones, "Harvard's home-schooling ban: the dangers of educational totalitarianism," *Washington Examiner*, April 29, 2020.
96 "Remarks by President Biden and First Lady Jill Biden at the 2023 National and State Teachers of the Year Celebration," White House Briefing Room, April 24, 2023.
97 twitter.com/tomselliott/status/1658537748809015313
98 Jonathan Turley, "Public education without students?" *The Hill*, January 28, 2023.
99 twitter.com/SecCardona/status/1659652692107468811
100 Madeleine Hubbard, "Education Secretary says he doesn't 'respect' parents thinking 'they know what's right for kids,'" JustTheNews.com, September 24, 2023.
101 twitter.com/AFTunion/status/1530241409478971393

Chapter 7

1 *City of St. Paul v. Robert Morris*, 258 Minn. 467 (1960).
2 *Youngstown Sheet & Tube Co. v. Sawyer*, 343 U.S. 579 (1952).
3 *American Banana Co. v. United Fruit Co.*, 213 U.S. 347, 356 (1907).
4 *Greene v. McElroy*, 79 S. Ct. 1400 (1907).
5 U.S. Treasury Department Office of Economic Policy, White House Council of Economic Advisers, and the U.S. Labor Department, "Occupational Licensing: A Framework for Policymakers," July 2015.
6 Shobhana Chandra, "It's the anti-Uber job market and it still has a grip on America," Bloomberg News, May 16, 2016.
7 Lisa Knepper, Darwyyn Deyo, Kyle Sweetland, Jason Tiezzi, and Alec Mena, "License to Work: A National Study of Burdens from Occupational Licensing," Institute for Justice, November 2022.
8 Chris Orchard, "Somerville Fortune Tellers Now Need a License and Background Check," Patch.com, April 16, 2012.

[9] Nicole Jones, "Did Fortune Tellers See This Coming? Spiritual Counseling, Professional Speech, and the First Amendment," Social Science Research Network, February 15, 2014.

[10] Luke Hilgemann and Russ Latino, "Does the Public Need Protection from Rogue Auctioneers?" *Wall Street Journal*, April 28, 2017.

[11] Shelley Shelton, "Creative license: When is a massage not a massage?" *Arizona Daily Star*, November 25, 2007.

[12] "Stop Unlicensed Massage Therapy," MoveOn.org.

[13] Michael Ganci, "Four Women Arrested in Massapequa Massage, Bribery Incident," Patch.com, October 6, 2013.

[14] Lindsey Blest and Hurubie Meko, "A massage parlor sting led to more training for a detective," *Lancaster Online*, July 8, 2019.

[15] Prachi Gupta, "This Woman Fought for 20 Years to Change the Rules for Hair Braiding in Texas. This Week She Scored a Major Victory," *Cosmopolitan*, June 10, 2015.

[16] Radley Balko, "Federal appeals court: Stop using SWAT-style raids for regulatory inspections," *Washington Post*, September 19, 2014.

[17] Robert McNamara, "Free to Speak for a Living," Institute for Justice, *Liberty and Law*, October 2018.

[18] Matt Cohen, "Court Rules D.C.'s Tour Guide Regulations Are 'Unconstitutional,'" DCist, June 27, 2014.

[19] Scott Shackford, "Judge Rules Florida Can Require a License to Give Out Diet Tips," *Reason*, July 18, 2019.

[20] Brian Doherty, "Victory over North Carolina Attempt to Ban Giving Unlicensed Paleo Dietary Advice Online," *Reason*, February 18, 2015.

[21] Altaf Saadi, "Larry Nassar isn't the only doctor accused of molesting patients. We need to do more to stop it," *STAT News*, February 5, 2018.

[22] Susan Schmidt, "Md. Moves to Punish Bad Doctors; Bill Would Toughen Physician Discipline," *Washington Post*, April 7, 1988.

[23] Tracy Weber and Charles Ornstein, "Board knew of nurses' criminal records but took years to act," *Los Angeles Times*, November 1, 2008.

[24] Andrea Estes, "Scores of sex offenders have state licenses to be electricians, manicurists, and more. The official who found out got fired," *Boston Globe*, December 14, 2019.

[25] Andrea Estes, "FBI investigating state's licensing of massage therapists with fake credentials," *Boston Globe*, February 20, 2020.

[26] Brian Meehan and Edward Timmons, "Reviving the American dream is going to require licensing reform," *The Hill*, April 19, 2018.

[27] J.D. Tuccille, "Can Even the President Reverse the Destructive Trend Toward Occupational Licensing?" *Reason*, August 18, 2015.

[28] U.S. Treasury Department Office of Economic Policy, White House Council of Economic Advisers, and the U.S. Labor Department, "Occupational Licensing: A Framework for Policymakers," July 2015.

[29] Alexander Acosta and Dennis Daugaard, "Make It Easier to Work Without a License," *Wall Street Journal*, January 8, 2018.

[30] *Ashish Patel et al. v. Texas Dept. of Licensing and Regulation*, Texas Supreme Court, No. 12-0657, June 26, 2015.

[31] Justin Gallagher, "Red Light Cameras May Not Make Streets Safer," *Scientific American*, August 16, 2018.

[32] John Moore Williams, "Are Red-Light Cameras Actually Causing Accidents?" Esurance.com, March 18, 2013.

[33] Dan King, "Red Light Cameras: Unfair, Unsafe, Unnecessary," *National Review*, January 11, 2018.

[34] Noah Pransky, "10 [News] investigates, discovers short yellow lights," WTSP, June 27, 2014.

[35] Ibid.

[36] Chris Papst, "Montgomery County turns off red-light camera responsible for $350K in fines," ABC 7, December 8, 2016.

[37] Jeff Zurschmeide, "Red-light cameras are producing profits more than protecting drivers," Digital Trends, March 12, 2016.

[38] James Bovard, "Red Light Robberies Across America," American Institute for Economic Research, September 14, 2021.

[39] Ari Ashe, "Rockville sees massive jump in red-light camera tickets," WTOP, February 11, 2013.

[40] "Government Transparency — Caution: Red Light Cameras Ahead," U.S. PIRG Education Fund, October 27, 2011.

[41] John Moore Williams, "Are Red-Light Cameras Actually Causing Accidents?" Esurance.com, March 18, 2013.

[42] Ashley Halsey, "New York Avenue at Bladensburg: Hit the gas, and speed cameras hit back," *Washington Post*, June 26, 2010.

[43] Ashley Halsey, "Single District speed camera: 116,734 tickets worth $11.6 million," *Washington Post*, October 23, 2012.

[44] "Federal Judge Declines to Intervene in DC Speed Camera Lawsuit," TheNewspaper.com, December 16, 2020.

[45] Ashley Halsey, "D.C. is the Wild West when enforcing tickets for traffic violators, audit finds," *Washington Post*, September 8, 2014.

[46] Justin Moyer, "One D.C. stop-sign camera brought in $1.3 million in tickets in 2 years," *Washington Post*, May 31, 2022.

[47] James Bovard, "'Governing as Looting' in Washington and Beyond," American Institute for Economic Research, May 18, 2021.

[48] Hannah Cox, "How Washington, DC Carjacked an Elderly Couple," Foundation for Economic Education, May 14, 2021.

[49] Anna Spiegel, "DC Mayor Hopes to Triple the Number of Traffic Enforcement Cameras," *Washington Post*, March 24, 2022.

[50] "DC Report Finds Racial Bias in Speed Camera Use," TheNewspaper.com, July 20, 2018.

[51] Jalonda Hill and Phylicia Brown, "Buffalo must return $1.84 million 'mined' from school zone speed camera program," *Buffalo News*, September 15, 2021.

[52] Emily Hopkins and Melissa Sanchez, "Chicago's 'Race-Neutral' Traffic Cameras Ticket Black and Latino Drivers the Most," ProPublica, January 11, 2022.

[53] Jeff Zurschmeide, "Red-light cameras are producing profits more than protecting drivers," Digital Trends, March 12, 2016.

[54] Robert Herguth and Tina Sfondeles, "Illinois comptroller calls red-light camera program 'broken and morally corrupt,' plans to halt ticket collections," *Chicago Sun-Times*, January 6, 2020.

[55] *Brief of Amicus Curiae National Cattlemen's Association and Affiliated Organizations in Support of Petitioners, Sackett v. EPA*, April 18, 2022.

[56] James Bovard, "More Wetlands Purgatory for American Landowners," American Institute for Economic Research, September 3, 2021.

[57] *National Mining Association v. U.S. Army Corps of Engineers*, 145 F.3d 1399 (1998).

[58] *Brief of Fourteen National Agricultural Organizations as Amici Curiae in Support of Petitioners, Sackett v. EPA*, April 2022.

[59] *Rapanos v. U.S.*, 547 U.S. 715 (2006).

[60] *Brief of Fourteen National Agricultural Organizations as Amici Curiae in Support of Petitioners, Sackett v. EPA*, April 2022.

[61] Debra Cassens Weiss, "Alito Concurrence Decries 'Notoriously Unclear' Clean Water Act in Landowner Rights Case," *ABA Journal*, March 21, 2012.

[62] Eric Lipton and Michael Shear, "E.P.A. Broke Law with Social Media Push for Water Rule, Auditor Finds," *New York Times*, December 14, 2015.

[63] "Environmental Protection Agency — Application of Publicity or Propaganda and Anti-Lobbying Provisions," Government Accountability Office, December 14, 2015.

[64] Juliet Eilperin and Abby Phillip, "Trump directs rollback of Obama-era water rule he calls 'destructive and horrible,'" *Washington Post*, February 28, 2017.

[65] "EPA and Army Deliver on President Trump's Promise to Issue the Navigable Waters Protection Rule — A New Definition of WOTUS," Environmental Protection Agency Press Office, January 23, 2020.

[66] Annie Snider, "Biden EPA to reverse Trump's sweeping Clean Water Act rollback," Politico, June 9, 2021.

[67] Scott Dance, "EPA broadens protections for U.S. waterways, reversing Trump," *Washington Post*, December 30, 2022.

[68] Todd Neeley, "Sacketts See Support on Wetlands Case," *Progressive Farmer*, April 22, 2022.

[69] James Bovard, "Supreme Court strikes blow against bureaucratic tyranny in EPA case," *New York Post*, May 26, 2023.

[70] *Sackett v. Environmental Protection Agency*, 598 U.S. (2023).

[71] "Remarks Commemorating the First Anniversary of the Signing of the Americans with Disabilities Act of 1990," *Public Papers of the Presidents, Vol. 27*, July 26, 1991, p. 1042.

[72] "Proclamation 6708 — Anniversary of the Americans with Disabilities Act, 1994," *Public Papers of the Presidents*, July 26, 1994.

[73] Congressional Research Service, "The Americans with Disabilities Act: Supreme Court Decisions," October 14, 2008. Also, see: Francis P. Alvarez and Joseph J. Lynett, "President Bush Signs Landmark Amendments to the Americans with Disabilities Act," EGBlaw.com, September 25, 2008.

[74] Congressional Research Service, "The Americans with Disabilities Act: Supreme Court Decisions," October 14, 2008.

[75] Mark Pulliam, "The ADA Litigation Monster," *City Journal*, Spring 2017.

[76] Julia Marsh and Ruth Brown, "Sleep apnea sufferers claim discrimination after losing jobs," *New York Post*, February 8, 2018.

[77] Ibid.

[78] Fox Rothschild, LLP, "Fired Sleep Apnea Sufferer Awarded $1 Million By Jury," Employment Discrimination Report, October 18, 2014.

[79] Eugene Volokh, "Short Circuit: A roundup of recent federal court decisions," *Washington Post*, June 27, 2016.

[80] Helen Jung, "Lawsuit by Gresham police officer who was fired for drunken driving dismissed," *The Oregonian*, August 12, 2014.

[81] Becky Jacobs, "Ex-Lake County cop convicted of hit-and-run sues sheriff's department," *Chicago Tribune*, May 16, 2018.

[82] Mario Loyola and Richard A. Epstein, "The Disabling of America," *American Interest*, June 2013.

[83] Mark Pulliam, "In Austin, the ADA Lawsuit Mill Grinds On," Misrule of Law, March 3, 2018.

[84] Mosi Secret, "Disabilities Act Prompts Flood of Suits Some Cite as Unfair," *New York Times*, April 16, 2012.

[85] Melanie Payne, "Are ADA lawsuit plaintiffs hucksters or heroes?" *News-Press* (Ft. Myers, Florida), March 30, 2017.

[86] Abigail Sterling and Allen Martin, "Serial Plaintiff Turns California ADA Lawsuits into a Lucrative Cottage Industry," KPIX 5, August 2, 2021.

[87] James Bovard, "After 30 Years, Did the Disabilities Act Work?" American Institute for Economic Research, July 22, 2020.

[88] "Pornhub Sued — You Make it Hard for Deaf to Enjoy!!!" TMZ, January 16, 2020.

[89] Robert Barnes, "Do protections for people with disabilities apply online? Domino's asks high court," *Washington Post*, July 20, 2019.

[90] Steven Melendez, "Domino's Pizza was just dealt a Supreme Court blow that could reshape the ADA in the digital era," Fast Company, October 7, 2019.

[91] John Mac Ghlionn, "Doctor who helped broaden autism spectrum 'very sorry' for over-diagnosis," *New York Post*, April 24, 2023.

[92] Ibid.

[93] "Psychiatric Disorders and the Americans with Disabilities Act: Reducing the Stigma of Mental Illness in the Workplace," *DLJ* Online.

[94] Douglas Belkin, "Colleges Bend the Rules for More Students, Give Them Extra Help," *Wall Street Journal*, May 24, 2018.

[95] American College Health Association, National College Health Assessment (2019).

[96] Alexa Schwerha, "Universities compounded the student mental health crisis during the pandemic," *Campus Reform*, August 29, 2022.

[97] Eric Boehm, "Department of Education Will Launch Investigations Targeting States that Banned Schools from Mandating Masks," *Reason*, August 30, 2021.

[98] *E.T. et al. v. Kenneth Paxton, Texas Attorney General*, Case: 21-51083, July 25, 2022.

[99] Eric Boehm, "Department of Education Will Launch Investigations Targeting States that Banned Schools from Mandating Masks," *Reason*, August 30, 2021.

[100] Daron Acemoglu and Joshua Angrist, "Consequences of Employment Protection? The Case of the Americans with Disabilities Act," NBER Working Paper No. 6670 (1998).

[101] Wendy Lu, "How Equity Is Lost When Companies Hire Only Workers with Disabilities," *New York Times*, July 23, 2020.

[102] Melanie Payne, "Are ADA lawsuit plaintiffs hucksters or heroes?" *News-Press* (Ft. Myers, Florida), March 30, 2017.

[103] Jay Schweikert, "Justice Gorsuch on Overcriminalization and Arbitrary Prosecution," Cato Institute, April 17, 2018.

[104] Paul M. Bator, "What Is Wrong with the Supreme Court?" *University of Pittsburgh Law Review*, Spring 1990, p. 673.

[105] Benjamin Constant, *Political Writings* (Cambridge: Cambridge University Press, 1988 [1815]), p. 291.
[106] Friedrich Hayek, *The Road to Serfdom* (Chicago: University of Chicago Press, 1944).

Chapter 8

[1] *Wickard v. Filburn*, 317 U.S. 111 (1942).
[2] *Lemon v. Kurtzman*, 403 U.S. 602, 621 (1970).
[3] Emily Gilbert, "Money as a 'weapons system' and the entrepreneurial way of war," *Critical Military Studies*, July 13, 2015.
[4] James Bovard, "Unfair Housing Acts," *American Spectator*, April 1999. Also, "Cuomo Says HUD Seeking to End Mortgage Lending Discrimination," HUD press release, August 6, 1998.
[5] "President Bush Signs American Dream Downpayment Act of 2003," White House Office of the Press Secretary, December 16, 2003.
[6] Jo Becker, Sheryl Gay Stolberg, and Stephen Labaton, "Bush drive for home ownership fueled housing bubble," *New York Times*, December 21, 2008.
[7] Peter Wallison, "Hey, Barney Frank: The Government Did Cause the Housing Crisis," *The Atlantic*, October 21, 2016.
[8] James Bovard, "Nothing Down: The Bush Administration's Wrecking-Ball Benevolence," *Barron's*, August 23, 2004.
[9] Jo Becker, Sheryl Gay Stolberg, and Stephen Labaton, "Bush drive for home ownership fueled housing bubble," *New York Times*, December 21, 2008.
[10] Peter Wallison, "Hey, Barney Frank: The Government Did Cause the Housing Crisis," *The Atlantic*, October 21, 2016.
[11] Jo Becker, Sheryl Gay Stolberg, and Stephen Labaton, "Bush drive for home ownership fueled housing bubble," *New York Times*, December 21, 2008.
[12] Lisa Lerer, "Fannie, Freddie spent $200M to buy influence," Politico, July 16, 2008.
[13] Don Layton, "The Homeownership Rate and Housing Finance Policy," Joint Center for Housing Studies, Harvard University, August 2021.
[14] Ylan Q. Mui, "For black Americans, financial damage from subprime implosion is likely to last," *Washington Post*, July 8, 2012.
[15] Mark Calabria, "Coming Full Circle on Mortgage Finance," Urban Institute Housing Finance Policy Center, April 21, 2016.
[16] Susan Schmidt and Maurice Tamman, "Housing Push for Hispanics Spawns Wave of Foreclosures," *Wall Street Journal*, January 5, 2009.
[17] "The Racial Wealth Gap: Latinos," Center for Global Policy Solutions, April 2014.
[18] Jonathan H. Adler, "D.C. Circuit concludes Recovery Act bars judicial review of suits against FHFA," *Washington Post*, February 21, 2017.
[19] Peter Wallison, "Hey, Barney Frank: The Government Did Cause the Housing Crisis," *The Atlantic*, October 21, 2016.
[20] Damian Paletta, "Federal government has dramatically expanded exposure to risky mortgages," *Washington Post*, October 2, 2019.
[21] Howard Husock, "Build Back Better's big breaks for illegal immigrants, drug dealers would hurt public housing," *New York Post*, November 11, 2021.
[22] James Bovard, "Biden's mortgage 'equity' will screw up the homebuying market," *New York Post*, April 25, 2023.

23 Katherine Fung, "Biden Raises Costs for Homebuyers With Good Credit to Help Risky Borrowers," *Newsweek*, April 21, 2023.

24 "The Impact of Source of Income Laws on Voucher Utilization and Locational Outcomes," HUD Office of Policy Development, February 2011.

25 U.S. General Accounting Office, "Section 8 Subsidized Housing — Some Observations on its High Rents, Costs, and Inequities," June 6, 1980.

26 Dawn Wotapka, "No More 'Slum, Slumming' for Section 8 Recipients," *Wall Street Journal*, August 2, 2010.

27 Alby Gallun, "CHA pays luxury rents; With 'supervouchers,' poor families can live in the city's priciest apartment buildings," *Crain's Chicago Business*, July 26, 2014.

28 Jennifer Levitz, "Public Housing Agencies Push to Impose Time Limits, Work Requirements for Aid Recipients," *Wall Street Journal*, May 6, 2013.

29 Brian A. Jacob and Jens Ludwig, "The Effects of Housing Assistance on Labor Supply: Evidence from a Voucher Lottery," *American Economic Review*, February 2012.

30 James Bovard, "How Baltimore Became Pottersville," *USA Today*, May 25, 2015.

31 Ibid.

32 Kim Horner, "Thousands line up, stampede to get on wait list for housing vouchers in Dallas County," *Dallas News*, July 2011.

33 Geetha Suresh and Gennaro F. Vito, "Homicide Patterns and Public Housing: The Case of Louisville, KY (1989–2007)," *Homicide Studies*, November 2009.

34 Dave Gossett, "Public housing questions asked," *Herald-Star* (Steubenville, Ohio), November 20, 2008.

35 Press Release 11-002, "Indianapolis Housing Agency Announces Final Results of U.S. Department of Justice Grant Targeting Violent Crime and Federally Assisted Housing in the City of Indianapolis," Indianapolis Housing Agency, June 5, 2011.

36 Tim Novak, Chris Fusco, Mick Dumke, and Brett Chase, "CHA danger zones — a Sun-Times/BGA Watchdogs special report," *Chicago Sun-Times*, September 14, 2016.

37 "Moving to Opportunity — Interim Impacts Evaluation," U.S. Department of Housing and Urban Development Office of Policy Development and Research, June 2003.

38 Jillian Carr and Vijetha Koppa, "The Effect of Housing Vouchers on Crime: Evidence from a Lottery," Texas A&M University, 2017.

39 Kristian Hernández, "Biden Wants to Offer More Housing Vouchers. Many Landlords Won't Accept Them," PewTrusts.Org, May 12, 2021.

40 Glenn Minnis, "Ald. Arena's Section 8 development means more crime, lower property values in Jefferson Park, says expert," *Chicago City Wire*, March 17, 2017.

41 Whet Moser, "Did the Destruction of Chicago's Public Housing Decrease Violent Crime, Or Just Move It Elsewhere?" *Chicago*, April 5, 2012.

42 Zeta Cross, "Landlords oppose bill to expand Section 8 housing in Illinois," Center Square, March 12, 2022.

43 James Bovard, "Raising Hell in Subsidized Housing," *Wall Street Journal*, August 18, 2011.

44 Ibid.

45 Annie Sciacca, "In costly Bay Area, even six-figure salaries are considered 'low income,'" *Mercury News* (San Jose, California), April 22, 2017.

46 *New York Times*, July 21, 1930.

[47] *New York Times*, March 12, 1933.

[48] Sharon LaFraniere, "'Windfall' Subsidies for Just Peanuts," *Washington Post*, June 14, 1993.

[49] James Bovard, "Politicians and Peanut Pilfering," *Washington Times*, August 25, 2016.

[50] James Bovard, "Oreo Closure Proof of Losing Trump Trade Policy," *USA Today*, March 23, 2016.

[51] James Bovard, "Rubio's Sweet but Wasted Victory," *USA Today*, August 12, 2015.

[52] James Bovard, "Why the California Raisins Have Stopped Singing," *Wall Street Journal*, May 26, 2014.

[53] James Bovard, "Fight for the Right to Grow Raisins," *USA Today*, April 5, 2013.

[54] *Horne v. U.S. Department of Agriculture*, 576 U.S. 350 (2015).

[55] Editorial, "Trump's trade war has cost billions and ensnared farmers in federal dependency," *St. Louis Post-Dispatch*, August 1, 2020.

[56] Ryan McCrimmon, "'Here's your check': Trump's massive payouts to farmers will be hard to pull back," Politico, July 14, 2020.

[57] Alan Rappeport, "Trump Funnels Record Subsidies to Farmers Ahead of Election Day," *New York Times*, October 12, 2020.

[58] Anne Schechinger, "Farm Subsidies Ballooned Under Trump — President Biden Should Not Make the Same Mistakes," Environmental Working Group, February 24, 2021.

[59] Ibid.

[60] Liz Knueven and Rickie Houston, "The average net worth in America by age, race, education, and location," *Business Insider*, June 15, 2022.

[61] "Inspector General, Overlap and Duplication in Food and Nutrition Service's Nutrition Programs," U.S. Department of Agriculture, June 2013.

[62] "Remarks by President Biden at the White House Conference on Hunger, Nutrition, and Health," White House Briefing Room, September 28, 2022.

[63] James Bovard, "Feeding Everybody," *Policy Review*, Fall 1983.

[64] Eli Saslow, "In Florida, a food-stamp recruiter deals with wrenching choices," *Washington Post*, March 23, 2013.

[65] "Supplemental Nutrition Assistance Program: Improved Oversight of State Eligibility Expansions Needed," U.S. Government Accountability Office, August 2, 2012.

[66] Jennifer Bleyer, "Hipsters on food stamps," *Salon*, March 15, 2010.

[67] Quoted in James Bovard, "The Food Stamp Crime Wave," *Wall Street Journal*, June 23, 2011.

[68] "Trump administration submits proposal to end food stamps 'loophole,'" *New York Post*, November 28, 2019.

[69] Alvin Powell, "Patterns of obesity prove resilient," *Harvard Gazette*, November 25, 2015.

[70] M. Pia Chaparro, Gail Harrison, May Wang, Edmund Seto, and Anne Pebley, "The unhealthy food environment does not modify the association between obesity and participation in the Supplemental Nutrition Assistance Program (SNAP) in Los Angeles County," BMC Public Health, January 14, 2017.

[71] Honor Whiteman, "Death risk may be higher for participants of U.S. food assistance program," *Medical News Today*, January 21, 2017.

72 Luma Akil and Anwar Ahmad, "Effects of Socioeconomic Factors on Obesity Rates in Four Southern States and Colorado," *Ethnicity & Disease*, Winter 2011.

73 Patricia Waldron, "Study shows banning soda purchases using food stamps would reduce obesity and type-2 diabetes," *Stanford Medicine*, June 2, 2014.

74 Robert Paarlberg, Dariush Mozaffarian, Renata Micha, and Carolyn Chelius, "Keeping Soda in SNAP: Understanding the Other Iron Triangle," *Society*, August 2018.

75 Hilary Hoynes and Diane Schanzenbach, "Work Incentives and the Food Stamp Program," *Journal of Public Economics*, 2010.

76 Mike Pomranz, "SDA Officially Drops SNAP Benefit Rule That Would Have Disqualified 700,000 Americans," *Yahoo News*, April 2, 2021.

77 twitter.com/RepBowman/status/1647951016988405760

78 "Thrifty Food Plan, 2021," Food and Nutrition Service, U.S. Department of Agriculture, August 2021.

79 Angela Rachidi, "Biden ignores Congress to increase SNAP," *The Hill*, August 19, 2021.

80 Jason DeParle, "Biden Administration Prompts Largest Permanent Increase in Food Stamps," *New York Times*, August 15, 2021.

81 "Children who eat school lunches more likely to be overweight," *Michigan Medicine*, March 13, 2010.

82 "Remarks by the President and First Lady at the Signing of the Healthy, Hunger-Free Kids Act," White House Office of the Press Secretary, December 13, 2010.

83 James Bovard, "Why expand school free food programs?" *USA Today*, September 26, 2012. More recently, Bettina Elias Siegel, "Why There Is So Much Sugar in Your Kid's School Breakfast," CivilEats.com, September 24, 2015.

84 "School Nutrition Dietary Assessment Study-IV, Summary of Findings, Office of Research and Analysis," U.S. Department of Agriculture, November 2012.

85 James Bovard, "Biden's cluelessness on hunger, food aid epitomized by gaffe on dead GOP rep," *New York Post*, September 28, 2022.

86 Mary Kay Fox, Elizabeth C. Gearan, and Colin Schwartz, "Added Sugars in School Meals and the Diets of School-Age Children," *Nutrients*, February 2021.

87 "Statement by the President on the Release of the Annual Household Food Security," White House Office of the Press Secretary, November 16, 2009.

88 David S. Ludwig, Susan J. Blumenthal, and Walter C. Willett, "Opportunities to Reduce Childhood Hunger and Obesity," *JAMA*, December 26, 2012.

89 "Food Insecurity and Hunger in the United States — An Assessment of the Measure," National Academies of Science, 2006.

90 "Statement by the President on the Release of the Annual Household Food Security," White House Office of the Press Secretary, November 16, 2009.

91 Matt Margolis, "Biden Admin Sued for Holding School Lunch Money Hostage Over Transgender Policies," PJ Media, July 27, 2022.

92 Robert Schmad, "Federal judge halts Biden's Title IX changes," *Campus Reform*, July 27, 2022.

93 Gary Taubes, "Unintended Consequences, Special Interests, and Our Problem with Sugar," Cato Institute, January 9, 2017.

94 "Cost of College Degree in U.S. Has Increased 1,120 Percent in 30 Years, Report Says," *Huffington Post*, August 15, 2012.

95 "Candidates Differ on Energy Policy," WSFA.com, July 23, 2008.

[96] Quoted in William Bennett, "Stop subsidizing soaring college costs," CNN.com, March 22, 2012.

[97] Kelley Beaucar Vlahos, "Study blames college tuition arms race on schools addicted to federal aid," Fox News, July 10, 2015.

[98] Editorial, "The Rolling Student Loan Bailout," *Wall Street Journal*, August 10, 2013.

[99] Editorial, "Obama's Student-Loan Fiasco," *Wall Street Journal*, January 22, 2017.

[100] Josh Mitchell, "New York Fed study faults government aid for letting colleges boost prices," *Wall Street Journal*, August 2, 2015.

[101] Neal McCluskey, "End the student loan-acy," *The Hill*, August 10, 2022.

[102] Hans Bader, "Biden Student Loan Write-Off Plan Will Cost over a Trillion Dollars, Not $300 Billion," Liberty Unyielding, August 24, 2022.

[103] twitter.com/LHSummers/status/1561701543644127232

[104] Catherine Rampell, "Biden's student debt plan is a Democratic version of 'trickle-down' economics," *Washington Post*, August 25, 2022.

[105] David Stockman, "Covid Invoked for More Redistribution from Workers to Doctors and Lawyers," Brownstone Institute, August 25, 2022.

[106] Daniel Dale, "Fact check: Biden falsely claims he got student debt forgiveness passed by Congress," CNN, October 24, 2022.

[107] James Bovard, "Biden bribed young voters with student loan bailouts he knew he couldn't give," *New York Post*, November 14, 2022.

[108] Catherine Rampell, "Biden's student debt jubilee likely hurt those it intended to help," *Washington Post*, June 30, 2023.

[109] "FACT SHEET: White House Calls on Congress to Provide Additional Support for Ukraine," White House Briefing Room, April 28, 2022.

[110] Victor Pickard and Timothy Neff, "Strengthen our democracy by funding public media," *Columbia Journalism Review*, June 2, 2021.

[111] Joshua Darr, "Government subsidies to save local news," NiemanLab, December 2021.

[112] James Bovard, "Scott Walker's Stadium Socialism," *USA Today*, April 10, 2015.

[113] "How George W. Bush scored big with the Texas Rangers," Center for Public Integrity, January 17, 2000.

[114] Ian Schwartz, "Biden: 'I Don't Want To Hear Any More Of These Lies About Reckless Spending,'" Real Clear Politics, June 14, 2022.

[115] Bertrand de Jouvenel, *The Ethics of Redistribution* (Indianapolis: Liberty Fund Press, 1989 [1950]), p. 73.

[116] John Stuart Mill, *Utilitarianism, Liberty, and Representative Government* (New York: E.P. Dutton, 1951 [1861]).

[117] Friedrich Hayek, *The Constitution of Liberty* (Chicago: University of Chicago, 1972 [1960]), p. 109.

[118] twitter.com/reverendwarnock/status/1345082524402393088

[119] Kate Sullivan, "Biden says electing Georgia's Ossoff and Warnock would lead to $2,000 stimulus checks," CNN, January 4, 2021.

[120] Plutarch, "Life of Cato the Younger," in *The Lives of the Noble Grecians and Romans* (New York: Modern Library, 1935 [early 2nd century AD]), p. 943.

[121] G. Warren Nutter, *Political Economy and Freedom* (Indianapolis: Liberty Press, 1983), p. 52.

Chapter 9

[1] Tim Cushing, "Third Circuit Says TSA Officers Can Be Sued Directly for Abuses and Rights Violations," Techdirt, September 6, 2019.

[2] Leslie Miller, "Marshal mantra: Dominate, Intimidate, Control," Associated Press, September 21, 2002.

[3] Ed O'Keefe, "TSA using pizza boxes to recruit new workers," *Washington Post*, July 14, 2010.

[4] "Transportation Security Administration's Checked Baggage Screener Training and Certification," Department of Homeland Security Inspector General, August 2003.

[5] James Bovard, "Bag It," *New York Times*, August 18, 2004.

[6] Leslie Miller, "Reports: Airport Screeners Still Do Poorly," Associated Press, April 15, 2005.

[7] *Federal Register*, February 17, 2002, p. 8339.

[8] James Bovard, "After pointlessly groping countless Americans, the TSA is keeping a secret watchlist of those who fight back," *Los Angeles Times*, May 28, 2018.

[9] Brock Meeks, "9/11 Panel's Report Critical of FAA," NBC News, January 27, 2004.

[10] "National Commission on Terrorist Attacks Upon the United States," January 27, 2004.

[11] Matthew Wald and John Schwartz, "Expansion Sank Terror Screening Program, Officials Say," *New York Times*, September 19, 2004.

[12] Joe Sharkey, "Many Women Say Airport Pat-Downs Are a Humiliation," *New York Times*, November 23, 2004.

[13] Ron Marsico, "Airport screeners fail to see most test bombs," *Seattle Times*, October 28, 2006.

[14] Thomas Frank, "Most Fake Bombs Missed by Screeners," *USA Today*, October 19, 2007.

[15] "Investigation Concerning TSA's Compromise of Covert Testing Methods," Department of Homeland Security Office of Inspector General, March 2009.

[16] "Petition for Suspension of TSA Full Body Scanner Program," letter from ACLU to DHS Secretary Janet Napolitano, April 21, 2010.

[17] Michael Scott, "False Choices and Airport Security," *CounterPunch*, November 24, 2010.

[18] Janice Kephart, "State Dept. Misled Us Again about the Christmas Day Bomber's Visa," Center for Immigration Studies, March 25, 2010.

[19] Derek Wallbank, "MSP airport security: Whole-body scanners are likely, but not everyone's on board," *MinnPost*, February 4, 2010.

[20] Jason Harrington, "Dear America, I Saw You Naked," Politico, January 30, 2014.

[21] Roni Caryn Rabin, "X-Ray Scans at Airports Leave Lingering Worries," *New York Times*, August 7, 2012.

[22] Gary Stoller, "Airport screeners get more aggressive with pat-downs," *USA Today*, November 2, 2010.

[23] Editorial, "Shut Up and Be Scanned," *Los Angeles Times*, November 17, 2010.

[24] Ruth Marcus, "Don't touch my junk? Grow up, America," *Washington Post*, November 24, 2010.

25 Sean J. Miller, "House Dem calls for 'beefed up' security, special treatment for members by TSA," *The Hill*, January 9, 2011.
26 Ibid.
27 Hugh Handeyside, "Government Placing Itself at Top of New Air Travel Caste System," American Civil Liberties Union, September 22, 2014.
28 Michael Grabell, "Body Scanners Risking Health to Secure Airports," ProPublica, December 22, 2011.
29 James Bovard, "My too intimate relations with the TSA," *USA Today*, March 21, 2016.
30 Ashley Halsey, "Homeland Security looking for leaker of report on airport checkpoint failures," *Washington Post*, June 9, 2015.
31 Ben Sasse, "There are TSA secrets worse than a 96% fail rate," *USA Today*, June 8, 2015.
32 James Bovard, "Thanksgiving travel: Trump's holiday gift is more invasive airport security," *USA Today*, November 17, 2017.
33 Zainab Merchant, "The TSA searches me every time I travel. I think I know why," *Washington Post*, August 14, 2018.
34 Jonathan Corbett, "TSA: Forced Strip-Search No More Offensive than Voluntarily Using a Locker Room," Professional-Troublemaker.com, August 19, 2019. (Corbett was the lawyer representing Mengert.)
35 Michael Grabell, "TSA Reveals Passenger Complaints... Four Years Later," ProPublica, May 4, 2012.
36 James Bovard, "After pointlessly groping countless Americans, the TSA is keeping a secret watchlist of those who fight back," *Los Angeles Times*, May 28, 2018.
37 Bart Jansen, "TSA keeps list of combative travelers as warning for checkpoint officers," *USA Today*, May 17, 2018.
38 TSA Chief John Pistole, "Letter to the Editor: TSA holds employees to highest standard," *Washington Times*, August 20, 2014.
39 Faiza Patel, "Does TSA Really Need a Watch List for 'Unruly' Travelers?" Brennan Center for Justice, May 23, 2018.
40 Michael S. Schmidt and Eric Lichtblau, "Racial Profiling Rife at Airport, U.S. Officers Say," *New York Times*, August 11, 2012.
41 Steve Strunsky, "Newark airport screeners targeted Mexicans," *Star-Ledger* (Newark, New Jersey), June 12, 2011.
42 "Aviation Security: TSA Does Not Have Valid Evidence Supporting Most of the Revised Behavioral Indicators Used in Its Behavior Detection Activities," Government Accountability Office, July 20, 2017.
43 Michael Grabell, "Air Marshals: Undercover and Under Arrest," ProPublica, November 13, 2008.
44 Kevin Rector, "Baltimore-based air marshal arrested, admits to taking pictures up women's dresses," *Baltimore Sun*, October 18, 2013.
45 Rene Marsh, "Federal Air Marshals allegedly solicited prostitutes," CNN, September 17, 2015.
46 Richard A. Serrano, "Critics say air marshals, much wanted after 9/11, have become 'bored cops' flying first class," *Los Angeles Times*, October 20, 2015.
47 Jana Winter, "TSA says air marshals don't follow 'ordinary' travelers," *Boston Globe*, August 18, 2018.
48 Ibid.

[49] James Bovard, "Have you gained or lost weight? Congrats, TSA is now tracking you for suspicious activity," *USA Today*, July 31, 2018.

[50] Jana Winter, "TSA admits 'Quiet Skies' surveillance snared zero threats," *Boston Globe*, August 3, 2018.

[51] Bart Jansen, "'Very effective': TSA supports controversial surveillance program despite civil-rights complaints," *USA Today*, August 8, 2018.

[52] "TSA Air Marshals for Members of Congress," Judicial Watch, May 26, 2021.

[53] William La Jeunesse and Lee Ross, "Maxine Waters among lawmakers accused of abusing privilege of air marshals on flights," Fox News, May 14, 2021.

[54] Ron Nixon, "Dozens Punished by T.S.A. for Whistle-Blowing Are Later Exonerated," *New York Times*, April 8, 2016.

[55] "U.S. Appeals Court Rules for TSA Screener Who Had Run-In with Flier," *U.S. News*, August 22, 2017.

[56] Alison Wade, "Runner Detained at Security Checkpoint Files Lawsuit," *Runner's World*, February 5, 2015.

[57] *Leuthauser v. U.S.*, No. 22-15402 9th Cir., June 26, 2023.

[58] Edward Hasbrouck, "TSA argues for impunity for checkpoint staff who rape travelers," *Papers, Please!*: The Identity Project, December 6, 2022.

[59] "Woman alleges TSA screener assaulted her," *Virginia Lawyers Weekly*, May 2, 2023.

[60] Joe Dodson, "Fourth Circuit grapples with role of airport security staff," Courthouse News Service, March 7, 2023. Jonathan Corbett was the lawyer for Osmon.

[61] David Koenig, "TSA insider claims agency kept masks from workers at start of outbreak," Associated Press, June 19, 2020.

[62] "Risch, Crapo, Rubio Introduce Bill to Prevent Illegal Immigrants from Using Arrest Warrants as TSA ID," Sen. James Risch, March 24, 2023.

[63] Geoffrey A. Fowler, "Don't smile for surveillance: Why airport face scans are a privacy trap," *Washington Post*, June 10, 2019.

[64] Shira Ovide, "You can say no to a TSA face scan. But even a senator had trouble," *Washington Post*, July 11, 2023.

[65] Geoffrey A. Fowler, "TSA now wants to scan your face at security," *Washington Post*, December 2, 2022.

[66] Ibid.

[67] Jay Stanley, "U.S. Customs and Border Protection's Airport Face Recognition Program," American Civil Liberties Union, February 2020.

[68] Nathan Sheard, "About Face: Ending Government Use of Face Surveillance," Electronic Frontier Foundation, November 22, 2019.

[69] Keith Laing, "Departing TSA chief touts 'risk-based' security approach," *The Hill*, December 8, 2014.

[70] Charles Kenny, "Airport Security Is Killing Us," Bloomberg News, November 19, 2012.

[71] Maria Santos, "The TSA is getting sued over its failure to follow procedures for invasive body scanners," *Washington Examiner*, July 16, 2015.

[72] Nicholas McEntyre, "Miami TSA officers seen stealing from travelers newly released footage," *New York Post*, September 14, 2023.

[73] Nathan Diller and Kinsey Crowley, "TSA agents in Miami appear to steal passenger items; what they're accused of taking," *USA Today*, September 15, 2023.

[74] Chris Edwards, "End the TSA," Cato Institute, May 4, 2014.

Chapter 10

1 *McCulloch v. Maryland* (1819).
2 David Pryor, "The Near Totalitarian I.R.S.," *New York Times*, April 15, 1988.
3 William Roth and William Nixon, *The Power to Destroy* (New York: Atlantic Monthly Press, 1999), p. 32.
4 "The Truth About Frivolous Arguments — Section I (A to C)," Internal Revenue Service, March 2022.
5 J.T. Manhire, "'What Does Voluntary Tax Compliance Mean?' a Government Perspective," *University of Pennsylvania Law Review*, 2015, p. 11.
6 David Burnham, *A Law Unto Itself: The IRS and the Abuse of Power* (New York: Random House, 1989), p. 162.
7 Kelly Heyboer, "Princeton University acquires records from 1944 tax fraud probe involving Lyndon Johnson," *Star-Ledger* (Newark, New Jersey), May 25, 2011.
8 Burnham, *A Law Unto Itself: The IRS and the Abuse of Power* (New York: Random House, 1989), p. 72.
9 "The Internal Revenue Service: An Intelligence Resource and Collector — Intelligence Activities and the Rights of Americans," U.S. Senate Select Committee to Study Governmental Operations with Respect to Intelligence Activities, Book II, April 26, 1976.
10 Burnham, *A Law Unto Itself: The IRS and the Abuse of Power* (New York: Random House, 1989), p. 268.
11 Ibid., p. 240.
12 Editorial, "Ask and Ye Shall Receive," *Wall Street Journal*, March 15, 2000.
13 Glenn Harlan Reynolds, "Tax Audits Are No Laughing Matter," *USA Today*, May 18, 2009.
14 Max Fisher, "Obama Finds Predator Drones Hilarious," *The Atlantic*, May 3, 2010.
15 Alexis Levinson, "Cantor: IRS actions 'hallmark of authoritarian nations,'" *Daily Caller*, February 26, 2014.
16 Wesley Bruer, "Court: IRS needs to prove it isn't targeting conservative groups," CNN, August 6, 2016.
17 Bradley A. Smith and David Keating, "Congress Abetted the IRS Targeting of Conservatives," *Wall Street Journal*, June 3, 2014.
18 James Bovard, "Is Biden, like past presidents, unleashing the IRS on his enemies?" *New York Post*, March 29, 2023.
19 Press Release, "Chairman Jordan Raises Alarm on Potential IRS Weaponization Against American Journalist," House Judiciary Committee, March 28, 2023.
20 Matt Taibbi, "Twitter Files Thread: The Spies Who Loved Twitter," *Racket News*, December 25, 2022.
21 Steven Nelson, "IRS opened Matt Taibbi tax probe on Christmas Eve following 'Twitter Files' document dump," *New York Post*, May 24, 2023.
22 James Bovard, "The IRS Mess," *American Spectator*, June 1998.
23 Dick M. Carpenter, "Seize First, Question Later," Institute for Justice, February 1, 2015.
24 James Bovard, "Know your banker: he may be working for big brother," *Playboy*, December 1996.
25 Shaila Dewan, "Law Lets I.R.S. Seize Accounts on Suspicion, No Crime Required," *New York Times*, October 25, 2014.

[26] Jason Clayworth, "Iowa forfeiture fight gets nation's attention," *Des Moines Register*, April 4, 2015.

[27] Edward Ericson, "South Mountain Creamery gets its money back from the IRS, and more," *Baltimore Sun*, July 1, 2016.

[28] Rachel Weiner, "Uncle Sam may have picked the wrong cash cow," *Washington Post*, April 14, 2015.

[29] Shaila Dewan, "Rules Change on I.R.S. Seizures, Too Late for Some," *New York Times*, April 30, 2015.

[30] Christopher Ingraham, "How the IRS seized a man's life savings without ever charging him with a crime," *Washington Post*, May 15, 2015.

[31] "Criminal Investigation Enforced Structuring Laws Primarily Against Legal Source Funds and Compromised the Rights of Some Individuals and Businesses," Treasury Inspector General for Tax Administration, March 30, 2017.

[32] "What is a statute of limitations on a debt?" Consumer Financial Protection Bureau, January 25, 2017.

[33] Marc Fisher, "Social Security, Treasury target taxpayers for their parents' decades old debts," *Washington Post*, April 10, 2014.

[34] Pedro Gonçalves, "IRS to revoke 260,000 American passports," InternationalInvestment.net, October 16, 2018.

[35] Kevin Williamson, "IRS Policy Targets U.S. Passports," *National Review*, February 15, 2018.

[36] GianCarlo Canaparo, Patrick McLaughlin, PhD, Jonathan Nelson, and Liya Palagashvili, "Count the Code: Quantifying Federalization of Criminal Statutes," Heritage Foundation and George Mason University Mercatus Center, January 7, 2022.

[37] Chris Edwards, "Our Complex Tax Code Is Crippling America," *Time*, April 11, 2016.

[38] Jason J. Fichtner and Jacob Feldman, "The Hidden Costs of Tax Compliance," George Mason University Mercatus Center, May 20, 2013.

[39] Demian Brady, "Increasing Complexity Brings Back Bigger Compliance Burdens," National Taxpayers Union, April 18, 2022.

[40] "Briefing Book," Tax Policy Center, May 2020.

[41] Stephen Moore, "An IRS that's armed and dangerous," *Washington Examiner*, August 11, 2022.

[42] Burnham, *A Law Unto Itself: The IRS and the Abuse of Power* (New York: Random House, 1989), p. 20.

[43] James Keightley, "Testimony before Restructuring Commission," Tax Notes Today, November 8, 1996.

[44] "Full Text: Treasury IRS 1992 Business Plan," *Tax Notes Today*, May 18, 1992.

[45] Lisa Rein, "Secret plan shows the IRS wants to 'get out of the business of talking with taxpayers,' advocate says," *Washington Post*, January 6, 2016.

[46] Ibid.

[47] "Americans visited IRS refund website 632 million times last year as challenges swamp tax agency 'in crisis,'" *Washington Post*, January 12, 2022.

[48] Lisa Rein and Tony Romm, "IRS backlog hits nearly 24 million returns, further imperiling the 2022 tax filing season," *Washington Post*, February 12, 2022.

[49] Paul Caron, "IRS Dangles Telework to Lure Workers to Beleaguered Agency," TaxProf blog, June 4, 2022.

[50] "Millions of Destroyed Tax Forms Deal Reviled IRS Fresh Black Eye," Bloomberg News, May 13, 2022.
[51] Kate Dore, "Tax professionals 'horrified' by IRS decision to destroy data on 30 million filers," CNBC, May 12, 2022.
[52] Dan Mangan, "Leading House Democrat Bill Pascrell demands Biden replace IRS chief over tax document destruction 'scandal,'" CNBC, May 13, 2022.
[53] Ibid.
[54] Stephen Barr, "IRS Computer Revamp Faulted by Study Panel," *Washington Post*, August 20, 1993.
[55] "IRS Security of Taxpayer Information: Characteristics of Employee Unauthorized Access and Disclosure Cases," Government Accountability Office, May 19, 2022.
[56] Farai Chideya, "Your Data Is Showing: Breaches Wreak Havoc While the Government Plays Catch Up," *The Intercept*, May 27, 2015.
[57] Ibid.
[58] Jesse Eisinger, Jeff Ernsthausen and Paul Kiel, "The Secret IRS Files: Trove of Never Before Seen Records Reveal How the Wealthiest Avoid Income Tax," ProPublica, June 8, 2021.
[59] Glenn Thrush and Alan Rappeport, "I.R.S. Contractor Charged with Leaking Tax Returns," *New York Times*, September 29, 2023.
[60] Jeff Stein, "White House seeks to make massive boost to IRS enforcement centerpiece of new spending plan," *Washington Post*, April 27, 2021.
[61] James Bovard, "Biden's Wrecking Ball for Financial Privacy," American Institute for Economic Research, September 22, 2021.
[62] Ibid.
[63] Daniel J. Pilla, "Three False Narratives Being Used in the IRS Funding Push," *National Review*, May 17, 2021.
[64] Darlene McCormick Sanchez, "Number of Low-Income Audits Could at Least Triple as IRS Grows, Data Show," *Epoch Times*, August 18, 2022.
[65] twitter.com/RepThomasMassie/status/1559157960957460482
[66] Travis Nix and Tyler Martinez, "The IRS and the Eighth Amendment," *Wall Street Journal*, November 2, 2022.
[67] Kelsey Reichmann and Megan Butler, "Justices limit fines for failing to report foreign bank accounts," Courthouse News Service, February 28, 2023.
[68] Travis Nix, "Congress Enacts a Tax Nobody Can Understand," *Wall Street Journal*, March 9, 2023.
[69] Editorial, "The IRS Makes Another House Call," *Wall Street Journal*, June 16, 2023.
[70] Press Release, "New Information Reveals IRS Agent Used Fake Name to Target Ohio Resident," House Judiciary Committee, June 16, 2023.
[71] Burnham, *A Law Unto Itself: The IRS and the Abuse of Power* (New York: Random House, 1989), p. 21.
[72] James Bovard, "IRS coverup of Hunter Biden could be scandal that sinks a presidency," *New York Post*, May 24, 2023.
[73] Press Release, "Six Key Takeaways from the Released IRS Whistleblower Transcripts," House Ways and Means Committee, July 12, 2023.
[74] Friedrich Hayek, *The Constitution of Liberty* (Chicago: University of Chicago, 1972 [1960]), p. 294.
[75] twitter.com/PerBylund/status/1533431908167712769

[76] Matt Welch, "I've abandoned free market principles to save the free market system," *Reason*, December 16, 2008.

[77] Matt Taibbi, "The Fed's Magic Money Printing Machine," *Rolling Stone*, October 8, 2010.

[78] Lawrence H. Summers, "It's time for the Fed to rethink quantitative easing," *Washington Post*, August 26, 2021.

[79] Alex J. Pollock, "Since 2008, Monetary Policy Has Cost American Savers about $4 Trillion," Mises Institute, November 15, 2021.

[80] "Full Transcript: Fed Chair Jerome Powell's 60 Minutes interview on economic recovery from the coronavirus pandemic," CBS *60 Minutes*, May 17, 2020. (Interview recorded May 13, 2020.)

[81] David J. Lynch, "Inflation has Fed critics pointing to spike in money supply," *Washington Post*, February 6, 2022.

[82] twitter.com/stlouisfed/status/1462176434420690946

[83] Caitlin Doornbos, "Stacey Abrams outrageously suggests abortion can help voters' wallet amid inflation fears," *New York Post*, October 19, 2022.

[84] Teresa Ghilarducci, "Inflation Stings Most If You Earn Less than $300K. Here's How to Deal," *Washington Post*, March 13, 2022. (Originally published by Bloomberg News.)

[85] James Bovard, "Inflation only goes up and will bankrupt Joe Biden and the Democrats," *New York Post*, January 24, 2022.

[86] Jenny Goldsberry, "Joy Reid claims Republicans 'taught people the word inflation,'" *Washington Examiner*, November 4, 2022.

[87] Kristine Parks and Nikolas Lanum, "Janet Yellen blames Americans' 'splurging' for record high inflation," Fox News, December 1, 2022.

[88] David Lin, "Inflation is really 15%, highest since 1947," Kitco, February 1, 2022.

[89] James Bovard, "Debunking 10 of Joe Biden's lies about the state of the US economy," *New York Post*, June 16, 2022.

[90] Robert Spencer, "Angry Biden Shouts, 'I'm Sick of This Stuff,' Lashes Out at Those Who Blame Him for Inflation," PJ Media, March 11, 2022.

[91] Ibid.

[92] Molly Nagle, Ben Gittleson, and Libby Cathey, "Biden blames 'Putin's price hike,' says gas prices shouldn't depend on his committing 'genocide,'" ABC News, April 12, 2022.

[93] Ariel Zilber, "Americans saw 'most severe' pay cut in 25 years under Biden," *New York Post*, October 6, 2022.

[94] Tom Schatz, "Interest on the debt is a huge threat," *The Hill*, May 25, 2022.

[95] *Burnet v. Wells*, 289 U.S. 670, 683 (1933).

Chapter 11

[1] *Berger v. State of New York*, 388 U.S. 41 (1967).

[2] James Bovard, "The feds are buying mountains of your personal data and one day could use it against you," *New York Post*, June 19, 2023.

[3] "Text of Judge Gesell's Decision in the Ellsberg Case," *New York Times*, May 25, 1974.

[4] Otto Friedrich, "The Individual Is Sovereign," *Time*, July 21, 1986.

[5] *Jones v. Securities Exchange Commission*, 298 U.S. 1 (1936).

[6] "The Internal Revenue Service: An Intelligence Resource and Collector — Intelligence Activities and the Rights of Americans," U.S. Senate Select Committee

to Study Governmental Operations with Respect to Intelligence Activities, Book II, April 26, 1976.

[7] James Bovard, "Federal Surveillance: The Threat to Americans' Security," *Freeman*, January 2004.

[8] "COINTELPRO: The FBI's Covert Action Programs Against American Citizens," U.S. Senate Select Committee to Study Governmental Operations with Respect to Intelligence Activities, Book III, April 26, 1976.

[9] "The Internal Revenue Service: An Intelligence Resource and Collector — Intelligence Activities and the Rights of Americans," U.S. Senate Select Committee to Study Governmental Operations with Respect to Intelligence Activities, Book II, April 26, 1976.

[10] James Bovard, "Property and Liberty," *Freeman*, September 2000.

[11] *Skinner v. Railway Labor Executive Association*, 489 U.S. 602, 641 (1989).

[12] *California v. Acevedo*, 111 S. Ct. 1982, 2002 (1991).

[13] Bob Sullivan, "FBI software cracks encryption wall," MSNBC, November 20, 2001.

[14] Kim Zetter, "New technologies, laws threaten privacy," *PC World*, March 1, 2002.

[15] Ashkan Soltani and Timothy B. Lee, "Research shows how MacBook Webcams can spy on their users without warning," *Washington Post*, December 18, 2013.

[16] Susan Baer, "Broader U.S. spy initiative debated," *Baltimore Sun*, January 5, 2003.

[17] Ted Rall, "The Right to Privacy Dies with a Whimper," *Yahoo News*, November 28, 2002.

[18] "Pentagon seeks to detect people by odor," Associated Press, December 19, 2002.

[19] Farhad Manjoo, "Total Information Awareness: Down, but not out," *Salon*, January 29, 2003.

[20] Barton Gellman, "The FBI's Secret Scrutiny," *Washington Post*, November 5, 2005.

[21] Ibid.

[22] Dan Froomkin, "FBI Flouts Obama Directive to Limit Gag Orders on National Security Letters," *The Intercept*, February 19, 2015.

[23] Barton Gellman, "The FBI's Secret Scrutiny," *Washington Post*, November 5, 2005.

[24] "FBI abused Patriot Act," *Chicago Tribune*, March 9, 2007.

[25] Adam Liptak, "Judge Voids F.B.I. Tool Granted by Patriot Act," *New York Times*, September 7, 2007.

[26] David G. Savage and Bob Drogin, "Legality of Wiretaps Remains in Question," *Los Angeles Times*, December 18, 2005.

[27] John Dean, "George W. Bush as the New Richard M. Nixon," FindLaw.com, December 30, 2005.

[28] James Bovard, "Nunes memo released: FBI objections lacked credibility given bureau's shady past," *USA Today*, February 2, 2018.

[29] James Risen, *State of War: The Secret History of the CIA and the Bush Administration* (New York: Free Press, 2006).

[30] Carol D. Leonnig and Dafna Linzer, "Judges on Surveillance Court to Be Briefed on Spy Program," *Washington Post*, December 22, 2005.

[31] James Bovard, "How Washington Protects Your Privacy and Liberty," *Freeman*, December 22, 2010.

[32] Lyle Denniston, "Analysis: Collision course on 'inherent power'?" SCOTUS Blog, December 19, 2005.

[33] "Administration Asserts No Fourth Amendment for Domestic Military Operations," Electronic Frontier Foundation, April 2, 2008.

[34] Andrea Stone, "Lawsuit over phone records may grow," *USA Today*, May 14, 2006.

[35] James Bovard, "Reach Out and Tap Someone," *American Conservative*, June 19, 2006.

[36] John O'Neil and Eric Lichtblau, "Qwest's Refusal of N.S.A. Query Is Explained," *New York Times*, May 12, 2006.

[37] James Bovard, "Robert Mueller's forgotten surveillance crime spree," *The Hill*, January 29, 2018.

[38] Bob Egelko, "U.S. opens assault on wiretap suit," *San Francisco Chronicle*, May 16, 2006.

[39] Zain Verjee, "This Week at War," CNN, August 19, 2006.

[40] Claire Cain Miller, "Secret Court Ruling Put Tech Companies in Data Bind," *New York Times*, June 13, 2013.

[41] "Barack Obama on surveillance, then and now," PolitiFact, June 13, 2013.

[42] Barton Gellman and Julie Tate, "In NSA-intercepted data, those not targeted far outnumber the foreigners who are," *Washington Post*, July 5, 2014.

[43] James Risen and Eric Lichtblau, "Extent of E-Mail Surveillance Renews Concerns in Congress," *New York Times*, June 17, 2009.

[44] Dana Priest, "A Hidden World Growing Beyond Control," *Washington Post*, July 19, 2010.

[45] Charlie Savage, *Power Wars: The Relentless Rise of Presidential Authority and Secrecy* (New York: Back Bay Books, 2017), p. 563.

[46] "Surveillance and Accountability," *New York Times*, October 28, 2012.

[47] Jesse Holland, "Court won't allow challenge to surveillance law," Associated Press, February 26, 2013.

[48] Adam Liptak, "Justices Turn Back Challenge to Broader U.S. Eavesdropping," *New York Times*, February 26, 2013.

[49] James Risen and Laura Poitras, "N.S.A. Gathers Data on Social Connections of U.S. Citizens," *New York Times*, September 23, 2013.

[50] Mike Masnick, "Mike Rogers: You Can't Have Your Privacy Violated If You Don't Know About It," Techdirt, October 30, 2013.

[51] Glenn Greenwald, "XKeyscore: NSA tool collects 'nearly everything a user does on the internet,'" *The Guardian*, July 31, 2013.

[52] Barton Gellman and Julie Tate, "In NSA-intercepted data, those not targeted far outnumber the foreigners who are," *Washington Post*, July 5, 2014.

[53] Glenn Greenwald, "XKeyscore: NSA tool collects 'nearly everything a user does on the internet,'" *The Guardian*, July 31, 2013.

[54] "Obama To Leno: 'There Is No Spying on Americans,'" National Public Radio, August 7, 2013.

[55] Barton Gellman and Julie Tate, "In NSA-intercepted data, those not targeted far outnumber the foreigners who are," *Washington Post*, July 5, 2014.

[56] Eric Lichtblau, "In Secret, Court Vastly Broadens Powers of N.S.A.," *New York Times*, July 7, 2013.

[57] Ellen Nakashima and Ann Marimow, "Judge: NSA's collecting of phone records is probably unconstitutional," *Washington Post*, December 16, 2013.

[58] "Turn Off the Data Vacuum," *New York Times*, December 18, 2013.

[59] James Bamford, "Every Move You Make," *Foreign Policy*, September/October 2016.

[60] Bob Goodlatte, "How the FBI uses laws to spy on foreign terrorists to spy on you," *The Hill*, June 10, 2022.

[61] Charlie Savage, "Court Chides F.B.I., but Re-Approves Warrantless Surveillance Program," *New York Times*, April 26, 2021.

[62] Ellen Nakashima, "Federal court approved FBI's continued use of warrantless surveillance power despite repeated violations of privacy rules," *Washington Post*, April 26, 2021.

[63] James Bovard, "Sham Surveillance Safeguards vs. Tucker Carlson," *American Conservative*, July 2, 2021.

[64] Erik Wemple, "NSA hits back at Tucker Carlson's surveillance allegations," *Washington Post*, June 30, 2021.

[65] Jonathan Swan, "Scoop: Tucker Carlson sought Putin interview at time of spying claim," Axios, July 7, 2021.

[66] "Annual Statistical Transparency Report for Calendar Year 2021," Office of the Director of National Intelligence, April 2022.

[67] James Bovard, "The FBI just got caught in yet more massive, outrageous FISA abuses," *New York Post*, May 22, 2023.

[68] "Declassified: Memorandum Opinion and Order," U.S. Foreign Intelligence Surveillance Court, April 21, 2022. intel.gov/assets/documents/702%20 Documents/declassified/21/2021_FISC_Certification_Opinion.pdf.

[69] James Bovard, "Democrats attack FBI whistleblowers — giving cover to the agency's abuses," *New York Post*, May 19, 2023.

[70] Jack Douglas, "U.S. Security Memos Warn of Little Things," *Fort Worth Star-Telegram*, May 25, 2003.

[71] Murtaza Hussain, "U.S. Military White Paper Describes Wearing Hijab as 'Passive Terrorism,'" *The Intercept*, February 24, 2016.

[72] James Osborne, "Pentagon Exam Calls Protests 'Low-Level Terrorism,' Angering Activists," Fox News, June 17, 2009.

[73] Tim Cushing, "The DHS and FBI Present: You Might Be a Terrorist If… (Hotel Guest Edition)," Techdirt, November 14, 2012.

[74] "Terrorism Awareness and Prevention," New Jersey Office of Homeland Security and Preparedness, 2012.

[75] Mike German and Jay Stanley, "Fusion Center Update," American Civil Liberties Union, July 2008.

[76] "Defining 'Suspicious Activity,'" PBS *Frontline*, January 18, 2011.

[77] "More About Fusion Centers," American Civil Liberties Union, June 25, 2010.

[78] "Recommendations for Fusion Centers: Preserving Privacy & Civil Liberties While Protecting Against Crime & Terrorism," Constitution Project, 2012.

[79] "U.S. Polls: Public Opinion and Right-Wing Extremism," Department of Homeland Security, April 2010.

[80] "Missouri Fusion Center Report on Extremists Raises Ruckus," *Homeland Security Today*, March 18, 2009.

[81] J.D. Tuccille, "Government Snoops Caught Spying on Peaceful Americans," *Reason*, January 6, 2023.

[82] Robert O'Harrow, "DHS 'fusion centers' portrayed as pools of ineptitude and civil liberties intrusions," *Washington Post*, October 2, 2012.

83 "FBI 'Communities Against Terrorism' Suspicious Activity Reporting Flyers," PublicIntelligence.net, February 1, 2012.
84 Ibid.
85 Elizabeth Nolan Brown, "Homeland Security Asking Hotel Staff to Report Customers for Too Many Condoms," *Reason*, Jan. 12, 2016.
86 Murtaza Hussain, Cora Currier, and Jana Winter, "Is Your Child a Terrorist? U.S. Government Questionnaire Rates Families at Risk for Extremism," *The Intercept*, February 9, 2015.
87 "National Strategy for Countering Domestic Terrorism," White House, June 2021.
88 "Background Press Call by Senior Administration Officials on the National Strategy for Countering Domestic Terrorism," White House, June 14, 2021.
89 Alexander Hall, "FBI documents associate internet slang like 'based' and 'red pill' with 'extremism,'" Fox News, April 9, 2023.
90 Zachary Cohen and Katie Bo Williams, "Biden team may partner with private firms to monitor extremist chatter online," CNN, May 3, 2021.
91 James Bovard, "Biden Plans Expansion of Feds' Army of Snitches in 'Dollars for Collars' Program," *American Conservative*, May 10, 2021.
92 James Bovard, "Uncle Scam wants you: could you be set up by the government to commit a crime?" *Playboy*, March 1995.
93 "Summary of the Terrorism Threat to the United States," National Terrorism Advisory System Bulletin, Department of Homeland Security, February 7, 2022.
94 Giselle Ruhiyyih Ewing, "Biden calls white supremacy 'most dangerous terrorist threat' in speech at Howard," Politico, May 13, 2023.
95 Jon Levine, "House Republicans say probe of DOJ, FBI will include Facebook," *New York Post*, December 24, 2022.
96 William M. Arkin, "FBI Ramps Up Spending to Fight MAGA Terrorism," *Newsweek*, December 5, 2022.
97 Brooke Singman, "FBI threat tag created after Supreme Court's Dobbs ruling 'shifted' to focus on pro-lifers, whistleblower says," Fox News, March 2, 2023.
98 Ellen Nakashima, "Travelers' Laptops May Be Detained at Border," *Washington Post*, August 1, 2008.
99 Drew Harwell, "Customs officials have copied Americans' phone data at massive scale," *Washington Post*, September 15, 2022.
100 James Bovard, "Technology does more to reduce environmental harm than emissions tests," *Washington Times*, July 7, 2016.
101 James Bovard, "Should Gun Owners Fear the Deep State?" *America's 1st Freedom*, National Rifle Association, August 10, 2018.
102 Devlin Barrett, "Gun-Show Customers' License Plates Come Under Scrutiny," *Wall Street Journal*, October 2, 2016.
103 Sam Blum, "That Radar Speed Road Sign Might Be Saving Your License Plate for Later," Quartz, October 1, 2018.
104 Devlin Barrett, "U.S. Spies on Millions of Drivers," *Wall Street Journal*, January 26, 2015.
105 "DEA Using License Plate Readers to Spy On Drivers," *All Things Considered*, National Public Radio, January 31, 2015.
106 Adam Liptak, "Supreme Court to Rule on GPS Surveillance, Addressing 'Big Brother' Claims," *New York Times*, September 10, 2011.

[107] James Bovard, "The feds are buying mountains of your personal data and one day could use it against you," *New York Post*, June 19, 2023.

[108] Theo Wayt, "CDC bought cellphone data to track vaccination, lockdown compliance: report," *New York Post*, May 4, 2022.

[109] Sara Sirota, "Why Have 14 of 15 U.S. Cabinet Departments Bought Phone Unlocking Technology? Few Will Say," *The Intercept*, February 3, 2023.

[110] Ken Klippenstein, "NSA Orders Employees to Spy on the World 'With Dignity and Respect.'" *The Intercept*, August 25, 2023.

[111] Charlie Savage, "D.E.A. Secretly Collected Bulk Records of Money-Counter Purchases," *New York Times*, March 30, 2019.

[112] Ed Pilkington, "9/11: 20 years later — Surveillance," September 4, 2021.

[113] Eleanor Hill, "Joint Inquiry Staff Statement – Hearing on the Intelligence Community's Response to Past Terrorist Attacks Against the United States from February 1993 to September 2001," October 8, 2002.

[114] James Bovard, "Ruby Ridge lessons for fighting right-wing extremism," *USA Today*, August 28, 2017.

[115] Karl E. Campbell, *Senator Sam Ervin, Last of the Founding Fathers* (Chapel Hill: University of North Carolina, 2007), p. 260.

[116] Chris Wallace, Patrick Leahy interview on "Fox News Sunday," Fox News, January 19, 2014.

[117] James Bamford, "NSA, the Agency That Could Be Big Brother," *New York Times*, December 25, 2005.

[118] James Risen and Laura Poitras, "N.S.A. Gathers Data on Social Connections of U.S. Citizens," *New York Times*, September 23, 2013.

[119] "The Internal Revenue Service: An Intelligence Resource and Collector — Intelligence Activities and the Rights of Americans," U.S. Senate Select Committee to Study Governmental Operations with Respect to Intelligence Activities, Book II, April 26, 1976.

[120] J.D. Tuccille, "NSA Likes Watching Radicals Watching Porn," *Reason*, November 27, 2013.

[121] *Brinegar v. U.S.*, 338 U.S. 160 (1949).

[122] Glenn Greenwald, "New Study Shows Mass Surveillance Breeds Meekness, Fear and Self-Censorship," *The Intercept*, April 28, 2016.

[123] "Heidi Boghosian on Self-Censorship and Expression," Literary Hub, July 15, 2021.

Chapter 12

[1] "Remarks at the Dedication of the Thomas J. Dodd Archives and Research Center in Storrs, Connecticut," *Public Papers of the Presidents*, October 15, 1995.

[2] *Grosjean v. American Press Co.*, 297 U.S. 233 (1936).

[3] Ronan Farrow, "The real concern: why are so many US government documents classified?" *The Guardian*, June 28, 2013.

[4] Editorial, "The government's 'unsustainable' avalanche of secrets," *Washington Post*, August 26, 2019.

[5] Ibid.

[6] John F. Kennedy, "The President and the Press," Address before the American Newspaper Publishers Association, April 27, 1961. jfklibrary.org/archives/other-resources/john-f-kennedy-speeches/american-newspaper-publishers-association-19610427.

[7] H.R. McMaster, "LBJ: A Texan in Camelot," *Washington Times*, November 16, 1997.

[8] Jon Schwarz, "Pentagon Official Once Told Morley Safer that Reporters Who Believe the Government Are 'Stupid,'" *The Intercept*, May 20, 2016.

[9] *New York Times Co. v. U.S.*, 403 U.S. 713 (1971).

[10] Tom Blanton, "The lie behind the secrets," *Los Angeles Times*, May 21, 2006.

[11] Beverly Gage, "The Strange Politics of 'Classified' Information," *New York Times*, August 22, 2017.

[12] James Bovard, *Terrorism and Tyranny* (New York: St. Martin's Press, 2003), pp. 302–5.

[13] Shaun Waterman, "Half of govt secrets shouldn't be secret," United Press International, August 24, 2004.

[14] Scott Shane, "Increase in the Number of Documents Classified by the Government," *New York Times*, July 3, 2005.

[15] Steven Aftergood, "President Obama Declares 'A New Era of Openness,'" Federation of American Scientists, January 22, 2009.

[16] Josh Gerstein, "Obama's hard line on leaks," Politico, March 7, 2011.

[17] Sam Sacks, "U.S. Government: We Can Classify Anything and Judges Can't Stop Us," *The Intercept*, May 8, 2015.

[18] James Bovard, "Federal Secrecy Protects the Crimes of Every President," *CounterPunch*, January 28, 2021.

[19] Bart Jansen, "Who has security clearance? More than 4.3M people," *USA Today*, June 6, 2017.

[20] Jameel Jaffer and Ramya Krishnan, "When Will We See Bolton's Book?" *New York Times*, January 30, 2020.

[21] Charlie Savage, "Ex-National Security Officials Sue to Limit Censorship of Their Books," *New York Times*, April 2, 2019.

[22] Meenakshi Krishnan, "New Documents Point to Special Treatment for Favored Officials," Knight First Amendment Institute at Columbia University, February 25, 2020.

[23] Eric Lichtblau and James Risen, "Government Tries to Keep Secret What Many Consider a Fraud," *New York Times*, February 20, 2011.

[24] James Risen, *State of War: The Secret History of the CIA and the Bush Administration* (New York: Free Press, 2006), p. 32.

[25] Karl Vick, "Judges Skeptical of State-Secrets Claim," *Washington Post*, August 16, 2007.

[26] Zachary Roth, "Obama Website Slams Secrecy Claim That Obama Now Invokes," Talking Points Memo, April 10, 2009.

[27] Ryan Singel, "'State Secrets' Can't Hide CIA Torture Program, Appeals Court Rules," *Wired*, April 28, 2009.

[28] James Bovard, "Assassin Nation," *American Conservative*, January 2011.

[29] Tom Blanton, "Freedom of Information at 40 — LBJ Refused Ceremony, Undercut Bill with Signing Statement," National Security Archive, July 4, 2006.

[30] Betty Medsger, "Our government is always hiding something," *USA Today*, March 29, 2014.

[31] *NLRB v. Robbins Tire Co.*, 437 U.S. 214, 242 (1978).

[32] "Memorandum for Heads of Departments and Agencies re: The Freedom of Information Act," White House, October 4, 1993.

[33] Attorney General John Ashcroft, "Memorandum on the Freedom of Information Act," Justice Department Office of Public Affairs, October 12, 2001.

[34] C.J. Ciaramella, "Justice Dept. proposes lying, hiding existence of records under new FOIA rule," *Daily Caller*, October 24, 2011.

[35] Josh Gerstein, "Watchdog suit: Obama White House slowing FOIA process," Politico, May 10, 2016.

[36] David Kravets, "Feds Embrace Lying in Response to Public-Record Requests," *Wired*, October 25, 2011.

[37] Justin Elliott, "Trying (and Trying) to Get Records from the Most Transparent Administration," Pro Publica, March 11, 2016.

[38] Sarah Westwood, "Lawmakers, reporters slam government secrecy," *Washington Examiner*, June 3, 2015.

[39] James Bovard, "Inspector general's report on FBI and Clinton's emails shows secrecy threatens democracy," *USA Today*, June 15, 2018.

[40] Dell Cameron, "The FBI Redacted the Names of DC Comic Book Characters to Protect Their Non-Existent Privacy," *Gizmodo*, April 30, 2018.

[41] Paul Bedard, "Judge suggests Justice, State colluded to protect Hillary Clinton in email scandal," *Washington Examiner*, December 7, 2018.

[42] James Bovard, "The Lies Aren't Secret," *American Conservative*, February 24, 2021.

[43] Craig Whitlock and Nate Jones, "U.S. fought to keep veterans' jobs with foreign governments secret," *Washington Post*, October 18, 2022.

[44] Andrew Kelly, "Wait what? FDA wants 55 years to process FOIA request over vaccine data," Reuters, November 18, 2021.

[45] Jenna Greene, "Federal Judge Tells FDA it Must Make Public 55,000 Pages a Month of Pfizer Vaccine Data," Reuters, January 10, 2022.

[46] James Bovard, "The contorted Presidential Records Act is a bipartisan scam to hide White House mischief," *USA Today*, February 20, 2022.

[47] Becky Little, "7 Revealing Nixon Quotes from His Secret Tapes," History.com, July 30, 2018.

[48] Kelley Shannon, "New Tapes Show LBJ Worried About Vietnam, Nixon," Associated Press, August 28, 2016.

[49] Marcy Lynn Karin, "Out of sight, but not out of mind: how Executive Order 13233 expands executive privilege while simultaneously preventing access to presidential records," *Stanford Law Review*, November 2002.

[50] James Bovard, "The contorted Presidential Records Act is a bipartisan scam to hide White House mischief," *USA Today*, February 20, 2022.

[51] Alex Thompson, Josh Gerstein, and Max Tani, "The Obama FOIA timebomb," Politico, March 31, 2022.

[52] James Bovard, "There's no sainthood for Obama, National Archives in Trump FBI raid uproar," *New York Post*, August 14, 2022.

[53] Jennifer Schuessler, "The Obama Presidential Library That Isn't," *New York Times*, February 20, 2019.

[54] James Bovard, "Trump indictment shows federal secrecy gone wild makes political lies harder to uncover," *New York Post*, June 13, 2023.

[55] Carol E. Lee, Monica Alba, and Michael Kosnar, "Biden classified documents investigation shows few signs of wrapping up soon," NBC News, June 8, 2023.

[56] James Bovard, "Endangering Washington's Divine Right to Deceive," Mises Institute, April 17, 2023.

[57] Editorial, "The Discord leaks show our nation's secrets at risk," *Washington Post*, April 13, 2023.

[58] Alexander Hall, "John Kirby warns press that leaked intelligence documents are 'not intended for public consumption,'" Fox News, April 10, 2023.

[59] twitter.com/David_Philipps/status/1647025184409542656

[60] Shane Harris, Souad Mekhennet, Loveday Morris, and Michael Birnbaum, "Investigators skeptical of yacht's role in Nord Stream bombing," *Washington Post*, April 3, 2023.

[61] James Bovard, "Hillary's Anti-Transparency Bargain," *Washington Times*, October 27, 2016.

[62] James Bovard, "The contorted Presidential Records Act is a bipartisan scam to hide White House mischief," *USA Today*, February 20, 2022.

[63] Bryan Bender, "White House launches new war on secrecy," Politico, August 23, 2022.

Chapter 13

[1] Ken Klippenstein and Lee Fang, "Truth Cops," *The Intercept*, October 31, 2022.

[2] *Memorandum Ruling on Request for Preliminary Injunction, Missouri et al. v. Biden et al.*, July 4, 2023.

[3] Amanda Seitz, "Disinformation board to tackle Russia, migrant smugglers," Associated Press, April 28, 2022.

[4] Lev Golinkin, "Meet the Head of Biden's New 'Disinformation Governing Board,'" *The Nation*, May 12, 2022.

[5] Ibid.

[6] James Bovard, "Team Biden dumps ditzy disinfo czar Nina Jankowicz — but its board remains a threat to free speech," *New York Post*, May 18, 2022.

[7] Taylor Lorenz, "How the Biden administration let right-wing attacks derail its disinformation efforts," *Washington Post*, May 18, 2022.

[8] twitter.com/mazemoore/status/1524049867315859463

[9] James Bovard, "Team Biden dumps ditzy disinfo czar Nina Jankowicz," *New York Post*, May 18, 2022.

[10] Emily Jacobs, "Former Biden disinformation chief Nina Jankowicz registers as foreign agent," *Washington Examiner*, November 28, 2022.

[11] Kate Conger and Lauren Hirsch, "Elon Musk Completes $44 Billion Deal to Own Twitter," *New York Times*, October 27, 2022.

[12] "Biden says Twitter spews lies across the world," Reuters, November 4, 2022.

[13] "Remarks by President Biden at a Democratic Congressional Campaign Committee Reception," White House Briefing Room, October 14, 2022.

[14] twitter.com/elonmusk/status/1601667312930590721

[15] Tom Tillison, "Musk: 'To be totally frank, almost every conspiracy theory people had about Twitter turned out to be true,'" *BizPac Review*, December 26, 2022.

[16] James Bovard, "How the feds spend $74M a year to try to censor Americans," *New York Post*, March 2, 2023.

[17] Jonathan Turley, "Twitter censorship is the modern-day red scare," *New York Post*, February 10, 2023.

[18] twitter.com/mtaibbi/status/1631338680676671488

[19] twitter.com/mtaibbi/status/1631338680676671488

[20] twitter.com/elonmusk/status/1622739987031552002

[21] Sharon Lerner, Mara Hvistendahl, and Maia Hibbett, "NIH Documents Provide New Evidence U.S. Funded Gain-of-Function Research in Wuhan," *The Intercept*, September 9, 2021.

[22] twitter.com/mtaibbi/status/1631338687718907904

[23] twitter.com/mtaibbi/status/1631338656144269315

[24] twitter.com/mtaibbi/status/1631338702440996880/photo/3

[25] "Russia's Pillars of Disinformation and Propaganda," U.S. State Department, August 4, 2020.

[26] James Bovard, "Inspector General report on FBI's FISA abuse tells us one thing: We need radical reform," *USA Today*, December 10, 2019.

[27] twitter.com/mtaibbi/status/1610372352872783872

[28] twitter.com/mtaibbi/status/1610394297727082499

[29] "Election Integrity Partnership," Stanford Internet Observatory and the University of Washington Center for an Informed Public, EIPartnership.net.

[30] twitter.com/mtaibbi/status/1610394315938992129

[31] twitter.com/mtaibbi/status/1610394281683959811

[32] twitter.com/mtaibbi/status/1606701405443874816

[33] Emily Crane, "FBI brass warned agents off Hunter Biden laptop due to 2020 election: whistleblowers," *New York Post*, August 24, 2022.

[34] Jerry Dunleavy, "Hunter Biden evidence wrongly labeled disinformation by FBI: Whistleblower," *Washington Examiner*, July 25, 2022.

[35] twitter.com/mtaibbi/status/1598831435288563712

[36] Jerry Dunleavy, "Top Twitter executive reveals key information on Hunter Biden censorship decision," *Washington Examiner*, February 8, 2023.

[37] Natasha Bertrand, "Hunter Biden story is Russian disinfo, dozens of former intel officials say," Politico, October 19, 2020. Also, James Bovard, "Spy letter about Hunter Biden shows how Dems are undermining democracy," *New York Post*, April 21, 2023.

[38] Carl Campanile, "Biden's false Hunter laptop letter interfered in election beyond 'anything China or Russia' could do: GOP pol," *New York Post*, April 23, 2023.

[39] Tim Murtaugh, "Media's suppression of Hunter Biden's laptop was election interference," *Washington Times*, March 24, 2022.

[40] twitter.com/elonmusk/status/1605219914813673473

[41] James Bovard, "Private-federal censorship machine targeted TRUE 'misinformation,'" *New York Post*, March 17, 2023.

[42] *Memorandum Ruling on Request for Preliminary Injunction, Missouri et al. v. Biden et al.*, July 4, 2023.

[43] twitter.com/Jim_Jordan/status/1687116316073930752

[44] twitter.com/Jim_Jordan/status/1684595382871785472

[45] "Hearing Before the United States House of Representatives Committee on the Judiciary, Select Subcommittee on the Weaponization of the Federal Government: Testimony of D. John Sauer," March 30. 2023.

[46] *Plaintiffs Proposed Findings of Fact, Missouri v. Biden*, Case No. 3:22-cv-01213, filed March 6, 2023.

[47] Email from Rob Flaherty to multiple Google staffers, in *Memorandum Ruling on Request for Preliminary Injunction, Missouri et al. v. Biden et al.*, July 4, 2023. Disclosed in the state attorney general lawsuit against the Biden administration, January 2023. nclalegal.org/wp-content/uploads/2023/01/Doc.-174-Plaintiffs-Supplemental-Brief-Addressing-Nondispositive-Order.pdf.

48 Jeff Landry, "Our lawsuit uncovers more shocking evidence Team Biden used Big Tech to censor," *New York Post*, January 23, 2023.
49 Flaherty email to Facebook official [name blocked out], May 12, 2021. From Missouri lawsuit disclosures. See: Tyler O'Neil, "Not Just Misinformation: In Emails to White House, Facebook Admits Suppressing 'Often-True Content' on COVID-19 Vaccines," *Daily Signal*, January 12, 2013.
50 twitter.com/Jim_Jordan/status/1687116316073930752
51 David Zweig, "How Twitter Rigged the Covid Debate," The Free Press, December 26, 2022.
52 "Confronting Health Misinformation: The U.S. Surgeon General's Advisory on Building a Healthy Information Environment," Department of Health and Human Services, July 2021.
53 Sheryl Gay Stolberg and Davey Alba, "Surgeon General Assails Tech Companies Over Misinformation on Covid-19," *New York Times*, July 15, 2021.
54 Zolan Kanno-Youngs and Cecilia Kang, "'They're Killing People': Biden Denounces Social Media for Virus Disinformation," *New York Times*, July 16, 2021.
55 twitter.com/davidzweig/status/1607186027269709026
56 David Zweig, "How Twitter Rigged the Covid Debate," The Free Press, December 26, 2022.
57 "NCLA Takes on U.S. Surgeon General's Censoring of Alleged Covid-19 'Misinformation' on Twitter," New Civil Liberties Alliance, March 25, 2022.
58 Davey Alba, "The surgeon general calls on Big Tech to turn over Covid-19 misinformation data," *New York Times*, March 3, 2022.
59 twitter.com/mtaibbi/status/1636729166631432195
60 James Bovard, "Private-federal censorship machine targeted TRUE 'misinformation,'" *New York Post*, March 17, 2023.
61 Jeff Landry, "Our lawsuit uncovers more shocking evidence Team Biden used Big Tech to censor," *New York Post*, January 23, 2023.
62 twitter.com/mtaibbi/status/1633830108321677315
63 "Fauxi: Undermining Authoritative Health Sources," Virality Project, June 25, 2021.
64 "Nixon Tapes: Oval Office Meeting with Bob Haldeman," Nixon Presidential Materials Project, June 14, 1971.
65 Alice Miranda Ollstein, "FDA Commissioner Califf sounds the alarm on health misinformation," Association of Health Care Journalists News, April 30, 2022.
66 Maryanne Demasi, "FDA chief sparks misinformation while vowing to fight misinformation," Maryanne Demasi's Substack, April 25, 2023.
67 twitter.com/Alexander_Tin/status/1650552199066398732?s=20
68 Maryanne Demasi, "FDA chief sparks misinformation while vowing to fight misinformation," Maryanne Demasi's Substack, April 25, 2023.
69 Gabriel Hays, "Zuckerberg says 'establishment' asked Facebook to censor COVID misinfo that ended up true," Fox News, June 9, 2023.
70 Ken Klippenstein and Lee Fang, "Truth Cops," *The Intercept*, October 31, 2022.
71 James Bovard, "Democrats desperate to censor anyone that disagrees with them," *New York Post*, November 1, 2022.
72 Ken Klippenstein and Lee Fang, "Truth Cops," *The Intercept*, October 31, 2022.
73 "National Strategy for Countering Domestic Terrorism," White House, June 2021.
74 Ken Klippenstein and Lee Fang, "Truth Cops," *The Intercept*, October 31, 2022.

75 twitter.com/mtaibbi/status/1603857603867598859
76 twitter.com/mtaibbi/status/1603857573219819529
77 James Bovard, "Democrats Champion Censorship and Smear Twitter Files Heroes," *New York Post*, March 10, 2023.
78 Joseph Clark, "House Democrat threatens Matt Taibbi with perjury charges for 'Twitter Files' testimony," *Washington Times*, April 20, 2023.
79 Editorial, "The Biden FTC muscles Musk for revealing Twitter's abuses," *New York Post*, March 8, 2023.
80 twitter.com/elonmusk/status/1633231562962780160
81 Joseph A. Wulfsohn, "Twitter Files: Rep. Adam Schiff's office requested tech giant to suspend accounts," Fox News, January 3, 2023.
82 "Suspected Accounts (Facebook)," document from the office of Senator Angus King, docs.google.com/spreadsheets/d/e/2PACX-1vS1PbfNEqDCKX7YFNEvXmm7Lil3Z5unKivX5SA5avFE9tF95kgkbDVJpeRhX4lCig/pubhtml#.
83 twitter.com/mtaibbi/status/1627098967237435396
84 Houston Keene, "Dem Gov Katie Hobbs requested Twitter censor critics of tweet comparing Trump supporters to Nazis," Fox News, August 10, 2023.
85 "23-30445 State of Missouri v. Biden, August 10, 2023," U.S. Court of Appeals, Oral Arguments, August 10, 2023, youtube.com/watch?v=_s7kcB-a4Bs.
86 James Bovard, "Biden censors battered — expect an epic Supreme Court showdown," *New York Post*, August 13, 2023.
87 *Missouri et al. v. Biden et al.*, U.S. Court of Appeals for the Fifth Circuit, No. 23-30445, September 8, 2023.
88 Lee Fang, "Twitter Aided the Pentagon in Its Covert Online Propaganda Campaign," *The Intercept*, December 20, 2022.
89 Ibid.
90 Javier E. David, "Ukraine gas producer appoints Biden's son to board," CNBC, May 13, 2014.
91 Victor Nava, "FBI facilitated social media 'takedown requests' made by Ukrainian spy agency: report," *New York Post*, July 10, 2023.
92 David Axe, "The 'Ghost of Kyiv,' Who Was Never Real, Just Got Killed in the Press," *Forbes*, April 30, 2022.
93 "Ukraine, Poland and six other countries call for Meta and other tech giants to fight disinformation," *New York Times*, March 29, 2023.
94 Hannah Arendt, *Between Past and Future* (New York: Penguin, 1961), p. 234.
95 Ibid., p. 229.
96 Christopher St. Aubin and Jacob Liedke, "Most Americans favor restrictions on false information, violent content online," Pew Research Center, July 20, 2023.
97 Carl M. Cannon, "POLL: Is Censorship a Partisan Issue?" Real Clear Politics, September 22, 2023.

Chapter 14

1 "Commerce, Justice, Science, and Related Agencies Appropriations for 2016," House Appropriations Committee, March 25, 2015.
2 "Longhand Note of President Harry S. Truman – May 12, 1945," Harry S. Truman Library and Museum, National Archives.
3 "Transcript: James Comey's interview with ABC News chief anchor George Stephanopoulos," ABC News, April 15, 2018.

[4] James Madison, "Letter to Thomas Jefferson – October 17, 1788," National Archives.

[5] Robert Suro, "Law Enforcement Ethics: A New Code for Agents," *Washington Post*, August 21, 1997.

[6] James Risen, "How, and How Not, to Fix the F.B.I.," *New York Times*, September 9, 2001.

[7] Richard Morin and Claudia Deane, "Poll: Americans' Trust in Government Grows," *Washington Post*, September 28, 2001.

[8] Eleanor Hill, "Joint Inquiry Staff Statement – Hearing on the Intelligence Community's Response to Past Terrorist Attacks Against the United States from February 1993 to September 2001," October 8, 2002.

[9] James Bovard, "A Stasi for America," *American Conservative*, May 30, 2012.

[10] Martin Weil and Petula Dvorak, "Woman Shot Dead Outside Fairfax Store," *Washington Post*, October 15, 2002.

[11] James Bovard, "Concrete lesson of the snipers," *Washington Times*, October 2, 2003.

[12] Tony Allen-Mills, "Money might have been only motive of the urban snipers," *The Times* (London), October 27, 2002.

[13] "Witnesses say sniper note went unread," United Press International, October 31, 2003.

[14] Adam Clymer, "Big Brother Joins the Hunt for the Sniper," *New York Times*, October 20, 2002.

[15] "Police Checked Suspects Plates at Least 10 Times," *Washington Post*, October 26, 2002.

[16] Stephen Braun and Mark Fineman, "Sniper Suspects Slipped Past Authorities Time and Again," *Los Angeles Times*, November 30, 2002.

[17] James Bovard, "Undue Process," *American Conservative*, October 11, 2004.

[18] Siobhan Roth, "Judiciary Pushes Back over Anti-Terror Tactics," *Recorder*, May 31, 2002.

[19] Mark Z. Barabak, Sebastian Rotella and Richard B. Schmitt, "In Oregon, Spain, Arrest Raises Doubts," *Los Angeles Times*, May 8, 2004.

[20] James Bovard, "Undue Process," *American Conservative*, October 11, 2004.

[21] David Stout, "Report Faults F.B.I.'s Fingerprint Scrutiny in Arrest of Lawyer," *New York Times*, November 17, 2004.

[22] Eric Lichtblau, "U.S. Will Pay $2 Million to Lawyer Wrongly Jailed," *New York Times*, November 30, 2006.

[23] Dan Eggen, "Judge Rules Law Gives Executive Branch Too Much Power," *Washington Post*, September 27, 2007.

[24] John Solomon, "FBI's Forensic Test Full of Holes," *Washington Post*, November 18, 2007.

[25] Spencer S. Hsu, "FBI admits flaws in hair analysis over decades," *Washington Post*, April 18, 2015.

[26] Spencer S. Hsu, "Judge orders D.C. to pay $13.2 million in wrongful FBI hair conviction case," *Washington Post*, February 28, 2016.

[27] Spencer Ackerman, "FBI Taught Agents They Could 'Bend or Suspend the Law,'" *Wired*, March 28, 2012.

[28] Trevor Aaronson, *The Terror Factory: Inside the FBI's Manufactured War on Terrorism* (New York: Ig Press, 2013).

[29] John O'Neil, "Plot Was in 'Earliest Stages,' Gonzales Says," *New York Times*, June 23, 2006.

[30] "Excerpt: Tim Weiner's 'Enemies: A History of the FBI,'" WNYC Studios, February 16, 2012.

[31] Simon Montlake, "Jury Deadlock Ends Terror Trial in Miami," *Christian Science Monitor*, December 14, 2007.

[32] Damien Cave and Carmen Gentile, "Five Convicted in Plot to Blow Up Sears," *New York Times*, May 12, 2009.

[33] "Aspirational Rather than Operational," Democracy Now, June 26, 2006.

[34] Ari Shapiro, "New Doc Looks at How Real the Liberty City Seven's Threat Actually Was," National Public Radio, August 24, 2021.

[35] Alice Speri, "The Most High-Profile Al Qaeda Plot Foiled After 9/11 Was an FBI Scam," *The Intercept*, August 14, 2021.

[36] Adam Andrzejewski, "FBI and Other Agencies Paid Informants $548 Million in Recent Years with Many Committing Authorized Crimes," *Forbes*, November 18, 2021.

[37] Michael Hill, "A judge called an FBI operative a 'villain,'" Associated Press, August 8, 2023.

[38] Andy Newman, Benjamin Weiser, William K. Rashbaum, "Limo Company Owner in Crash Revealed as F.B.I. Informant, Recruiter of Terrorists, Fraudster," *New York Times*, October 9, 2018.

[39] James Bovard, "Pathetic Unite the Right and angry Antifa sputter. There's still time to heed Rodney King," *USA Today*, August 12, 2018.

[40] Dean Seal, "KKK leader seeking Charlottesville rally has history as FBI informant," *Daily Progress* (Charlottesville, Virginia), June 6, 2017.

[41] Matthew, Gault, "FBI Bankrolled Publisher of Occult Neo-Nazi Books, Feds Claim," *Vice*, August 25, 2021.

[42] Ben Norton, "'Tear up Texas': How the FBI played a central role in the first ISIS attack on U.S. soil," *Salon*, March 30, 2017.

[43] James Bovard, "Ruby Ridge lessons for fighting right-wing extremism," *USA Today*, August 28, 2017.

[44] Ryan Devereaux and Trevor Aaronson, "The Bizarre Story Behind the FBI's Fake Documentary About the Bundy Family," *The Intercept*, May 16, 2017.

[45] Robert Anglen, "Bundy Ranch standoff trial ends with zero guilty verdicts," *Arizona Republic*, August 22, 2017.

[46] James Bovard, "Cliven Bundy — FBI debacle: Another example of why the feds need to be leashed," *USA Today*, January 5, 2018.

[47] Maxine Bernstein, "BLM investigator alleges misconduct by feds in Bundy ranch standoff," *The Oregonian*, December 15, 2017.

[48] John L. Smith, "After discovery dustup, Bundy prosecution works to refocus its case," *Nevada Independent*, December 20, 2017.

[49] Trevor Aaronson and Ryan Devereaux, "How the Government Botched the Case Against Cliven Bundy," *The Intercept*, December 22, 2017.

[50] Rebecca Shabad, "FBI Director Comey: 'highly confident' Orlando shooter radicalized through internet," CBS News, June 13, 2016.

[51] "Omar Mateen was taken off a terrorist watch list, but keeping him on it wouldn't have stopped him from buying guns," *Los Angeles Times*, June 12, 2016.

[52] James Comey, "Press Briefing on Orlando Mass Shooting," June 13, 2016.

53 James Bovard, "FBI Pulse shooting failures shatters James Comey's credibility," *USA Today*, April 3, 2018.

54 Rebecca Shabad, "FBI Director Comey: 'highly confident' Orlando shooter radicalized through internet," CBS News, June 13, 2016.

55 Ellen Nakashima, "FBI wants access to Internet browser history without a warrant in terrorism and spy cases," *Washington Post*, June 6, 2016.

56 Adam Goldman, "FBI has found no evidence that Orlando shooter targeted Pulse because it was a gay club," *Washington Post*, July 16, 2016.

57 James Bovard, "Biden Demagogues Florida Massacre to Demonize Gun Owners," Libertarian Institute, June 13, 2023.

58 Trevor Aaronson, "The Father of Pulse Attacker Omar Mateen Was an FBI Informant," *The Intercept*, March 26, 2018.

59 Glenn Greenwald and Murtaza Hussain, "At Trial of Omar Mateen's Wife, Judge's Questioning Reveals a Huge Hole in Prosecution's Case," *The Intercept*, March 22, 2018.

60 Patricia Mazzei, "Noor Salman Acquitted in Pulse Nightclub Shooting," *New York Times*, March 30, 2018.

61 Tim Cushing, "Your Word Against Ours: How the FBI's 'No Electronic Recording' Policy Rigs the Game... And Destroys Its Credibility," Techdirt, May 20, 2013.

62 James Bovard, "Beyond Perjury," *Playboy*, May 1999.

63 Eric Felten, "Are Unrecorded FBI Interviews a G-Man's License to Lie?" Real Clear Investigations, March 21, 2019.

64 Rhodri Jeffreys-Jones, "A brief history of the FBI's meddling in US politics," *Vox*, November 5, 2016.

65 Lee Edwards, "The FBI Spied for LBJ's Campaign," *Wall Street Journal*, May 24, 2018.

66 "FBI agreed to destroy laptops of Clinton aides with immunity deal, lawmaker says," Fox News, October 3, 2016.

67 Sarah Westwood, "Immunity deals stopped FBI from investigating BleachBit use in Clinton email case," *Washington Examiner*, October 5, 2016.

68 James Bovard, "Inspector general's report on FBI and Clinton's emails shows secrecy threatens democracy," *USA Today*, June 15, 2018.

69 James Bovard, "Comey firing justly knocks FBI off its pedestal," *USA Today*, May 11, 2017.

70 James Bovard, "Durham proves that Hillary and the FBI tried to rig the 2016 election," *New York Post*, May 16, 2023.

71 Jesse O'Neill, "FBI offered ex-UK spy $1M to prove Trump dossier claims, agent testifies," *New York Post*, October 12, 2022.

72 John Solomon, "New Durham bombshell: FBI paid Russian accused of lying as a confidential informant against Trump," JustTheNews.com, September 13, 2022.

73 Jill Colvin, "DNC, Clinton campaign agree to Steele dossier funding fine," CNN, March 31, 2022.

74 James Bovard, "Inspector General report on FBI's FISA abuse tells us one thing: We need radical reform," *USA Today*, December 10, 2019.

75 James Bovard, "FISA and the Still Too Secret Police," *American Conservative*, April 30, 2021.

76 Adam Goldman, "Comey Is Criticized by Justice Dept. Watchdog for Violating F.B.I. Rules," *New York Times*, August 29, 2019.

[77] "Growing Partisan Differences in Views of the FBI; Stark Divide Over ICE," Pew Research Center, July 24, 2018.

[78] James Bovard, "Democrats attack FBI whistleblowers — giving cover to the agency's abuses," *New York Post*, May 19, 2023.

[79] Alexander Hall, "Purported FBI document suggests agency may be targeting Catholics who attend Latin Mass," Fox News, February 9, 2023.

[80] William M. Arkin, "Exclusive: Donald Trump Followers Targeted by FBI as 2024 Election Nears," *Newsweek*, October 4, 2023.

[81] James Bovard, "Is the FBI turning Trump supporters into terrorist targets?" *New York Post*, October 6, 2023.

[82] William M. Arkin, "Exclusive: Donald Trump Followers Targeted by FBI as 2024 Election Nears," *Newsweek*, October 4, 2023.

[83] *Congressional Record*, April 27, 1971, p. 11562.

Chapter 15

[1] *Associated Press v. National Labor Relations Board* (1937).

[2] *Youngstown Sheet & Tube Co. v. Sawyer*, 343 U.S. 579 (1952).

[3] *Nixon v. Sirica*, 487 F.2d 700, 711 (1973).

[4] John Taylor, *Construction Construed, and Constitutions Vindicated* (Richmond: Shepherd & Pollard, 1820).

[5] Thomas Jefferson, *The Works of Thomas Jefferson, Vol. 8* (New York: Putnam, 1902 [1798]), p. 475.

[6] *West Virginia State Board of Education v. Barnette*, 319 U.S. 624 (1943).

[7] John Locke, *Two Treatises of Government* (Cambridge: Cambridge University Press, 1960 [1689]), p. 320.

[8] Thomas Macaulay, *History of England, Vol. 2* (Philadelphia: 1848).

Index

Kane, Thomas, 115

Kansas, 15, 57, 141, 187, 295

Kant, Immanuel, 279

Katzmann, Robert, 252

Kennedy, Anthony, 138

Kennedy, John F., 194, 242

Kennedy, Robert, 194

Kentucky, 20, 22, 55, 81, 131, 229

Kessler, Gladys, 249

Kessler, Glenn, 32

Kiley, Kevin, 84

King George, 46

King, Angus, 274

Kittens Gentlemen's Club, 84

Kleck, Gary, 42

Kodak Black, 30

Komie, Stephen, 12

Koskinen, John, 203

Kozbial, Matt, 21–2

Kozinski, Alex, 64

Kraska, Peter, 55, 58

Krauthammer, Charles, 31

Ku Klux Klan Act, 61

Ku Klux Klan, 61, 289

LaHood, Darin, 228

Lamberth, Royce, 251

Lancet, 54, 78, 99, 101

Landry, Jeff, 271

Las Vegas Review Journal, 52, 67

Las Vegas, 38, 52, 67, 186, 220

Leahy, Patrick, 238

Lehrman, Lewis, 211

Lemp, Duncan, 33, 60–1

Lemp, Mercedes, 61

Leon, Richard, 226

Leonard, William, 243

Leuthauser, Michele, 186

Levin, Carl, 197

Liberty City Seven, 287–8

License plate readers, 234–5

Licensing, 2, 45, 128–33, 157

Lightfoot, Lori, 43

Lincicome, Scott, 97

Linlor, James, 185

Litt, Robert, 244

Lockdowns, 42, 48, 77–86, 88, 90, 102–4, 211–3, 235–6

Locke, John, 48, 305

Long, Huey, 194

Long, Jennifer, 197

Los Angeles, 2, 15, 51, 70, 82, 95, 115, 120, 176, 229

Louis C.K., 112

Lynch, Loretta, 53, 293, 295

Macaulay, Thomas, 279, 305

Mackinac Center for Public Policy, 19, 81

Madison, James, 241, 281

Maharrey, Mike, 40, 189

Maine, 28

Malcolm, Joyce Lee, 47–8

Malone, Rachel, 28

Manhattan Institute, 120

Manion, Daniel, 137

Marcus, Ruth, 178

Acknowledgments

I want to thank Scott Horton, the president of the Libertarian Institute, for enthusiastically embracing my pitch for *Last Rights*. I've known Scott for 20 years, and I'm most happy to see him rise from pirate radio host to a think tank founder and leading foreign policy critic. I want to thank Hunter DeRensis for his deft editing of my pieces for the Libertarian Institute. I especially want to thank Mike Dworski and Grant F. Smith for transforming a rough-edged manuscript into a final polished product. And I want to thank Ben Parker for his excellent copyediting of this book and for bringing order out of the chaos of MS Word software debacles.

I want to thank Jeffrey Tucker, the president of the Brownstone Institute, which provided a 2023 fellowship which provided me the time to finish this book. Jeffrey also spurred me to write early and often about COVID boondoggles while he was editorial director at the American Institute for Economic Research (AIER). I also had the pleasure of working with AIER editors Lucio Saverio-Eastman, David Waugh, and James Harrigan.

I would like to thank my old friend Kelly Torrance, the op-ed editor at the *New York Post*. Dozens of assignments from her spurred me to dig fast and furiously into the most amusing absurdities of the Biden era.

At *USA Today*, commentary editor David Mastio published some of my favorite smackdowns of the FBI and TSA, and editor Kelsey Bloom opened the door to my COVID critiques.

At *The American Conservative*, editors Arthur Bloom, Kelley Beaucar Vlahos, Dan McCarthy, and Micah Meadowcroft provided plenty of chances to toss bouquets to bureaucrats since the magazine's founding in the glorious George W. Bush era.

At the Mises Institute, editors Ryan McMaken and Bill Anderson have been great to work with for more than a decade.

At *CounterPunch*, Jeffrey St. Clair kindly provided an open door for my broadsides and bipartisan batterings. Writing for *CounterPunch* spurred the only rave review I ever received from a Hollywood femme fatale.

I've been writing monthly articles for the Future of Freedom Foundation for almost 30 years, and I appreciate my friend, FFF President Jacob Hornberger, for giving me plenty of opportunities to flog the statist targets of my choice.

My friend Dan Alban, a lawyer with the Institute for Justice, provided invaluable insights into federal forfeiture follies during hikes and/or boozing.

I especially would like to thank Patricia Kearney for sharing plenty of laughter, camaraderie, and good times while I hammered this book into shape. I especially appreciated her patience, her humor, and her tolerance of my periodic profanity spurred by researching this book.

Also by James Bovard

Public Policy Hooligan (Sixth Street Books) 2012

Attention Deficit Democracy (Palgrave Macmillan) 2006

The Bush Betrayal (Palgrave Macmillan) 2004
   *Arabic edition 2006

Terrorism & Tyranny: Trampling Freedom, Justice, and Peace to Rid the World of Evil (Palgrave Macmillan) 2003
   *Spanish edition 2004

Feeling Your Pain: The Explosion and Abuse of Government Power in the Clinton-Gore Years (St. Martin's/Palgrave) 2000

Freedom in Chains: The Rise of the State and the Demise of the Citizen (St. Martin's) 1999

Shakedown (Viking Penguin) 1995

Lost Rights: The Destruction of American Liberty (St. Martin's) 1994

The Fair Trade Fraud (St. Martin's) 1991
   *Japanese edition 1992
   *Korean edition 1992

The Farm Fiasco (ICS Press) 1989
   *Japanese edition 1990

The Libertarian Institute

Check out the Libertarian Institute at LibertarianInstitute.org. It's Scott Horton, Sheldon Richman, Laurie Calhoun, James Bovard, Kyle Anzalone, Keith Knight and the best libertarian writers and podcast hosts on the Internet. We are a 501(c)(3) tax-exempt charitable organization. EIN 83-2869616.

Help support our efforts — including our project to purchase wholesale copies of this book to send to important congressmen and women, antiwar groups and influential people in the media. We don't have a big marketing department to push this effort. We need your help to do it. And thank you.

LibertarianInstitute.org/donate or
The Libertarian Institute
612 W. 34th St.
Austin, TX 78705

Check out all of our other great books at LibertarianInstitute.org/books:

Hotter Than the Sun: Time to Abolish Nuclear Weapons by Scott Horton

Enough Already: Time to End the War on Terrorism by Scott Horton

Fool's Errand: Time to End the War in Afghanistan by Scott Horton

Diary of a Psychosis: How Public Health Disgraced Itself During Covid Mania by Thomas E. Woods, Jr.

Questioning the COVID Company Line: Critical Thinking in Hysterical Times by Laurie Calhoun

Domestic Imperialism: Nine Reasons I Left Progressivism by Keith Knight

Voluntaryist Handbook by Keith Knight

The Fake China Threat and Its Very Real Danger by Joseph Solis-Mullen

The Great Ron Paul: The Scott Horton Show Interviews 2004–2019

No Quarter: The Ravings of William Norman Grigg, edited by Tom Eddlem

Coming to Palestine by Sheldon Richman

What Social Animals Owe to Each Other by Sheldon Richman

Keep a look out for more great titles to be published in 2023 and 2024.

Printed in the USA
CPSIA information can be obtained
at www.ICGtesting.com
LVHW011935200424
777776LV00005B/151/J